Lecture Notes of the Institute for Computer Sciences, Social Informatics and Telecommunications Engineering 691

The LNICST series publishes ICST's conferences, symposia and workshops.

LNICST reports state-of-the-art results in areas related to the scope of the Institute.

The type of material published includes

- Proceedings (published in time for the respective event)
- Other edited monographs (such as project reports or invited volumes)

LNICST topics span the following areas:

- General Computer Science
- E-Economy
- E-Medicine
- Knowledge Management
- Multimedia
- Operations, Management and Policy
- Social Informatics
- Systems

Anne Remke · Katinka Wolter · Gethin Norman
Editors

Performance Evaluation Methodologies and Tools

18th EAI International Conference, Valuetools 2025
Glasgow, UK, December 11–12, 2025
Proceedings

Springer

Editors
Anne Remke
University of Münster
Münster, Germany

Katinka Wolter
Free University Berlin
Berlin, Germany

Gethin Norman
University of Glasgow, UK
Glasgow, UK

ISSN 1867-8211 ISSN 1867-822X (electronic)
Lecture Notes of the Institute for Computer Sciences, Social Informatics and Telecommunications Engineering
ISBN 978-3-032-23900-6 ISBN 978-3-032-23901-3 (eBook)
https://doi.org/10.1007/978-3-032-23901-3

This Springer imprint is published by the registered company Springer Nature Switzerland AG
The registered company address is: Gewerbestrasse 11, 6330 Cham, Switzerland

Preface

As General and Program Chairs we would like to welcome the reader to the proceedings of Valuetools 2025, the 18th EAI International Conference on Performance Evaluation, Methodologies and Tools, which took place in Glasgow, UK on December 11–12, 2025.

The University of Glasgow generously hosted Valuetools 2025 at their Advanced Research Center, providing excellent facilities and technical support in a beautiful area of the city.

The aim of the Valuetools series is to provide a focused platform for sharing new methods and tools to evaluate and optimize complex systems as well as present new application domains and open problems. Valuetools 2025 brought together experts from fields such as Optimisation, Networks, Operations Research, Control, Formal Methods and Probability. Lively discussions were facilitated by a cosy athmosphere created by the large Christmas tree in the big open space at the university and the scenic city of Glasgow.

The technical program of Valuetools 2025 consisted of 18 full papers selected from 46 submissions, complemented by an invited talk by William Knottenbelt on sophisticated mechanisms to control the timing behaviour of Proof of Work blockchains. Each of the 46 submissions was reviewed by at least three reviewers following a single-blind review process.

We thank the members of the program committee for their reviews and for their effort in selecting high quality papers.

We are grateful to the Conference Coordinators Natasha Onofrei and Radka Vasileiadis for their help and invaluable advice before and during the conference. Moreover, we are grateful to Springer for publishing the proceedings of Valuetools 2025. We hope all participants enjoyed the friendly scientific discussions at this edition of the event. When reading these proceedings you may find valuable new insights that support your research and its uptake.

Gethin Norman
Anne Remke
Katinka Wolter

Organization

Steering Committee

Eitan Altman	INRIA, Sophia-Antipolis, France
Dieter Fiems	Gent University, Belgium
William Knottenbelt	Imperial College London, UK

Organizing Committee

General Chair

Gethin Norman	University of Glasgow, UK

TPC Chair and Co-Chair

Anne Remke	University of Münster, Germany
Katinka Wolter	Free University of Berlin, Germany

Technical Program Committee

Anne Remke	University of Münster, Germany
Armin Zimmermann	Technische Universität Ilmenau, Germany
Dieter Fiems	Ghent University, Belgium
Douglas Down	McMaster University, Canada
Gethin Norman	University of Glasgow, UK
Giuliana Franceschinis	Politecnico di Milano, Italy
Giuliano Casale	Imperial College London, UK
Han Wu	University of Southampton, UK
Josu Doncel	University of the Basque Country, Spain
Marco Gribaudo	Politecnico di Milano, Italy
Marco Paolieri	University of Southern California, USA
Mauro Iacono	Università degli Studi della Campania, Italy
Nihal Pekergin	Paris-East Créteil University, France
Sabina Rossi	Università Cà Foscari di Venezia, Italy
Tuan Phung-Duc	University of Tsukuba, Japan
William Knottenbelt	Imperial College London, UK
Yezekael Hayel	University of Avignon, France

Contents

Cyber attacks

Tools

Networks and Routing

Queueing Models

A Queueing Model Under a Threshold Balking Strategy Based on Recent Customers' Decisions

Antonis Economou[1], Odysseas Kanavetas[2], Athanasia Manou[1], and Sotiris Tzinakis[1](✉)

[1] National and Kapodistrian University of Athens, Department of Mathematics, Panepistemiopolis, 15784 Athens, Greece
{aeconom,amanou,sotitzin}@math.uoa.gr
[2] Leiden University, Mathematical Institute, Einsteinweg 55, 2333 CC Leiden, The Netherlands
o.kanavetas@math.leidenuniv.nl
https://en.math.uoa.gr/ ,
https://www.universiteitleiden.nl/en/science/mathematics

Abstract. We consider a Markovian single-server queue where arriving customers face the dilemma of whether to join or balk. Customers are informed about the number of consecutive recent arrivals who have balked (after the last arrival who joined) and make their decisions according to a threshold balking strategy, i.e., they balk if the number of consecutive recent balking arrivals is below a threshold. This model is motivated by modern service facilities, where customers seeking for service through a website are routed to one of several alternative service systems. In such cases, although the administrator of the website usually does not have information about the congestion in the service systems, he has information about the joining decisions of the arriving customers (which service system they have chosen, if any). Based on this information, customers make their joining decisions. In the present paper, we focus on the performance evaluation of the system, computing its stationary distribution and other measures associated with the sojourn times of the joining customers. These are the first steps towards a more thorough study concerning the strategic customer behavior and optimization issues. Apart from being valuable from a managerial viewpoint, the present model is mathematically interesting. Indeed, the state process of the model is a continuous-time QBD process which is amenable to closed-form solutions for the main performance measures of the system.

Keywords: queueing · balking · strategic customers · mixed threshold strategy · stationary distribution

1 Introduction

The study of queueing models with some kind of balking and the associated performance evaluation computations is a classical topic in Queueing Theory.

A. Remke et al. (Eds.): Valuetools 2025, LNICST 691, pp. 3–21, 2027.
https://doi.org/10.1007/978-3-032-23901-3_1

Most introductory textbooks contain the Markovian single-server queue with arrival rate λ and service rate μ, where a customer who finds n customers in the system balks with probability q_n, $n = 0, 1, 2, \ldots$ (see e.g. Kleinrock [14] Sect. 3.3 or Shortle, Thompson, Gross and Harris [17] Sect. 3.10.1). The number of customers in this system constitutes a birth-death process with birth rates $\lambda_n = \lambda(1 - q_n)$, $n = 0, 1, 2, \ldots$, and death rates $\mu_n = \mu$, $n = 1, 2, \ldots$. In the case where the balking probabilities q_n have an appropriate algebraic form, the stationary distribution of the number of customers in the system is known in closed form. A classical example is when $q_n = \frac{n}{n+1}$ (i.e., when the joining probability is inversely proportional to the number of customers in the system - including the arriving customer). Then, the stationary distribution of the number of customers in the system is known to be Poisson. Another example is when $q_n = 1_{\{n \geq \bar{n}\}}$ (i.e., when the customers follow a threshold joining strategy and enter as long as the number of customers in the system is below a threshold $\bar{n}$), in which case the stationary distribution of the queue length is truncated geometric etc.

Apart from studies where the balking probabilities are exogenously given, there is a mature literature on queueing systems with strategic customers who face the join-or-balk dilemma upon arrival. Such problems belong to the so-called area of Rational Queueing, i.e., the branch of Queueing Theory that treats problems of economic flavor where the various agents (customers and/or administrators-servers) are strategic. This area goes back to the pioneering work of Naor [16] who studied the join-or-balk dilemma of arriving customers at the M/M/1 queue with service value R and unit waiting cost C. Naor [16] focused on the observable case, where arriving customers observe the queue length before making their decisions. He proved that the customers adopt a threshold strategy, i.e., $q_n = 1_{\{n \geq n_e\}}$, where $n_e = \lfloor \frac{R\mu}{C} \rfloor$, when the service rate is μ. Moreover, he discussed the pricing of the system so that the customers follow the socially optimal strategy or the profit maximizing strategy for a monopolist. A few years later, Edelson and Hildebrand [8] considered the unobservable case, where the decisions are based solely on the knowledge of the parameters of the system. Since then there is a growing part of the literature that deals with strategic considerations in queueing. The fundamental models, problems and results in this area have been summarized in the monograph by Hassin and Haviv [12]. Subsequently, Hassin [11] provided an overview of more recent contributions. Moreover, Stidham [18] presented optimal design problems in queueing systems with strategic customers.

In queueing systems where strategic customers face the join-or-balk dilemma, after observing the number of present customers, the equilibrium joining/balking strategies are usually of (mixed) threshold type (see e.g. Burnetas and Economou [1], Economou and Kanta [6], Guo and Hassin [9,10], Economou, Logothetis and Manou [7]). Therefore, a great deal of literature is devoted to the performance evaluation of the corresponding systems when customers adopt threshold strategies. More generally, the study of the systems under threshold strategies is important, since customers tend to adopt such strategies, even when the equilibrium strategies are not of this type. However, information on the number of present customers is not always available to the arriving customers. In this paper, we consider the case where arriving customers are not informed about the number of present customers, but are informed about the number of consecutive recently arriving customers who have balked. Therefore, our work is related to the research thread that deals with the impact of information that is provided to the customers on their behavior and, consequently, on the performance of the system. Several recent works summarize some important findings and challenges regarding this question; see, e.g., Chap. 4 in the book of Hassin [11] and the review papers by Ibrahim [13] and Economou [2,3].

More specifically, this paper focuses on the study of the performance of a system where customers follow a mixed threshold strategy after being informed about the number of consecutive recent arrivals who balked after the last arrival who had joined. This constitutes the first step towards a more thorough study of systems that provide such information to the customers. The study is motivated by webplatforms that direct customers to alternative service providers. In such cases, the webplatform can inform the customer about the previous decisions of the customers, in particular about the number of customers that have not been routed towards a given service provider. However, they cannot provide information about the congestion that will be faced in the chosen service provider. In the current study, we consider strategic customer behavior when the arriving customer is informed about the number of customers who have balked since the last joining customer. Economou [4] presents several models where customers are aware of the recent customers' decisions and in [5] he studies their strategic behavior when they observe the decision of the last customer.

To keep a simple framework, we consider the Markovian single-server queue (i.e., the M/M/1 queue) and assume that the customers adopt a mixed threshold balking strategy given the aforementioned information. In this case, a mixed threshold strategy is specified by a nonnegative real number $J + b$, where J is a non-negative integer and b is a real number in $[0, 1)$. Under such a strategy

- an arrival balks if the number of consecutive balking customers, i, is at most $J - 1$,
- balks with probability b when i equals J, and
- joins when i is at least $J + 1$.

Our main contributions are the following:

- We derive the stability condition of the model.
- We obtain the joint steady-state distribution of the number of customers in the system and the number of consecutive recent balked arrivals, when the system is stable.
- We compute some performance measures.
- We study numerically the social welfare generated by the system as a function of the threshold.

The paper is structured as follows: In Sect. 2, we describe the dynamics and the operational parameters of the queueing model under study. Subsequently, in Sect. 3, we derive the stability condition of the system and the joint steady-state distribution of the number of customers and the number of consecutive recent balked customers. We then use this distribution to compute the main performance measures of the system, in Sect. 4. In Sect. 5, we exploit the results and run a number of numerical experiments that reveal the behavior of the social welfare generated by the model when its parameters change. Finally, Sect. 6 presents some conclusions and directions for future research.

2 The Model

We consider a single-server queue with infinite waiting space and the First-Come-First-Served (FCFS) discipline. Customers arrive according to a Poisson process with rate λ and have independent exponential service times with rate μ.

Each customer, at the instant of her arrival, is informed about the number of customers who have balked since the last joining customer. We assume that arriving customers balk if they observe that less than the last J customers have balked, balk with probability b if they observe that the last J customers have balked, and join if they observe that more than J consecutive customers have balked. This type of mixed threshold strategy will be referred to as the $J + b$ strategy. Note that under a $J + b$ strategy, at most $J + 1$ customers may have balked since the last entrance.

This system can be described by a continuous-time Markov chain $\{(Q(t), I(t)) : t \geq 0\}$, where $Q(t)$ is the number of customers in the system at time t and $I(t)$ is the number of balking customers since the last entrance at time t. The state space of the Markov chain is given by

$$S = \{(n, i) : n = 0, 1, 2, \ldots, \quad i = 0, \ldots, J + 1\},$$

and its non-zero transition rates are

$$\begin{aligned}
q_{(n,i),(n,i+1)} &= \lambda, \quad n = 0, 1, 2, \ldots, \quad i = 0, \ldots, J - 1, \\
q_{(n,J),(n,J+1)} &= \lambda b, \quad n = 0, 1, 2, \ldots, \\
q_{(n,J),(n+1,0)} &= \lambda(1 - b), \quad n = 0, 1, 2, \ldots, \\
q_{(n,J+1),(n+1,0)} &= \lambda, \quad n = 0, 1, 2, \ldots, \\
q_{(n,i),(n-1,i)} &= \mu, \quad n = 1, 2, 3 \ldots, \quad i = 0, \ldots, J + 1.
\end{aligned}$$

The transition diagram is given in Fig. 1.

The Markov chain $\{(Q(t), I(t)) : t \geq 0\}$ is a quasi birth-and-death (QBD) process with partitioned transition rate matrix given as

$$Q = \begin{pmatrix}
B_{0,0} & B_{0,1} & 0 & 0 & 0 & \cdots \\
B_{1,0} & A_1 & A_0 & 0 & 0 & \cdots \\
0 & A_2 & A_1 & A_0 & 0 & \cdots \\
0 & 0 & A_2 & A_1 & A_0 & \cdots \\
\vdots & \vdots & \vdots & \vdots & \vdots & \ddots
\end{pmatrix}, \tag{1}$$

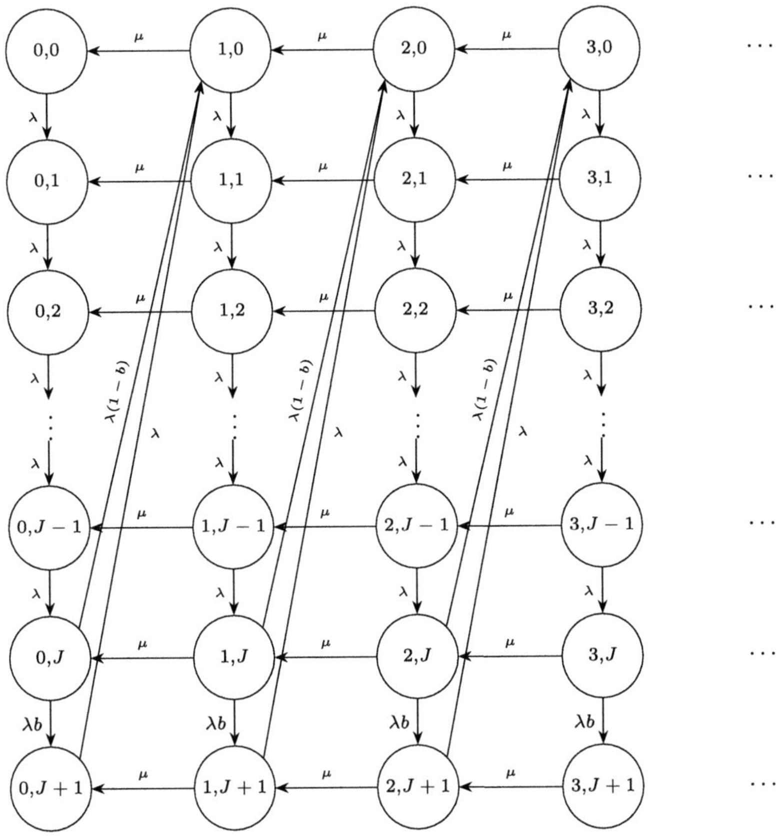

Fig. 1. Transition rate diagram of $\{(Q(t), I(t))\}$.

where the matrix $B_{0,0}$, of order $(J+2) \times (J+2)$, is

$$B_{0,0} = \begin{pmatrix} -\lambda & \lambda & 0 & \cdots & 0 & 0 & 0 \\ 0 & -\lambda & \lambda & \cdots & 0 & 0 & 0 \\ 0 & 0 & -\lambda & \cdots & 0 & 0 & 0 \\ \vdots & \vdots & \vdots & \ddots & \vdots & \vdots & \vdots \\ 0 & 0 & 0 & \cdots & -\lambda & \lambda & 0 \\ 0 & 0 & 0 & \cdots & 0 & -\lambda & \lambda b \\ 0 & 0 & 0 & \cdots & 0 & 0 & -\lambda \end{pmatrix},$$

the matrices $B_{0,1}$ and A_0, each of order $(J+2) \times (J+2)$, are

$$B_{0,1} = A_0 = \begin{pmatrix} 0 & 0 \cdots 0 \\ 0 & 0 \cdots 0 \\ \vdots & \vdots \ddots \vdots \\ 0 & 0 \cdots 0 \\ \lambda(1-b) & 0 \cdots 0 \\ \lambda & 0 \cdots 0 \end{pmatrix},$$

the matrix A_1, of order $(J+2) \times (J+2)$, is

$$A_1 = \begin{pmatrix} -(\lambda+\mu) & \lambda & 0 & \cdots & 0 & 0 & 0 \\ 0 & -(\lambda+\mu) & \lambda & \cdots & 0 & 0 & 0 \\ 0 & 0 & -(\lambda+\mu) & \cdots & 0 & 0 & 0 \\ \vdots & \vdots & \vdots & \ddots & \vdots & \vdots & \vdots \\ 0 & 0 & 0 & \cdots & -(\lambda+\mu) & \lambda & 0 \\ 0 & 0 & 0 & \cdots & 0 & -(\lambda+\mu) & \lambda b \\ 0 & 0 & 0 & \cdots & 0 & 0 & -(\lambda+\mu) \end{pmatrix},$$

and the matrices $B_{1,0}$ and A_2, each of order $(J+2) \times (J+2)$, are

$$B_{1,0} = A_2 = \begin{pmatrix} \mu & 0 & \cdots & 0 \\ 0 & \mu & \cdots & 0 \\ \vdots & \vdots & \ddots & \vdots \\ 0 & 0 & \cdots & \mu \end{pmatrix}.$$

Note that $B_{0,0} = A_1 + A_2$ and $A_2 = \mu I$.

3 The Steady-State Distribution

Let $p(n,i)$ be the steady-state probability that the system is in state (n,i), for $n = 0, 1, 2, \ldots$ and $j = 0, 1, \ldots, J+1$. Moreover, let $\underline{p}_n$ be the column-vector of the steady-state probabilities that correspond to level n of the QBD, i.e.,

$$\underline{p}_n = (p(n,0), p(n,1), \cdots, p(n,J+1))^T, \quad n = 0, 1, 2, \ldots.$$

Then, the matrix-analytic approach (see e.g., Latouche and Ramaswami [15], Theorem 6.4.1, Proposition 6.4.2 and Lemma 6.4.3) is applicable and the steady-state distribution $\underline{p}^T = (\underline{p}_0^T, \underline{p}_1^T, \ldots)$ has the matrix-geometric form

$$\underline{p}_n^T = \underline{p}_0^T R^n, \quad n = 0, 1, 2, \ldots, \tag{2}$$

where R is the minimal solution of the equation

$$X^2 A_2 + X A_1 + A_0 = 0, \tag{3}$$

in the set of non-negative matrices and $\underline{p}_0^T$ is the unique solution of

$$\underline{p}_0^T (I-R)^{-1}\underline{e} = 1, \tag{4}$$

$$\underline{p}_0^T (B_{0,0} + RA_2) = \underline{0}^T, \tag{5}$$

where $\underline{e} = (1,1,\cdots,1)^T$ denotes a $(J+2)$-column-vector of ones and I is the identity matrix of order $J+2$.

The process $\{I(t)\}$ is itself a continuous-time Markov chain, since its evolution is not influenced by $\{Q(t)\}$. The next proposition gives its steady-state distribution.

Proposition 1. *Consider the M/M/1 queue with arrival rate λ and service rate μ, operating under the $J+b$ strategy. Then, the steady-state distribution of $\{I(t)\}$ is $\underline{\alpha} = (\alpha_0, \alpha_1, \alpha_2, \ldots, \alpha_{J+1})^T$, with*

$$\alpha_i = \frac{1}{J+1+b}, \quad i = 0, \ldots, J, \tag{6}$$

$$\alpha_{J+1} = \frac{b}{J+1+b}. \tag{7}$$

Proof. The transition rate matrix of the continuous-time Markov chain $\{I(t)\}$ is clearly the matrix

$$A = A_0 + A_1 + A_2 = \begin{pmatrix} -\lambda & \lambda & 0 & \cdots & 0 & 0 & 0 \\ 0 & -\lambda & \lambda & \cdots & 0 & 0 & 0 \\ 0 & 0 & -\lambda & \cdots & 0 & 0 & 0 \\ \vdots & \vdots & \vdots & \ddots & \vdots & \vdots & \vdots \\ 0 & 0 & 0 & \cdots & -\lambda & \lambda & 0 \\ \lambda(1-b) & 0 & 0 & \cdots & 0 & -\lambda & \lambda b \\ \lambda & 0 & 0 & \cdots & 0 & 0 & -\lambda \end{pmatrix},$$

with transition rate diagram given in Fig. 2.

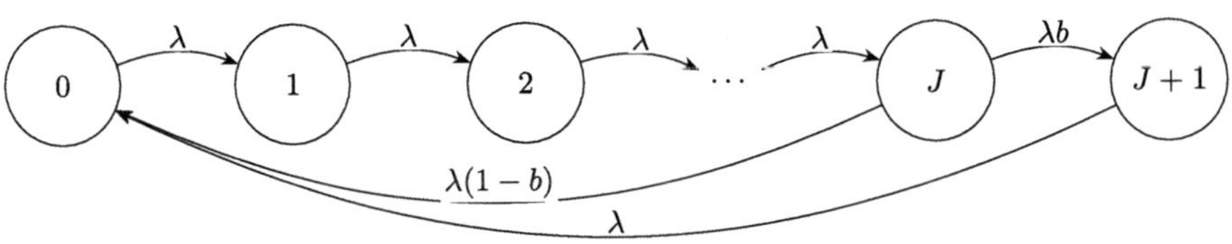

Fig. 2. Transition rate diagram of $\{I(t)\}$.

The balance equations of this CTMC are

$$\lambda\alpha_0 = \lambda(1-b)\alpha_J + \lambda\alpha_{J+1},$$

$$\lambda\alpha_i = \lambda\alpha_{i-1}, \quad i = 1, \ldots, J, \tag{8}$$

$$\lambda\alpha_{J+1} = \lambda b\alpha_J. \tag{9}$$

Equations (8) and (9) yield

$$\alpha_0 = \alpha_1 = \ldots = \alpha_J, \tag{10}$$

$$\alpha_{J+1} = b\alpha_J. \tag{11}$$

Then, the normalization equation, and equations (10), (11) yield (6) and (7). □

The next proposition states the stability condition for $\{(Q(t), I(t)) : t \geq 0\}$.

Proposition 2. *Consider the M/M/1 queue with arrival rate λ and service rate μ, operating under the $J + b$ strategy. The process $\{(Q(t), I(t))\}$ is stable (i.e., positive recurrent), if and only if*

$$\frac{\lambda}{J+1+b} < \mu. \tag{12}$$

Proof. We use the standard drift condition for the stability of continuous-time QBD processes (see e.g., Latouche and Ramaswami [15] Theorem 7.2.4)). According to this result, the process $\{(Q(t), I(t)) : t \geq 0\}$ is positive recurrent if and only if

$$\underline{\alpha}^T A_0 \underline{e} < \underline{\alpha}^T A_2 \underline{e}. \tag{13}$$

Because of the sparse nature of the matrices A_0 and A_2, condition (13) is written equivalently as

$$\lambda(1-b)\alpha_J + \lambda\alpha_{J+1} < \mu \sum_{i=0}^{J+1} \alpha_i,$$

which reduces to (12), taking into account (6) and (7). □

The stability condition can be intuitively explained. Indeed, suppose that an entrance to the system has just occurred. Then, under the $J + b$ strategy, before the next entrance to the system, either J (with probability $1 - b$) or $J + 1$ (with probability b) consecutive arrivals will balk. Thus, one entrance in the system corresponds to $(J + 1)(1 - b) + (J + 2)b = J + 1 + b$ total arrivals. In other words, the fraction of customers that enter the system is $1/(J + 1 + b)$ and the effective arrival rate is $\lambda/(J+1+b)$. Then, the stability condition merely states that the service rate should exceed the effective arrival rate, which is exactly the condition (12).

We will now derive the steady-state distribution of $\{(Q(t), I(t))\}$. The derivation relies on the very special form of the matrix A_0. To exploit this fact, we adapt a known result for discrete-time QBDs (see e.g., Latouche and Ramaswami [15] Theorem 8.5.2)) in the continuous-time framework.

Lemma 1. *Consider a QBD process with transition rate matrix given by (1). Assume that*

$$A_0 = \underline{c}\,\underline{r}^T, \tag{14}$$

with

$$\underline{r}^T \underline{e} = 1, \tag{15}$$

where $\underline{c}$, $\underline{r}$ are column-vectors. Then, the matrix R in (2) is given as

$$R = \underline{c}\underline{\xi}^T, \tag{16}$$

where

$$\underline{\xi}^T = \underline{r}^T(-A_1 - \eta A_2)^{-1}, \tag{17}$$

and η is the unique root in $(0, 1)$ of

$$z = \underline{r}^T(-zA_2 - A_1)^{-1}\underline{c}. \tag{18}$$

Proof. From the characteristic equation $R^2A_2 + RA_1 + A_0 = 0$ of R (see (3)), we have that

$$R = A_0(-RA_2 - A_1)^{-1} \overset{(14)}{=} \underline{c}\underline{r}^T(-RA_2 - A_1)^{-1} = \underline{c}\underline{\xi}^T, \tag{19}$$

where

$$\underline{\xi}^T = \underline{r}^T(-RA_2 - A_1)^{-1}.$$

However,

$$R^n = \left(\underline{c}\underline{\xi}^T\right)^n = \underline{c}\left(\underline{\xi}^T\underline{c}\right)^{n-1}\underline{\xi}^T = \eta^{n-1}\underline{c}\underline{\xi}^T = \eta^{n-1}R, \tag{20}$$

with $\eta = \underline{\xi}^T\underline{c}$. Then, the characteristic equation $R^2A_2 + RA_1 + A_0 = 0$ can be written equivalently as

$$\eta RA_2 + RA_1 + A_0 = 0 \overset{(19),(14)}{\Leftrightarrow} \eta\underline{c}\underline{\xi}^T A_2 + \underline{c}\underline{\xi}^T A_1 + \underline{c}\underline{r}^T = 0 \Leftrightarrow \underline{c}\left[\underline{\xi}^T(\eta A_2 + A_1) + \underline{r}^T\right] = 0.$$

Premultiplying with $\underline{\xi}^T$ yields

$$\underline{\xi}^T\underline{c}\left[\underline{\xi}^T(\eta A_2 + A_1) + \underline{r}^T\right] = 0 \Rightarrow \eta\left[\underline{\xi}^T(\eta A_2 + A_1) + \underline{r}^T\right] = 0 \Rightarrow \underline{\xi}^T(\eta A_2 + A_1) + \underline{r}^T = 0,$$

and solving for $\underline{\xi}^T$ yields (17).

Now it is easy to see that η is the spectral radius of R. Postmultiplying $R = \underline{c}\underline{\xi}^T$ (see (19)) with $\underline{c}$ yields $R\underline{c} = \underline{c}\underline{\xi}^T\underline{c} = \eta\underline{c}$, which shows that η is an eigenvalue of R with right eigenvector $\underline{c}$. Similarly, premultiplying $R = \underline{c}\underline{\xi}^T$ with $\underline{\xi}^T$ yields $\underline{\xi}^T R = \underline{\xi}^T\underline{c}\underline{\xi}^T = \eta\underline{\xi}^T$, which shows that η is an eigenvalue of R with left eigenvector $\underline{\xi}$. Hence, η is the eigenvalue of the non-negative matrix R which corresponds to the right eigenvector $\underline{c}$ and the left eigenvector $\underline{\xi}$ which are both non-negative, since $R = \underline{c}\underline{\xi}^T$. However, a non-zero $n \times n$ matrix, which is the product of a column and a row vector has one non-zero eigenvalue with multiplicity one and the zero eigenvalue with multiplicity $n - 1$. Therefore, η is the unique non-zero eigenvalue of R which is given as $\underline{\xi}^T\underline{c}$ and taking into account (17), we have that it is the unique root in $(0, 1)$ of (18). □

We now apply Lemma 1 to obtain the matrix R for the queueing model of interest, since A_0 is of the required special form.

Theorem 1. *Consider the M/M/1 queue with arrival rate λ and service rate μ, operating under the $J+b$ strategy. The matrix R in (2) is given by*

$$R = \begin{pmatrix} 0 & 0 & \cdots & 0 & 0 \\ 0 & 0 & \cdots & 0 & 0 \\ \vdots & \vdots & \ddots & \vdots & \vdots \\ 0 & 0 & \cdots & 0 & 0 \\ \lambda(1-b)\xi_0 & \lambda(1-b)\xi_1 & \cdots & \lambda(1-b)\xi_J & \lambda(1-b)\xi_{J+1} \\ \lambda\xi_0 & \lambda\xi_1 & \cdots & \lambda\xi_J & \lambda\xi_{J+1} \end{pmatrix}, \tag{21}$$

where

$$\xi_i = \frac{1}{\lambda} \cdot \alpha^{i+1}, \quad i = 0, \ldots, J, \tag{22}$$

$$\xi_{J+1} = \frac{b}{\lambda} \cdot \alpha^{J+2}, \tag{23}$$

with

$$\alpha = \frac{\lambda}{\lambda + \mu(1-\eta)}, \tag{24}$$

and η being the unique root in $(0,1)$ of

$$[\lambda + \mu(1-z)]^{J+2} \cdot z - \lambda^{J+2} - \lambda^{J+1}(1-b)\mu(1-z) = 0. \tag{25}$$

Proof. We note that $A_0 = \underline{c}\,\underline{r}^T$, where

$$\underline{c} = (0, 0, \cdots, 0, \lambda(1-b), \lambda b)^T,$$
$$\underline{r} = (1, 0, \cdots, 0, 0, 0)^T.$$

Let $\underline{\xi} = (\xi_0, \xi_1, \ldots, \xi_{J+1})^T$. Equation (17) can equivalently be written as

$$\underline{\xi}^T(-\eta A_2 - A_1) = \underline{r}^T,$$

which gives

$$\xi_0[\lambda + \mu(1-\eta)] = 1,$$
$$-\lambda\xi_{i-1} + [\lambda + \mu(1-\eta)]\xi_i = 0, \quad i = 1, 2, \ldots, J,$$
$$-\lambda b\xi_J + [\lambda + \mu(1-\eta)]\xi_{J+1} = 0.$$

Solving recursively yields

$$\xi_0 = \frac{1}{\lambda + \mu(1-\eta)},$$

$$\xi_i = \left(\frac{\lambda}{\lambda + \mu(1-\eta)}\right)^i \cdot \frac{1}{\lambda + \mu(1-\eta)}, \quad i = 1, \ldots, J,$$

$$\xi_{J+1} = b\left(\frac{\lambda}{\lambda + \mu(1-\eta)}\right)^{J+1} \cdot \frac{1}{\lambda + \mu(1-\eta)}.$$

which shows (22) and (23) with α given by (24).

As we have proved, η is the unique root in $(0,1)$ of the equation (18). In this case, we have to solve the equation

$$\begin{aligned}
& z = c_J\xi_J + c_{J+1}\xi_{J+1} \\
\Leftrightarrow\ & z = \lambda(1-b)\left(\frac{\lambda}{\lambda+\mu(1-z)}\right)^J \cdot \frac{1}{\lambda+\mu(1-z)} + \lambda b\left(\frac{\lambda}{\lambda+\mu(1-z)}\right)^{J+1} \cdot \frac{1}{\lambda+\mu(1-z)} \\
\Leftrightarrow\ & [\lambda+\mu(1-z)]^{J+2}\cdot z - \lambda^{J+2} - \lambda^{J+1}(1-b)\mu(1-z) = 0. \qquad (26)
\end{aligned}$$

Applying Lemma 1, we have

$$R = \underline{c}\,\underline{\xi}^T = (0,0,\ldots,0,\lambda(1-b),\lambda b)^T \cdot (\xi_0,\xi_1,\ldots,\xi_{J-1},\xi_J,\xi_{J+1}),$$

which shows (21). □

The next result concerns the steady-state distribution of $\{(Q(t),I(t)) : t \geq 0\}$.

Theorem 2. *Consider the M/M/1 queue with arrival rate λ and service rate μ, operating under the $J+b$ strategy. The steady-state distribution of $\{(Q(t),I(t)) : t \geq 0\}$ is*

$$p(0,i) = \frac{1}{J+1+b}\cdot(1-\alpha^{i+1}), \quad i = 0,\ldots,J, \qquad (27)$$

$$p(0,J+1) = \frac{b}{J+1+b}\cdot(1-\alpha^{J+2}), \qquad (28)$$

$$p(n,i) = \frac{1}{J+1+b}\cdot(1-\eta)\eta^{n-1}\alpha^{i+1}, n = 1,2,\ldots,\ i = 0,1,\ldots,J, \qquad (29)$$

$$p(n,J+1) = \frac{b}{J+1+b}\cdot(1-\eta)\eta^{n-1}\alpha^{J+2}, n = 1,2,\ldots, \qquad (30)$$

where α is given by (24) and η is the unique root in $(0,1)$ of (25).

Proof. Note that equation (20) implies

$$(I-R)^{-1} = \sum_{n=0}^{\infty} R^n = I + \sum_{n=1}^{\infty} R^n = I + \sum_{n=1}^{\infty} \eta^{n-1}R = I + \frac{1}{1-\eta}R.$$

Hence,

$$\begin{aligned}
(I-R)^{-1}\underline{e} &= \left(I + \frac{1}{1-\eta}R\right)\underline{e} \\
&= \underline{e} + \frac{1}{1-\eta}R\underline{e} \\
&= \begin{pmatrix} 1 \\ 1 \\ \vdots \\ 1 \\ 1+\frac{1}{1-\eta}\lambda(1-b)\sum_{i=0}^{J+1}\xi_i \\ 1+\frac{1}{1-\eta}\lambda\sum_{i=0}^{J+1}\xi_i \end{pmatrix}. \qquad (31)
\end{aligned}$$

Now,

$$\sum_{i=0}^{J+1}\xi_i = \frac{\alpha}{\lambda}\left(\sum_{i=0}^{J}\alpha^i + b\alpha^{J+1}\right) = \frac{\alpha}{\lambda}\left(\frac{1-\alpha^{J+1}}{1-\alpha} + b\alpha^{J+1}\right) = \frac{\alpha}{\lambda}\cdot\frac{1-\alpha^{J+1}+b\alpha^{J+1}-b\alpha^{J+2}}{1-\alpha}$$
$$= \frac{1}{\mu(1-\eta)}\cdot\left[1-(1-b)\alpha^{J+1}-b\alpha^{J+2}\right]. \tag{32}$$

Plugging (24) in the middle equation of (26), we get

$$\eta = (1-b)\alpha^{J+1} + b\alpha^{J+2}. \tag{33}$$

Inserting (33) into (32) yields

$$\sum_{i=0}^{J+1}\xi_i = \frac{1}{\mu(1-\eta)}\cdot(1-\eta) = \frac{1}{\mu}. \tag{34}$$

Hence, plugging (34) into (31) yields

$$(I-R)^{-1}\underline{e} = \begin{pmatrix} 1 \\ 1 \\ \vdots \\ 1 \\ 1+\frac{\lambda(1-b)}{\mu(1-\eta)} \\ 1+\frac{\lambda}{\mu(1-\eta)} \end{pmatrix}. \tag{35}$$

Equations (35) and (4) imply

$$\sum_{i=0}^{J+1}p(0,i) + \frac{\lambda(1-b)}{\mu(1-\eta)}p(0,J) + \frac{\lambda}{\mu(1-\eta)}p(0,J+1) = 1$$
$$\Leftrightarrow \sum_{i=0}^{J+1}p(0,i) + \frac{\lambda}{\mu(1-\eta)}\left[(1-b)p(0,J) + p(0,J+1)\right] = 1. \tag{36}$$

On the other hand, equation (5) can equivalently be written as

$$\underline{p}_0^T(A_1 + \mu I + \mu R) = \underline{0}^T,$$

or, taking into account the forms of the various matrices, as

$$\underline{p}_0^T\cdot\begin{pmatrix} -\lambda & \lambda & \cdots & 0 & 0 & 0 \\ 0 & -\lambda & \cdots & 0 & 0 & 0 \\ 0 & 0 & \cdots & 0 & 0 & 0 \\ \vdots & \vdots & \ddots & \vdots & \vdots & \vdots \\ 0 & 0 & \cdots & -\lambda & \lambda & 0 \\ \mu\lambda(1-b)\xi_0 & \mu\lambda(1-b)\xi_1 & \cdots & \mu\lambda(1-b)\xi_{J-1} & -\lambda+\mu\lambda(1-b)\xi_J & \lambda b+\mu\lambda(1-b)\xi_{J+1} \\ \mu\lambda\xi_0 & \mu\lambda\xi_1 & \cdots & \mu\lambda\xi_{J-1} & \mu\lambda\xi_J & -\lambda+\mu\lambda\xi_{J+1} \end{pmatrix} = \underline{0}^T.$$

We can divide all entries by λ and obtain

$$\underline{p}_0^T \cdot \begin{pmatrix} -1 & 1 & \cdots & 0 & 0 & 0 \\ 0 & -1 & \cdots & 0 & 0 & 0 \\ 0 & 0 & \cdots & 0 & 0 & 0 \\ \vdots & \vdots & \ddots & \vdots & \vdots & \vdots \\ 0 & 0 & \cdots & -1 & 1 & 0 \\ \mu(1-b)\xi_0 & \mu(1-b)\xi_1 & \cdots & \mu(1-b)\xi_{J-1} & -1+\mu(1-b)\xi_J & b+\mu(1-b)\xi_{J+1} \\ \mu\xi_0 & \mu\xi_1 & \cdots & \mu\xi_{J-1} & \mu\xi_J & -1+\mu\xi_{J+1} \end{pmatrix} = \underline{0}^T.$$

By equating the entries of the two row-vectors, we obtain the equations

$$-p(0,0) + \mu(1-b)\xi_0 p(0,J) + \mu\xi_0 p(0,J+1) = 0, \tag{37}$$

$$p(0,i-1) - p(0,i) + \mu(1-b)\xi_i p(0,J) + \mu\xi_i p(0,J+1) = 0, \quad i=1,\ldots,J-1, \tag{38}$$

$$p(0,J-1) - (1-\mu(1-b)\xi_J)p(0,J) + \mu\xi_J p(0,J+1) = 0, \tag{39}$$

$$(b+\mu(1-b)\xi_{J+1})p(0,J) - (1-\mu\xi_{J+1})p(0,J+1) = 0. \tag{40}$$

Define

$$p(0,J+b) = (1-b)p(0,J) + p(0,J+1). \tag{41}$$

Then, the equations (37)-(40) can be written more compactly as

$$\begin{aligned} p(0,0) &= \mu\xi_0 p(0,J+b), \\ p(0,i) &= p(0,i-1) + \mu\xi_i p(0,J+b), \quad i=1,\ldots,J, \\ p(0,J+1) &= bp(0,J) + \mu\xi_{J+1} p(0,J+b). \end{aligned}$$

Hence,

$$p(0,i) = \mu\sum_{k=0}^{i}\xi_k p(0,J+b), \quad i=0,\ldots,J \tag{42}$$

$$p(0,J+1) = \mu\left(b\sum_{k=0}^{J}\xi_k + \xi_{J+1}\right)p(0,J+b). \tag{43}$$

Then, from equations (22) and (23) we deduce

$$\sum_{k=0}^{i}\xi_k = \frac{1}{\lambda}\sum_{k=0}^{i}\alpha^{k+1} = \frac{\alpha}{\lambda}\cdot\frac{1-\alpha^{i+1}}{1-\alpha}, \quad i=0,\ldots,J, \tag{44}$$

$$b\sum_{k=0}^{J}\xi_k + \xi_{J+1} = \frac{b}{\lambda}\sum_{k=0}^{J}a^{k+1} + \frac{b}{\lambda}a^{J+2} = \frac{b}{\lambda}\sum_{k=0}^{J+1}a^{k+1} = \frac{b\alpha}{\lambda}\cdot\frac{1-\alpha^{J+2}}{1-\alpha}. \tag{45}$$

Now (36), in light of (41), yields

$$\sum_{i=0}^{J+1}p(0,i) + \frac{\lambda}{\mu(1-\eta)}p(0,J+b) = 1.$$

Substituting $p(0,i)$, $i=0,1,\dots,J$ and $p(0,J+1)$ using (42), (43), (44) and (45) yields

$$\mu\sum_{i=0}^{J}\frac{\alpha}{\lambda}\cdot\frac{1-\alpha^{i+1}}{1-\alpha}\cdot p(0,J+b)+\mu\frac{b\alpha}{\lambda}\cdot\frac{1-\alpha^{J+2}}{1-\alpha}p(0,J+b)+\frac{\lambda}{\mu(1-\eta)}p(0,J+b)=1.$$

After computing the geometric sums and grouping similar terms, we deduce

$$\frac{1}{\mu(1-\eta)}\left(\mu(J+1+b)-\mu\alpha\left(\frac{1-\alpha^{J+1}}{1-\alpha}+b\alpha^{J+1}\right)+\lambda\right)p(0,J+b)=1. \quad (46)$$

By (32) and (34)

$$\begin{aligned}\frac{1-\alpha^{J+1}}{1-\alpha}+b\alpha^{J+1}&=\frac{1-(1-b)\alpha^{J+1}-b\alpha^{J+2}}{1-\alpha}=\frac{\mu(1-\eta)}{1-\alpha}\sum_{i=1}^{J+1}\xi_i\\&=[\lambda+\mu(1-\eta)]\sum_{i=1}^{J+1}\xi_i=\frac{\lambda}{\mu}+1-\eta.\end{aligned} \quad (47)$$

Hence, (46) is written equivalently as

$$\frac{1}{\mu(1-\eta)}\left(\mu(J+1+b)-\alpha\lambda-\mu\alpha(1-\eta)+\lambda\right)p(0,J+b)=1,$$

and substituting α by (24) yields

$$\frac{1}{\mu(1-\eta)}\left(\mu(J+1+b)+\lambda\frac{\mu(1-\eta)}{\lambda+\mu(1-\eta)}-\mu\frac{\lambda}{\lambda+\mu(1-\eta)}\cdot(1-\eta)\right)p(0,J+b)=1.$$

Simplifying and solving for $p(0,J+b)$ yields

$$p(0,J+b)=\frac{1-\eta}{J+1+b}. \quad (48)$$

Substituting (44), (45) and (48) into (42) and (43) yields immediately (27) and (28).

We now focus on the derivation of (29) and (30). Note that equations (2) and (20) imply that

$$\underline{p}_n^T=\underline{p}_0^T R^n=\underline{p}_0^T\eta^{n-1}R,\quad n\geq 1.$$

Therefore, using (21), we have that

$$\begin{aligned}p(n,i)&=\eta^{n-1}(p(0,J)\lambda(1-b)\xi_i+p(0,J+1)\lambda\xi_i),\quad n=1,2,\dots,\quad i=0,1,\dots,J,\\p(n,J+1)&=\eta^{n-1}(p(0,J)\lambda(1-b)\xi_{J+1}+p(0,J+1)\lambda\xi_{J+1}),\quad n=1,2,\dots.\end{aligned}$$

We can now substitute $p(0,J)$, $p(0,J+1)$, ξ_i, $i=0,1,\dots,J$ and ξ_{J+1} by (27), (28), (22) and (23), respectively, and we deduce (29) and (30). □

4 The Mean Measures

In this section, we focus on the performance of an M/M/1 queue operating under the $J+b$ balking strategy, where customers entrances depend on recent balking history. We derive the conditional and unconditional expected numbers of customers in the system, as well as the effective arrival rate under such a strategy. These results highlight how the queue length depends on the number of balked customers since the last entrance and provide insight into the system's performance under controlled entry dynamics.

Proposition 3. *Consider the M/M/1 queue with arrival rate λ and service rate μ, operating under the $J+b$ strategy. Let η be the unique root in $(0,1)$ of (25) and α be given by (24).*

The conditional expected number of customers in the system given that i customers have balked since the last entrance is

$$E[Q|I=i] = \frac{\alpha^{i+1}}{1-\eta}, \quad i=0,1,\ldots,J+1. \tag{49}$$

The expected number of customers in the system is

$$E[Q] = \frac{\lambda}{\mu(1-\eta)(J+1+b)}. \tag{50}$$

The effective arrival rate is

$$\lambda_{eff} = \frac{\lambda}{J+1+b}. \tag{51}$$

Proof. Using (29) (30), (6) and (7), we have

$$E[Q|I=i] = \sum_{n=1}^{\infty} n \cdot \frac{p(n,i)}{\alpha_i} = \sum_{n=1}^{\infty} n(1-\eta)\eta^{n-1}\alpha^{i+1} = \frac{\alpha^{i+1}}{1-\eta}.$$

For deducing $E[Q]$, we condition on I:

$$\begin{aligned}
E[Q] &= \sum_{i=0}^{J} E[Q|I=i]\alpha_i + E[Q|I=J+1]\alpha_{J+1} \\
&= \sum_{i=0}^{J} \frac{\alpha^{i+1}}{1-\eta} \cdot \frac{1}{J+1+b} + \frac{\alpha^{J+2}}{1-\eta} \cdot \frac{b}{J+1+b} \\
&= \frac{\alpha}{(1-\eta)(J+1+b)} \left(\frac{1-\alpha^{J+1}}{1-\alpha} + b\alpha^{J+1} \right).
\end{aligned}$$

Using (47) we get

$$\begin{aligned}
E[Q] &= \frac{\alpha}{(1-\eta)(J+1+b)} \left(\frac{\lambda}{\mu} + 1 - \eta \right) = \frac{\lambda\alpha}{(1-\eta)(J+1+b)} \cdot \frac{\lambda+\mu(1-\eta)}{\lambda\mu} \\
&= \frac{\lambda\alpha}{(1-\eta)(J+1+b)} \cdot \frac{1}{\mu\alpha} = \frac{\lambda}{\mu(1-\eta)(J+1+b)}.
\end{aligned}$$

Moreover, the effective arrival rate is

$$\lambda_{eff} = \lambda(1-b)\alpha_J + \lambda\alpha_{J+1} = \lambda(1-b)\frac{1}{J+1+b} + \lambda\frac{b}{J+1+b} = \frac{\lambda}{J+1+b}.$$

□

An intuitive interpretation of the effective arrival rate is given after the derivation of the stability condition in Proposition 2. Moreover, we see that $E[Q|I=i]$ is a decreasing function of i. This is expected because as i increases, more customers have balked after the last entrance. Hence, the elapsed time after the last entrance stochastically increases in i and the number of customers that have been served after the last entrance increases. As a result, the expected queue length decreases in i.

5 The Social Welfare

In this section we assume that there is a social planner who acts as the administrator of the system. The service reward per customer who joins the system is r utility units, whereas the waiting cost is c per customer and time unit. Hence, the social welfare generated by the system (per time unit), when the strategy $J+b$ is imposed (or induced via a pricing mechanism), is

$$SW(J+b) = \lambda_{eff} \cdot r - \cdot E[Q].$$

The social planner's objective is to determine the strategy $J+b$ that maximizes the expected social welfare. By formula (51), we see that λ_{eff} is decreasing in $J+b$. Moreover, one can easily show using the characteristic equation of η (middle equation of (26)) that η is decreasing in $J+b$ and, therefore, $E[Q]$ decreases with $J+b$. Hence, $SW(J+b)$ is influenced by two opposite effects as the threshold $J+b$ increases. On the one hand, more customers balk and the total reward ($\lambda_{eff}r$) decreases. On the other hand, the congestion decreases so the total waiting cost ($c \cdot E[Q]$) decreases. Thus, the monotonicity behavior of $SW(J+b)$ as function of the threshold $J+b$ is not clear.

Figure 3 illustrates the effect of $J+b$ on the expected social welfare, $SW(J+b)$, for three different service rates: $\mu = 0.4,\ 1.4,\ 3$. In all cases, we fix the other parameters at $\lambda = 1$, $r = 2$, and $c = 1$.

The behavior of the expected social welfare function, is non-monotonic. When service is slow ($\mu = 0.4$), unrestricted or partially restricted entry leads to excessive congestion and negative welfare that increases in $J+b$. In this case, the optimal strategy requires that all customers balk ($J+b=\infty$). When the service rate is fast ($\mu = 3$), delay costs are negligible, social welfare decreases in $J+b$ and immediate entry $J+b=0$ (all join) maximizes social welfare. For intermediate service rates ($\mu = 1.4$), social welfare is non-monotonic: welfare increases for more permissive strategies but peaks at a finite value of $J+b$, after which it begins to decline due to rising congestion.

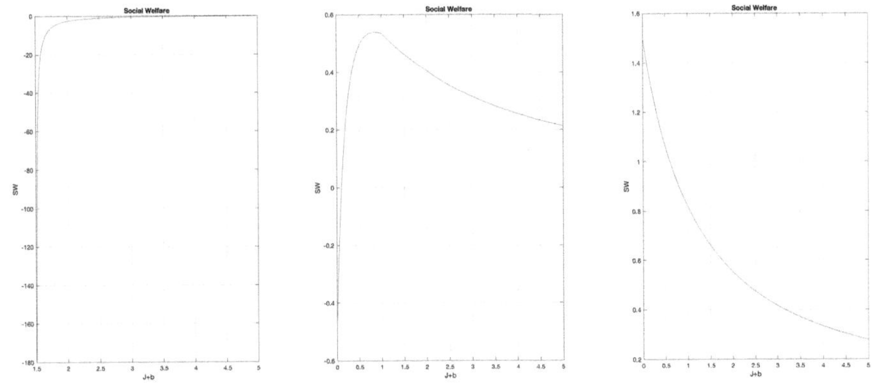

(a) $\mu = 0.4$ (b) $\mu = 1.4$ (c) $\mu = 3$

Fig. 3. Social Welfare under varying strategies $J + b$, when $r = 2$, $c = 1$, $\lambda = 1$ and $\mu = 0.4,\ 1.4,\ 3$.

These trends are consistent with the values presented in Table 1, which shows the optimal $J + b$ and corresponding maximum social welfare for a wider range of μ. As the service rate increases, the optimal strategy becomes less restrictive, and the achievable social welfare improves. Finally, we observe that all customers join when the system has relatively high service rate ($\mu = 3$) and that all balk when the service rate is relatively small ($\mu = 0.4$).

Table 1. Maximum social welfare and optimal strategy $J + b$ for different service rates μ.

μ	0.4	0.7	0.9	1.1	1.4	2	3
Optimal strategy $J + b$	∞	3.99	2.001	1.37	0.86	0	0
Maximum SW	0	0.089	0.207	0.332	0.539	1	1.5

6 Conclusions and Directions for Future Research

Nowadays, in complex multi-level service systems, the administrator of the first level who handles the arrival/entrance process may not have information regarding the congestion of the system in upper levels. Therefore, he makes his decisions regarding the control of the arrivals of the customers based solely on information about the recent joining history of the customers. In a similar manner, in decentralized systems, where the customers make their join-or-balk decisions, the customers may be informed about the recent customers' balking decisions but not about the real congestion. The objective of the present paper was the study of a simple system that lies in this framework under a mixed threshold strategy.

The paper shows a path for the modeling and the study of the performance of such a system. In particular, it shows that such systems can be typically modeled as QBD processes, where the phase process corresponds to the information about recent customers decisions and the level process corresponds to the number of the customers in the system. The special structure of the phase process allows simplifications that lead to elegant and useful formulas about the main performance measures of the system. The next step is the economic analysis of such a system (equilibrium customer strategies, social and revenue optimization).

A more general question concerns the performance evaluation and the economic analysis of systems where the customers' decisions are based on the history of other recently arrived customers' decisions. This seems an important research direction for the study of the behavior of decentralized systems where the customers infer the congestion using other customers' decisions or experiences.

References

1. Burnetas, A., Economou, A.: Equilibrium customer strategies in a single server Markovian queue with setup times. Queueing Syst. **56**, 213–228 (2007)
2. Economou, A.: The impact of information structure on strategic behavior in queueing systems. In: Anisimov, V., Limnios, N. (eds.) Queueing Theory 2, Advanced Trends, Series 'Mathematics and Statistics', Sciences. ISTE & J. Wiley, London (2021)
3. Economou, A.: How much information should be given to the strategic customers of a queueing system? Queueing Syst. **100**(3-4), 421–423 (2022)
4. Economou, A.: Communicating recent customers' decisions to strategic customers of a service system: the join or balk dilemma. In: Dimitras, A., Peppas, G., Mitsi, C.(eds.) Proceedings of the International Conference on Business and Economics, Hellenic Open University ICBE 2024, vol. 4 No. 1 (2024)
5. Economou, A.: The impact of information about last customer's decision on the join-or-balk dilemma in a queueing system. Ann. Oper. Res., forthcoming (2024)
6. Economou, A., Kanta, S.: Equilibrium balking strategies in the observable single-server queue with breakdowns and repairs. Oper. Res. Lett. **36**(6), 696–699 (2008)
7. Economou, A., Logothetis, D., Manou, A.: The value of reneging for strategic customers in queueing systems with server vacations/failures. Eur. J. Oper. Res. **299**(3), 960–976 (2022)
8. Edelson, N.M., Hildebrand, K.: Congestion tolls for Poisson queueing processes. Econometrica **43**, 81–92 (1975)
9. Guo, P., Hassin, R.: Strategic behavior and social optimization in Markovian vacation queues. Oper. Res. **59**(4), 986–997 (2011)
10. Guo, P., Hassin, R.: Strategic behavior and social optimization in Markovian vacation queues: the case of heterogeneous customers. Eur. J. Oper. Res. **222**, 278–286 (2012)
11. Hassin, R.: Rational Queueing. CRC Press, Taylor and Francis Group, Boca Raton (2016)

12. Hassin, R., Haviv, M.: To Queue or Not to Queue: Equilibrium Behavior in Queueing Systems. Kluwer Academic Publishers, Boston (2003)
13. Ibrahim, R.: Sharing delay information in service systems: a literature survey. Queueing Syst.**89** , 49–79 (2018)
14. Kleinrock, L.: Queueing Systems, Volume I: Theory. John Wiley and Sons Inc (1975)
15. Latouche, G., Ramaswami, V.: Introduction to matrix analytic methods in stochastic modeling. ASA-SIAM Series Stat. Appl. Probab. (1999)
16. Naor, P.: The regulation of queue size by levying tolls. Econometrica **37**, 15–24 (1969)
17. Shortle, J.F., Thompson, J.M., Gross, D., Harris, C.M.: Fundamentals of Queueing Theory, 5th Edition. Wiley (2018)
18. Stidham, S., Jr.: Optimal Design of Queueing Systems. CRC Press, Taylor and Francis Group, Boca Raton (2009)

A Simulation Study of the Sojourn Time in Queueing Systems with Stochastically Delayed Information

Kazuma Abe[1(✉)], Tuan Phung-Duc[2], and Masaki Onishi[2,3]

[1] Graduate School of Science and Technology, University of Tsukuba, Ibaraki, Japan
abe.kazuma.su@alumni.tsukuba.ac.jp

[2] Institute of Systems and Information Engineering, University of Tsukuba, Ibaraki, Japan
tuan@sk.tsukuba.ac.jp, onishi-masaki@aist.go.jp

[3] National Institute of Advanced Industrial Science and Technology (AIST), Ibaraki, Japan

Abstract. In this paper, we consider a queueing model with delayed information, in which the routing decision is based on a multinomial logit model. Many studies have analyzed queue length oscillations caused by herd behavior under the join-the-shortest-queue (JSQ) policy. However, there has been limited research on how two key factors—the sensitivity parameter θ, which influences the server routing preference, and the delay Δ, which represents the time required to enter a server—affect the performance. This study aims to characterize the relationship between them when the delay Δ follows some particular probability distributions. Simulation examples illustrate that the constant delay case yields the worst performance in terms of mean sojourn time. Moreover, we demonstrate that there exists an optimal sensitivity parameter that minimizes the sojourn time, and that as the expectation of Δ increases, this optimal sensitivity parameter approaches zero, corresponding to random allocation.

Keywords: Queueing system · Sojourn time · Multinomial logit model · Simulation

1 Introduction

Spatially distributed service systems arise in a wide range of real-world applications, where service seekers and providers coexist within the same geographical space. Representative examples include patients selecting hospitals based on proximity and capacity [3], mobile users connecting to wireless base stations in cellular networks [2], and evacuees seeking shelter or transportation hubs in the event of a natural disaster.

A. Remke et al. (Eds.): Valuetools 2025, LNICST 691, pp. 22–36, 2027.
https://doi.org/10.1007/978-3-032-23901-3_2

These systems are inherently complex due to the interplay among spatial geometry, system dynamics (e.g., queueing, congestion, and mobility), and decision-making under uncertainty. Analyzing and optimizing such systems requires careful modeling of spatial factors, such as distance, coverage, interference, and travel time, which are often coupled with stochastic elements, including random arrivals and time-varying service capacities. A key factor that influences system performance is the delay incurred in accessing services, as spatial separation inherently causes latency and can significantly degrade the overall efficiency.

Acknowledging the importance of delay on system efficiency, recent studies on spatial service systems have extensively examined how queue length and waiting time information, particularly delay announcements, affect user behavior. Mitzenmacher [8] investigated that while the join-the-shortest-queue (JSQ) policy is optimal in the absence of travel delays, outdated information can lead to significant queue imbalance and even cause random allocation to outperform the JSQ under sufficiently large information delays. However, this foundational work primarily focused on specific deterministic delay scenarios and did not extensively explore the implications of various stochastic delay distributions on system stability and performance.

In such cases, the use of outdated information in the JSQ can lead to oscillatory behavior. Building on this, Ibrahim [6] further examined a model in which service providers routinely share information about upcoming waiting times with their customers through delayed announcements. To characterize the relationship between queue oscillation and information delay, Pender et al. [11] analyzed a fluid model for a two-queue system with an infinite buffer, where customers select their queues according to a multinomial logit model. They identified the critical delay under which oscillation of the queue lengths can be observed indefinitely. Pender et al. established a rigorous stochastic foundation in [10], deriving fluid and diffusion limits and characterizing critical delay thresholds that determine system stability by proving heavy traffic limits. Building on this line of inquiry, [7] employed nonlinear dynamical systems techniques to approximate oscillation amplitudes and frequencies, and extended the framework to multi-queue settings.

Further extending this line of inquiry, the work in [12] analyzed the model with time-varying arrivals. Their asymptotic analysis revealed that the critical delay remains unaffected unless the frequency of the time-varying arrival rate is double that of the critical delay. Novitzky et al. [9] considered situations when the delay follows some probability distributions and derived a condition for Hopf bifurcation.

While many studies have focused on characterizing queue oscillations, another stream of work has explored strategies to mitigate these effects. For instance, [4] introduced the randomized join-the-shortest-queue (RJSQ) policy, in which jobs are dispatched to servers in proportion to their service capacities, such that only a small fraction of the jobs are assigned to the server with the least capacity. They derived the optimal fraction to select the server with the smallest number of jobs in the heavy traffic regime.

While these mitigation strategies offer potential solutions, accurately analyzing the expected change in queue lengths during the delay remains a significant challenge. Most studies utilize the asymptotic analysis to circumvent these difficulties (for example, [1,4,5]). However, a comprehensive understanding of how various delay distributions impact system performance remains limited, particularly in scenarios where analytical solutions are intractable. This intractability necessitates the use of computational approaches.

In this paper, we comprehensively capture the sojourn time through Monte Carlo simulations, representing it by performance evaluation indicators under delay scenarios governed by probability distributions. Here, the sojourn time refers to the total time from when a job is transferred to when it finishes being processed by a server. We demonstrate that the specific characteristics of the delay distribution play a critical role in shaping the queueing dynamics.

The remainder of this paper is organized as follows. Section 2 presents the queueing model based on the multi-logit routing. In Sect. 3, we present the simulation results and investigate how the sensitivity parameter affects the system performance under information delay, where the delay is assumed to follow various probability distributions. Finally, we conclude this work with a discussion of future directions in Sect. 4.

2 Multinomial Logit Model

In this section, we present a multinomial logit model, which is widely used in discrete choice theory, machine learning, and probabilistic routing in queueing systems. Our mathematical representation follows Pender et al. (e.g., [10,11], and [12]). While their selection rule is based on delayed queue lengths, our derivation focuses on the server's expected processing time.

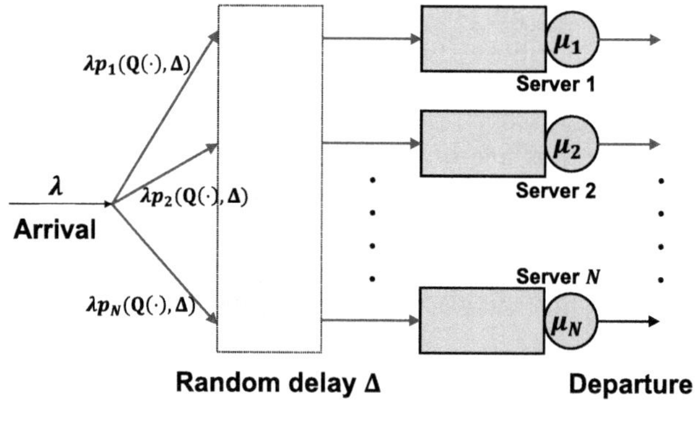

Fig. 1. System model. The dispatcher selects a server when a job arrives in front of the gray rectangle that represents the delay. (Color figure online)

We assume a queueing system, which is composed of N spatially distributed servers, as in Fig. 1. Each server has an infinitely sized buffer and a service rate

μ_i, $i \in \{1, 2, \ldots, N\}$. We denote by $Q_i(t)$ the queue length at server i at time t. The total arrival rate to the dispatchers, also interpreted here as service seekers, is denoted by λ. We now consider the situation in which jobs experience a delay Δ to enter the server after being selected by the dispatcher, where Δ follows a probability distribution that is common to all queues.

The probability that a job is routed to server i at time t is given by

$$p_i(Q(t)) = \frac{\exp\{-\theta \cdot \frac{Q_i(t)}{\mu_i}\}}{\sum_{j=1}^{N} \exp\left\{-\theta \cdot \frac{Q_j(t)}{\mu_j}\right\}} \quad \text{for } \theta \in \mathbb{R}_+, \tag{1}$$

where $Q(t) = \{Q_1(t), \ldots, Q_N(t)\}$, and θ is the sensitivity parameter that controls the preference of the servers. The larger θ is, the more likely a job is assigned to the shortest expected delay.

While the server selection is based on the current queue length $Q_i(t)$, which reflects the number of jobs already present at server i at time t, the actual number of jobs upon arrival at server i is $Q_i(t + \Delta)$. This value may differ from $Q_i(t)$ due to possible arrivals and departures during the delay period Δ.

Since one server is chosen upon arrival, $\sum_{i=1}^{N} p_i(Q(t)) = 1$. It should be noted that equation (1) can be rewritten as

$$p_i(Q(t)) = \frac{1}{1 + \sum_{j \neq i} \exp\left\{-\theta(\frac{Q_j(t)}{\mu_j} - \frac{Q_i(t)}{\mu_i})\right\}} \quad \text{for } \theta \in \mathbb{R}_+, \tag{2}$$

which states that the routing probability is determined by the difference between the number of jobs assigned to the server and the number of jobs assigned to other servers, not the queue length (see Fig. 2). Now, if one takes the limit $\theta \to \infty$, then the choice function behaves like the shortest expected delay (SED) rule, which generalizes the JSQ policy to heterogeneous service rates and reduces to the JSQ when $\mu_1 = \cdots = \mu_N$. This behavior follows from the fact that the second term of the denominator vanishes if the number of jobs handled by server 1 is smaller than that of the other servers. And, if θ is close to 0, the routing probability becomes more uniform and approaches $\frac{1}{N}$.

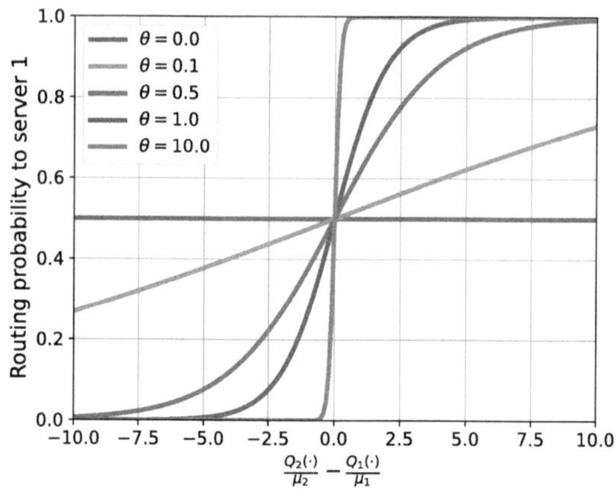

Fig. 2. The probability that a job is routed to server 1 for various θ in case of $\mu_1 = \mu_2 = 1.0$ and $N = 2$.

3 Numerical Simulation

Each simulation in this section is conducted using SimPy, a discrete-event simulation library in Python, running up to time 10^6, with the first 5×10^5 jobs are discarded as a burn-in period. For each of the 10 independent runs, we collect the mean and the standard deviation of the sojourn time for each job. These 10 samples are then used to estimate a 95% confidence interval for the population mean using Student's t-distribution.

3.1 Identical Servers Case

We conduct a simulation example for the queueing model with two identical servers. In this setting, jobs are generated spatially in a certain domain according to a Poisson process with rate λ. Upon job generation, there is a constant delay Δ before the job enters a server. Two identical servers with infinite buffers process jobs whose lengths follow the exponential distribution with rate $\mu = 1.0$. We focus on the sojourn time of each job in the system, which is the total time from job generation to the completion of service at a server.

Constant delay

Figure 3 shows the mean and standard deviation of the sojourn time over θ for three job arrival rates λ when the delay is constant. The shaded area represents a 95% confidence interval using Student's t-distribution, which is sufficiently narrow, and the sample mean lies within this range, indicating that the results are consistent. The x-axis represents the sensitivity parameter, where $\theta = 0$ is equivalent to random allocation, and as $\theta \to \infty$, a job is more likely to be routed

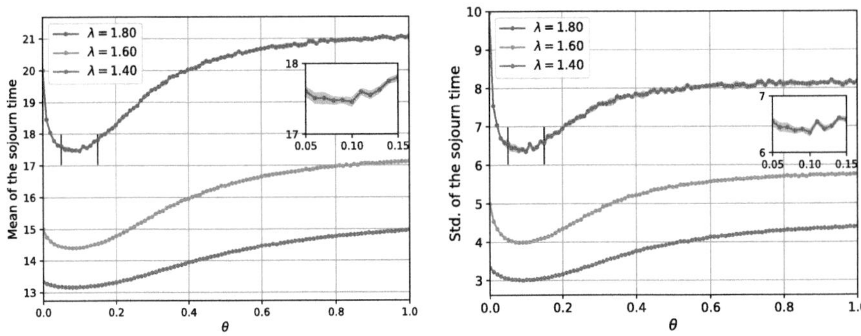

Fig. 3. The sojourn time against θ for $\Delta = 10$.

to the server that has the fewest jobs, and the sojourn time approaches the value that would obtain under the JSQ policy (see Table 1).

Both curves show a similar pattern over θ, suggesting that the standard deviation evolves in close correspondence with the mean over time. For $\lambda = 1.80$, we clearly observe a minimum in both the mean and the standard deviation of the sojourn time near $\theta = 0.10$. When the arrival rate is smaller, the observed pattern is similar to that at higher arrival rates, and the distinction between the curves becomes less apparent.

Table 1. Sojourn times for constant Δ and λ under the JSQ policy ($\theta = \infty$) obtained from simulation.

Δ	$\lambda = 1.40$		$\lambda = 1.60$		$\lambda = 1.80$	
	Mean	Std.	Mean	Std.	Mean	Std.
0	2.110	2.045	3.002	2.922	5.451	5.192
1.0	3.556	2.308	4.473	3.129	7.198	5.674
5.0	8.908	3.377	10.239	4.326	13.436	6.666
10	15.506	4.641	17.575	5.904	21.342	8.168
20	28.548	6.782	32.385	9.042	37.845	11.997
50	67.266	12.459	76.807	17.850	89.048	24.610

Figure 4 illustrates the mean and standard deviation of the sojourn time against θ for three arrival rates when the constant delay $\Delta = 20$. Compared to $\Delta = 10$ in Fig. 3, the curves exhibit a similar behavior, including a point where the sojourn time reaches its minimum. Moreover, as Δ increases, the value θ^*—where sojourn time is minimized—shifts toward 0. This observation is supported by the work in [4], which demonstrates that introducing randomness in server selection can outperform pure deterministic routing.

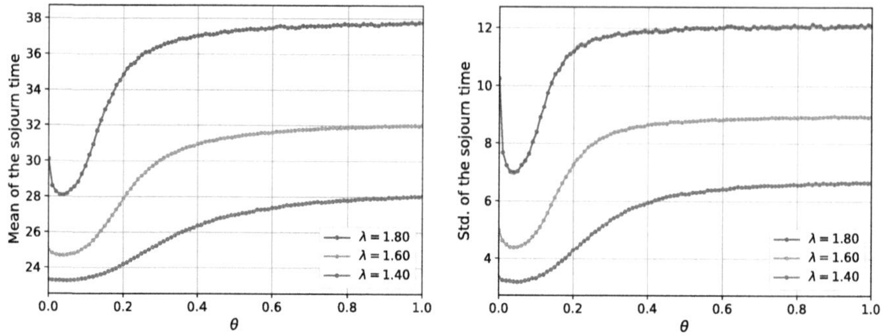

Fig. 4. Changes in sojourn time with θ for $\Delta = 20$.

Throughout the remainder of the section, we fix $\lambda = 1.80$, unless otherwise specified. Figure 5 illustrates the behavior of the mean of the sojourn time when θ changes for a slight delay (left) and a large delay (right). For better visualization and comparison, the results are separated into two plots. First, when the delay is small (i.e., $\Delta = 1.0$), the curve exhibits a downward trend, which suggests that the information delay does not significantly affect the load balancing, and the JSQ policy is still optimal to minimize sojourn time. As Δ increases, there exists some value θ^* to minimize the sojourn time, because delayed information eventually becomes invalid. Indeed, when the delay is sizeable (as when $\theta = 10$ and 20), θ^* shifts toward 0, which indicates that adding randomness to server routing improves performance.

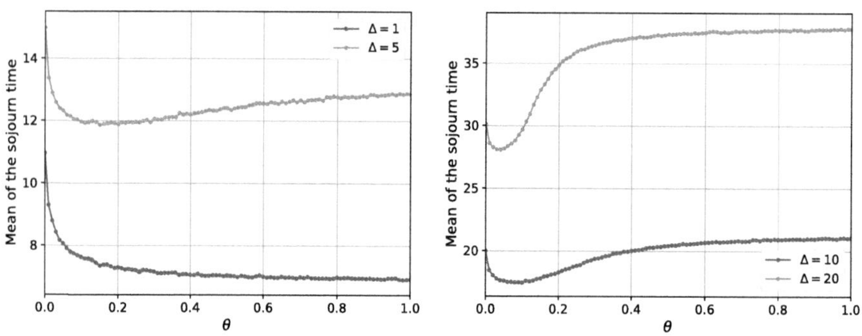

Fig. 5. The sojourn time against θ for several constant delays.

Figure 6 shows histograms of the sojourn time. Here, the red circle and the blue triangle denote the mean and the maximum sojourn time (observed from the simulationz), respectively. The top row corresponds to random allocation (i.e., $\theta = 0$), which follows an exponential distribution with rate $\mu - \lambda$, shifted to the right by Δ.

In Fig. 6, the two histograms in the middle row correspond to the optimal values of θ obtained from the simulations, with $\theta = 0.1$ for $\Delta = 10$ (left) and $\theta = 0.04$ for $\Delta = 20$ (right). Both subplots show improved performances in terms of the mean and standard deviation of the sojourn time, compared to other θ values.

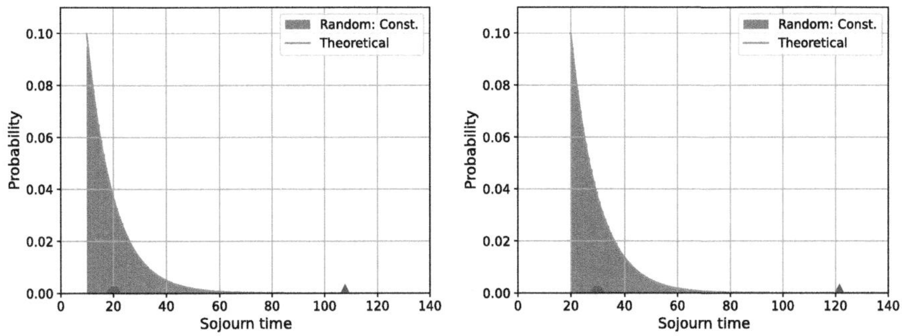

(a) Random allocation ($\theta = 0$).

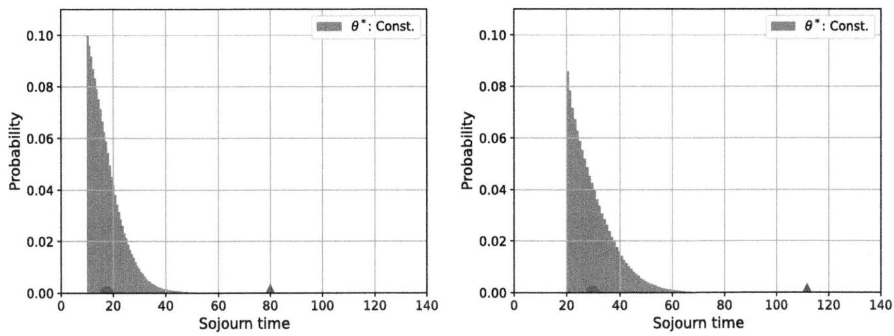

(b) Optimal value of θ obtained from the simulations.

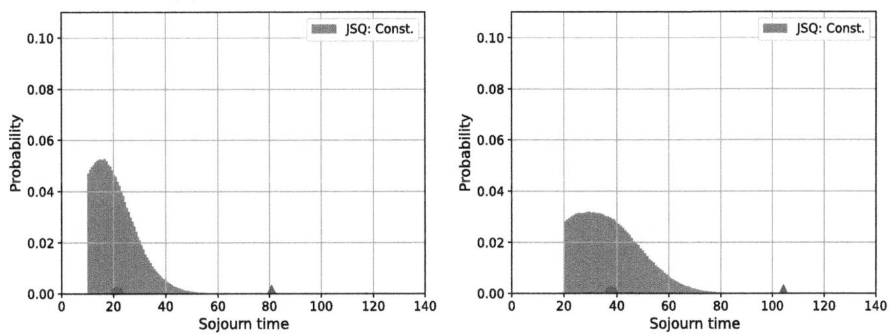

(c) JSQ policy ($\theta = \infty$).

Fig. 6. Histograms of sojourn time. The left column corresponds to $\Delta = 10$, and the right column to $\Delta = 20$.

The bottom row of histograms depicts the distribution under the JSQ policy (i.e., $\theta = \infty$), and the center subplots show the results for the optimal θ value obtained from the simulation. When $\Delta = 10$, the JSQ policy shows better performance than random allocation in terms of the mean sojourn time and its standard deviation (also see Fig. 3). On the contrary, when $\Delta = 20$, the mean sojourn time under the JSQ policy is larger than that under random allocation. Conversely, concerning the maximum sojourn time, random allocation is worse than the JSQ policy. Evaluating the tail behavior of a queue with delayed information using probabilistic techniques remains an open problem.

Uniform delay

The assumption of constant delay simplifies the analysis of the system. However, in practical situations, access delays are unlikely to be constant; they typically fluctuate based on various factors, including service congestion and geographical location. To extend to a delay following a probability distribution, [9] introduced a queueing system where M discrete constant delays are imposed proportionally on incoming jobs, and M is very large. This causes the delay distribution to approximate a continuous one.

Inspired by the work in [9], we investigate a routing policy under which the delay distribution is assumed to be uniformly distributed over the interval $[0, 2\Delta]$ when there are M discrete delay values with equal weights, and M approaches infinity.

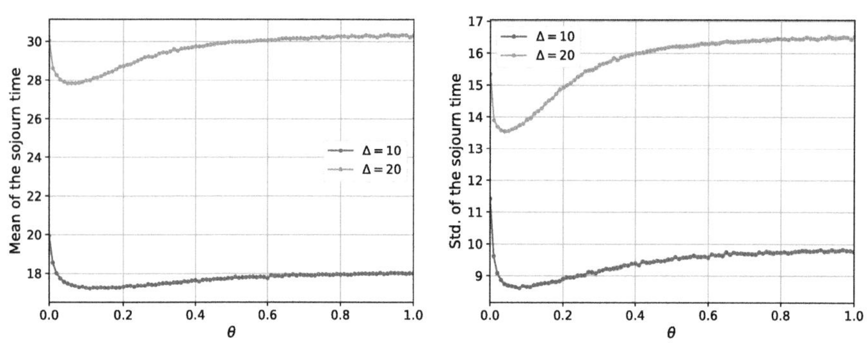

Fig. 7. The mean and standard deviation of sojourn time against θ when Δ follows a uniform distribution.

Figure 7 illustrates the mean and standard deviation of the sojourn time when the delay distribution is a uniform distribution. The observed patterns resemble those of the constant delay case, although the curves appear less distinct. In particular, both plots exhibit sojourn time minima, for which θ^* approaches 0 when Δ becomes large.

Figure 8 shows the histograms of sojourn times when the delay is a uniform distribution. The top, middle and bottom rows correspond to random allocation ($\theta = 0$), the optimal value θ^* obtained from the simulations, and the JSQ policy ($\theta = \infty$), respectively. As discussed for Fig. 6, we observe a similar distributional shape.

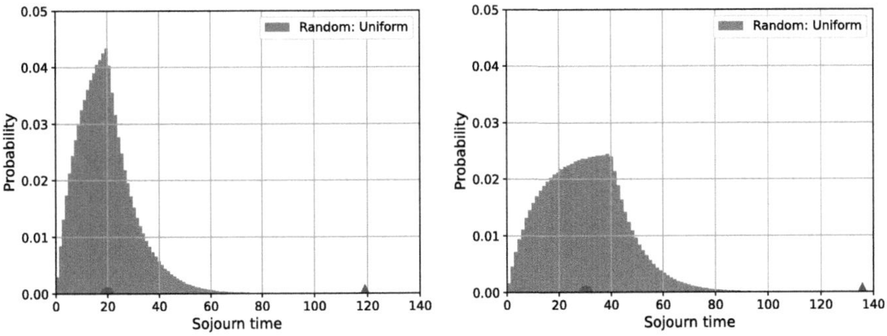

(a) Random allocation ($\theta = 0$).

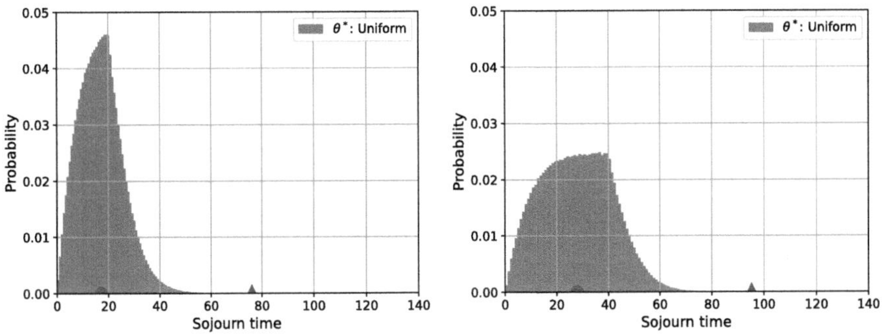

(b) Optimal value of θ obtained from the simulations.

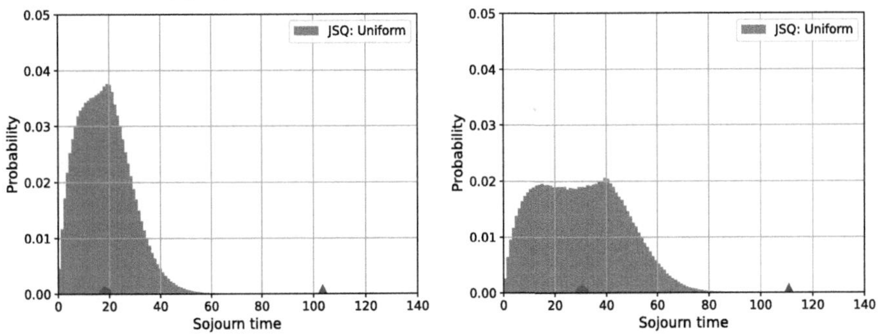

(c) JSQ policy ($\theta = \infty$).

Fig. 8. Histograms of sojourn times when the delay follows a uniform distribution with the support $[0, 20]$ (the left column), and $[0, 40]$ (the right column).

From the perspective of the mean and the standard deviation of the sojourn time, the difference between random allocation and the JSQ policy when $\Delta = 10$ is not substantial (see Fig. 7). However, in terms of the maximum sojourn time, the JSQ policy achieves better performance than random allocation.

Whereas the mean sojourn time under the JSQ policy is larger than that under random allocation when $\Delta = 20$, random allocation is a worse policy than JSQ in terms of the maximum sojourn time.

Gamma distribution

The gamma distribution is another important continuous distribution. Unlike the uniform distribution, it has an unbounded support and provides a broader variety of probability density shapes. Its form is specified by two parameters: the shape parameter $k > 0$ and the rate parameter $\alpha > 0$.

For a random variable $\Delta \sim \text{Gamma}(k, \alpha)$, the probability density function is:

$$f_\Delta(x) = \begin{cases} \dfrac{\alpha^k}{\Gamma(k)} x^{k-1} e^{-\alpha x}, & \text{for } x > 0, \\ 0, & \text{for } x \leq 0, \end{cases}$$

where $\Gamma(k)$ is the gamma function.

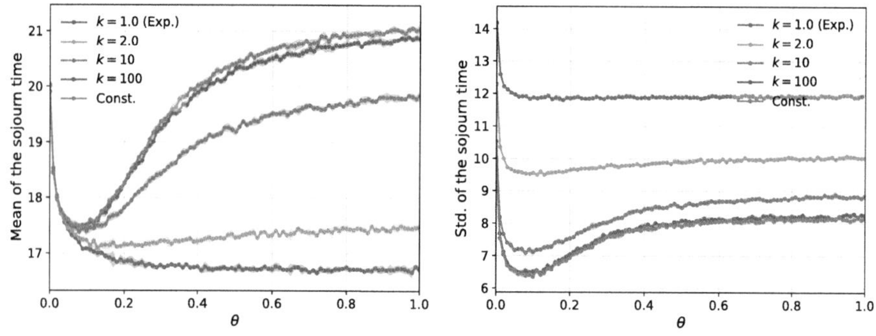

Fig. 9. Changes in the mean and standard deviation of the sojourn time against θ when Δ follows a gamma distribution.

Figure 9 shows how the mean and the standard deviation of the sojourn time vary with θ when the delay distribution follows a gamma distribution. $k = 1$ represents an exponential distribution, which achieves the smallest sojourn time among the curves (also see Fig. 10).

We can also notice that the curve converges to the case of the constant delay as k becomes large. This observation is justified, since the gamma distribution converges to a Dirac delta function as $k \to \infty$, indicating that the delay asymptotically approaches a deterministic value. This insight highlights the importance of variability in delay, which significantly impacts the mean sojourn time. In other words, as the fluctuation in delay Δ decreases, the mean sojourn time increases.

Exponential delay

When $k = 1$, the gamma distribution reduces to the exponential distribution. Here, we examine the relationship between delay and sojourn time under this particular case.

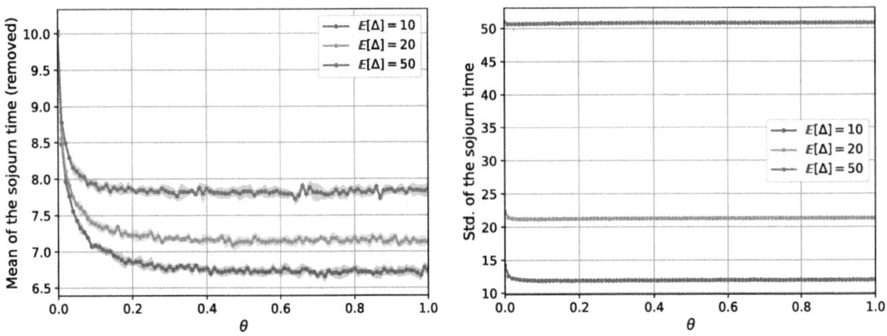

Fig. 10. The mean and standard deviation of the sojourn time against θ with an exponentially distributed delay.

Figure 10 shows the sojourn time with respect to θ when the delay is exponentially distributed. The left subplot shows the mean time after removing delays Δ from the sojourn time for clarity of visualization. We can hence confirm that the longer the delay, the longer it takes for jobs to be completed, indicating that the timeliness of information affects the system performance.

3.2 Heterogeneous Servers Case

In this subsection, we consider a three-server queueing system with heterogeneous service capacities. Jobs arrive at the system according to a Poisson process with rate $\lambda = 3.6$. The service rates are defined as $\mu_1 = \mu_2 = 1.0$ and $\mu_3 = 2.0$ for servers $i = 1, 2, 3$, where each server has an infinite buffer. Under these settings, the traffic intensity yields $\rho = 0.90$.

The upper two figures in Fig. 11 show the mean of the sojourn time against $\Delta = 10$. We notice a similar pattern to the case of identical servers. Random allocation ($\theta = 0$) leads to the system instability because the server with $\mu = 1.0$ receives a proportion of jobs that exceeds its capacity. In this sense, the effect of introducing randomness into the selection of servers is clearly distinct.

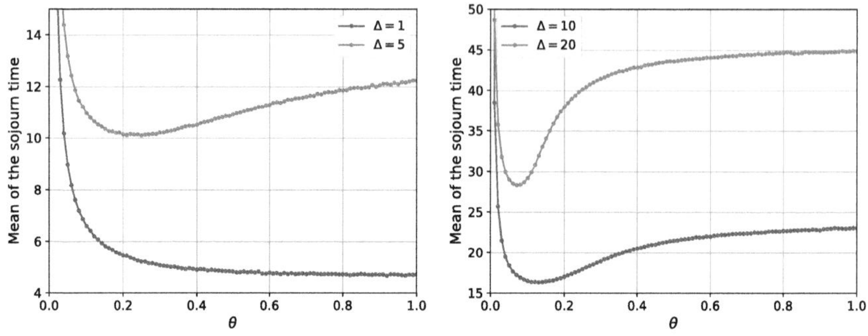

(a) The mean of the sojourn time.

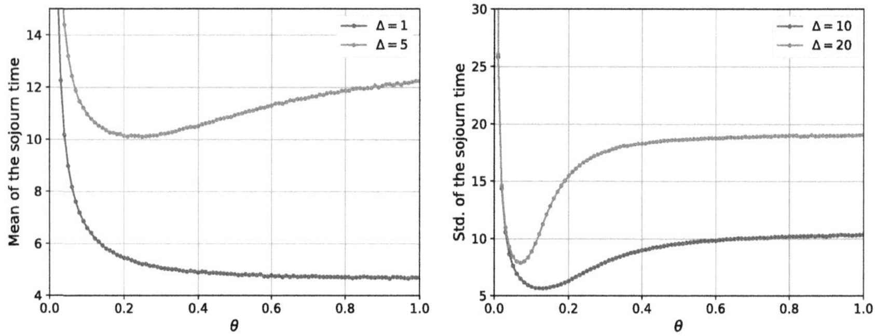

(b) The standard deviation of the sojourn time.

Fig. 11. The mean and standard deviation of the sojourn time against θ for several constant delays.

Furthermore, the larger the value of θ, the smaller the sojourn time when Δ is small, meaning that the JSQ policy is still an effective policy. However, the larger value of θ degrades the performance for large Δ.

The bottom plots Fig. 11 illustrate the standard deviation of the sojourn time for various Δ. The observed patterns resemble those of the mean sojourn time.

4 Conclusion

In this work, we studied a queueing model where information delays follow various probability distributions. Through Monte Carlo simulations, we found that the case with constant delay results in the worst performance in terms of mean sojourn time.

For server routing, we employed a multinomial logistic function parameterized by a sensitivity parameter θ. When the delay is small, delayed information remains useful, and the join-the-shortest-queue (JSQ) policy ($\theta = \infty$) outperforms random allocation ($\theta = 0$). This result is consistent with the findings of [8]. In contrast, when the delay becomes large, the JSQ policy performs worse than other choices of θ. Furthermore, there exists an optimal sensitivity parameter θ^* that minimizes the sojourn time, and as Δ increases, θ^* converges to zero, corresponding to random allocation.

These conclusions were previously established through analytical studies that examined mean values. The value of this simulation study is in showing the standard deviation and distribution of sojourn times under the proposed model. The standard deviation of the sojourn time reflects how much individual values typically deviate from the mean. When combined with the mean and the overall distribution, it helps reveal underlying patterns in the system's performance. In addition, the distribution of the sojourn time can be used to design service-level agreements. For instance, the system can be configured to ensure that the probability of a job's sojourn time exceeding a specified threshold remains below 5%.

For future work, it would be desirable to derive additional performance measures, such as the tail of the distribution and the maximum sojourn time, using extreme value theory. It would also be of interest to investigate methods for obtaining θ^* in analytical form, as well as to explore the assumptions and conditions required for asymptotic analysis.

Acknowledgement. KA was supported by JSPS KAKENHI Grant Number 25KJ0675. TP was supported in part by JSPS KAKENHI Grant Number 21K11765, F-MIRAI: R&D Center for Frontiers of MIRAI in Policy and Technology, the University of Tsukuba and Toyota Motor Corporation Collaborative R&D center, and Kayamori Foundation of Informational Science Advancement.

References

1. Atar, R., Lipshutz, D.: Heavy traffic limits for join-the-shortest-estimated-queue policy using delayed information. Math. Oper. Res. **46**(1), 268–300 (2021)
2. Baccelli, F., Klein, M., Lebourges, M., Zuyev, S.: Stochastic geometry and architecture of communication networks. Telecommun. Syst. **7**, 209–227 (1997)
3. Dong, J., Yom-Tov, E., Yom-Tov, G.B.: The impact of delay announcements on hospital network coordination and waiting times. Manage. Sci. **65**(5), 1969–1994 (2019)
4. He, S., Yang, Y., Yu, Y.: Randomized routing to remote queues. arXiv preprint arXiv:2505.04942 (2025)
5. He, Y.T., Down, D.G.: On accommodating customer flexibility in service systems. INFOR: Inf. Syst. Oper. Res. **47**(4), 289–295 (2009)
6. Ibrahim, R.: Sharing delay information in service systems: a literature survey. Queueing Syst. **89**(1), 49–79 (2018)
7. Lakrad, F., Pender, J., Rand, R.: Queues with delayed information: a dynamical systems perspective. SIAM J. Appl. Dyn. Syst. **21**(1), 676–713 (2022)
8. Mitzenmacher, M.: How useful is old information? In: Proceedings of the Sixteenth Annual ACM Symposium on Principles of Distributed Computing, pp. 83–91 (1997)
9. Novitzky, S., Pender, J.: Queues with delayed information: a probabilistic perspective. Cornell University, Ithaca NY **14853** (2020)

10. Pender, J., Rand, R., Wesson, E.: A stochastic analysis of queues with customer choice and delayed information. Math. Oper. Res. **45**(3), 1104–1126 (2020)
11. Pender, J., Rand, R.H., Wesson, E.: Queues with choice via delay differential equations. Int. J. Bifurcation Chaos **27**(04), 1730016 (2017)
12. Pender, J., Rand, R.H., Wesson, E.: An analysis of queues with delayed information and time-varying arrival rates. Nonlinear Dyn. **91**(4), 2411–2427 (2018)

Social Welfare Optimization in a Queueing Game with Heterogeneous Customers and Partial Information

Fehmina Malik[1] and Yezekael Hayel[2](✉)

[1] Institute of Management Technology Ghaziabad, Ghaziabad, India
fmalik@imt.edu
[2] Avignon University, Avignon, France
yezekael.hayel@univ-avignon.fr

Abstract. Information has a critical impact on the behavior of strategic customers in queueing systems. While prior literature has largely focused on comparing fully observable and unobservable queues, this paper examines a partial information disclosure policy for a system with heterogeneous customers. We consider a threshold-based rule where the queue length is revealed only when the number of customers is below a specified threshold D. For this setting, we characterize equilibrium customer strategies and analyze how the disclosure threshold affects system performance. Our main result identifies the social welfare maximizing disclosure policy and shows how it depends on the degree of customer heterogeneity and system parameters. These findings provide valuable insights for designing efficient information disclosure policies in service systems with strategic, heterogeneous customers.

Keywords: Queuing games · Heterogeneous customers · Strategic customers · Mixed observation structure

1 Introduction

Queueing systems are central to modern service economies, spanning telecommunications, cloud computing, healthcare, and transportation. A key challenge in their design is modeling the behavior of strategic customers, who weigh service benefits against waiting costs. Their decentralized joining decisions shape congestion and system performance, making strategic queueing games a natural framework.

Customer behavior depends critically on information disclosure. Two classical extremes dominate the literature: the fully observable queue of [11], where customers follow threshold joining rules, and the unobservable queue of [5], where decisions are probabilistic. This dichotomy provides foundational insights [8] but misses practical cases where providers disclose state information selectively to balance congestion control with demand.

A. Remke et al. (Eds.): Valuetools 2025, LNICST 691, pp. 37–48, 2027.
https://doi.org/10.1007/978-3-032-23901-3_3

Most canonical models also assume homogeneous customers with identical valuations and waiting costs. Real systems, however, feature heterogeneity: passengers of different classes, emergency versus scheduled patients, or premium versus standard customers. Such heterogeneity fundamentally changes equilibrium structures, often creating hierarchical joining behaviors [1,4].

This paper combines these two dimensions—partial disclosure and heterogeneity—by analyzing a mixed observation structure. A service provider adopts a threshold-based Information Disclosure Policy (IDP): the queue length is revealed if and only if it does not exceed a threshold D. Customers above this threshold receive no information and decide based on beliefs, creating two distinct modes of decision-making.

Our model includes multiple customer classes with distinct waiting costs, each with its own Naor threshold n_j. This leads to a state-dependent arrival process and a rich equilibrium structure. We derive equilibrium strategies, the stationary distribution, and address the provider's problem of selecting D to maximize social welfare. Closed-form results are obtained for fully observable and certain mixed scenarios; in more complex cases, we characterize equilibrium conditions for joining probabilities.

Our contributions are:

- A general model integrating heterogeneity with threshold-based disclosure, not previously studied.
- Characterization of symmetric equilibrium strategies and mixed joining probabilities under the IDP.
- Explicit formulas for stationary distributions and welfare across scenarios defined by D and class thresholds.
- A welfare maximization result proving existence of an optimal finite disclosure threshold D^*, with asymptotic properties depending on heterogeneity and load.

In doing so, we extend [12], which analyzed homogeneous populations, to heterogeneous systems. We show that heterogeneity is not a minor complication but a structural feature that reshapes optimal disclosure, providing providers with sharper tools for system design.

2 Literature Review

The seminal work of Naor [11] established the observable queue, where customers adopt threshold joining rules and inefficiencies arise from congestion externalities. The unobservable case, formalized by [5], yields mixed-strategy equilibria based on system parameters. These two extremes of information—full and none—form the basis of the literature [8].

A key extension concerns the value of partial information disclosure. Rather than choosing between extremes, providers can strategically reveal information to influence behavior. [2,7] showed that the impact depends on load: disclosure can reduce throughput under light traffic but raise it under heavy traffic. This initiated the study of information design, where disclosure is a decision variable. Closest to our work, [12] analyzed a threshold-based policy for homogeneous customers and proved that partial disclosure can dominate both extremes.

The simplifying assumption of homogeneous customers has also been challenged. [1,4] studied heterogeneous classes differing in waiting costs or valuations, showing that heterogeneity generates hierarchical equilibria and complicates welfare analysis. Further complexity arises when information is costly or delayed: [9] considered customers who may acquire information at a price, while [13] examined delayed, stale data. Relatedly, retrial-type models [3,10] incorporate multi-stage decision processes with distinct action and cost structures.

Despite these advances, the intersection of heterogeneity and information design remains underexplored. [12] solved for the optimal threshold in homogeneous systems, while [4] studied heterogeneous populations under fixed scenarios. Our work synthesizes these streams by investigating optimal threshold-based disclosure in heterogeneous queues. We show how a single threshold D is interpreted differently across classes, derive the resulting equilibrium and welfare, and solve for the provider's optimal policy D^*.

3 Model and Preliminaries

3.1 System Overview and Heterogeneous Customer Classes

We consider an $M/M/1$ queue system that serves heterogeneous customers. J classes of users exist in the system and they are served based on First-Come First-Served (FCFS) priority. The arrival rate is a Poisson process for each j-customer at rate λ_j, where $j \in \{1, 2, ..., J\}$. The service time for each customer is exponentially distributed with the same rate μ. We denote $\rho_j = \lambda_j/\mu$.

We assume that all customers have the same service valuation $R > 0$, and they incur a waiting cost $C_j > 0$ per unit of time. The waiting costs for each class are increasing, satisfying the relation $C_1 < C_2 < \cdots < C_J$, meaning that customers of class 1 are the least sensitive to waiting time while customers of class J are the most sensitive to waiting.

Informed customers observe the system state and make joining decisions based on the observed queue length. A customer who observes i customers in the queue (including the one in service) will join if their net benefit $R - \frac{(i+1)C_j}{\mu}$ is positive; otherwise, they balk. Consequently, the best response of an observing j-customer is to join the system if $i + 1 \leq n_j$, where

$$n_j = \left\lfloor \frac{\mu R}{C_j} \right\rfloor \tag{1}$$

is Naor's threshold for the observable queue. Due to the increasing waiting costs, each class has its own threshold, yielding the relation $n_1 > n_2 > \cdots > n_J$. Under this strategy, a j-customer joins the queue if and only if they observe $n_j - 1$ or fewer customers.

The system structure is illustrated in Fig. 1, which shows the queueing system with J classes of users.

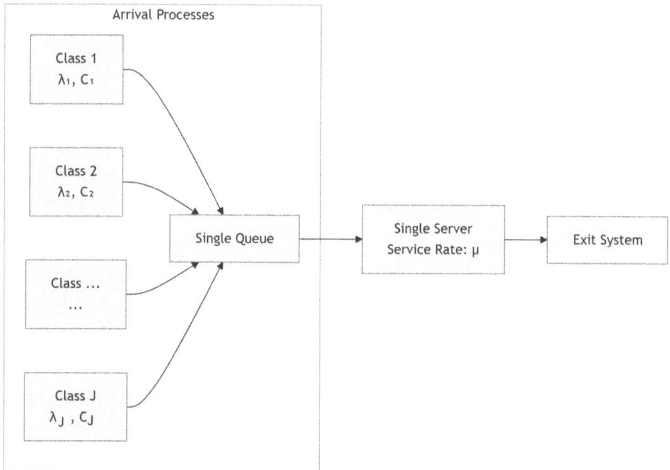

Fig. 1. Queue system with J classes of users.

3.2 Mixed Observation Structure Under Threshold-Based Information Disclosure

We analyze the strategic behavior of customers in a queueing system where queue length information is selectively disclosed under a threshold-based Information Disclosure Policy (IDP). The policy is defined by a threshold parameter $D \in \mathbb{N}$, which determines whether arriving customers receive real-time queue length information.

- **Informed Customers:** If an arrival finds $i \leq D$ customers in the system, the provider reveals the exact queue length. The customer then follows Naor's rule: a class-j customer joins if and only if $i \leq n_j - 1$, i.e., when the net benefit condition $R - \frac{(i+1)C_j}{\mu} \geq 0$ holds.
- **Uninformed Customers:** If an arrival finds $i > D$, the provider withholds information. The customer, lacking state knowledge, adopts a mixed strategy as in [5]: a class-j customer joins with probability $q_j \in [0, 1]$, determined in equilibrium from expected waiting costs.

Thus, the IDP induces a hybrid system that alternates between observable and unobservable scenarios depending on whether the state exceeds D. The central question is how a welfare-maximizing provider should choose the optimal disclosure threshold D^*, trading off the benefits of transparency against the congestion effects of strategic behavior.

4 Analysis of Queueing Models Under Threshold-Based Information Disclosure

4.1 Model Specifications and Classification

For the remainder of this analysis, we focus on a system with two classes of heterogeneous customers ($J = 2$). The system behavior varies significantly based on the relationship between the information disclosure threshold D and the Naor thresholds n_1 and n_2, leading to three distinct operational scenarios.

4.2 Complete Information Scenario ($D \geq n_1 - 1$)

When the disclosure threshold satisfies $D \geq n_1 - 1$, all arriving customers receive complete queue length information. In this scenario, the system operates as a standard $M/M/1/n_1$ queue with state-dependent arrival rates, where customers of class j join only if they observe $i \leq n_j - 1$ customers in the system (Fig. 2).

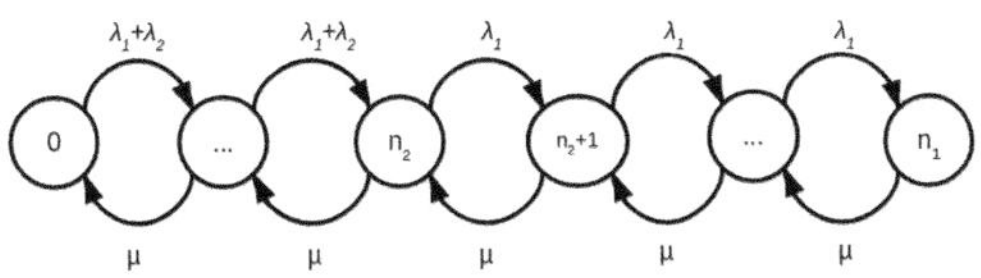

Fig. 2. Markov chain representation of system evolution under complete information disclosure ($D \geq n_1 - 1$).

Proposition 1 (Stationary Distribution - Complete Information). *The stationary probability of an empty system in the complete information scenario is given by:*

$$\pi_0 = \frac{(1 - (\rho_1 + \rho_2))(1 - \rho_1)}{1 - \rho_1 - (\rho_1 + \rho_2)^{n_2+1}(1 - \rho_1^{n_1-n_2+1}) + (\rho_1 + \rho_2)^{n_2}\rho_1(1 - \rho_1^{n_1-n_2})} \tag{2}$$

Proof. From the balance equations of the underlying birthâĂŞdeath process (state-dependent arrivals), we obtain for $i > 0$:

$$\pi_i = \begin{cases} (\rho_1 + \rho_2)^i \pi_0 & \text{for } 0 \leq i \leq n_2 \\ (\rho_1 + \rho_2)^{n_2} \rho_1^{i-n_2} \pi_0 & \text{for } n_2 < i \leq n_1 \end{cases}$$

Normalizing the sum of probabilities yields:

$$\pi_0 \left[\sum_{i=0}^{n_2} (\rho_1 + \rho_2)^i + \sum_{i=n_2+1}^{n_1} (\rho_1 + \rho_2)^{n_2} \rho_1^{i-n_2} \right] = 1$$

Evaluating the geometric sums:

$$\sum_{i=0}^{n_2}(\rho_1+\rho_2)^i = \frac{1-(\rho_1+\rho_2)^{n_2+1}}{1-(\rho_1+\rho_2)}$$

$$\sum_{i=n_2+1}^{n_1}(\rho_1+\rho_2)^{n_2}\rho_1^{i-n_2} = (\rho_1+\rho_2)^{n_2}\rho_1\frac{1-\rho_1^{n_1-n_2}}{1-\rho_1}$$

Substituting and solving for π_0 provides the desired result. ■

Performance Measures The expected number of customers in the system is given by:

$$\begin{aligned} L =& \pi_0\left[(\rho_1+\rho_2)\left(\frac{(1-(\rho_1+\rho_2))(n_2+1)(\rho_1+\rho_2)^{n_2}+(1-(\rho_1+\rho_2)^{n_2+1})}{(1-(\rho_1+\rho_2))^2}\right)\right] \\ &+\pi_0\left[(\rho_1+\rho_2)^{n_2}\rho_1^{n_2+2}\left(\frac{(1-\rho_1)(n_1+1)\rho_1^{n_1}+(1-\rho_1^{n_1+1})}{(1-\rho_1)^2}\right)\right]. \end{aligned}$$

4.3 Mixed Information Scenario ($D < n_1 - 1$)

When $D < n_1 - 1$ (i.e., $D \leq n_1 - 2$), the system exhibits more complex behavior with partial information disclosure. We distinguish between two subcases based on the relationship between D and n_2.

Equilibrium Analysis In the mixed information scenario, uninformed customers (those arriving when $i > D$) employ mixed strategies. The equilibrium joining probabilities p_j^* are determined by solving the system of equations that equalizes expected utility to zero.

Proposition 2 (Equilibrium Joining Probabilities). *The equilibrium joining probabilities for uninformed customers are:*

$$p_1^* = \frac{\mu(R\mu-(D+2)C_1)}{\lambda_1(R\mu-(D+1)C_1)} \tag{3}$$

$$p_2^* = \frac{\mu(R\mu-(D+2)C_2)}{\lambda_2(R\mu-(D+1)C_2)} - \frac{\lambda_1}{\lambda_2} \tag{4}$$

Proof. The expected sojourn time for uninformed customers is:

$$W_D(p^*) = \frac{D+1}{\mu} + \frac{1}{\mu-\sum_{j=1}^{2}\lambda_j p_j^*}$$

The equilibrium conditions require that for each class j:

$$U_j(p^*) = R - C_j W_D(p^*) = 0$$

Solving these equations simultaneously yields the expressions for p_1^* and p_2^*. ■

These equilibrium probabilities reflect the strategic behavior of customers who must decide whether to join without observing the current queue length. The expressions capture how joining decisions depend on both the disclosure threshold D and the system parameters. Specifically, higher waiting costs C_j reduce the joining probability, while a higher service reward R increases it. The additional term $-\lambda_1/\lambda_2$ in p_2^* accounts for the congestion effect caused by class-1 customers, highlighting how strategic interactions between different customer classes shape equilibrium behavior. This formulation extends the classic threshold strategies in observable queues to settings with partial information disclosure.

Scenario 1: $D \leq n_2 - 1$: In this scenario where $D \leq n_2 - 1$, the queue length is observable to an arriving class-j customer only when $i \leq D$. For $i > D$, the queue becomes unobservable to all customers. In such cases, a class-j customer joins with probability p_j, which corresponds to the equilibrium joining strategy p_j^* derived earlier.

Proposition 3 (Stationary Distribution - Scenario 1). *The stationary probability of an empty system when $D \leq n_2 - 1$ is:*

$$\pi_0 = \frac{(1-(\rho_1+\rho_2))(\mu-(\lambda_1 p_1+\lambda_2 p_2))}{\mu(1-(\rho_1+\rho_2)^{D+1})-(\lambda_1 p_1+\lambda_2 p_2)+(\rho_1+\rho_2)^D(\lambda_1 p_1+\lambda_2 p_2)} \tag{5}$$

Proof. The proof follows the same reasoning as Proposition 1. From the balance equations of the underlying birthâĂŞdeath process (state-dependent arrivals), we obtain for $i > 0$:

$$\pi_i = \begin{cases} \pi_0(\rho_1+\rho_2)^i & \text{if } i \leq D \\ \pi_0(\rho_1+\rho_2)^D(\frac{\lambda_1 p_1+\lambda_2 p_2}{\mu})^{i-D} & \text{if } i > D \end{cases} \tag{6}$$

Normalizing the probabilities and evaluating the geometric sums yields the expression for π_0.

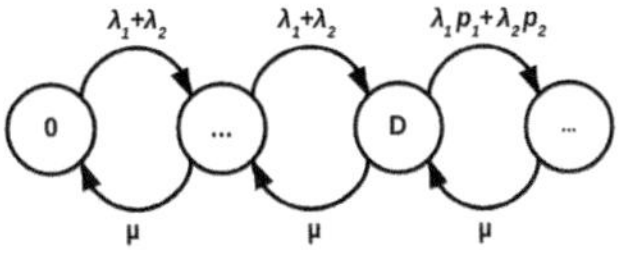

Fig. 3. Markov chain representation for Scenario 1 ($D \leq n_2 - 1$).

Scenario 2: $n_2 \leq D \leq n_1 - 2$: In this scenario where $n_2 \leq D \leq n_1 - 2$, the queue length is observable to an arriving class-j customer only when $i \leq D$. For $i > D$, the queue becomes unobservable. In such cases, class-2 customers balk as per their threshold n_2, while class-1 customers join with probability p_1, which corresponds to the equilibrium joining strategy p_1^* derived earlier (Fig. 3).

Proposition 4 (Stationary Distribution - Scenario 2). *The stationary probability of an empty system when $n_2 \leq D \leq n_1 - 2$ is:*

$$\pi_0 = \frac{(1-(\rho_1+\rho_2))(1-\rho_1)(1-\rho_1 p_1)}{(1-\rho_1 p_1)(1-\rho_1-\rho_2(\rho_1+\rho_2)^{n_2}) + (\rho_1+\rho_2)^{n_2}(p_1-1)\rho_1^{D-n_2+1}(1-(\rho_1+\rho_2))} \quad (7)$$

Proof. The proof follows the same reasoning as Proposition 1. From the balance equations of the underlying birthâĂŞdeath process (state-dependent arrivals), we obtain for $i > 0$:

$$\pi_i = \begin{cases} \pi_0(\rho_1+\rho_2)^i & \text{if } i \leq n_2 \\ \pi_0(\rho_1+\rho_2)^{n_2}\rho_1^{i-n_2} & \text{if } n_2+1 \leq i \leq D \\ \pi_0(\rho_1+\rho_2)^{n_2}\rho_1^{D-n_2}(p_1\rho_1)^{i-D} & \text{if } i > D \end{cases} \quad (8)$$

Normalizing the probabilities and evaluating the geometric sums yields the expression for π_0. ■

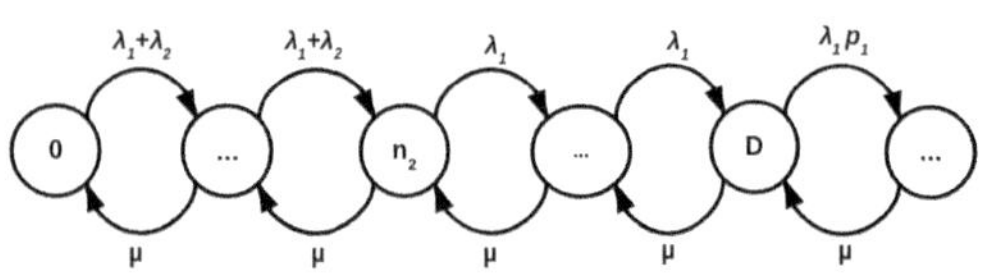

Fig. 4. Markov chain representation for Scenario 2 ($n_2 \leq D \leq n_1 - 2$).

4.4 Social Welfare

Let $S_j(i) = R - \dfrac{(i+1)C_j}{\mu}$ be the surplus of a class-j customer arriving when the state is i and the state is observable. By PASTA, the steady-state social welfare rate equals the total rate of admitted arrivals times their expected per-customer surplus. Using the decomposition (observable part + uninformed tail) we derive Social Welfare for both scnerios (Fig. 4):

Lemma 1. *For a two-class queue with information disclosure threshold D, the social welfare SW under different observability scenarios is given by:*

1. ***Full observability*** *($D \geq n_1 - 1$):*

$$SW_{full} = \sum_{j=1}^{2} \lambda_j \sum_{i=0}^{n_j-1} \pi_i \left(R - \frac{(i+1)C_j}{\mu} \right)$$

where π_i follows the birth-death structure:

$$\pi_i = \begin{cases} \pi_0(\rho_1+\rho_2)^i & 0 \leq i \leq n_2 \\ \pi_0(\rho_1+\rho_2)^{n_2}\rho_1^{i-n_2} & n_2 < i \leq n_1 \end{cases}$$

2. ***Scenario 1*** *($D \leq n_2 - 1$): Both classes uninformed when $i > D$*

$$SW_1(D) = \sum_{j=1}^{2} \lambda_j \sum_{i=0}^{\min(D,n_j-1)} \pi_i S_j(i) + \left(\sum_{i=D+1}^{\infty} \pi_i \right) \sum_{j=1}^{2} \lambda_j p_j^*(R - C_j W_D)$$

where $W_D = \frac{D+1}{\mu} + \frac{1}{\mu-(\lambda_1 p_1^* + \lambda_2 p_2^*)}$ *and stationary probabilities are:*

$$\pi_i = \begin{cases} \pi_0(\rho_1 + \rho_2)^i & 0 \leq i \leq D \\ \pi_0(\rho_1 + \rho_2)^D \left(\frac{\lambda_1 p_1^* + \lambda_2 p_2^*}{\mu}\right)^{i-D} & i > D \end{cases}$$

3. ***Scenario 2*** *($n_2 \leq D \leq n_1 - 2$): Only class 1 uninformed when $i > D$*

$$SW_2(D) = \sum_{i=0}^{n_2-1} \pi_i[\lambda_1 S_1(i) + \lambda_2 S_2(i)] + + \sum_{i=n_2}^{D} \pi_i \lambda_1 S_1(i) + \left(\sum_{i=D+1}^{\infty} \pi_i \right) \lambda_1 p_1^*(R - C_1 W_D)$$

where $W_D = \frac{D+1}{\mu} + \frac{1}{\mu-\lambda_1 p_1^*}$ *and stationary probabilities are:*

$$\pi_i = \begin{cases} \pi_0(\rho_1 + \rho_2)^i & 0 \leq i \leq n_2 \\ \pi_0(\rho_1 + \rho_2)^{n_2} \rho_1^{i-n_2} & n_2 < i \leq D \\ \pi_0(\rho_1 + \rho_2)^{n_2} \rho_1^{D-n_2} (p_1^* \rho_1)^{i-D} & i > D \end{cases}$$

Theorem 1 (Existence of Optimal Threshold). *For any parameter configuration $(\lambda_1, \lambda_2, \mu, R, C_1, C_2)$ with $C_1 < C_2$, there exists an optimal threshold $D^* \in \{0, 1, \ldots, n_1 - 1\}$ that maximizes social welfare.*

Proof. The social welfare function $SW(D)$ is defined on a finite discrete domain and is piecewise continuous in D within each scenario. The function is continuous at the boundaries between scenarios, as verified through the stationary distributions. By the extreme value theorem for discrete functions, $SW(D)$ attains a maximum at some D^* in its domain. ∎

Full and zero disclosure are seldom optimal because full transparency can deter customers in high states, while complete opacity may cause excess congestion. An intermediate threshold balances belief-driven caution and information-driven precision.

Theorem 2 (Asymptotic Properties of D^*). *The optimal disclosure threshold D^* exhibits the following asymptotic properties:*

1. $\lim_{R \to \infty} D^* = n_1 - 1$
2. $\lim_{C_2 \to C_1} D^* = 0$
3. $\lim_{(\lambda_1 + \lambda_2) \to 0} D^* = n_1 - 1$
4. $\lim_{\mu \to \infty} D^* = n_1 - 1$

Proof. 1. $R \to \infty$: As the service reward increases, Naor's thresholds $n_j = \lfloor \mu R / C_j \rfloor \to \infty$. Waiting costs become negligible relative to the reward, and social welfare approximates $SW(D) \approx R \cdot T(D)$, where $T(D)$ is throughput, i.e., the long-run average service completion rate under threshold D, given by $T(D) = \mu \cdot (1 - \pi_0(D))$. In this throughput-dominant regime, revealing more information increases joining behavior and improves system performance [6]. Thus, full disclosure ($D = n_1 - 1$) maximizes throughput by eliminating balking in the observable region and driving $p_j^* \to 1$ in the unobservable region.

2. $C_2 \to C_1$: As the waiting costs converge, customer heterogeneity diminishes ($n_1 = n_2$). The system reduces to the classical setting of [5], where no disclosure ($D = 0$) is optimal. By continuity of $SW(D)$ in C_2, $D^* \to 0$.
3. $\lambda_1 + \lambda_2 \to 0$: Under light traffic conditions, the queue remains empty with high probability ($\pi_0 \to 1$), congestion effects vanish, and waiting costs become negligible. Throughput dominates, and more information increases joining [6], so $D^* \to n_1 - 1$.
4. $\mu \to \infty$: As service rate increases, waiting times vanish ($W \to 0$), and social welfare approaches $SW(D) \approx R \cdot T(D)$. Throughput is maximized under full disclosure, which eliminates all balking.

■

The optimal threshold D^* balances revealing information to avoid unnecessary waiting costs with concealing it to limit excessive balking. The asymptotic results show how this balance shifts under extreme parameter values. When rewards dominate or congestion is negligible, full disclosure becomes optimal, whereas when customer types converge and strategic differences fade, limited or no disclosure emerges as the efficient choice. This highlights how system conditions shape the optimal information policy.

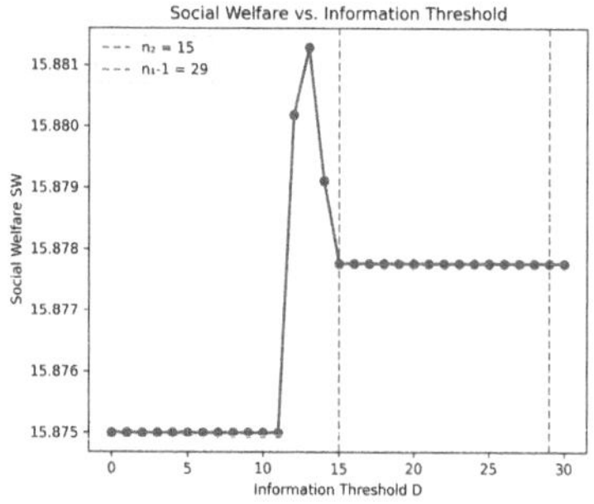

Fig. 5. Impact of information disclosure threshold D on Social Welfare ($\lambda_1 = 0.7, \lambda_2 = 0.5, \mu = 2, R = 15, C_1 = 1, C_2 = 2$).

Figure 5 shows social welfare SW versus D curve. Social welfare reaches its maximum at $D \approx 12$, reflecting the trade-off between system efficiency and individual customer costs. The vertical dashed lines mark the Naor thresholds ($n_1 - 1 = 29$, $n_2 = 15$), showing where different customer classes gain full information. The significant difference between n_1 and n_2 highlights substantial customer heterogeneity, which the optimal information policy successfully accommodates.

5 Conclusion

This paper analyzed strategic queueing games with heterogeneous customers under a threshold-based information disclosure policy. By combining classical insights from observable and unobservable regimes, we showed that selective disclosure can strictly improve social welfare relative to the two extremes. The analysis revealed that system load and customer heterogeneity jointly determine the welfare-maximizing disclosure threshold, with partial disclosure often outperforming full observability.

Our results highlight the value of information design as an operational lever: carefully calibrated disclosure policies can improve throughput and welfare in realistic service systems where customers differ in delay sensitivity. This work extends prior models to heterogeneous populations and provides a foundation for future studies on dynamic disclosure, richer service environments, and empirical validation.

This analysis provides guidance for real-world systems such as call centers, cloud services, hospital triage systems, and mobility platforms where customer delay sensitivities vary. When congestion is moderate and customer types differ substantially, partial disclosure is beneficial: it prevents excessively impatient users from abandoning while still using information to discourage inefficient arrivals. In contrast, transparency is preferred in light-load or high-service-speed environments. These findings demonstrate the value of calibrated information disclosure as a lever for improving system efficiency.

References

1. Burnetas, A., Economou, A.: Equilibrium customer strategies in a single server markovian queue with setup times. Queueing Syst. **56**(3–4), 213–228 (2007)
2. Chen, H., Frank, M.Z.: Monopoly pricing when customers queue. IIE Trans. **36**(6), 569–581 (2004)
3. Cui, S., Su, X., Veeraraghavan, S.K.: A model of rational retrials in queues. Oper. Res. **67**(6), 1699–1718 (2019)
4. Economou, A., Kanta, S.: Equilibrium balking strategies for a clearing queueing system in alternating environment. Ann. Oper. Res. **186**(1), 83–97 (2011)
5. Edelson, N.M., Hildebrand, D.K.: Congestion tolls for poisson queuing processes. Econometrica **43**(1), 81–92 (1975)
6. Guo, P., Zipkin, P.: Analysis and comparison of queues with different levels of delay information. Manage. Sci. **53**(6), 962–970 (2007)

7. Hassin, R.: Consumer information in markets with random product quality: the case of queues and balking. Econometrica **54**(5), 1185–1195 (1986)
8. Hassin, R., Haviv, M.: To queue or not to queue: equilibrium behavior in queueing systems. Kluwer Academic Publishers (2003)
9. Hassin, R., Roet-Green, R.: The impact of inspection cost on equilibrium, revenue, and social welfare in a single-server queue. Oper. Res. **65**(3), 804–820 (2017)
10. Mandelbaum, A., Yechiali, U.: Optimal entering rules for a customer with wait option at an m/g/1 queue. Manage. Sci. **29**(2), 174–187 (1983)
11. Naor, P.: The regulation of queue size by levying tolls. Econometrica **37**(1), 15–24 (1969)
12. Simhon, E., Hayel, Y., Starobinski, D., Zhu, Q.: Optimal information disclosure policies in strategic queueing games. Oper. Res. Lett. **44**(1), 109–113 (2016)
13. Wang, J., Hu, M.: Efficient inaccuracy: user-generated information sharing in a queue. Manage. Sci. **66**(10), 4648–4666 (2020)

Stochastic Models

There are Several Ways out of the Hospital. And into.

Dominic Zimmer(✉) and Holger Hermanns

Saarland University, Saarland Informatics Campus, Saarbrücken, Germany
{zimmer,hermanns}@depend.uni-saarland.de

Abstract. Phase-Type distributions describe the time to absorption in an absorbing continuous-time Markov chain (CTMC). This paper develops the model of multi-exit multi-entry acyclic phase-type distributions (MXMEs), a novel CTMC-based model. This generalizes applied work on stochastic models for competing risks. Several aspects of MXMEs are explored: representations, transient behavior, closure properties, and semantics in the realm of monoidal categories. In addition, the usefulness of MXMEs is illustrated.

Keywords: Acyclic Phase-Type Distributions · Canonical Representations · Composition · Monoidal Categories

1 Introduction

Phase-type distributions are a class of continuous probability distributions that are often used in statistics, stochastics, and data science. In particular, they allow the modeling of data that is influenced by continuously varying quantities as time progresses. Typical use cases include, for instance, the modeling of the length of stay in hospital [16,20,21].

A phase-type distribution (PD) can be thought of as describing the time to absorption in an absorbing continuous-time Markov chain (CTMC). These distributions can, in principle, represent any distributions on the positive axis with arbitrary precision [26]. This is true even if restricting to acyclic representations. Such acyclic phase-type distributions (APD) are very well studied, among others, with respect to normal forms, minimality, composability, approximability [3,6,14,24,25].

In applications of PD modeling, an important aspect is flexibility in developing integrated models that describe and predict important features, such as the movements of patients through hospital. However, patient pathways and the corresponding length of stay distributions are highly heterogeneous, particularly with regard to patient diagnosis, age, gender, and outcome. This topic has been pioneered by McClean and coworkers [20,21], who looked at the evaluation of *competing risks*, which on the modeling level corresponds to CTMCs with multiple distinct options for absorption. If one were to use these structures to model

A. Remke et al. (Eds.): Valuetools 2025, LNICST 691, pp. 51–69, 2027.
https://doi.org/10.1007/978-3-032-23901-3_4

the inter-arrival times between distinct types of events, one would observe similarities with marked Markovian arrival processes [12].

The focus of this paper, however, is very different. We revisit the APD model family underlying the competing risks phenomena, which we call multi-exit (MX). We establish new results regarding canonical representations of MXs. We then move on to generalize the model towards APD with multiple exits as well as multiple entries (MXME). The presence of entries and exits makes it natural to consider MXMEs as components in a composition formalism that supports the identification of one component's absorbing states with the initial states of another. We provide an algebraic embedding that allows expression of system composition in terms of monoidal categories and string diagrams.

Section 2 gives a brief overview of the established results of APDs. We reiterate the competing risks model in Section 3 and present our novel canonical form. Section 4 introduces the class of MXME distributions, and Section 5 discusses their composition. The category theoretical view on MXMEs is presented in Section 6 before we conclude with Section 7.

2 Preliminaries

Notation and Definitions We denote matrices in bold face $\mathbf{M}$, column vectors with an overset arrow $\vec{A}$, and row vectors underlined $\underline{\alpha}$. Matrix entries are denoted as $\mathbf{M}_{i,j}$ or $\mathbf{M}(i,j)$, their rows as $\mathbf{M}(i,\bullet)$ and columns as $\mathbf{M}(\bullet,j)$. The vector of all ones is denoted $\vec{\mathbb{1}}$, whereas the unit column (row) vectors are denoted as $\vec{e_i}$ ($\underline{e_i}$). We call a vector $\underline{v}$ (sub)stochastic if its entries $v_i \in [0,1]$ add up to (at most) one. A measurable real-valued function is called a (sub)stochastic, if its image is non-negative and the integral over its support is (at most) one. A matrix $\mathbf{M}$ is called bidiagonal if its only nonzero entries are on the diagonal or first superdiagonal. We use δ to denote the probability distribution that assigns all probability mass to a single point. In the continuous case, this is the Dirac delta function, assigning the probability mass of one to zero, and in the discrete case, it corresponds to any unit stochastic vector.

Continuous-Time Markov Chains We assume the reader to be familiar with time-homogeneous, continuous-time Markov Chains (CTMCs) [11,28] over a finite set of states $\mathbb{S}$, represented by a square generator matrix $\mathbf{Q}$ of dimension $|\mathbb{S}|$, where $\mathbf{Q}_{ij}$ $(i \neq j)$ is the rate parameter of the exponential distribution describing the transition probability from state i to j over time, and $\mathbf{Q}_{ii}$ is the negative sum of all outgoing rates $\sum_{j=1,j\neq i}^{|\mathbb{S}|} -\mathbf{Q}_{ij}$.

Throughout this paper, we will assume all CTMCs to be acyclic. We denote the unconditional time to absorption by the $\mathbb{R}$-valued random variable X, and initiation and absorption in the CTMC by the $\mathbb{S}$-valued random variables S and A. We assume the states $\mathbb{S}$ to be identified by Latin and Greek letters, and $\mathbb{S}$ to be partitioned into $\mathcal{E} \cup \mathcal{I} \cup \mathcal{X}$, read *entry*, *inner*, and *exit*, where $\mathcal{E}$ are states that may be assigned a nonzero initial probability, $\mathcal{I}$ are transient states that are always assigned zero initial probability[1], and $\mathcal{X}$ are absorbing states. [2] We impose the canonical ordering $\prec$ on $\mathbb{S}$, given by the lexicographic ordering of (i) $\mathcal{E} \prec \mathcal{I} \prec \mathcal{X}$, (ii) Latin alphabet before Greek alphabet, and (iii) position of the letter in the alphabet. Using $\prec$, we can express the $\mathbf{Q}$ matrix as block matrix over the bases of $\mathcal{E}$, $\mathcal{I}$, and $\mathcal{X}$, appearing in eq. (1). Moreover, this ordering permits the notation $s_i \in S \subseteq \mathbb{S}$ for the i-th state of a subset S of $\mathbb{S}$. Notably, we have chosen this ordering for the sake of presentation. The theory to be developed does not depend on this choice. Throughout this paper, we depict initial and transient states white (t), and absorbing states black (a).

Phase-Type Distributions A Phase-Type distribution (PD) [3,6,14,24,25] describes the time to absorption in a finite, absorbing Markov chain. The focus of this work is the class APD of phase-type distributions arising from absorbing, acyclic CTMCs. A named pair $\mathtt{APD}(\underline{\alpha}, \mathbf{A})$ is called a representation of probability density $f \in \mathtt{APD}$, if $\underline{\alpha}$ is a (sub)stochastic vector, $f(t) = \underline{\alpha} e^{\mathbf{A}t} \vec{A}$, and if the matrix

$$\mathbf{Q} = \left(\begin{array}{cc|c} \mathbf{Q}_{\mathcal{E}\to\mathcal{E}} & \mathbf{Q}_{\mathcal{E}\to\mathcal{I}} & \mathbf{Q}_{\mathcal{E}\to\mathcal{X}} \\ \mathbf{0} & \mathbf{Q}_{\mathcal{I}\to\mathcal{I}} & \mathbf{Q}_{\mathcal{I}\to\mathcal{X}} \\ \hline \mathbf{0} & \mathbf{0} & \mathbf{0} \end{array}\right) = \left(\begin{array}{c|c} \mathbf{A} & \vec{A} \\ \hline \mathbf{0} & \mathbf{0} \end{array}\right) \tag{1}$$

is the generator matrix of the underlying CTMC, where $\vec{A} = -\mathbf{A}\vec{\mathbb{1}}$. We call $\mathbf{A}$ the PD-generator and $\underline{\alpha}$ the initial probability distribution over the states $\mathbb{S}$. The cumulative distribution function $F(t) = \int_0^t f(x)\,dx = \underline{\alpha}(\mathbf{1} - e^{\mathbf{A}t})\mathbf{U}\vec{A}$ describes the (sub)probability of absorption within t units of time, where $\mathbf{U} = (-\mathbf{A})^{-1}$. Lastly, the Laplace-Stieltjes transform of f is given by $\mathcal{L}\{f\}(s) = \underline{\alpha}(s\mathbf{I} - \mathbf{A})^{-1}\vec{A}$. $\mathcal{L}\{f\}(s)$ is a rational polynomial in s with only negative poles and a unique maximal pole. The poles of $\mathcal{L}\{f\}(s)$ agree with the eigenvalues of $\mathbf{A}$.

Acyclic phase-type distributions are closed under formation of minimum, maximum, summation, and finite mixtures [22]. The density of the sum of two APD distributed random variables $f \sim X$ and $g \sim Y$ is given by their convolution $(f \circledast g) \sim X + Y$. In the Laplace domain, the convolution $\mathcal{L}\{f \circledast g\}$ equals the product $\mathcal{L}\{f\}\mathcal{L}\{g\}$ of polynomials. The family of all exponential distributions $f(t) = \lambda e^{-\lambda t}$ with Laplacian $\mathcal{L}\{\mathrm{Exp}(\lambda)\}(s) = \frac{\lambda}{s+\lambda}$ is contained in APD.

APD Representations If $\lambda_n \leq \cdots \leq \lambda_1$ are the eigenvalues of $\mathbf{A}$, we call the n-dimensional vector $\vec{\mathcal{B}}$ with $\mathcal{B}_i = \circledast_{j=n}^{n+1-i} \mathrm{Exp}(\lambda_j)$ the *basic series* of $\mathtt{APD}(\underline{\alpha}, \mathbf{A})$. For any $f \in \mathtt{APD}$, there exist representations $f_b \sim \mathtt{APD}(\underline{\beta}, \mathbf{B})$ and $f_c \sim \mathtt{APD}((\alpha\vec{\mathbb{1}})\underline{\delta}, \mathbf{C})$ of equal dimension with bidiagonal generators $\mathbf{B}$ and $\mathbf{C}$, whose densities f_b and f_c agree with f. We call the latter a *Coxian* representation, and the former a *bidiagonal* representation, provided absorption can only take place from the last transient state. A bidiagonal representation $\mathtt{APD}(\underline{\beta}, \mathbf{B})$ can be obtained from from $\mathcal{L}\{f\}(s)$, by solving the system of linear equations

[2] The latter is no restriction. Inverse lumpability can be applied to a model where some transient state has initial probability to turn it into one where this is not the case, at the price of adding a fresh state to $\mathcal{E}$, echoing the state's one-step behavior.

$\underline{\beta}\vec{\mathcal{B}} = f$ in the Laplace domain, which is also known as Cumani's algorithm [7]. It is well-known that a bidiagonal representation can be transformed into a Coxian in linear time [7].

3 Phase-Type Models with Multiple Exits

In this section, we will break the fundamental assumption that there can only be a single terminal state in the Markov chain underlying a phase-type distributed random variable. That is, will we consider models with multiple absorbing states (or "exits"). Multi-exit PDs capture the joint probability (sub)densities of absorption into each available absorbing state, as introduced by McClean et al., who call them phase-type distributions for competing risks [21]. "Competing risks" refers to the Markov chain offering mutually exclusive options for absorption. A loosely related formalism is that of multivariate phase-type distributions (MPDs) [4], which describe the accumulated rewards until absorption in a Markov reward model. Based on the same underlying Markov chain, these reward structures give rise to products of correlated phase-type distributed random variables, while we are interested in strictly mutually exclusive options for absorption.

Definition 1 (Multi-Exit Phase-Type). *We call an $|\mathcal{X}|$-dimensional vector of probability subdensities $\underline{f}$ a multi-exit phase-type distribution (MX), if*

$$\underline{f}_j(t) = \mathbb{P}(X = t \cap A = j)$$

expresses the density of the time to absorption into state $\textcircled{j}$.

As is the case in acyclic phase-type distributions, the subspace of the $\mathbf{Q}$ matrix associated with the $\mathcal{X}$-states is void. Hence, MXs permit a representation very similar to that of APD representations.

Definition 2 (Multi-Exit Phase-Type Representation [21]). *Let $\underline{\alpha} \in \mathbb{R}^{1\times n}$ be the initial probability vector, $\mathbf{A} \in \mathbb{R}^{n\times n}$ be the real-valued rate-matrix, and $\mathbf{L} = (\vec{L}_1 \mid \cdots \mid \vec{L}_k) \in \mathbb{R}^{n\times k}$ be the nonnegative exit-matrix. We call MX$(\underline{\alpha}, \mathbf{A}, \mathbf{L})$ a (matrix)* representation *of $\underline{f} \in$ MX, if the densities are given by $\underline{f}_j(t) = \underline{\alpha} e^{\mathbf{A}t}\vec{L}_j$, and*

(i) $\underline{\alpha}$ has nonnegative entries $\underline{\alpha}_i$ and $\underline{\alpha}\vec{\mathbb{1}} = 1$,
(ii) the entries $\mathbf{A}_{ij}$, for $i \neq j$, and the entries $\mathbf{L}_{ij}$ are non-negative, and
(iii) it holds that $\mathbf{A}\vec{\mathbb{1}} + \mathbf{L}\vec{\mathbb{1}} = \vec{0}$, i.e. the diagonal entries $\mathbf{A}_{ii}$ are the negative sums of all rates exiting state i.

Transient Behavior Given a representation $\underline{f} \sim$ MX$(\underline{\alpha}, \mathbf{A}, \mathbf{L})$, the vector of density functions of the time to absorption into the absorbing states is given by $\underline{\alpha} e^{\mathbf{A}t}\mathbf{L}$ with components $\underline{f}_i(t) = \mathbb{P}(X = t \cap A = i) = \underline{\alpha} e^{\mathbf{A}t}\vec{L}_i$. Note how this formula coincides with the PDF of the 1-exit MX distribution APD$(\underline{\alpha}, \mathbf{A})$, where the exit vector is $\vec{A} = \mathbf{L}\vec{\mathbb{1}}$, that is, all absorbing states have been merged into one.

Recall the definition $\mathbf{U} = (-\mathbf{A})^{-1}$. The vector of CDFs is given by $\underline{F}(t) = \underline{\alpha}(1 - e^{\mathbf{A}t})\mathbf{UL}$, ensuring that $\underline{F}_i(t) = \mathbb{P}(X \leq t \cap A = i) = \int_0^t \underline{f}_i(t)\, dt = \underline{\alpha}(1 - e^{\mathbf{A}t})\mathbf{U}\vec{L}_i$. The limit $\lim_{t\to\infty} \underline{F}(t) = \underline{\alpha}\mathbf{UL}$ yields the vector of marginals $\underline{\mathbb{P}(A)}$ whose entries are given by $\mathbb{P}(A = i) = \int_0^\infty f_{X_i}(t)\, dt = \underline{\alpha}\mathbf{U}\vec{L}_i$. It is straightforward to obtain conditionals such as $\mathbb{P}(X \mid A)$ or $\mathbb{P}(A \mid X)$.

Example 1 (Running Example) Imagine a fairly new disease D. We want to model the time a patient has to stay hospitalized using multi-exit `APDs`. From past observations, we know that patients newly suspected to have disease D originate with equal probability (50%) from the emergency reception (ER) and from general practitioners (GP).

Once a patient is suspected to have disease D, they undergo a screening to identify whether they have the benign variant D-β, the malignant variant D-μ, or whether they were a false-positive and actually are healthy. We model this process by a `MX` distribution, illustrated in fig. 1, where rate values are of purely hypothetical nature.

$$\alpha = \begin{pmatrix} \frac{1}{2} & \frac{1}{2} & 0 \end{pmatrix}$$
$$(\mathbf{A} \mid \mathbf{L}) = \left(\begin{array}{ccc|ccc} -3 & 1 & 1 & 1 & & \\ & -6 & 1 & & 2 & 3 \\ & & -4 & 2 & 2 & \end{array}\right)$$

(a) Representation of the `MX`

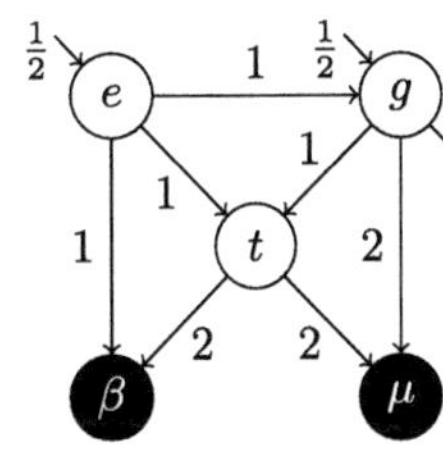

(b) Underlying absorbing CTMC

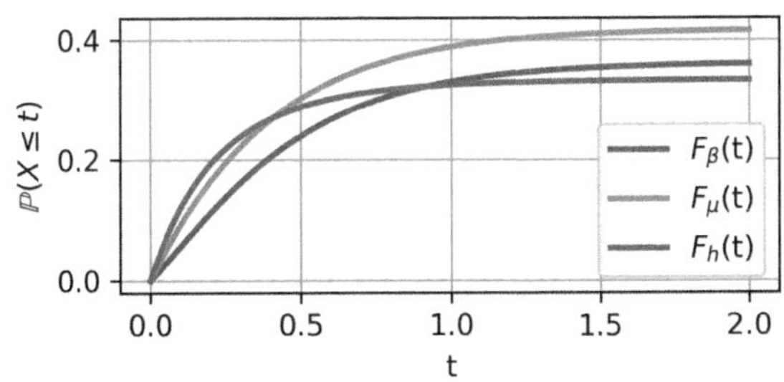

(c) Cumulative density functions of the individual times to absorption

Fig. 1. Illustration of the multi-exit phase-type distribution $\underline{f}$ modeling the patient flow spelled out in example 1. Figure 1(a) shows a representation of $\underline{f} \sim$ `MX`$(\underline{\alpha}, \mathbf{A}, \mathbf{L})$. In fig. 1(b), the initial states (e) and (g) represent the ER and GP, (t) a transient state internal to the model, and states (h) through (μ) represent the respective diagnose outcome. Figure 1(c) illustrates the subdensities of absorption occurring within t time units.

3.1 Canonical Representations of Multi-Exit Phase-Type

Acyclic phase-type distributions enjoy various canonical representations, most notably the bidiagonal and Coxian representations. Each canonical representation comes with its unique benefits, namely, canonicity of the graph structure and canonicity of the initial probability distribution, respectively.

Bidiagonal Representation Functions of the MX class are vectors of substochastic APDs [18, 23], permitting the same analysis via basic series that APD permits. That is, given $\underline{f} \sim \mathtt{MX}(\underline{\alpha}, \mathbf{A}, \mathbf{L})$ and a vector of basic series $\vec{\mathcal{B}}$ consisting convolutions of exponential distributions of increasing lengths over the eigenvalues of $\mathbf{A}$, we can find a matrix $\mathbf{\Pi}$, such that $\underline{f} = (\mathbf{\Pi}\vec{\mathcal{B}})^T$.

The coefficient $\mathbf{\Pi}_{ij}$ gives the initial probability assigned to the state of a bidiagonal generator matrix that absorbs with certainty into ⓙ after exactly i transitions.

Coxian Mixture Representation Given $\underline{f} \sim \mathtt{MX}(\underline{\alpha}, \mathbf{A}, \mathbf{L})$, its Coxian mixture representation [20, Appendix] explicitly spells out the relation between joint and conditional probability, expressing the joint probability as a mixture of conditionals:

$$\begin{aligned}\mathbb{P}(X \cap A) \sim \mathtt{MX}(\underline{\beta}, \mathbf{B}, \mathbf{L}) &= \mathtt{MX}(\underline{\gamma}, \bigoplus_i \mathbf{C}_i, \bigoplus_i \vec{C}_i) \\ &= \bigoplus_i \mathtt{APD}(\underline{\gamma}_i, \mathbf{C}_i) = \bigoplus_i \alpha_i \cdot \mathtt{APD}(\underline{\delta}_i, \mathbf{C}_i) = \mathbb{P}(A)\,\mathbb{P}(X \mid A)\end{aligned}$$

Starting from the bidiagonal representation $\underline{f} \sim \mathtt{MX}(\underline{\beta}, \mathbf{B}, \mathbf{L})$, applying the Coxian transformation for APDs to each component $\underline{f}_j \sim \mathtt{APD}(\underline{\gamma}_i, \mathbf{C}_i)$, where $\underline{\gamma}_i = \alpha_i \underline{\delta}_i$ with $\underline{\delta}_i$ the Dirac-vector of appropriate dimension. We get a block matrix of Coxian generators $\mathbf{C} = \mathbf{C}_1 \oplus \cdots \oplus \mathbf{C}_n$, initial probability vector $\underline{\gamma} = (\underline{\gamma}_1 \cdots \underline{\gamma}_n)$, and block diagonal exit matrix $\mathbf{K} = \vec{C}_1 \oplus \cdots \oplus \vec{C}_n$, where $\vec{C}_i = \mathbf{C}_i \vec{\mathbb{1}}$.

Example 2. Figure 2 illustrates the Coxian mixture representation of the running example. Note that the marginal probabilities are reflected in the initial probability vector $\underline{\gamma}$.

Coxian Representation Recall that a Coxian representation $\mathtt{APD}(\underline{\gamma}, \mathbf{C})$ consists of a bidiagonal generator matrix $\mathbf{C}$ and a distribution $\underline{\gamma}$ that assigns the total initial probability mass to one state. We extend this definition to the class of MX functions under the same restrictions.

Definition 3 (Coxian Representation). *We call a multi-exit representation* $\mathtt{MX}(\underline{\alpha}, \mathbf{A}, \mathbf{L})$ Coxian*, if* $\mathbf{A}$ *is bidiagonal and* $\underline{\alpha} = c\underline{\delta} \in \mathbb{R}^n$*, for some* $c \in (0, 1]$.

$$\gamma = \left(\tfrac{11}{36} \;\; 0 \;\; 0 \;\; \tfrac{13}{36} \;\; 0 \;\; 0 \;\; \tfrac{12}{36} \;\; 0 \;\; 0 \right)$$

$$(\mathbf{C} \mid \mathbf{K}) = \left(\begin{array}{ccc|ccc|ccc|ccc}
-6 & \frac{18}{11} & & & & & & & & \frac{48}{11} & & \\
 & -4 & \frac{11}{8} & & & & & & & \frac{21}{8} & & \\
 & & -3 & & & & & & & 3 & & \\
\hline
 & & & -6 & \frac{42}{13} & & & & & & \frac{36}{13} & \\
 & & & & -4 & \frac{10}{7} & & & & & \frac{18}{7} & \\
 & & & & & -3 & & & & & 3 & \\
\hline
 & & & & & & -6 & \frac{3}{2} & & & & \frac{9}{2} \\
 & & & & & & & -4 & 3 & & & 1 \\
 & & & & & & & & -3 & & & 3
\end{array}\right)$$

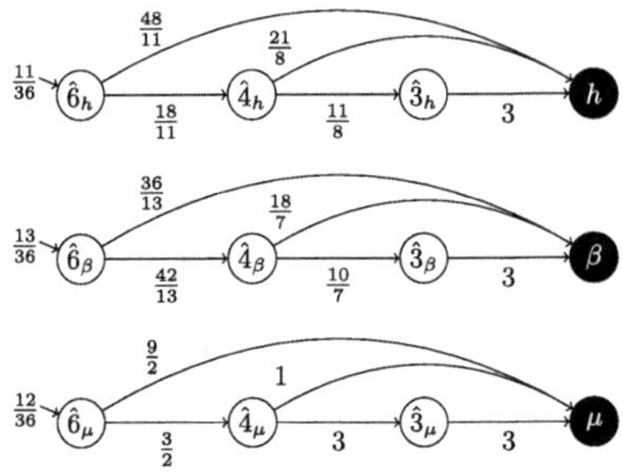

Fig. 2. Coxian mixture representation of example 1, separating the behaviors of the joint distribution into three disjoint subdistributions. The transient states are labeled according to their associated eigenvalues and state of eventual absorption. Instead of applying the canonical order $\prec$, we here present the transient states ordered by eventual state of absorption and corresponding eigenvalues.

Observe that the definition of a Coxian representation does not impose additional restrictions on the structure of $\mathbf{L}$. Instead, a Coxian multi-exit phase-type representation is already characterized by its diagonal entries $\lambda_1, \ldots, \lambda_n$, as well as the matrix of transition probabilities $\mathbf{T}_{ij}$, describing the transition probabilities from the i-th transient state into the j-th absorbing state. From this information, one can recover the entries of the exit rate matrix $\mathbf{L}_{ij} = -\lambda_i \mathbf{T}_{ij}$. The inter-phase rates Λ_i from state i to $i+1$ is given by $\Lambda_i = -\lambda_i(1 - \sum_{j=1}^{k} \mathbf{T}_{ij})$.

The existence of the Coxian representation as canonical representation for MX distributions has been suggested by Lindqvist [18, sec. 3.4], yet, in the upcoming section, we make this statement explicit by providing a constructive proof of the theorem ahead, showing that any given MX representation $\vec{f} \sim \mathtt{MX}(\underline{\alpha}, \mathbf{A}, \mathbf{L})$ can be transformed into an equivalent Coxian representation. This result lets us express any MX distribution as a distribution that starts with all its probability mass in the first state.

Theorem 1 (Canonicity of Coxian Representations). *Given any k-exit representation $\mathtt{MX}(\underline{\alpha}, \mathbf{A}, \mathbf{L})$, there exists a Coxian representation $\mathtt{MX}(\underline{\gamma}, \mathbf{C}, \mathbf{K})$ that agrees in distribution.*

Proof. ***Construction.*** *Given $\underline{f} \sim \mathtt{MX}(\underline{\alpha}, \mathbf{A}, \mathbf{L})$, we will construct an equivalent Coxian representation $\underline{g} \sim \mathtt{MX}(\underline{\gamma}, \mathbf{C}, \mathbf{K})$. Let $\lambda_n \leq \cdots \leq \lambda_1$ be the ordered eigenvalues of $\mathbf{A}$, $\vec{\mathcal{B}}$ denote its basic series, and $\mathbf{\Pi} \in \mathbb{R}^{n \times n}$ be the coefficient matrix, such that we can construct the vector of bidiagonal representations $\underline{f} = (\mathbf{\Pi}\vec{\mathcal{B}})^T$. In particular, $\mathbf{\Pi}_{ij}$ is the probability of absorption into ⓙ after traversing exactly i many phases, namely the states whose rates are the i eigenvalues of largest absolute value. Towards the Coxian representation, we construct its transition probability matrix $\mathbf{T}$ and bidiagonal generator $\mathbf{B}$ as follows:*

$$\mathbf{B} = \begin{pmatrix} \lambda_n & \Lambda_n & & \\ & \ddots & \ddots & \\ & & \lambda_2 & \Lambda_2 \\ & & & \lambda_1 \end{pmatrix} \qquad \mathbf{T}(i,\bullet) = \begin{cases} \mathbf{\Pi}(1,\bullet) & \text{if } i = 1 \\ \frac{1}{\sum_{a=i}^{n}\sum_{b=1}^{k} \mathbf{\Pi}(a,b)} \cdot \mathbf{\Pi}(i,\bullet), & \text{else} \end{cases}$$

One should interpret the entry $\mathbf{T}(i,j)$ as the probability of absorbing from the i-th transient state into the j-th absorbing state, assuming prior arrival in the i-th transient state. To obtain the rate matrix $\mathbf{K}$, we scale the absorption probabilities $\mathbf{T}$ by their respective eigenvalues, i.e. $\mathbf{K} = \mathbf{T} \cdot \mathbf{D}$, where $\mathbf{D} = Diag(\lambda_n, \dots, \lambda_1)$. The superdiagonal entries of $\mathbf{B}$ are given by $\Lambda_i = \lambda_i + \mathbf{K}(i,\bullet)\vec{\mathbb{1}}$, and the initial probability distribution $\underline{\gamma} = \underline{\alpha}\vec{\mathbb{1}} \cdot \underline{\delta}$.

Correctness. *Next, we show that the probability distribution $\underline{g} \sim \mathtt{MX}(\underline{\gamma}, \mathbf{C}, \mathbf{K})$ agrees with $\underline{f}$ by showing that there is a one-to-one mapping between the paths from initiation to absorption in both underlying CTMCs. Assume the bidiagonal representation $\underline{f} = (\mathbf{\Pi}\vec{\mathcal{B}})^T$. By construction, the sojourn times along paths from initial states to absorbing states in both diagonal and Coxian representations are exactly described by the basic series. Thus, it suffices to show that the paths corresponding to the same basic series agree in their occurrence probabilities.*

Let $(T = i)$ denote the event that absorption occurs after visiting exactly i transient states. Note that $\mathbb{P}(A = j \cap T = i) = \mathbf{\Pi}_{ij}$ and, from the definition of $\mathbf{T}$, that $\mathbf{T}_{ij} = \mathbb{P}(T = i \cap A = j \mid T \geq i) = \mathbb{P}(T = i \cap A = j) \,/\, \mathbb{P}(T \geq i)$. Lastly, note that $\mathbb{P}(T \geq a \mid T \geq a-1) = \mathbb{P}(T \geq a) \,/\, \mathbb{P}(T \geq a - i)$.

Let us now assume a path in the Coxian representation that visits exactly i states before absorbing into j. We must show that its path probability ρ_{ij} agrees with the probability of starting in state $\mathbf{\Pi}_{ij}$ in the bidiagonal representation. Observe that ρ_{ij} is composed of the probability of absorption, given arrival in the i-th transient state, and of the reachability probability of the i-th transient state.

$$\rho_{ij} = \mathbb{P}(A = j \cap T = i \mid T \geq i) \cdot \prod_{a=2}^{i} \frac{\mathbb{P}(T \geq a)}{\mathbb{P}(T \geq a-1)} = \frac{\mathbb{P}(A = j \cap T = i)}{\mathbb{P}(T \geq 1)} = \mathbf{\Pi}_{ij}$$

□

Example 3. Figure 3 illustrates the results of theorem 1, applied to the running example. We obtain a model that starts with certainty in a single state and exhibits the same stochastic behavior, albeit at the cost of weakened interpretability with regard to the roles of the transient states appearing in fig. 1(b).

4 Phase-Type Models with Multiple Exits and Entries

In the context of APDs and MXs, an initial distribution singles out one or several states by assigning them an initial probability. These distinguished states can be viewed as serving as an entry to the model, in the same way as absorbing states can be viewed as providing exits. In this section, we will study the model

$$\alpha = \begin{pmatrix} 1 & 0 & 0 \end{pmatrix}$$
$$\mathbf{A} \mid \mathbf{L} = \left(\begin{array}{ccc|ccc} -6 & 6/2 & & 1/2 & 2/2 & 3/2 \\ & -4 & 8/6 & 7/6 & 6/6 & 3/6 \\ & & -3 & 11/8 & 10/8 & 3/8 \end{array}\right)$$

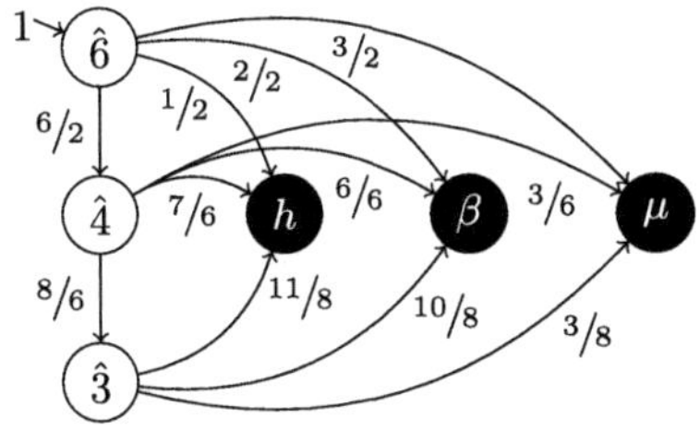

Fig. 3. Coxian representation of example 1, condensing the total probability mass into the initial state. Instead of the canonical order $\prec$, we here order the transient states by their corresponding eigenvalues.

of absorbing CTMCs with distinguished states for initialization and absorption, loosening the connection between initial probability distribution and entry states. We thereby obtain a model of phase-type models with multiple entries and (possibly) multiple exits.

We call CTMCs whose states are partitioned into the sets $\mathcal{E}$, $\mathcal{I}$, and $\mathcal{X}$, for *Entry*, *Inner*, and *eXit*) permitting solely transitions within $\mathcal{E}$, within $\mathcal{I}$, from $\mathcal{E}$ to $\mathcal{I}$, and from $\mathcal{I}$ to $\mathcal{X}$, *multi-exit multi-entry phase-type distributions* (MXME, read *mix-me*). Its generator matrix bears the structure depicted in eq. (2).

Evidently, given a CTMC that meets these criteria, we can characterize the Markov chain by conditioning its behavior on each of its initial states $(i) \in \mathcal{E}$, thereby obtaining a multi-exit representation for every initial state. Consequently, we can characterize the entire CTMC by a (column) vector of multi-exit distributions $(\underline{f}_i)_i$. We turn this observation into the following definition:

Definition 4 (Multi-Entry Multi-Exit Phase-Type). *We call a matrix of probability subdensities* $\mathbf{F}$ *a* multi-entry multi-exit *phase-type distribution (MXME), if*

$$\mathbf{F}_{ij} = \mathbb{P}\left(X = t \cap A = j \mid S = i\right)$$

is the density of the time to absorption into state ● j, *given initiation in* (i).

Definition 5 (Multi-Entry Multi-Exit Phase-Type Representation). *Let* $\mathbf{A} \in \mathbb{R}^{n\times n}$ *be a real-valued rate matrix, and* $\mathbf{L} = (\vec{L}_1 \mid \cdots \mid \vec{L}_k) \in \mathbb{R}^{n\times k}$ *be the nonnegative exit-matrix. We call the named pair* MXME$(\mathbf{A}, \mathbf{L})$ *a representation of* $\mathbf{F} \in$ MXME, *written* $\mathbf{F} \sim$ MXME$(\mathbf{A}, \mathbf{L})$, *if, given an initial distribution* $\underline{\pi}$ *over* $\mathcal{E}$, *the subdensities* $\mathbb{P}\left(X = t \cap A = j \mid S = i\right)$ *are given by* $\mathbf{F}_{ij} = \underline{\pi} e^{\mathbf{A}t}\vec{L}_j$.

Recalling that the canonical order on $\mathbb{S}$ requires $\mathcal{E} \prec \mathcal{I} \prec \mathcal{X}$, we obtain the following relation between generator matrix $\mathbf{Q}$, and matrices $\mathbf{A}$ and $\mathbf{L}$:

$$\mathbf{Q} = \left(\begin{array}{cc|c} \mathbf{Q}_{\mathcal{E}\to\mathcal{E}} & \mathbf{Q}_{\mathcal{E}\to\mathcal{I}} & \mathbf{Q}_{\mathcal{E}\to\mathcal{X}} \\ \mathbf{0} & \mathbf{Q}_{\mathcal{I}\to\mathcal{I}} & \mathbf{Q}_{\mathcal{I}\to\mathcal{X}} \\ \hline \mathbf{0} & \mathbf{0} & \mathbf{0} \end{array}\right) = \left(\begin{array}{c|c} \mathbf{A} & \mathbf{L} \\ \hline \mathbf{0} & \mathbf{0} \end{array}\right). \tag{2}$$

Example 4. Figure 4(a) illustrates a matrix representation for the subdensity matrix $\mathbf{D}$ of the running example 1. In fig. 4(b), we introduce a visualization of MXMEs, which we will refer to as its *topology*.

A MXME's topology hides the precise implementation of the Markov chain and only exhibits its initial and absorbing states.

$$\mathbf{D} = \begin{pmatrix} f_{e\to h} & f_{e\to\beta} & f_{e\to\mu} \\ f_{g\to h} & f_{g\to\beta} & f_{g\to\mu} \end{pmatrix} \quad (\mathbf{A} \mid \mathbf{L}) = \left(\begin{array}{ccc|ccc} -3 & 1 & 1 & 1 & & \\ & -6 & 1 & & 2 & 3 \\ & & -4 & 2 & 2 & \end{array}\right)$$

(a) The underlying multi-entry multi-exit distribution $\mathbf{D} \sim \texttt{MXME}(\mathbf{A}, \mathbf{L})$ of example 1.

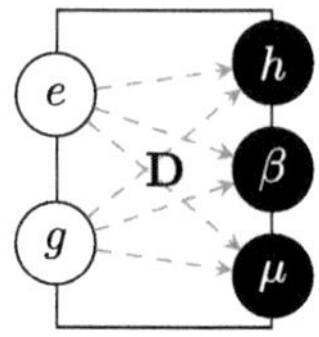

(b) Topology of $\mathbf{D}$

Fig. 4. Forgetting the initial distribution assumed in fig. 1 yields the depicted MXME $\mathbf{D}$. For any pair $s_i \in \mathcal{E}$ and $d_j \in \mathcal{X}$, the subdistribution of the time to absorption in d_j, given initialization in s_i, is given by $f_{s_i \to d_j} \sim \texttt{MX}(\underline{e_i}, \mathbf{A}, \mathbf{L})\vec{e_j}$. Figure 4(b) shows the topology of $\mathbf{D}$, abstracting away the implementations of the individual components while only depicting the parts essential to MXME composition.

Transient Behavior A multi-exit multi-entry distribution $\mathbf{F} \sim \texttt{MXME}(\mathbf{A}, \mathbf{L})$ describes a family of CTMCs, in which the initial probability distribution over the states in $\mathcal{E}$ is unknown. It is characterized by the family of functions $\mathbf{F}_{ij}$ which describe the subprobability of, given start in ⓘ, absorption occurs in ⓙ. Given an initial probability distribution $\underline{\pi} \in \mathbb{R}^k$ over $\mathcal{E}$, where $\underline{\pi}_i = \mathbb{P}(S = i)$, we obtain the mixture of multi-exit phase-type distributions $\underline{\pi}\mathbf{F}$, which reifies one member of the family of distributions. Note how the vector-matrix product $\underline{\pi}\mathbf{F}$ corresponds to mixing the individual multi-exit components of $\mathbf{F}$, yielding $\texttt{MX}(\underline{\pi}, \mathbf{A}, \mathbf{L})$, whence the name "mix-me"s.

Insights regarding cumulative distribution function, Laplace transformation, and limiting distributions transfer from multi-exit distributions.

Coxian Representation Each component $\mathbf{F}_{ij}$ of a MXME is a substochastic phase-type distribution. A known result in the representations of phase-type distributions is that substochastic, acyclic phase-type distributions permit the same canonical representation that stochastic phase-type distributions do [23]. In particular, this allows us to represent each component by an equivalent Coxian representation $\mathbf{F}_{ij} \sim \texttt{APD}(\alpha_{ij} \cdot \underline{\delta}, \mathbf{A}_{ij})$, where α_{ij} is the total probability mass of the (sub)distribution, and $\mathbf{A}_{ij}$ is the APD-generator matrix.

Hadamard Representation In what follows, we will denote Coxian representations $f \sim \mathtt{APD}(\alpha\underline{\delta}, \mathbf{C}x)$ by their total probability mass α and *stochastic* probability density $\tilde{f} \sim \mathtt{APD}(\underline{\delta}, \mathbf{C}x)$ by what we will call the *Hadamard pair* $f \sim (\!(\alpha, \tilde{f})\!)$. As long as PDFs are concerned, it is clear that the relationship $\alpha\tilde{f} = f$ holds.

Representing APDs using Hadamard pairs allows us to factor a MXME $\mathbf{F}$ via the Hadamard product $\bullet$ into its probability masses $\boldsymbol{\alpha}_{ij}$ and *stochastic* phase-type distributions $\mathbf{f}_{ij}$, such that $\mathbf{F} = \boldsymbol{\alpha} \bullet \mathbf{f} := \{\boldsymbol{\alpha}_{ij} \cdot \mathbf{f}_{ij}\}_{ij}$. We refer to the product $\boldsymbol{\alpha} \bullet \mathbf{f}$ as Hadamard representation of $\mathbf{F}$, denoted $(\!(\boldsymbol{\alpha}, \mathbf{f})\!)$. Since all functions $\mathbf{f}_{ij}$ are stochastic, the marginal probabilities of $\mathbf{F}_{ij}$ are exactly $\boldsymbol{\alpha}_{ij}$. Since absorption in a MXME is certain, $\boldsymbol{\alpha}$ is a stochastic matrix.

Note the similarity between Coxian and Hadamard representations: the essence of both representations is to factor out the total probability mass – Coxian describing APD representations, Hadamard describing probability (sub)densities. Since both the Coxian and Hadamard representations always exist, we will assume the most convenient representation of a MXME $\mathbf{F}$.

5 Composition of MXME Representations

MXMEs encapsulate the behavior of directed, acyclic CTMCs as a whole, disconnecting the algebraic object of an APD from the implementation in the underlying Markov chain. This section will illustrate that besides APDs [24], MXMEs exhibit well-behaved compositional behavior, too. First, we will formalize the algebraic structure underlying acyclic phase-type measures. Then, we will introduce an orthogonal ($\perp\!\!\!\perp$) and sequential (;) composition operator. In section 6, we will embed these operations into the framework of monoidal categories, which allow for a streamlined notion of composition.

Orthogonal Composition Composing two MXMEs orthogonally, denoted $\mathbf{F} \perp\!\!\!\perp \mathbf{G}$, formally merges the graphs of their underlying CTMCs, obtaining the vertices and edges as the respective disjoint unions of the vertices and edges of $\mathbf{F}$ and $\mathbf{G}$. The term *orthogonal* is used to signal that the underlying CTMCs are unrelated, distinguishing this operation from parallel interleaving of CTMCs.

Definition 6 (Orthogonal Composition of MXMEs). *Given two multi-entry multi-exit phase-type distributions* $\mathbf{F} \in \mathit{APD}^{\ell \times m}$ *and* $\mathbf{G} \in \mathit{APD}^{n \times o}$ *with respective matrix representations* $\mathbf{F} \sim \mathit{MXME}(\mathbf{A}, \mathbf{L})$ *and* $\mathbf{G} \sim \mathit{MXME}(\mathbf{B}, \mathbf{K})$*, we call the direct sum* $\mathbf{F} \oplus \mathbf{G}$ *of their subdensity matrices their orthogonal composition* $\mathbf{F} \perp\!\!\!\perp \mathbf{G}$*. Its matrix representation is given by* $\mathbf{F} \oplus \mathbf{G} \sim \mathit{MXME}(\mathbf{A} \oplus \mathbf{B}, \mathbf{L} \oplus \mathbf{K})$*, where* $\mathbf{A} \oplus \mathbf{B}$ *and* $\mathbf{L} \oplus \mathbf{K}$ *refers to the direct sum of the matrix representations.*

Sequential Composition Sequential composition of the CTMCs described by two MXMEs $\mathbf{F} \in \mathtt{APD}^{\ell \times m}$ and $\mathbf{G} \in \mathtt{APD}^{n \times o}$ should be understood as joining the two CTMCs by their interfacing sets $\mathcal{X}_\mathbf{F}$ and $\mathcal{E}_\mathbf{G}$. Intuitively, this operation should only be defined if the output dimension of $\mathbf{F}$ agrees with the input dimension of $\mathbf{G}$, i.e. $|\mathcal{X}_\mathbf{F}| = m = n = |\mathcal{E}_\mathbf{G}|$. Absorbing states $d_k \in \mathcal{X}_\mathbf{F}$ become associated with their corresponding state $s_k \in \mathcal{E}_\mathbf{G}$, making them transient. A path from $\mathcal{E}$ to $\mathcal{X}$ in the graph of the sequential composition $\mathbf{F}\,;\mathbf{G}$ consists of two paths in $\mathbf{F}$ and $\mathbf{G}$, respectively, that join at a state on the interface.

Paths Before we continue with the formal definition of sequential composition of MXMEs $\mathbf{F};\mathbf{G}$, we will discuss the fundamental ideas of the composition of paths – interpreted as substochastic APDs – in the underlying Markov chain.

A path $(i) \overset{f}{\rightsquigarrow} (k) \overset{g}{\rightsquigarrow} (j)$ starting in $(i) \in \mathcal{E}_\mathbf{F}$, through $(k) \in \mathcal{E}_\mathbf{G}$ to $(j) \in \mathcal{X}_\mathbf{G}$ can be represented by the two APDs $f \sim (\!(\alpha, \tilde{f})\!)$ and $g \sim (\!(\beta, \tilde{g})\!)$. The path probability of the composed path $f \circ g$ is $\alpha \cdot \beta$, and – up to normalization – the probability distribution of absorption in (j) is $\tilde{f} \circledast \tilde{g}$. We can express the composed path by the Hadamard pair representation $f \circ g \sim (\!(\alpha \cdot \beta, \tilde{f} \circledast \tilde{g})\!)$.

Using the Chapman-Kolmogorov equations, we can generalize this idea to capture all possible paths from (i) to (j) by summing the composed subdistributions over all possible intermediate states (k). We consolidate this insight in the following definition – lifting path composition $\circ$ from APDs to MXMEs.

Definition 7 (Sequential Composition of MXMEs). *Given MXMEs $\mathbf{F} \in \mathtt{APD}^{\ell \times m}$ and $\mathbf{G} \in \mathtt{APD}^{m \times n}$, their sequential composition is given by*

$$\mathbf{F}\,;\mathbf{G} := \left\{ \sum_{k=1}^{m} \mathbf{F}_{ik} \circ \mathbf{G}_{kj} \right\}_{ij} \in \mathtt{APD}^{\ell \times n}, \tag{3}$$

where $\circ$ acts on the Hadamard representations of the phase-type distributions $\mathbf{F}_{ik}$ and $\mathbf{G}_{kj}$. Given respective generator matrices $\mathbf{Q}$ and $\mathbf{R}$ of $\mathbf{F}$ and $\mathbf{G}$, we obtain the following matrix representation of $\mathbf{F}\,;\mathbf{G} \sim \mathtt{MXME}(\mathbf{C}, \mathbf{D})$:

$$(\mathbf{C} \mid \mathbf{D}) = \left(\begin{array}{ccccc|c} \mathbf{Q}_{\mathcal{E}\to\mathcal{E}} & \mathbf{Q}_{\mathcal{E}\to\mathcal{I}} & \mathbf{Q}_{\mathcal{E}\to\mathcal{X}} & & & \\ & \mathbf{Q}_{\mathcal{I}\to\mathcal{I}} & \mathbf{Q}_{\mathcal{I}\to\mathcal{X}} & & & \\ & & \mathbf{R}_{\mathcal{E}\to\mathcal{E}} & \mathbf{R}_{\mathcal{E}\to\mathcal{I}} & & \mathbf{R}_{\mathcal{E}\to\mathcal{X}} \\ & & & \mathbf{R}_{\mathcal{I}\to\mathcal{I}} & & \mathbf{R}_{\mathcal{I}\to\mathcal{X}} \end{array}\right).$$

Note that the resulting source and sink states become $\mathcal{E} = \mathcal{E}_\mathbf{F}$ and $\mathcal{X} = \mathcal{X}_\mathbf{G}$.

Example 5. Recall the diagnosis procedure discussed in example 1 and assume it to be described by $\mathbf{D} \sim \mathtt{MXME}(\mathbf{A}, \mathbf{L}) \in \mathtt{APD}^{2\times 3}$. Once diagnosed, an ill patient will receive in-hospital treatment depending on the diagnosed disease variant. We model the length-of-stay in the hospital of this treatment as a MXME $\mathbf{T} \in \mathtt{MXME}^{2\times 3}$. Patients deemed healthy in example 1 should not receive such treatment. We model this fact by composing the healthy population with the Dirac δ function. Figure. 5 illustrates the resulting algebraic expression $\mathbf{D}\,;(\delta \perp\!\!\!\perp \mathbf{T})$. The initial distribution $\underline{\alpha} = \left(1/2\ 1/2\right)$ from example 1 does not play into the model of this system, only into its transient behavior.

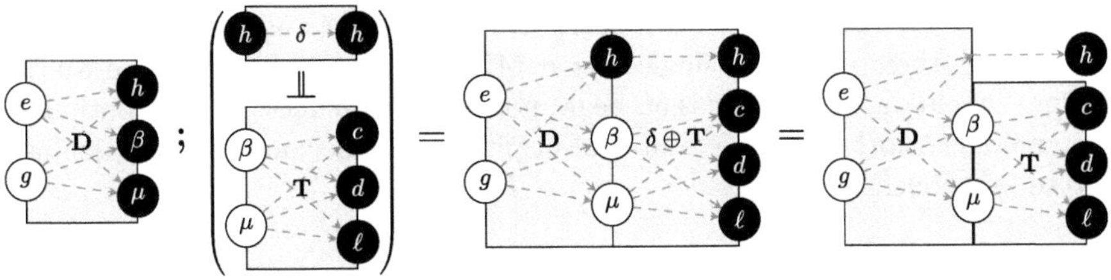

Fig. 5. Illustration of the algebraic expression $\mathbf{D} ; (\delta \perp\!\!\!\perp \mathbf{T})$ from example 5 by its MXMEs' topologies, hiding the specific implementations. A superset of the nonzero APDs between initial and absorbing states are drawn as dashed arrows. Patients arriving at the four absorbing states are deemed healthy, cured, deceased, and under long-term observation – thus their respective names h, c, d, and ℓ. Note that the orthogonal composition operator merges the CTMCs without introducing any interaction between the disjoint parts. The degenerate APD δ is depicted to connect two absorbing states, highlighting the fact that during this phase, no time passes. Hence, we omit the intermediate state h in the third picture.

Algebraic Structure Before we move on, we would like to observe that the set of acyclic phase-type measures on $\mathbb{R}^{\geq 0}$ together with the ordinary addition $+$ on functions, and sequential composition $\circ$ as multiplication forms a *rig*, or semiring, $\mathcal{R}_{\texttt{APD}} = (\texttt{APD}, +, \circ, 0, 1)$, which is a ring without negation. Its zero element $0_{\mathcal{R}}$ is the constant zero function, and the one element $1_{\mathcal{R}}$ is the Dirac-delta function δ that assigns the probability mass 1 to zero. Moreover, we can straightforwardly multiply the elements of $\mathcal{R}_{\texttt{APD}}$ by scalars $s \in \mathbb{R}^{\geq 0}$, making $\mathcal{R}_{\texttt{APD}}$ an $\mathcal{R}$-algebra.

We carefully chose the elements of $\mathcal{R}_{\texttt{APD}}$ to be *measures* as opposed to distributions, since measures are closed under the operations mentioned above, whereas distributions are not. However, the operations we typically perform on APDs are closed under the set of (sub)stochastic distributions.

In this setting, we can understand MXMEs to be matrices over $\mathcal{R}$, whose row sums integrate to one. Their components $\mathbf{F}_{ij}$ capture the probability subdensities of absorption into state j at time t, given initiation in (i). The formula given in eq. (3) for the sequential composition $\mathbf{F} ; \mathbf{G}$ of two MXMEs is exactly the matrix-matrix product over $\mathcal{R}_{\texttt{APD}}$.

Although MXMEs understood as matrices of a fixed square size, say $n \times n$, form a rig structure, this structure is not preserved if non-$n \times n$ matrices are brought into the mix. In the upcoming section, we will amend this limitation and discuss the category theoretical structure required to support a theory in which a liberal orthogonal and sequential composition is allowed.

6 Category Theoretical View on MXMEs

In this section, we will use the framework of monoidal categories to model arbitrary composition of (acyclic) multi-entry multi-exit phase-type distributions. We take inspiration from Watanabe et. al [30], who used traced, symmetric monoidal categories to model compositional model checking for MDPs. In fact, specializing their model to single-action MDPs – hence, discrete-time Markov chains – yields a framework that bears strong resemblance to our continuous-time model. Another notable source of inspiration is the composition calculus of Fettke and Reisig [8,9].

6.1 Background

Monoidal Categories A category $\mathcal{C}$ consists of a collection of objects $\mathrm{Ob}(\mathcal{C})$ and morphisms $\mathrm{Mor}(\mathcal{C})$ between objects. It is required that two morphisms between triplets of objects $a \xrightarrow{f} b$ and $b \xrightarrow{g} c$ be composable, as follows:

$$\circ\colon (b \xrightarrow{g} c) \circ (a \xrightarrow{f} b) \longrightarrow a \xrightarrow{g \circ f} c.$$

Moreover, for each object o of $\mathrm{Ob}(\mathcal{C})$, a special morphism $Id_o : o \to o$ must exist, which acts as the identity element under $\circ$. We denote the collection of morphisms between two objects a and b by $\mathrm{Hom}(a, b)$.

A category $\mathcal{C}$ becomes *monoidal*, if it is equipped with an associative bifunctor $\otimes : \mathcal{C} \times \mathcal{C} \to \mathcal{C}$, also called (tensor) product, and an identity object I that serves as the left and right identity under $\otimes$ [19,27].

We have previously hinted at the fact that matrices over a (semi)ring $\mathcal{R}$ do not straightforwardly form a (semi)ring of matrices $\mathcal{R}$, since matrix multiplication in general does not preserve the shape of the matrices involved. Switching from rings to categories alleviates this issue. Thinking about the morphisms of a category as matrices, we can see that the type signature of the composition operator $\circ : \mathrm{Hom}(a, b) \times \mathrm{Hom}(b, c) \to \mathrm{Hom}(a, c)$ precisely mirrors how matrix dimensions behave under the ordinary matrix product.

Category Prop Fixing $\mathcal{R}$, the category Prop($\mathcal{R}$) reifies this insight in the language of category theory [10]. Its objects are the natural numbers, and the morphisms in $\mathrm{Hom}(m, n)$ are the $\mathcal{R}$-matrices of dimensions $m \times n$. The composition of two morphisms is given by the matrix multiplication over $\mathcal{R}$. Furthermore, Props come equipped with a monoidal product. The product on objects computes the sum on integers $m \otimes n = m + n$, on morphisms it is given by the direct sum of matrices

$$\otimes\colon (k \xrightarrow{\mathbf{F}} \ell) \otimes (m \xrightarrow{\mathbf{G}} n) \longrightarrow (k + m) \xrightarrow{\mathbf{F} \oplus \mathbf{G}} (\ell + n),$$

and the monoidal unit I is given by the 0×0 matrix over $\mathcal{R}$. Note that the identity elements regarding composition $\circ$ are given by the identity matrices of suitable dimensions.

The name Prop is an abbreviation of "products and permutations", where product refers to the monoidal product and permutation refers to permutation matrices over $\mathcal{R}$.

Prop($\boldsymbol{\mathcal{R}}_{\mathtt{APD}}$) In the context of MXMEs, a morphism $m \xrightarrow{\mathbf{F}} n$ describes an m-entry n-exit acyclic phase-type distribution, that is, an element of $\mathtt{APD}^{m \times n}$. The composition of morphisms $\mathbf{G} \circ \mathbf{F}$ is given by the sequential composition of MXMEs

$\mathbf{F} ; \mathbf{G}$. Note that this definition flips the usual order of function composition, allowing us a more natural graphical representation of sequential composition in the upcoming section. The monoidal product of morphisms $\mathbf{F} \otimes \mathbf{G}$ is given by the orthogonal composition $\mathbf{F} \perp\!\!\!\perp \mathbf{G}$. Since the one element of $\mathcal{R}_{\mathtt{APD}}$ is the Dirac-delta function δ, the identities of composition are the identity matrices over $\mathcal{R}_{\mathtt{APD}}$ whose diagonal entries are δ.

String Diagrams Monoidal categories enjoy the particularly rich [27] framework of string diagrams, which serve as graphical illustrations for many different domains. String diagrams find applications in the modeling of in electronic circuits [15], concurrency theory [1], databases [5], quantum circuits [2], Markov decision processes [29,30], and many more. They serve as an intuitive graphical language to express abstract algebraic expressions. Figure 6 shows an example of the composition of two MXMEs $\mathbf{F}, \mathbf{G} \in \mathtt{APD}^{2\times 2}$ in the language of string diagrams, illustrating the category theoretical expression $(I \otimes \mathbf{F}) \circ (\mathbf{G} \otimes I)$ graphically.

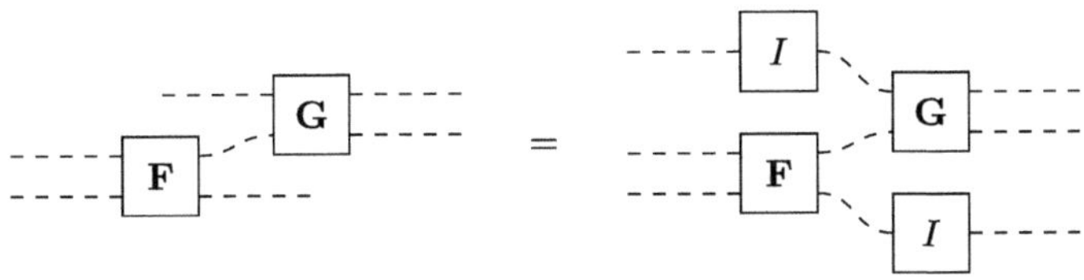

Fig. 6. Illustration of a non-straightforward MXME composition of $\mathbf{F}, \mathbf{G} \in \mathtt{APD}^{2\times 2}$. To realize the composition, auxiliary identities of sequential composition I are used.

6.2 Compositional Calculus for MXMEs

Next, we will illustrate the utility of the framework of monoidal categories for MXMEs by modeling many fundamental operations on acyclic phase-type distributions in said framework. The representation of these operations will be matrices over $\mathcal{R}$, which can be applied to a MXME using the ; operator.

Mixtures We elaborated in section 4 how we can transform the family of distributions $\mathbf{F}$, into *one* multi-exit phase-type distribution by mixing it with a probability distribution $\underline{\alpha}$ over $\mathcal{E}$. To be exact, we expect initial distributions $\underline{\alpha}$ to be vectors in $\mathbb{R}^{1\times n}$, however when talking about the morphisms in our PROP, we must lift the scalar entries $\alpha_i \in \mathbb{R}$ of $\underline{\alpha}$ to functions $\underline{\alpha}_i\delta \in \mathtt{APD}$. Since this mapping is simply the embedding of the (vectors of) scalars into the algebra $\underline{\alpha} \mapsto \underline{\alpha}\mathbf{Id}$, we will do this lifting implicitly.

Then, in our categorical framework, the initialization is given by the composition of the row-vector $\underline{\alpha}$ as a morphism $\underline{\alpha} : 1 \to n$ and the matrix $\mathbf{F} : n \to m$, obtaining the familiar result $\underline{\alpha} ; \mathbf{F} = \underline{\alpha}\mathbf{F}$. More generally, we can use arbitrary row-stochastic, real-valued matrices $\mathbf{A}$, lifted to APD, to rewire the inputs and outputs of our system by left- and right-composition, respectively.

Permutations, Merging and Marginalization As implied by their name, PROPs have access to permutation matrices over $\mathcal{R}$, which rearrange the order of sink states of a MXME. An $n \times n$ matrix $\mathbf{\Pi}$, represented by the morphism $n \to n$, is called a permutation matrix, iff every row and every column contains exactly one $1_{\mathcal{R}}$ and zeros everywhere else. We can associate $\mathbf{\Pi}$ with the function $\sigma(i) = j$, where j is the nonzero column index of the i-th row of $\mathbf{\Pi}$, and denote it $\mathbf{\Pi}_\sigma$.

It is sometimes desired to merge multiple absorbing states into one, reducing the output dimension of a MXME. Given a partition $P = P_1 \cup \cdots \cup P_k = \mathcal{X}$ of absorbing states to merge, we define the merging matrix $\mathbf{Merg}_P$ to have a $1_{\mathcal{R}}$ in $\mathbf{Merg}_P(i, j)$, if i belongs to the partition P_j and zeros else.

If we care about the marginal distributions $\mathbb{P}(X = t \cap A \in E)$ of absorption in a subset $E \subseteq \mathcal{X}$, we can use a very similar construction as for merging matrices: The matrix $\mathbf{Marg}_E \in \mathtt{APD}^{n \times 1}$ has ones exactly in rows j, where j belongs to E, and zeros elsewhere.

To apply the effects of all aforementioned matrices $\mathbf{M}$ to a MXME $\mathbf{F}$, we compose them from the right $\mathbf{F} \,;\, \mathbf{M}$.

Reachability Probability Functor If we recall that the entries of a MXME $\mathbf{F}_{ij}$ describe the probability distribution $\mathbb{P}(X = t \cap A = j \mid S = i)$, we see that we can marginalize out the time variable t, obtaining the limiting behavior of the component. This idea has been captured by Watanabe et al., who have defined the reachability probability functor $\mathbb{E}$ in the context of discrete-time Markov-chains, or rather, stochastic matrices [29].

Adapted to our setting, $\mathbb{E} : \text{PROP}(\mathcal{R}_{\mathtt{APD}}) \Rightarrow \text{PROP}(\mathcal{R}_{\mathbb{R}})$ maps a MXME to the marginal probability matrix $\boldsymbol{\alpha}$ with real entries. The functor $\mathbb{E}$ acts as the identity on $\text{Ob}(\mathcal{R}_{\mathtt{APD}})$, and assigns a morphism $a \xrightarrow{f} b \in \mathtt{APD}^{a \times b}$ the probability matrix $\boldsymbol{\alpha}$ of its Hadamard representation $f \sim (\!(\boldsymbol{\alpha}, A)\!)$. The Chapman-Kolmogorov equations express $\mathbb{E}(\mathbf{F} \,;\, \mathbf{G}) = \mathbb{E}(\mathbf{F}) \cdot \mathbb{E}(\mathbf{G})$, stating that $\mathbb{E}$ is a functor.

Example 6. We continue our running example. Assume that later into the clinical trials, it has been observed that the diagnosis stage results in false-positives and false-negatives for D-β and D-μ diagnoses. Statistical data indicate that we should correct the results of the old diagnosis model by a mixture matrix $\mathbf{C}$ of the assigned classes. Moreover, we merge the classification of both healthy and cured patients into one group using the matrix $\mathbf{M}$. In the algebraic language of MXMEs, this model can be expressed by the following expression

$$\mathbf{D} \,;\, (\mathbf{Id} \perp\!\!\!\perp (\mathbf{C} \,;\, \mathbf{T})) \,;\, (\mathbf{M} \perp\!\!\!\perp \mathbf{Id}).$$

Find below the – up to distributivity of $;$ and $\perp\!\!\!\perp$– same expression depicted as matrices. Note how the real scalars of $\mathbf{C}$ have been embedded into our algebra by multiplication with δ.

$$\underbrace{\begin{pmatrix} f_{e\to h} & f_{e\to\beta} & f_{e\to\mu} \\ f_{g\to h} & f_{g\to\beta} & f_{g\to\mu}\end{pmatrix}}_{\mathbf{D}} \cdot \underbrace{\left(\begin{array}{c|cc} \delta & & \\ \hline & 0.9\cdot\delta & 0.1\cdot\delta \\ & 0.2\cdot\delta & 0.8\cdot\delta \end{array}\right)}_{\mathbf{Id}\oplus\mathbf{C}} \cdot \underbrace{\left(\begin{array}{c|ccc} \delta & & & \\ \hline & g_{\beta\to c} & g_{\beta\to d} & g_{\beta\to\ell} \\ & g_{\mu\to c} & g_{\mu\to d} & g_{\mu\to\ell}\end{array}\right)}_{\mathbf{Id}\oplus\mathbf{T}} \cdot \underbrace{\left(\begin{array}{c|cc} \delta & & \\ \delta & & \\ \hline & \delta & \\ & & \delta \end{array}\right)}_{\mathbf{M}\oplus\mathbf{Id}}$$

Given an initial distribution over ER and GP statistics, we can use this model to analyze the length-of-stay in the hospital setting.

Example 7. Lastly, taking full advantage of the monoidal category semantics, we depict our example in the language of string diagrams in fig. 7.

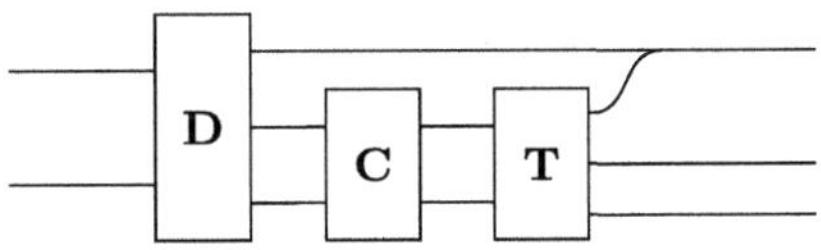

Fig. 7. String diagrammatic illustration of our running example. For clarity, coefficients of wires representing Dirac deltas have been omitted.

7 Conclusion

This paper has discussed construction and composition aspects of continuous-time phase-type distributions with multiple entries and multiple exits. This model world generalizes traditional phase-type distributions, as well as their multi-exit generalizations proposed to model competing risks.

Central to the paper is the novel `MXME` framework of multi-exit multi-entry (acyclic) phase-type models. `MXME`s are equipped with an algebraic formalism supporting several operations. The latter can be embedded into the language of monoidal categories, allowing depiction via string diagrams. Several theoretical aspects have been shed light on, and the applicability of `MXME`s has been demonstrated by a running example. Prototypical tool support for `MXME` is in the making. Since the `MXME` formalism essentially wires up component CTMCs, we can use established back-end solvers such as Prism [17] or Storm [13] to carry out numerical analysis of the resulting CTMC model. These solvers are known to support transient analysis of CTMCs with millions of states.

Regarding future work, we are currently looking into the question of how to enhance the so far monoidal setting to bimonoidal categories, so as to support a generalization of minimum and maximum of distributions to `MXME`s. We are also working on modeling support for closing loops from exit to entry, taking inspiration from ribbon categories [29]. Moreover, we intend to investigate ways of leveraging matrix geometric approaches for our purposes.

Acknowledgement. This research is supported by the German Research Foundation (DFG) grant 389792660 as part of TRR 248 – CPEC (see https://perspicuous-computing.science).

References

1. S. Abramsky: Retracing some paths in Process Algebra. CoRR abs/1401.5113 (2014)
2. MISC
3. A. Bies, H. Hermanns, M.A. Köhl, and A. Schmidt: Matching Distributions Under Structural Constraints. In: Quantitative Evaluation of Systems, pp. 221–237. Springer Nature Switzerland, Cham (2023)
4. M. Bladt and B.F. Nielsen: Matrix-exponential distributions in applied probability. Springer (2017)
5. F. Bonchi, J. Seeber, and P. Sobocinski: Graphical Conjunctive Queries. In: 27th EACSL Annual Conference on Computer Science Logic (CSL 2018). Leibniz International Proceedings in Informatics (LIPIcs), 13:1–13:23. Schloss Dagstuhl – Leibniz-Zentrum für Informatik, Dagstuhl, Germany (2018). DOI: https://doi.org/10.4230/LIPIcs.CSL.2018.13
6. P. Buchholz, J. Kriege, and I. Felko: Input Modeling with Phase-Type Distributions and Markov Models: Theory and Applications. Springer (2014)
7. A. Cumani: On the canonical representation of homogeneous markov processes modelling failure - time distributions. Microelectronics Reliability 22(3), 583–602 (1982). DOI: https://doi.org/10.1016/0026-2714(82)90033-6
8. P. Fettke and W. Reisig: Modelling Service-Oriented Systems and Cloud Services with Heraklit. In: Advances in Service-Oriented and Cloud Computing - International Workshops of ESOCC 2020, Heraklion, Crete, Greece, September 28-30, 2020, Revised Selected Papers. Communications in Computer and Information Science, pp. 77–89. Springer (2020). DOI: https://doi.org/10.1007/978-3-030-71906-7_7
9. P. Fettke and W. Reisig: Understanding the Digital World - Modeling with HERAKLIT. Springer (2024)
10. P. Hackney and M. Robertson: On the Category of Props. Applied Categorical Structures 23(4), 543–573 (2014). DOI: https://doi.org/10.1007/s10485-014-9369-4
11. B.R. Haverkort: Performance of computer communication systems. John Wiley & Sons, Chichester, England (1998)
12. Q.-M. He and M.F. Neuts: Markov chains with marked transitions. Stochastic Processes and their Applications 74(1), 37–52 (1998). DOI: https://doi.org/10.1016/S0304-4149(97)00109-9
13. C. Hensel, S. Junges, J. Katoen, T. Quatmann, and M. Volk: The probabilistic model checker Storm. Int. J. Softw. Tools Technol. Transf. 24(4), 589–610 (2022). DOI: https://doi.org/10.1007/S10009-021-00633-Z
14. G. Horváth and M. Telek: On the canonical representation of phase type distributions. Performance Evaluation 66(8), 396–409 (2009). DOI: https://doi.org/10.1016/j.peva.2008.11.002
15. G. Hotz: Eine Algebraisierung des Syntheseproblems von Schaltkreisen I. J. Inf. Process. Cybern. 1(3), 185–205 (1965)

16. B. Jones, S. McClean, and D. Stanford: Modelling mortality and discharge of hospitalized stroke patients using a phase-type recovery model. Health Care Management Science 22(4), 570–588 (2018). DOI: https://doi.org/10.1007/s10729-018-9446-6
17. M.Z. Kwiatkowska, G. Norman, and D. Parker: PRISM 4.0: Verification of Probabilistic Real-Time Systems. In: Computer Aided Verification - 23rd International Conference, CAV 2011, Snowbird, UT, USA, July 14-20, 2011. Proceedings. LNCS, vol. 6806, pp. 585–591. Springer, Heidelberg (2011). DOI: https://doi.org/10.1007/978-3-642-22110-1_47
18. B.H. Lindqvist: Phase-type models for competing risks, with emphasis on identifiability issues. Lifetime Data Anal. 29(2), 318–341 (2023)
19. S. MacLane: Natural Associativity and Commutativity. Rice Univ. Studies 49(4), 28–46 (1963)
20. S. McClean, M. Barton, L. Garg, and K. Fullerton: A modeling framework that combines markov models and discrete-event simulation for stroke patient care. ACM Transactions on Modeling and Computer Simulation (TOMACS) 21(4), 1–26 (2011). DOI: https://doi.org/10.1145/2000494.2000498
21. S. McClean, L. Garg, M. Barton, and K. Fullerton: Using mixed phase-type distributions to model patient pathways. In: 2010 IEEE 23rd International Symposium on Computer-Based Medical Systems (CBMS), pp. 172–177 (2010). DOI: https://doi.org/10.1109/CBMS.2010.6042636
22. M.F. Neuts: Matrix-geometric Solutions in Stochastic Models: An Algorithmic Approach. Johns Hopkins University Press, Baltimore (1981)
23. C.A. O'Cinneide: On non-uniqueness of representations of phase-type distributions. Communications in Statistics. Stochastic Models 5(2), 247–259 (1989). DOI: https://doi.org/10.1080/15326348908807108
24. MISC
25. P. Reinecke, T. Krauß, and K. Wolter: Phase-Type Fitting Using HyperStar. In: Computer Performance Engineering - 10th European Workshop, EPEW 2013, Venice, Italy, September 16-17, 2013. Proceedings. LNCS, vol. 8168, pp. 164–175. Springer, Heidelberg (2013). DOI: https://doi.org/10.1007/978-3-642-40725-3_13
26. R. Schassberger: Warteschlangen. Springer (1973)
27. P. Selinger: "A Survey of Graphical Languages for Monoidal Categories". In: New Structures for Physics. Berlin, Heidelberg: Springer Berlin Heidelberg, 2011, pp. 289–355. DOI: https://doi.org/10.1007/978-3-642-12821-9_4
28. W.J. Stewart: Introduction to the Numerical Solution of Markov Chains. Princeton University Press, Princeton (1995)
29. K. Watanabe, C. Eberhart, K. Asada, and I. Hasuo: Compositional Probabilistic Model Checking with String Diagrams of MDPs. In: Computer Aided Verification - 35th International Conference, CAV 2023, Paris, France, July 17-22, 2023, Proceedings, Part III. LNCS, vol. 13966, pp. 40–61. Springer, Heidelberg (2023). DOI: https://doi.org/10.1007/978-3-031-37709-9_3
30. K. Watanabe, M. van der Vegt, I. Hasuo, J. Rot, and S. Junges: Pareto Curves for Compositionally Model Checking String Diagrams of MDPs. In: Tools and Algorithms for the Construction and Analysis of Systems, pp. 279–298. Springer Nature Switzerland, Cham (2024)

Exact Persistent Stochastic Non-interference

Riccardo Romanello[1(✉)], Carla Piazza[2], Michele Bugliesi[1], and Sabina Rossi[1]

[1] Università Ca' Foscari Venezia, Venice, Italy
{riccardo.romanello,bugliesi,sabina.rossi}@unive.it
[2] Università degli Studi di Udine, Udine, Italy
carla.piazza@uniud.it

Abstract. Persistent Stochastic Non-Interference (PSNI) has been introduced to capture a quantitative security property in stochastic process algebras, ensuring that a high-level process does not influence the observable behaviour of a low-level component, as formalised via lumpable bisimulation. In this work, we revisit PSNI from a performance-oriented perspective and propose a new characterisation based on a refined behavioural relation. We introduce *exact lumpable bisimulation*, which extends exact equivalence with a relaxed treatment of internal (τ) actions, enabling precise control over quantitative observables while accommodating unobservable transitions. Based on this, we define *Exact PSNI* (EPSNI), a variant of PSNI, characterised via exact lumpable bisimilarity. EPSNI admits the same bisimulation-based and unwinding-style characterisations as PSNI, and enjoys analogous compositionality properties. These results confirm exact lumpable bisimilarity as a robust foundation for reasoning about non-interference in stochastic systems.

Keywords: Process Algebra · Non-Interference · Stochastic models · Exact Equivalence

1 Introduction

Formal notions of non-interference have long been central to the specification and analysis of information flow properties in secure systems [9,10,12]. Traditionally studied in deterministic or nondeterministic process models, non-interference ensures that high-level (secret) actions do not affect the observable behaviour of low-level (public) components [6,8]. Recently, attention has turned to quantitative settings, where systems are described using stochastic process algebras, and the need arises to reason not only about qualitative properties, but also about

The work described in this paper has been partially supported by PRIN project NiRvAna—Noninterference and Reversibility Analysis in Private Blockchains" (20202FCJMH, CUP G23C22000400005) and by PNRR project SERICS—Security and Rights in the CyberSpace (CUP H73C22000890001).

A. Remke et al. (Eds.): Valuetools 2025, LNICST 691, pp. 70–87, 2027.
https://doi.org/10.1007/978-3-032-23901-3_5

the performance and probabilistic characteristics of a system execution. In this context, the recent work by Hillston, Piazza, and Rossi [15] introduced the notion of *Persistent Stochastic Non-Interference* (PSNI), a security property formulated within the PEPA process algebra [13,17,21]. PSNI leverages the theory of lumpability for Markov chains [18,19] to define a compositional and performance-aware form of non-interference. Specifically, PSNI ensures that the behaviour of a low-level process remains indistinguishable to an external observer regardless of the high-level environment in which it is placed. The notion is persistent in that it requires this indistinguishability to hold at every reachable state, not just at the initial configuration. PSNI admits multiple characterisations, including a bisimulation-based formulation and a set of unwinding-style local conditions, and it has been shown to be preserved under key operations of the PEPA calculus. Building on this foundation, the aim of this work is to re-express PSNI using a behavioural equivalence that captures the quantitative structure of stochastic systems. Our starting point is the classical notion of *exact equivalence* [1,5,11], which requires two processes to exhibit the same apparent rates and to be reachable by the same incoming rates. Exact equivalence provides a strong notion of behavioural indistinguishability, particularly suited to performance modelling, as it ensures that two processes to be equiprobable with respect to their equivalence class. It thus seemed a natural candidate for reformulating the PSNI property in a more stochastic fashion. However, applying exact equivalence directly to the setting of non-interference raises a subtle challenge. In particular, the presence of internal (τ) actions, which are intended to be unobservable, clashes with the strict matching requirements of exact equivalence. When internal transitions differ across components, exact equivalence is too rigid to identify them, even if their observable behaviour is identical. As a consequence, exact equivalence fails to support the abstraction necessary for reasoning about security properties in systems where internal actions encode confidential or implementation-specific behaviours. To overcome this limitation, we introduce a new equivalence relation, which we call *Exact Lumpable Bisimilarity.* This relation extends exact equivalence by relaxing its requirements for τ-transitions. While it continues to enforce matching of apparent rates and incoming transition rates for visible actions, it allows for a controlled discrepancy in internal behaviour, provided that such differences do not affect observability at the level of equivalence classes. The key intuition is that exact lumpable bisimulation preserves the precise quantitative structure of a system, while abstracting from internal transitions in a way that remains compatible with security analysis. With this new equivalence in place, we define a corresponding security property, *Exact Persistent Stochastic Non-Interference* (EPSNI), which mimicks the structure of PSNI, but uses exact lumpable bisimilarity as its semantics foundation. We show that EPSNI admits the same threefold characterisations as PSNI: a semantic definition quantifying over high-level contexts, a bisimulation-based reformulation that avoids universal quantification, and a local unwinding condition [16] that enables compositional reasoning about the property. The above properties, allow also for a fast prototyping of an efficient procedure to verify whether EPSNI is fulfilled [20].

We further prove that EPSNI is preserved under PEPA operators such as prefix, hiding, and cooperation on low-level actions, and that it supports a notion of steady-state independence between high-level behaviour and low-level observations. These results demonstrate that EPSNI provides a robust and expressive framework for reasoning about non-interference in stochastic systems, with strong guarantees on both performance preservation and security. Compared to PSNI, EPSNI offers a form of behavioural indistinguishability which ensures underlying properties, maintaining compatibility with internal abstraction. At the same time, the similarity of its structural and compositional properties confirms that Exact Lumpable Bisimilarity is well-suited as a semantic foundation for quantitative security analysis in stochastic models.

Structure of the Paper. In Sect. 2, we introduce the process algebra PEPA, its structural operational semantics, and the observation equivalence named *Exact Lumpable Bisimilarity.* The notion of *Exact Persistent Stochastic Non-Interference (EPSNI)* and its characterizations are presented in Sect. 4. In Sect. 5, we prove some compositionality results and other properties of *EPSNI*. Section 6 concludes the paper. The proofs of the statements are in the Appendix section for sake of readability.

2 The Calculus

PEPA (Performance Evaluation Process Algebra) [13] is an algebraic formalism enriched with stochastic timing information. The core entities of PEPA are *activities* and *components*. An activity is a pair (α, r), where α is the *action type* (a label) and r is the *activity rate*. The rate r serves as the parameter of a negative exponential distribution, defining the activity's duration. We assume a countable set of action types $\mathcal{A}$, among which a special type τ is reserved for *unobservable* actions. Rates may be any positive real number or the special symbol $\top$, which stands for *unspecified*. The syntax of PEPA is described by the grammar:

$$N ::= (\alpha, r).N \mid N + N \mid X$$
$$P ::= N \mid P/A \mid P \underset{A}{\bowtie} P$$

Here N denotes a *sequential component*, X is a constant from a countable set $\mathcal{X}$, and $A \subset \mathcal{A}$ is a set of action types. A general *model component* is written P. We write $\mathcal{C}$ for the set of all well-formed components.

Structural Operational Semantics. The transition rules for PEPA are reported in Table 1. A component of the form $(\alpha, r).N$ executes activity (α, r) and then behaves as N. Writing $a = (\alpha, r)$, we sometimes abbreviate $(\alpha, r).N$ as $a.N$. The choice operator $N + M$ allows the system to proceed as either N or M, depending on which activity completes first. All enabled activities of both components are available, but once one completes, the other branch is discarded. Constants are introduced by defining equations $X \stackrel{def}{=} N$, which assign the behaviour of N

Table 1. Operational semantics of PEPA components

$$\frac{}{(\alpha, r).N \xrightarrow{(\alpha,r)} N} \qquad \frac{N \xrightarrow{(\alpha,r)} N'}{X \xrightarrow{(\alpha,r)} N'} \ (X \stackrel{def}{=} N)$$

$$\frac{N \xrightarrow{(\alpha,r)} N'}{N + M \xrightarrow{(\alpha,r)} N'} \qquad \frac{M \xrightarrow{(\alpha,r)} M'}{N + M \xrightarrow{(\alpha,r)} M'}$$

$$\frac{P \xrightarrow{(\alpha,r)} P'}{P/A \xrightarrow{(\alpha,r)} P'/A} \ (\alpha \notin A) \qquad \frac{P \xrightarrow{(\alpha,r)} P'}{P/A \xrightarrow{(\tau,r)} P'/A} \ (\alpha \in A)$$

$$\frac{P \xrightarrow{(\alpha,r)} P'}{P \underset{A}{\S} Q \xrightarrow{(\alpha,r)} P' \underset{A}{\S} Q} \ (\alpha \notin A) \qquad \frac{Q \xrightarrow{(\alpha,r)} Q'}{P \underset{A}{\S} Q \xrightarrow{(\alpha,r)} P \underset{A}{\S} Q'} \ (\alpha \notin A)$$

$$\frac{P \xrightarrow{(\alpha,r_1)} P' \quad Q \xrightarrow{(\alpha,r_2)} Q'}{P \underset{A}{\S} Q \xrightarrow{(\alpha,R)} P' \underset{A}{\S} Q'} \qquad R = \frac{r_1}{r_\alpha(P)} \frac{r_2}{r_\alpha(Q)} \min(r_\alpha(P), r_\alpha(Q)) \ (\alpha \in A)$$

to X. Every constant must have exactly one definition, and all definitions must be *guarded*: immediate recursion is forbidden (for instance, $X \stackrel{def}{=} Y + (\alpha, r).Z$ is not permitted if Y is unguarded). Hiding is written P/A, where actions in A are relabelled as τ. The cooperation operator $P \underset{A}{\S} Q$ enforces synchronization on action types in $A \subseteq \mathcal{A} \setminus \{\tau\}$. For action types not in A, the two components proceed independently (*individual activities*). If $\alpha \in A$, both P and Q must offer α simultaneously to enable the shared activity. The resulting rate reflects the slower partner [13]. If a sequential component contains an action with unspecified rate $\top$, then it is *passive* with respect to that action type. In this case all occurrences of that action type in the component must also be passive. The rate of the shared activity is then determined entirely by the cooperating partner.

The *apparent rate* of action type α in process P, denoted $r_\alpha(P)$, is defined as the sum of the rates of all currently enabled α-activities in P. The last rule of Table 1 makes use of apparent rates. When $\top$ is involved, the conventions of [13, Section 3.3.5] apply, including $r < \top$ for any positive r.
The semantics of PEPA terms is presented by means of a labelled *multi-transition system*, in which the multiplicity of transitions is relevant. Each syntactic term of the language corresponds to a state, also called a *derivative*. Arcs are labelled with activities and indicate the evolution of one derivative into another. The set of all derivatives reachable from a model P is denoted $ds(P)$ and forms the nodes of the *derivation graph* $\mathcal{D}(P)$, obtained by the rules in Table 1.

We use $\mathcal{A}(P)$ to denote the set of all *current action types* enabled by P, and $\mathcal{A}ct(P)$ for the multiset of currently enabled *activities*. Likewise, $\boldsymbol{\mathcal{A}}(P)$ is the union of all $\mathcal{A}(P')$ with $P' \in ds(P)$, that is, all action types appearing syntactically in P. The *exit rate* of a component P is the sum of the rates of all enabled activities, i.e., $q(P) = \sum_{a \in \mathcal{A}ct(P)} r_a$, where r_a is the rate of activity a. If multiple activities are enabled, the execution is governed by a *race condition*. Nondeterministic choice is replaced with probabilistic branching: activity a completes with probability $r_a/q(P)$.

Underlying Stochastic Process. A PEPA model P is said to be *complete* if every derivative of P has a strictly positive, real-valued exit rate. Completeness ensures that passive actions are either hidden or synchronised with active ones. As proved in [13], any finite complete PEPA model P with derivative set $ds(P) = \{P_0, \dots, P_n\}$ corresponds to a continuous-time Markov chain (CTMC). Define $X(t)$ to be the stochastic process such that $X(t) = P_i$ means the system behaves as P_i at time t. Then $X(t)$ is a CTMC. The *transition rate* from P_i to P_j is $q(P_i, P_j) = \sum_{a \in \mathcal{A}ct(P_i|P_j)} r_a$, where $\mathcal{A}ct(P_i \mid P_j) = \{\!| a \in \mathcal{A}ct(P_i) \mid P_i \xrightarrow{a} P_j |\!\}$ and $P_i \neq P_j$. If P_j is not a direct derivative of P_i, then $q(P_i, P_j) = 0$. The values $q(P_i, P_j)$ (also denoted q_{ij}) form the off-diagonal entries of the infinitesimal generator $\mathbf{Q}$. Diagonal elements are set as $q_{ii} = -q(P_i)$, where $q(P_i) = \sum_{j \neq i} q(P_i, P_j)$. For finite irreducible models, the steady-state distribution Π exists and satisfies the normalization and balance equations:

$$\sum_{P_i \in ds(P)} \Pi(P_i) = 1, \qquad \Pi\,\mathbf{Q} = \mathbf{0}\,.$$

For any process $Q \notin ds(P)$, we set $q(P_i, Q) = q(P_i, Q, \alpha) = 0$. The *conditional transition rate* from P_i to P_j via action type α is $q(P_i, P_j, \alpha) = \sum_{P_i \xrightarrow{(\alpha, r_\alpha)} P_j} r_\alpha$.. The *total conditional transition rate* from P to a set of components $S \subseteq \mathcal{C}$ is $q[P, S, \alpha] = \sum_{P' \in S} q(P, P', \alpha)$. Symmetrically, the rate from S to P is $q[S, P, \alpha] = \sum_{P' \in S} q(P', P, \alpha)$. and the total rate of outgoing α-transitions from P is $q[P, a] = \sum_{P' \in C} q(P, P', \alpha)$.

Observation Equivalence. In [7], the notion of Stochastic Non-Interference was introduced as a security property for process algebras. This property ensures that secret (high-level) actions do not influence the observable behaviour of a system in a probabilistic setting. Later, in [15], the concept of Persistency was incorporated, requiring that the non-interference property hold not only initially but at all reachable states of the system, obtaining Persistent Stochastic Non-Interference (PSNI). The key idea behind these properties is the inability of an observer to detect any information flow through protected (i.e., confidential) actions. To formalise this behaviour, the authors of [15] adopted an equivalence relation known as lumpable bisimilarity [14], defined over PEPA components. This relation was chosen because it induces a strong equivalence over the underlying CTMC, preserving both behavioural and performance properties.

In this work, we revisit the approach proposed in [15], shifting the focus from strong equivalence to exact equivalence [11]. While both notions are defined over CTMCs, their perspectives differ: strong equivalence compares the rates leaving a state, whereas exact equivalence focuses on the rates entering a state. Our goal is to reformulate PSNI using this more precise, incoming-rateoriented view.

Since exact equivalence is originally defined at the CTMC level [11], a key step in our development is to lift this notion to the level of PEPA components.

Two PEPA components are said to be *exact equivalent* if for any action type α the total conditional transition rates from any equivalence class to those components, via activities of this type, are the same. Moreover, it must hold that the total outgoing rates are the same.

Definition 1. (Exact equivalence) *An equivalence relation over PEPA components, $\mathcal{R} \subseteq \mathcal{C} \times \mathcal{C}$ is an* exact equivalence *if whenever $(P, Q) \in \mathcal{R}$ then for all $\alpha \in \mathcal{A}$ and for all $S \in \mathcal{C}/\mathcal{R}$ it holds $q[P, \alpha] = q[Q, \alpha]$ and $q[S, P, \alpha] = q[S, Q, \alpha]$.*

It is clear that the identity relation is an exact equivalence. We are interested in the relation which is the largest exact equivalence, formed by the union of all exact equivalences. It was proven in [1] that the transitive closure of a union of exact equivalences is still an exact equivalence. Hence, the maximal exact equivalence, denoted $\sim_e$, is defined as the union of all exact equivalences and it is an equivalence relation.

3 Exact Lumpable Bisimilarity

The equivalence relation we have just introduced does not distinguish between τ and non-τ actions. However, in [15], the very first step was to weaken strong equivalence so as to treat unobservable actions differently. For this reason, the notion of lumpable bisimulation was introduced.

Definition 2. (Lumpable bisimulation) *An equivalence relation over PEPA components $\mathcal{R} \subseteq \mathcal{C} \times \mathcal{C}$ is a* lumpable bisimulation *if*

$$q[P, S, \alpha] = q[Q, S, \alpha]$$

for any $(P, Q) \in \mathcal{R}$, for any $\alpha \in \mathcal{A}$, and for any class S in the equivalence partition $\mathcal{C}/\mathcal{R}$ such that either $\alpha \neq \tau$ or $\alpha = \tau$ and $P, Q \notin S$.

Similarly, in this paper, we introduce the notion of Exact Lumpable Bisimulation.

Definition 3. (Exact lumpable bisimulation) *An equivalence relation over PEPA components, $\mathcal{R} \subseteq \mathcal{C} \times \mathcal{C}$ is an* exact lumpable bisimulation *if whenever $(P, Q) \in \mathcal{R}$ then for all $\alpha \in \mathcal{A}$:*

- *either $\alpha \neq \tau$ and:*
  - $q[P, \alpha] = q[Q, \alpha]$
  - $\forall S \in \mathcal{C}/\mathcal{R} \quad q[S, P, \alpha] = q[S, Q, \alpha]$
- *or $\alpha = \tau$ and:*
  - $\forall S \in \mathcal{C}/\mathcal{R}, P, Q \notin S \quad q[S, P, \tau] = q[S, Q, \tau]$
  - $P, Q \in S \quad q[S, P, \tau] - q[P, \tau] = q[S, Q, \tau] - q[Q, \tau]$

While this new relation may seem counterintuitive, its properties have been derived from the conditions for the exact equivalence stated in [2]. This relation treats unobservable actions differently, while still preserving the equiprobability of the states that are related to each other. This property is usually related to the state partition induced by exact equivalence on CTMCs.

Definition 4. (Exact lumpable bisimilarity) *Two PEPA components P and Q are* exact lumpably bisimilar, *written $P \approx_e Q$, if $(P, Q) \in \mathcal{R}$ for some exact lumpable bisimulation $\mathcal{R}$, i.e.,*

$$\approx_e = \bigcup \{\mathcal{R} \mid \mathcal{R} \textit{ is an exact lumpable bisimulation}\}.$$

$\approx_e$ is called exact lumpable bisimilarity *and it is the largest symmetric exact lumpable bisimulation over PEPA components.*

Example 1. In this example we provide some insights about exact lumpable bisimilarity. Consider the model introduced in [1], regarding processors and jobs. A finite version of such example is depicted in Fig. 1. It represents a system with two identical processors, named κ_1 and κ_2. Each process can receive some jobs. Each job is assigned to one of the processors which are assumed not to work in parallel. At each service completion event of processor κ_i, the next job is assigned to κ_j, for $i \neq j$, with probability p, and is assigned to processor κ_i with probability $1 - p$. States in Fig. 1 labelled $n\kappa_i$, for $n > 0$ and $i = 1, 2$, denote those state in which processor κ_i is being used and there are n customers waiting to be served. State $0\kappa_i$ denotes the empty queue.

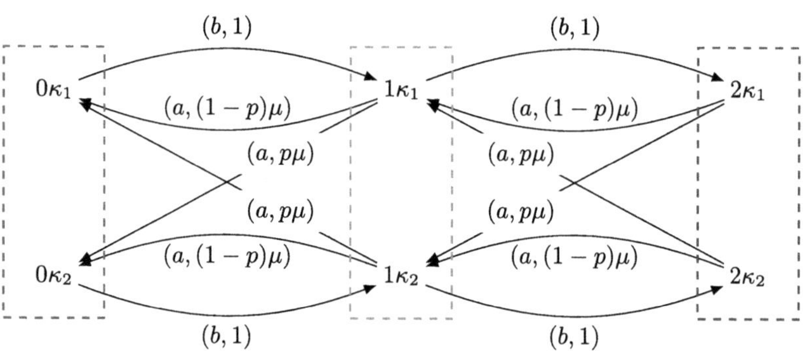

Fig. 1. Model introduced in [1].

The colours refer to the partition of the states according to Exact lumpable bisimilarity. Assume S_0, S_1, and S_2 are the red, green, and blue classes, respectively. We focus ourselves on the green class, namely S_1. For sake of readability, we denote by A the upper state and by B the lower state of S_1. We show how these states are compliant with the notion of $\approx_e$. First, we investigate the symbols $\alpha \neq \tau$. By definition of exact lumpable bisimilarity, the following constraints must be satisfied:

- $q[A, \alpha] = q[B, \alpha]$
- $\forall S \in \mathcal{C}/\approx_e, \quad q[S, A, \alpha] = q[S, B, \alpha]$.

The two symbols that appear in the example are a and b. Hence:

$$q[A, b] = 1 = q[B, b] \qquad q[A, a] = (1-p)\mu + p\mu = \mu = q[B, a].$$

For what concerns the incoming weights, we must consider S_0 and S_2, the only two classes that are directly connected to S_1. We have:

$$\begin{array}{ll} q[S_0, A, a] = 0 = q[S_0, B, a] & q[S_0, A, b] = 1 = q[S_0, B, b] \\ q[S_2, A, a] = \mu = q[S_2, B, a] & q[S_2, A, b] = 0 = q[S_2, B, b]. \end{array}$$

Hence, since all the conditions are met, it holds that $A \approx_{\mathrm{e}} B$. Moreover, notice that the classes cannot be enlarged because, for example, if S_1 and S_2 were to be combined, it is straightforward to see that no states in S_2 has incoming edges from S_0 while the ones in S_1 have.

We now assume that symbol a is substituted with τ, for instance if a is an high level action and we aim to analyze the process were all such actions are hidden. Clearly, all the conditions we checked above about b remain unchanged. However, we have to ensure that the definition of $\approx_{\mathrm{e}}$ is respected for the symbol τ as well. Indeed, the first condition for τ is:

$$\forall S \in \mathcal{C}/\approx_e, A, B \notin S \quad q[S, A, \tau] = q[S, B, \tau]e.$$

The only class (different from S_1) that has edges labelled τ that ends in states belonging to S_1 is S_2. This yields to:

$$q[S_2, A, \tau] = (1-p)\mu + p\mu = \mu = q[S_2, B, \tau].$$

The last condition to check for proving $A \approx_{\mathrm{e}} B$ in the case of τ is:

$$A, B \in S \quad q[S, A, \tau] - q[A, \tau] = q[S, B, \tau] - q[A, \tau].$$

Since $A, B \in S_1$ we can rewrite the above constraint as:

$$q[S_1, A, \tau] - q[A, \tau] = 0 - [(1-p)\mu - p\mu] = -\mu = q[S_1, B, \tau] - q[B, \tau].$$

This proves that A, B remain exactly lumpable bisimilar even if a is replaced with τ.

It is straightforward to verify that the red and blue classes, S_0 and S_2, respectively, are correct with respect to exact lumpable bisimulation as well.

□

Notably, exact lumpable bisimilarity induces an exact equivalence on the underlying Markov chain of the system. This follows directly from the fact that all conditions defining exact lumpable bisimulation over PEPA components correspond to sufficient conditions for exact equivalence on Markov chains, as presented in [11]. Therefore, exact lumpable bisimilarity on PEPA components guarantees exact equivalence in the associated CTMC.

Theorem 1. *Exact lumpable bisimilarity induces an exact equivalence on the underlying CTMC.*

To the best of our knowledge, this is the very first time such notion is adopted in the literature. Therefore, we prove its compositional properties. To obtain such endeavour, we first define the notion of equivalence *up to* [13].

Definition 5. (Exact lumpable bisimulation up to) $\mathcal{R}$ *is* an exact lumpable bisimulation up to $\approx_e$ *if* $\mathcal{R}$ *is an equivalence relation over* $\mathcal{C}$ *and* $(P,Q) \in \mathcal{R}$ *implies that for all* $\alpha \in \mathcal{A}$*:*

- *either* $\alpha \neq \tau$ *and:*
  - $q[P,\alpha] = q[Q,\alpha]$
  - $\forall T \in \mathcal{C}/(\approx_e \mathcal{R} \approx_e) \quad q[T,P,\alpha] = q[T,Q,\alpha]$
- *or* $\alpha = \tau$ *and:*
  - $\forall T \in \mathcal{C}/(\approx_e \mathcal{R} \approx_e), P,Q \notin T \quad q[T,P,\tau] = q[T,Q,\tau]$
  - $P,Q \in T \quad q[T,P,\tau] - q[P,\tau] = q[T,Q,\tau] - q[Q,\tau]$

We recall that $P \approx_e \mathcal{R} \approx_e Q$ if and only if there exist P_1, Q_1 such that $P \approx_e P_1$, $P_1 \mathcal{R} Q_1$, and $Q_1 \approx_e Q$. In some sense, we are considering different equivalence classes induced by $\approx_e$ and joining them via $\mathcal{R}$. Because of this, the classes induced by $\approx_e \mathcal{R} \approx_e$ are actually union of classes induced by $\approx_e$.

The above definition is useful in proving properties of exact lumpable bisimulation by looking at smaller relations, as proved in the following Lemma.

Lemma 1. *If* $\mathcal{R}$ *is an exact lumpable bisimulation up to* $\approx_e$*, then the relation* $\approx_e \mathcal{R} \approx_e$ *is an exact lumpable bisimulation.*

Proposition 1. *If* $P_1 \approx_e P_2$ *then:*

1. $P_1 \underset{L}{\S} Q \approx_e P_2 \underset{L}{\S} Q$
2. $P_1 \setminus L \approx_e P_2 \setminus L$

4 Exact Persistent Stochastic Non-Interference

The security property named *Persistent Stochastic Non-Interference (PSNI)* was introduced in [15]. Informally, it aims to capture every possible information flow from a *classified (high)* level of confidentiality to an *untrusted (low)* one. The property was derived from the classical notion of Non-Interference, enriched with the idea of *persistency*, meaning that the security property must hold for all reachable processes of the system.

In their proposal, the authors defined PSNI as follows. First, they partitioned the set $\mathcal{A} \setminus \{\tau\}$ of visible action types into two disjoint sets, $\mathcal{H}$ and $\mathcal{L}$, representing high- and low-level action types, respectively. A high-level PEPA component H is a PEPA term such that for all $H' \in ds(H)$, $\mathcal{A}(H') \subseteq \mathcal{H}$, i.e., every derivative of H may engage only in high-level actions. The set of all such high-level PEPA components is denoted by $\mathcal{C}_H$. Additionally, they extended the PEPA grammar by adding the $\mathbf{0}$ symbol to denote a component that performs no activity. With these notions in place, the authors introduced the following:

Definition 6. (Stochastic Non-Interference, SNI) *Let P be a PEPA component.*

$$P \in \mathit{SNI} \text{ iff } \forall H \in \mathcal{C}_H,\ (P \underset{\mathcal{H}}{\S} \mathbf{0})/\mathcal{H} \approx_l (P \underset{\mathcal{H}}{\S} H)/\mathcal{H}.$$

Here, $\approx_l$ is the equivalence relation called *lumpable bisimilarity*, the union of all possible lumpable bisimulations (see Definition 2). However, this definition did not enforce propagation of the security property across all process derivatives. To address this, the authors introduced the notion of *reachable* processes and extended the property to account for persistency, yielding the definition of Persistent SNI:

Definition 7. (Persistent Stochastic Non-Interference) *Let P be a PEPA component. $P \in \mathit{PSNI}$ iff $\forall P' \in ds(P)$, $P' \in \mathit{SNI}$.*

In [15], the following characterisation of PSNI was also provided:

$$P \in \mathit{PSNI} \text{ iff } \forall P' \in ds(P),\ \forall H \in \mathcal{C}_H,\ P' \setminus \mathcal{H} \approx_{\mathrm{e}} (P' \underset{\mathcal{H}}{\S} H)/\mathcal{H}.$$

It is evident that all the above definitions rely on the equivalence called *lumpable bisimilarity*, which is built upon the notion of lumpable bisimulation. However, as discussed in previous sections, alternative equivalence relations can also be considered. The aim of this paper is to characterise a new security property, which we call *Exact PSNI*, abbreviated as *EPSNI*.

We begin by adapting the definition of SNI to obtain *Exact SNI*:

Definition 8. (Exact Stochastic Non-Interference, ESNI) *Let P be a PEPA component.*

$$P \in \mathit{ESNI} \text{ iff } \forall H \in \mathcal{C}_H,\ (P \underset{\mathcal{H}}{\S} \mathbf{0})/\mathcal{H} \approx_e (P \underset{\mathcal{H}}{\S} H)/\mathcal{H}.$$

Following the same reasoning applied in the definition of *PSNI*, we add the persistency, resulting in *Exact Persistent Stochastic Non-Interference* (*EPSNI*):

Definition 9. (Exact Persistent Stochastic Non-Interference) *Let P be a PEPA component. $P \in \mathit{EPSNI}$ iff $\forall P' \in ds(P)$, $P' \in \mathit{ESNI}$.*

This property implies that all states of the Markov chain belonging to the same equivalence class under $\approx_{\mathrm{e}}$ are equiprobable in the stationary distribution. The use of the hiding operator on both sides of the equivalence ensures that indistinguishability is defined with respect to the low-level view of the system. Due to the properties of $\approx_{\mathrm{e}}$, we conclude that for a low-level observer, the probability of being in a particular state does not depend on high-level interactions.

Indeed, high-level activities may be present in the process $(P \underset{\mathcal{H}}{\S} H)$, but are absent in $(P \underset{\mathcal{H}}{\S} \mathbf{0})$. This does not mean the system lacks high-level actions altogether, but rather that such actions cannot be inferred by a low-level observer.

Observe that $(P' \mathbin{\S_{\mathcal{H}}} \mathbf{0})$ cannot perform any high-level activity. Therefore, the derivation graphs of $(P' \mathbin{\S_{\mathcal{H}}} \mathbf{0})$ and $(P' \mathbin{\S_{\mathcal{H}}} \mathbf{0})/\mathcal{H}$ are isomorphic as labelled transition systems. More precisely, $(P' \mathbin{\S_{\mathcal{H}}} \mathbf{0})$ behaves as the component P' constrained from engaging in any high-level action. Thus, we adopt the notation $P \setminus \mathcal{H}$ to denote the system $(P' \mathbin{\S_{\mathcal{H}}} \mathbf{0})/\mathcal{H}$, in analogy with the restriction operator in CCS. From this, we can restate the property as:

$$P \in \mathit{EPSNI} \text{ iff } \forall P' \in ds(P),\ \forall H \in \mathcal{C}_H,\ P' \setminus \mathcal{H} \approx_{\mathrm{e}} (P' \mathbin{\S_{\mathcal{H}}} H)/\mathcal{H}.$$

Our first result is that *EPSNI* is preserved by exact lumpable bisimilarity.

Lemma 2. *If P and Q are two PEPA components such that $P \approx_{\mathrm{e}} Q$ and $P \in$ EPSNI, then also $Q \in$ EPSNI.*

Subsequently, we introduce a novel bisimulation-based equivalence relation over PEPA components, named $\approx_{\mathrm{e}}^{hc}$, that allows us to give a first characterization of *EPSNI* in which the quantification over all possible high level components H is hidden inside the equivalence. In particular, we show that $P \in \mathit{EPSNI}$ if and only if $P \setminus \mathcal{H}$ and P are not distinguishable with respect to $\approx_{\mathrm{e}}^{hc}$. Intuitively, two processes are $\approx_{\mathrm{e}}^{hc}$-equivalent if they can simulate each other in any possible high context $C[\_]$ of the form $(\_ \mathbin{\S_{\mathcal{H}}} H)/\mathcal{H}$ where $H \in \mathcal{C}_H$. Observe that for any high context $C[\_]$ and PEPA model P, all the states reachable from $C[P]$ have the form $C'[P']$ with $C'[\_]$ being a high context too and $P' \in ds(P)$.

We now introduce the concept of *exact lumpable bisimulation on high contexts*: the idea is that, given two PEPA models P and Q, when a high level context $C[\_]$ filled with P executes a certain activity moving P to P' then the same context filled with Q is able to simulate this step moving Q to Q' so that P' and Q' are again exact lumpable bisimilar on high contexts, and vice-versa. This must be true for every possible high context $C[\_]$. It is important to note that the quantification over all possible high contexts is re-iterated for P' and Q'. For a PEPA model P, $\alpha \in \mathcal{A}$, $S \subseteq \mathcal{C}$ and a high context $C[\_]$ we define $q_C(P, P', \alpha) = \sum_{C[P] \xrightarrow{(\alpha, r_\alpha)} C'[P']} r_\alpha$ and $q_C[S, P, \alpha] = \sum_{P' \in S} q_C(P', P, \alpha)$. *Exact lumpable bisimilarity on high contexts* is defined as follows.

Definition 10. (Exact lumpable bisimilarity on high contexts) *An equivalence relation over PEPA components, $\mathcal{R} \subseteq \mathcal{C} \times \mathcal{C}$, is an* exact lumpable bisimulation on high contexts *if $(P, Q) \in \mathcal{R}$ implies that for all high context $C[\_]$ and $\alpha \in \mathcal{A}$*

- *either $\alpha \neq \tau$ and:*
  - $q_C[P, \alpha] = q_C[Q, \alpha]$
  - $\forall S \in \mathcal{C}/\mathcal{R} \quad q_C[S, P, \alpha] = q_C[S, Q, \alpha]$
- *or $\alpha = \tau$ and:*
  - $\forall S \in \mathcal{C}/\mathcal{R}, P, Q \notin S \quad q_C[S, P, \tau] = q_C[S, Q, \tau]$
  - $P, Q \in S \quad q_C[S, P, \tau] - q_C[P, \tau] = q_C[S, Q, \tau] - q_C[Q, \tau]$

P and Q are exact lumpably bisimilar on high contexts, *written $P \approx_e^{hc} Q$, if $(P, Q) \in \mathcal{R}$ for some exact lumpable bisimulation on high contexts $\mathcal{R}$, i.e.,*

$$\approx_e^{hc} = \bigcup \{\mathcal{R} \mid \mathcal{R} \text{ is an exact lumpable bisimulation on high contexts}\}.$$

$\approx_e^{hc}$ *is called* exact lumpable bisimilarity on high contexts *and it is the largest exact lumpable bisimulation on high contexts over PEPA components.*

Theorem 2 gives a characterization of *EPSNI* in terms of $\approx_e^{hc}$. Notice that $\approx_e^{hc}$ still contains a universal quantification over all high level contexts. However, the characterization of *EPSNI* given in Theorem 2 gives insights into the meaning and the properties of *EPSNI*. As a matter of fact, the persistency requirement is now absorbed in the notion of exact lumpable bisimulation on high contexts which is in a sense persistent by definition, as usual for lumpability notions.

Theorem 2. *Let P be a PEPA component. $P \in$ EPSNI iff $P \setminus \mathcal{H} \approx_e^{hc} P$.*

We show how it is possible to give a characterization of *EPSNI* avoiding both the universal quantification over all the possible high level components and the universal quantification over all the possible reachable states.

Previously, we have shown how the idea of "being secure in every state" can be directly moved inside the exact lumpable bisimulation on high contexts notion ($\approx_e^{hc}$). However, this bisimulation notion implicitly contains a quantification over all possible high contexts. We now prove that $\approx_e^{hc}$ can be expressed in a rather simpler way by exploiting local information only. This can be done by defining a novel equivalence relation which focuses only on observable actions that do not belong to $\mathcal{H}$. More in detail, we define an observation equivalence where actions from $\mathcal{H}$ *may* be ignored. We first introduce the notion of *exact lumpable bisimilarity* up to $\mathcal{H}$.

Definition 11. (Exact lumpable bisimilarity up to $\mathcal{H}$) *An equivalence relation over PEPA components, $\mathcal{R} \subseteq \mathcal{C} \times \mathcal{C}$, is an* exact lumpable bisimulation up to $\mathcal{H}$ *if whenever $(P, Q) \in \mathcal{R}$ then for all $\alpha \in \mathcal{A}$:*

- *either $\alpha \notin \mathcal{H} \cup \{\tau\}$ and:*
  - $q[P, \alpha] = q[Q, \alpha]$
  - $\forall S \in \mathcal{C}/\mathcal{R} \quad q[S, P, \alpha] = q[S, Q, \alpha]$
- *or $\alpha \in \mathcal{H} \cup \{\tau\}$ and:*
  - $\forall S \in \mathcal{C}/\mathcal{R}, P, Q \notin S \quad q[S, P, \alpha] = q[S, Q, \alpha]$
  - $P, Q \in S \quad q[S, P, \alpha] - q[P, \alpha] = q[S, Q, \alpha] - q[Q, \alpha]$

Two PEPA components P and Q are exact lumpably bisimilar up to $\mathcal{H}$, *written $P \approx_e^{\mathcal{H}} Q$, if $(P, Q) \in \mathcal{R}$ for some exact lumpable bisimulation up to $\mathcal{H}$, i.e.,*

$$\approx_e^{\mathcal{H}} = \bigcup \{\mathcal{R} \mid \mathcal{R} \text{ is an exact lumpable bisimulation up to} \mathcal{H}\}.$$

$\approx_e^{\mathcal{H}}$ *is called* exact lumpable bisimilarity up to $\mathcal{H}$ *and it is the largest symmetric exact lumpable bisimulation up to $\mathcal{H}$ over PEPA components.*

Theorem 3 shows that binary relations $\approx_e^{hc}$ and $\approx_e^{\mathcal{H}}$ are equivalent.

Theorem 3. *$P \approx_e^{hc} Q$ if and only if $P \approx_e^{\mathcal{H}} Q$.*

Theorem 3 allows us to identify a local property of processes (with no quantification on the states and on the high contexts) which is a necessary and sufficient condition for *EPSNI*. This is stated by the following corollary.

Corollary 1. *Let P be a PEPA component. Then $P \in EPSNI$ iff $P \setminus \mathcal{H} \approx_e^{\mathcal{H}} P$.*

We now study some compositionality properties of exact lumpable bisimilarity up to $\mathcal{H}$. These will allow us both to provide characterizations of *EPSNI* in terms of unwinding conditions and to prove compositionality results for *EPSNI*.

Lemma 3. *Let $\mathcal{T}$ be a symmetric and transitive binary relation over $\mathcal{C}$ and let $\mathcal{T}_{\mathcal{H}}^*$ be the symmetric and transitive closure of $\mathcal{T} \cup \approx_e^{\mathcal{H}}$. $\mathcal{T}_{\mathcal{H}}^*$ is an exact lumpable bisimulation up to $\mathcal{H}$ if and only if for all $(P, Q) \in \mathcal{T}$ it holds that:*

- *either $\alpha \notin \mathcal{H} \cup \{\tau\}$ and:*
  - $q[P, \alpha] = q[Q, \alpha]$
  - $\forall S \in \mathcal{C}/\mathcal{T}_{\mathcal{H}}^* \quad q[S, P, \alpha] = q[S, Q, \alpha]$
- *or $\alpha \in \mathcal{H} \cup \{\tau\}$ and:*
  - $\forall S \in \mathcal{C}/\mathcal{T}_{\mathcal{H}}^*, P, Q \notin S \quad q[S, P, \alpha] = q[S, Q, \alpha]$
  - $P, Q \in S \quad q[S, P, \alpha] - q[P, \alpha] = q[S, Q, \alpha] - q[Q, \alpha]$

We recall that $\mathcal{L} = \mathcal{A} \setminus \{\tau\} \cup \mathcal{H}$ is the set of low level action types.

Lemma 4. *Let P_1, P_2, Q, be PEPA components. Let $\alpha \in \mathcal{A}$, $A \subseteq \mathcal{A}$, and $L \subseteq \mathcal{L}$. If $P_1 \approx_e^{\mathcal{H}} P_2$, then:*

1. $P_1 \setminus A \approx_e^{\mathcal{H}} P_2 \setminus A$;
2. $P_1/A \approx_e^{\mathcal{H}} P_2/A$;
3. $P_1 \underset{L}{\bowtie} Q \approx_e^{\mathcal{H}} P_2 \underset{L}{\bowtie} Q$.

The following relationships between $\approx_e$ and $\approx_e^{\mathcal{H}}$ are useful to obtain both an unwinding characterization in terms of $\approx_{we}^{\mathcal{H}}$ and one in terms of $\approx_e$.

Lemma 5. *Let P and Q be PEPA components that do not perform high level activities, then it holds $P \approx_e Q$ if and only if $P \approx_e^{\mathcal{H}} Q$.*

As a consequence of Lemma 4 and Lemma 5 we get the following result.

Corollary 2. *$P \approx_e^{\mathcal{H}} Q$, then $P \setminus \mathcal{H} \approx_e Q \setminus \mathcal{H}$.*

Finally, we provide a characterization of *EPSNI* in terms of *unwinding conditions* [3,4]. In practice, whenever a state P' of a *EPSNI* PEPA model P may execute a high level activity leading it to a state P'', then P' and P'' are indistinguishable in the sense that both $P' \approx_e^{\mathcal{H}} P''$ and $P' \setminus \mathcal{H} \approx_e P'' \setminus \mathcal{H}$.

Theorem 4. *Let P be a PEPA component. The following are equivalent:*

a. $P \in EPSNI$;
b. $\forall h \in \mathcal{H}$, $\forall P' \in ds(P)$, $P' \xrightarrow{(h,r)} P''$ *implies* $P' \approx_e^{\mathcal{H}} P''$;
c. $\forall h \in \mathcal{H}$, $\forall P' \in ds(P)$, $P' \xrightarrow{(h,r)} P''$ *implies* $P' \setminus \mathcal{H} \approx_e P'' \setminus \mathcal{H}$.

Corollary 1 and Theorem 4 give different characterizations of *EPSNI* which lead to efficient methods for the verification and construction of secure systems.

5 Properties of EPSNI

In this section, we prove some interesting properties of *EPSNI*.

Proposition 2. *Let P and Q be two PEPA components. If $P, Q \in EPSNI$, then*

- $P \setminus A \in EPSNI$ *for all* $A \subseteq \mathcal{A}$
- $P/A \in EPSNI$ *for all* $A \subseteq \mathcal{A}$
- $P \underset{L}{\bowtie} Q \in EPSNI$ *for all* $L \subseteq \mathcal{L}$

Proof. Proofs are exactly the same as the one provided in [15]. The major difference is the absence of the prefix operator for which the notion of exact lumpable bisimilarity we introduce in this work is not compositional.

Example 2. In this example we want to provide some intuitions about the security property we proposed, namely EPSNI.

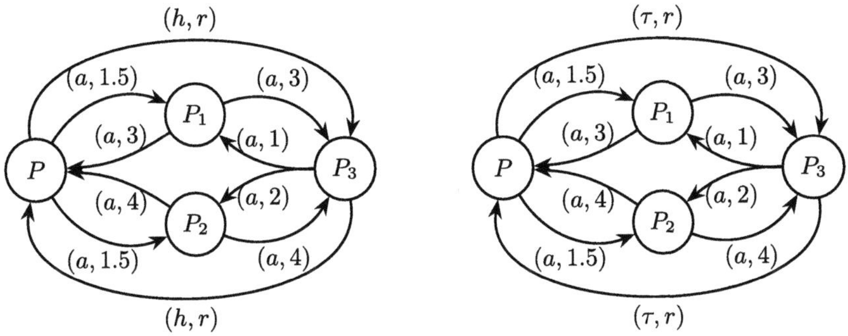

(a) A simple four states process.

(b) Process after hiding.

Fig. 2. A three state process and its version with high level actions forbidden.

In Fig. 2a, we present a simple process with four states. We show that state P satisfies EPSNI. By Theorem 4, we know that $P \in EPSNI$ if and only if

$$\forall h \in \mathcal{H},\ \forall P' \in ds(P),\ P' \xrightarrow{(h,r)} P'' \implies P' \setminus \mathcal{H} \approx_{\mathrm{e}} P'' \setminus \mathcal{H}.$$

In our setting:

- there is only one high-level action, namely h,
- the set of derivatives of P contains all four states.

Thus, we must show that whenever $P' \in ds(P)$ and there exists an edge $P' \xrightarrow{(h,r)} P''$, then $P' \setminus \mathcal{H} \approx_{\mathrm{e}} P'' \setminus \mathcal{H}$. The only two edges labeled with the high-level action are those connecting P and P_3. Therefore, it suffices to prove that $P \setminus \mathcal{H} \approx_{\mathrm{e}} P_3 \setminus \mathcal{H}$.

Recalling that $P\backslash\mathcal{H}$ is a shorthand for $(P \underset{\mathcal{H}}{\S} \mathbf{0})/\mathcal{H}$, the process with high level actions hidden is shown in Fig. 2b. It is immediate to observe that both states P_1 and P_2 form singleton classes. This follows since $q[P_1, a] = 6$ while $q[P_2, a] = 8$. Hence, the very first condition of exact lumpable bisimulation (with $\alpha \neq \tau$) is violated, and therefore the two states are not equivalent.

For states P and P_3, we instead obtain:

$$q[P, a] = 1.5 + 1.5 = 3 \qquad q[P_3, a] = 2 + 1 = 3,$$

which shows that $q[P, a] = q[P_3, a]$. The same equality clearly holds for $P \setminus \mathcal{H}$ and $P_3 \setminus \mathcal{H}$. Moreover, considering the incoming rates of $P \setminus \mathcal{H}$ and $P_3 \setminus \mathcal{H}$, we see that they both have two incoming edges, one from the class $S_1 := \{P_1\}$ and another from the class $S_2 := \{P_2\}$. We obtain:

$$q[S_1, P \setminus \mathcal{H}, a] = q[S_1, P_3 \setminus \mathcal{H}, a] = 3,$$

$$q[S_2, P \setminus \mathcal{H}, a] = q[S_2, P_3 \setminus \mathcal{H}, a] = 4.$$

The equalities above satisfy the requirements of exact lumpable bisimulation for symbols that are not τ. For what concerns the τ actions, we have to verify two conditions. The first, related to classes P and P_3 does not belong to, trivially holds since there are no τ-labelled edges from S_1 and S_2 towards the two above mentioned states. On the other hand, if we consider the class S to which we assume P and P_3 belong to, it is easy to verify that $q[S, P \setminus \mathcal{H}, \tau] - q[P \setminus \mathcal{H}, \tau] = q[S, P_3 \setminus \mathcal{H}, \tau] - q[P_3 \setminus \mathcal{H}, \tau]$. In our examples, we have:

$$q[S, P \setminus \mathcal{H}, \tau] - q[P \setminus \mathcal{H}, \tau] = r - r = 0$$

The same value is obtained for $q[S, P_3 \setminus \mathcal{H}, \tau] - q[P_3 \setminus \mathcal{H}, \tau]$. Hence, since all of the four conditions have been met, we can conclude that $P \setminus \mathcal{H} \approx_e P_3 \setminus \mathcal{H}$.

By Theorem 4, and since $P_3 \in ds(P)$, we should also verify that the edge labeled h from P_3 to P implies $P_3 \setminus \mathcal{H} \approx_e P \setminus \mathcal{H}$.

However, since $\approx_e$ is symmetric, this holds automatically. Thus, we have proved that state $P \in EPSNI$. Informally, we can say that the two states P and P_3 are indistinguishable to a low-level observer and can therefore be interchanged without altering the observable behavior. Furthermore, since exact lumpable bisimilarity induces an exact equivalence on the underlying Markov chain, this implies that P and P_3 contribute symmetrically to the steady-state distribution, making them equiprobable from the perspective of the aggregated system.

On the other hand, if we attempt to prove the equivalence between $P \setminus \mathcal{H}$ and $P_3 \setminus \mathcal{H}$ using lumpable bisimulation (see Definition 2), the outcome is different. First, it is clear that both P_1 and P_2 must be placed in singleton classes by lumpable bisimulation, hence we set $S_1 = \{P_1\}$ and $S_2 = \{P_2\}$. Then, by inspecting the values of $q[P \setminus \mathcal{H}, S_1, a]$ and $q[P_3 \setminus \mathcal{H}, S_1, a]$, we get:

$$q[P \setminus \mathcal{H}, S_1, a] = q[P, P_1, a] = 1.5, \qquad q[P_3 \setminus \mathcal{H}, S_1, a] = q[P_3, P_1, a] = 1.$$

This discrepancy in the outgoing rates is enough to conclude that $P \setminus \mathcal{H}$ and $P_3 \setminus \mathcal{H}$ are not equivalent according to lumpable bisimulation.

This example highlights the key distinction between PSNI and EPSNI. Under lumpable bisimulation (the basis for PSNI), the local mismatch in the outgoing rates towards class S_1 prevents $P \setminus \mathcal{H}$ and $P_3 \setminus \mathcal{H}$ from being identified, and thus PSNI fails. In contrast, exact lumpable bisimulation (underlying EPSNI) abstracts from such local discrepancies while preserving the global quantitative behavior. As a result, the two states are indistinguishable to a low-level observer, and EPSNI holds.

□

6 Conclusion

In this work, we revisited the notion of Persistent Stochastic Non-Interference (PSNI) [15] and proposed a new property, named Exact Persistent Stochastic Non-Interference (EPSNI), grounded on the exact lumpable bisimilarity relation. EPSNI refines the treatment of internal actions while preserving the quantitative accuracy of observable behaviours, thus providing a more precise semantic foundation for reasoning about non-interference in stochastic systems.

We presented three characterisations of EPSNI: a semantic formulation based on high-level contexts, a bisimulation-style definition that avoids explicit universal quantification, and an unwinding characterisation relying on local conditions. These multiple perspectives not only clarify the meaning of EPSNI but also provide complementary proof techniques for establishing the property. In particular, the unwinding-style characterisation yields both necessary and sufficient conditions for EPSNI, ensuring its applicability to compositional verification.

We further established that EPSNI enjoys strong compositionality properties. Specifically, the property is preserved under hiding, restriction, and cooperation on low-level actions, thereby supporting modular reasoning in the construction of complex systems.

From a practical standpoint, EPSNI enables efficient and precise verification of information flow properties in stochastic process algebras, bridging quantitative performance considerations with formal security guarantees. To the best of our knowledge, this work constitutes the first application of exact lumpable bisimilarity in the security setting, highlighting its robustness as a foundation for quantitative non-interference.

As future work, we plan to investigate a concrete Alice-and-Bob communication scenario in which EPSNI provides an appropriate framework for reasoning about information leakage. In addition, we aim to further explore the connections between EPSNI and other security properties defined through alternative equivalence relations.

References

1. Alzetta, G., Marin, A., Piazza, C., Rossi, S.: Lumping-based equivalences in markovian automata: algorithms and applications to product-form analyses. Inf. Comput. **260**, 99–125 (2018). https://doi.org/10.1016/j.ic.2018.04.002
2. Baarir, S., Beccuti, M., Dutheillet, C., Franceschinis, G., Haddad, S.: Lumping partially symmetrical stochastic models. Perf. Eval. **68**(1), 21–44 (2011)
3. Bossi, A., Focardi, R., Macedonio, D., Piazza, C., Rossi, S.: Unwinding in information flow security. Electron. Notes Theor. Comput. Sci. **99**, 127–154 (2004)
4. Bossi, A., Focardi, R., Piazza, C., Rossi, S.: Bisimulation and unwinding for verifying possibilistic security properties. In: Zuck, L.D., Attie, P.C., Cortesi, A., Mukhopadhyay, S. (eds.) VMCAI 2003. LNCS, vol. 2575, pp. 223–237. Springer, Heidelberg (2003). https://doi.org/10.1007/3-540-36384-X_19
5. Buchholz, P.: Exact and ordinary lumpability in finite markov chains. J. Appl. Probab. **31** (1995). https://doi.org/10.2307/3215235
6. Focardi, R., Gorrieri, R., Martinelli, F.: Information flow analysis in a discrete-time process algebra. In: Computer Security Foundations Workshop (CSFW-13 2000). 13th IEEE Computer Security Foundations Workshop, IEEE (2000)
7. Focardi, R., Gorrieri, R.: A classification of security properties for process algebras. J. Comput. Secur. **3**(1), 5–33 (1994/1995). https://doi.org/10.3233/JCS-1994/1995-3103
8. Focardi, R., Gorrieri, R., Martinelli, F.: Classification of security properties. In: Focardi, R., Gorrieri, R. (eds.) Foundations of Security Analysis and Design II, pp. 139–185. Springer, Berlin, Heidelberg (2004). https://doi.org/10.1007/978-3-540-24631-2_4
9. Focardi, R., Martinelli, F.: A uniform approach for the definition of security properties. In: FM'99 — Formal Methods, pp. 794–813. Springer, Berlin, Heidelberg (1999). https://doi.org/10.1007/3-540-48119-2_44
10. Focardi, R., Rossi, S.: Information flow security in dynamic contexts. J. Comput. Secur. **14**(1) (2006-02-01)
11. Franceschinis, G., Muntz, R.R.: Bounds for quasi-lumpable markov chains. Perf. Eval. **20**(1–3), 223–243 (1994)
12. Goguen, J.A., Meseguer, J.: Security policies and security models. In: 1982 IEEE Symposium on Security and Privacy, pp. 11–11 (1982). https://doi.org/10.1109/SP.1982.10014
13. Hillston, J.: A Compositional Approach to Performance Modelling. Cambridge Press, Cambridge (1996)
14. Hillston, J., Marin, A., Piazza, C., Rossi, S.: Contextual lumpability. In: Proceedings of Valuetools 2013 Conference, pp. 194–203. ACM Press (2013)
15. Hillston, J., Marin, A., Piazza, C.P., Rossi, S.: Persistent stochastic non-interference. Fundam. Inf. **181**(1), 1–35 (2021). https://doi.org/10.3233/FI-2021-2049
16. Mantel, H.: Unwinding possibilistic security properties. In: Proceedings of the European Symposium on Research in Computer Security (ESoRiCS'00). LNCS, vol. 2895, pp. 238–254. Springer-Verlag (2000). https://doi.org/10.1007/10722599_15
17. Marin, A., Piazza, C., Rossi, S.: A Process Algebra for (Delimited) Persistent Stochastic Non-Interference, Quantitative Evaluation of Systems, vol. 11785. Springer International Publishing (2019)

18. Marin, A., Piazza, C., Rossi, S.: Proportional lumpability and proportional bisimilarity. Acta Inform. **59**(2), 211–244 (2022)
19. Milios, D., Gilmore, S.: Component aggregation for PEPA models: an approach based on approximate strong equivalence. Perform. Eval. **94**, 43–71 (2015)
20. Piazza, C., Pivato, E., Rossi, S.: Cops - checker of persistent security. In: Tools and Algorithms for the Construction and Analysis of Systems, 10th International Conference (TACAS'04), pp. 144–152 (2004). https://doi.org/10.1007/978-3-540-24730-2_11
21. Ryan, P.Y.A., Schneider, S.: Process algebra and non-interference. J. Comput. Secur. **9**(1/2), 75–103 (2001). https://doi.org/10.3233/JCS-2001-91-204

Performance Paradox in Matching Models with Abandonment

Ana Busic[1,2], Jean-Michel Fourneau[1,3], and Shu Li[1,2(✉)]

[1] INRIA Paris, Paris, France
[2] DI ENS, PSL University, Paris, France
shu.li@inria.fr
[3] DAVID, UVSQ, Université Paris Saclay, Versailles, France
https://shuligraph.github.io

Abstract. Motivated by the kidney exchange problem, we add to the general matching model the possibility for the waiting items to leave the system because receivers have been transplanted or because of illness. This is denoted as an abandonment in queueing theory. Recently, performance paradoxes have been observed in stochastic matching models. In a matching model, the compatibility graph represents the possibility of a simultaneous and instantaneous departure of a couple of compatible items. Thus, one may expect that adding an edge in the compatibility graph, the expected total number of items decreases at equilibrium. A performance paradox occurs when this number increases. We state, with some numerical examples, that performance paradoxes also exist for matching models with abandonment.

Keywords: Matching models · Performance paradoxes · Abandonment

1 Introduction

We investigate a new model for general stochastic matching, motivated by the kidney exchange program [1,2]. The kidney exchange system is due to the biological compatibility between donors and receivers during a kidney transplantation. Most of these transplants use a kidney from a deceased donor. Some countries have legalized the possibility of cross-exchange of kidneys between pairs. This is modeled as follows: an item is a pair of donor and receiver. The receiver is ill and the donor has two kidneys. Unfortunately, they are not biological compatible. Then they registered into a database [14] as item A, and wait for another pair (say B) of donor and receiver which are cross-compatible: the receiver of pair A is compatible with donor of pair B while donor of pair A is compatible with receiver B. The cross transplant can then be done. In the model these transplants are instantaneous.

Assuming that the arrivals of item follow some stochastic processes, this leads to a new type of stochastic models where items arrive, check if a compatible item

A. Remke et al. (Eds.): Valuetools 2025, LNICST 691, pp. 88–103, 2027.
https://doi.org/10.1007/978-3-032-23901-3_6

is present. If it is present, they both leave immediately, otherwise it waits until the arrival of a compatible item. The model represents the number of items of each type and their order of arrivals. When the arrivals follow independent Poisson arrivals, and the choice of matched items are only based on the items waiting and their order of arrivals, the associated model is a continuous Markov chain (CTMC in the following). More formally, a general matching model in continuous time is described by:

- a compatibility graph $G = (V, E)$ where V is the set of items, and E represents the compatibility between items. (u, v) is an edge in E, if type u and type v items are compatible;
- a family of independent Poisson process to model the arrivals, with α_i denoting the arrival rate of type i items;
- a matching discipline which explains which couple of items disappears if several couples are compatible. Most of the papers so far assume that the matching discipline is First Come First Math (FCFM), an analog of FCFS in queueing theory.

Note that at each state the sum of the rates is equal to $\sum_{i \in V} \alpha_i$ which is constant. Therefore these chains are uniformizable.

We stress here the term "general" to avoid the confusion with Bipartite Matching models [7], where the compatibility graph is bipartite and the arrivals occur simultaneously at both subsets of the nodes of the bipartite graph.

We add the possibility for items to leave the system before being matched. Such an event is called an abandonment in the queuing literature. Here we assume that this abandonment rate is proportional to the number of items: in a state with n_i items of type i, the abandonment rate for items of type i is $n_i \delta_i$. In the kidney exchange problem, an item is a pair of donor and ill receiver which are not biological compatible. They must wait for a cross-compatible item to exchange the safe kidney. The abandonment in the model for kidney exchange represents the fact that due to illness or another transplantation process, the receiver does not need (or cannot receive) a safe kidney. As a consequence of these abandonment rules, the chains are not uniformizable anymore. Indeed, abandonment rates are not bounded. Finally let us assume in this paper that the matching discipline is First Come First Match (FCFM for short).

Matching models without abandonment were shown in [5,8] to exhibit the following performance paradox: adding a new edge in the compatibility graph will increase the expected total number of items at equilibrium, while one may expect that this expectation decreases as we add new possible matchings. One open question that we address here is the existence of performance paradox for matching with abandonment.

The technical part of the paper is as follows. In Sect. 2, we present a brief introduction on performance paradoxes in matching model without abandonment based on the literature on stochastic matching and performance paradoxes. Section 3 is devoted to the computation of the expectation of the total number of items when the compatibility graph are simple. Finally in Sect. 4, we explain the numerical algorithms we use and we show that performance paradoxes still exist. The abandonments which are sufficient to obtain stability, do not forbid the existence of performance paradoxes.

2 Performance Paradox in Matching Models Without Abandonment

Let $G = (\mathcal{V}, \mathcal{E})$ be the matching (or compatibility) graph and let n be the size of $\mathcal{V}$. The nodes in $\mathcal{V}$ are usually denoted as letters. A state of the system is an ordered list of letters and is and is called a word.

We first define some notation. Assume that x is a letter from $\mathcal{V}$, $\Gamma(x)$ is the set of neighbors of x in G. Let G be a graph and a, b two vertices of V such that (a, b) is not an edge of G, we will denote as $G + e$, the graph G where we have added edge $e = (a, b)$. Similarly, $G - (u, v)$ where (u, v) is an edge of G, is the graph obtained after removing edge (u, v). $\mathbb{E}[G, \alpha]$ will denote the expected number of items for compatibility graph G and vector of arrival rates α. As usual K_n will denote the complete graph with n nodes.

The analysis of the stability and the steady-state distribution when the chain is ergodic relies on the Independent Sets of the compatibility graph.

Definition 1 (Independent Set) *Let $G = (\mathcal{V}, \mathcal{E})$ be a graph, an independent set of G is a subset of nodes $\mathcal{I}$ such that for all u, v in $\mathcal{I}$, (u, v) is not an edge of $\mathcal{E}$. $\mathbb{I}$ will denote the set of Independent Sets of the compatibility graph.*

A necessary and sufficient condition of ergodicity is established in [12]. The steady-state distribution of the Markov chain is proved in [13] up to a normalizing factor that is difficult to compute. In fact, it is proved in [13] that it is based on a summation of the independent sets. As the number of independent sets can be exponential on $|\mathcal{V}|$, such an algorithm is in practice limited to a compatibility graph with a small number of vertices.

Definition 2 (Performance Paradox) *For some arrival rates α, we have a performance paradox if $\mathbb{E}[G + e, \alpha] > \mathbb{E}[G, \alpha]$. We will also use the following criteria: $\mathbb{E}[G - e, \alpha] < \mathbb{E}[G, \alpha]$.*

Property 1 (First Performance Paradox [8]). *Let K_4 be the complete graph with 4 nodes. For some arrival rates α which are given in [8], we have stated that*

$$\mathbb{E}[K_4 - (1, 2), \alpha] < \mathbb{E}[K_4, \alpha].$$

We have proved in [5] some "lifting theorems" to explain how one can build large compatibility graphs and arrival rates based on small compatibility graphs and the JOIN operation on compatibility graphs. We have proved that the existence of performance paradoxes on small graphs implies the existence of paradoxes on large graphs. Thus, from the initial seed graph (i.e. $K_4 - (1, 2)$ in [8]) we have obtained an infinite set of graphs with paradoxes.

Definition 3 (JOIN $\bowtie$). *Let $G1 = (V1, E1)$ and $G2 = (V2, E2)$ two arbitrary graphs, the join of $G1$ and $G2$ (denoted as $G1 \bowtie G2$) is defined by the set of vertices $V1 \cup V2$ and the set of edges $E1 \cup E2 \cup V1 \times V2$, where $\times$ is the Cartesian product.*

Property 2 (Construction of Performance Paradox [5]). *Performance paradoxes exist for graphs $IN_n \bowtie (K_4 - (1,2))$ where IN_n is the graph with n isolated nodes.*

In [6] we have also shown performance paradoxes for small graphs which are not included in the construction described in [5].

3 Matching with Abandonment

Matching models with abandonment have not yet been solved for any compatibility graph. Therefore, we restrict ourselves to two very simple compatibility graphs: complete graphs K_n and $K_n - (1,2)$, the same graph where we have removed edge $(1,2)$. These graphs are so simple that we can find the steady-state distributions for the associated Markov chains and study the ergodicity of the chains. Note that both graphs were used in [8] to prove the performance paradox on matching model without abandonment.

3.1 Presentation of the First Model

We first model the matching with a complete compatibility graph (i.e. K_n). For each class i, the system can be in a countably infinite number of states, indexed by a non-negative integer m. We denote the state corresponding to class i having m entities by (i, m), and let $\pi_{i,m}$ represent the steady-state probability of being in this state. The chain is rather simple. All the states contain at most only one type of items. From a non empty state, we only have transitions to state with one item more or one item less. From empty state, transitions exist to all states with one item of any type. Therefore, the Continuous Time Markov chain is a collection of Birth and Death processes connected by the empty state. As the graph of the chain is a tree, the chain is reversible [9]. Therefore, we only have to consider local balance equations. The balance equation governing transitions between these states is given by

$$\pi_{i,m-1}\alpha_i = (\beta_i + m\delta)\pi_{i,m}, \tag{1}$$

where α_i is the rate of arrival of class i items (i.e., the transition rate from state $(i, m-1)$ to (i, m)), and $(\beta_i + m\delta)$ is the departure rate from state (i, m) to $(i, m-1)$, with β_i being the matching rate and δ representing the abandonment rate per entity (see Fig. 1). Note that we assume, in that paper, that the abandonment rate is the same for all types of items and it is positive. As the graph is complete, we have:

$$\beta_k = \sum_{j=1/j \neq k}^{n} \alpha_j, \quad \forall k. \tag{2}$$

Furthermore, as node 1 and 2 play a special role in the next section, we assume that

$$\beta_1 = \beta_2. \tag{3}$$

Note that this constraint will only be used in the next section and for the comparison of the expectations. Finally, the balance equation for the empty state is:

$$\pi_\emptyset \sum_{i=1}^{n} \alpha_i = \sum_{i=1}^{n} \pi_{i,1}(\beta_i + \delta) \tag{4}$$

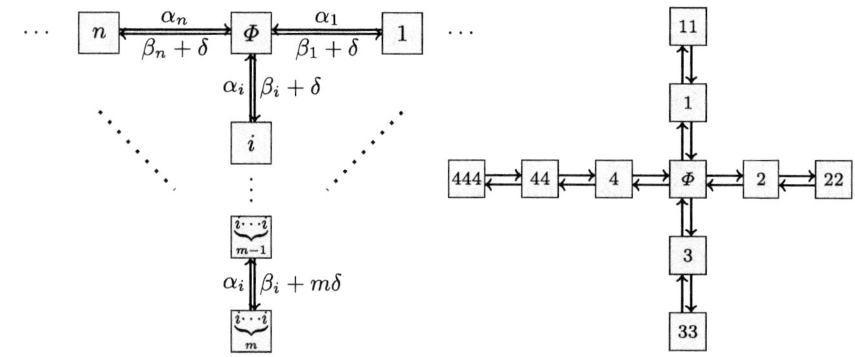

Fig. 1. Markov Chain for K_n(left) and a small example with 4 vertices(right).

Ergodicity Conditions. As the Markov chain is a collection of Birth and Death processes, it is clearly irreducible. Furthermore, it is ergodic, if all the Birth and Death processes have a stationary distribution. Let us consider the process associated to the words with only type n items. At state m, the birth rate is α_i and the death rate is $\sum_{j \neq i} \alpha_j + m\delta$.

The recurrence relation for the steady-state probabilities is derived as follows:

$$\pi_{i,m} = \frac{\alpha_i}{\beta_i + m\delta} \pi_{i,m-1}, \tag{5}$$

which, after iterating from 1 to m, becomes

$$\pi_{i,m} = \pi_\emptyset \prod_{k=1}^{m} \frac{\alpha_i}{\beta_i + k\delta}. \tag{6}$$

And this provides the invariant distribution of the chain.

Property 3 *If $\delta > 0$ then the Markov chain is ergodic.*

Proof. As $\beta_i > 0$, for all i we clearly have:

$$\frac{\alpha_i}{\beta_i + m\delta} < \frac{\alpha_i}{m\delta}$$

Thus,

$$\sum_{m>0} \prod_{k=1}^{m} \frac{\alpha_i}{\beta_i + k\delta} < \sum_{m>0} \prod_{k=1}^{m} \frac{\alpha_i}{k\delta} = \sum_{m>0} (\frac{\alpha_i}{\delta})^m \frac{1}{m!} < \infty,$$

as the summation on the r.h.s. always converges to $exp(\frac{\alpha_i}{\delta})$. Therefore the invariant distribution is summable and the chain is ergodic.

Steady-State Distributions. As the chain is ergodic, π_0 is the steady-state probability for state $\emptyset$. To ensure the total probabilities sum to 1, we need to normalize the distribution. The total probability across all states and classes must sum up to 1. Thus, we require

$$\sum_{i=1}^{n} \left[\sum_{m=1}^{\infty} \prod_{k=1}^{m} \frac{\alpha_i}{\beta_i + k\delta} \right] \pi_0 + \pi_0 = 1. \tag{7}$$

This yields the following expression for the normalizing constant π_0:

$$\pi_0 = \left(\sum_{i=1}^{n} \sum_{m=1}^{\infty} \prod_{k=1}^{m} \frac{\alpha_i}{\beta_i + k\delta} + 1 \right)^{-1}. \tag{8}$$

Finally, the steady-state probability for being in state (i, m) is given by:

$$\pi_{i,m} = \pi_0 \prod_{k=1}^{m} \frac{\alpha_i}{\beta_i + k\delta} \quad \text{for } i = 1, 2, \ldots, n. \tag{9}$$

The expected total population in the system, denoted by $\mathbb{E}[N_1 + N_2 + \cdots + N_n]$, is the sum of the expected number of individuals in each class. This can be expressed as:

$$\mathbb{E}[N_1 + N_2 + \cdots + N_n] = \sum_{i=1}^{n} \sum_{m=1}^{\infty} m\pi_{i,m}. \tag{10}$$

Substituting the expression for $\pi_{i,m}$:

$$\mathbb{E}[K_n, \alpha] = \sum_{i=1}^{n} \sum_{m=1}^{\infty} m \ \pi_0 \prod_{k=1}^{m} \frac{\alpha_i}{\beta_i + k\delta}. \tag{11}$$

This provides the expected number of individuals in the system by summing over the states of all classes, weighted by the steady-state probabilities. We will propose in Sect. 4 an algorithm to bound this expectation.

3.2 Presentation of the Second Model

We now consider the Markov chain associated with a compatibility graph K_n where one edge has been removed. For the clarity of the presentation, we assume that we have removed edge $(1, 2)$ but all the edges are equivalent. Remember that we have assumed accordingly that $\beta_1 = \beta_2$. Let β be equal to both rates. We now have:

$$\beta = \sum_{i>2} \alpha_i.$$

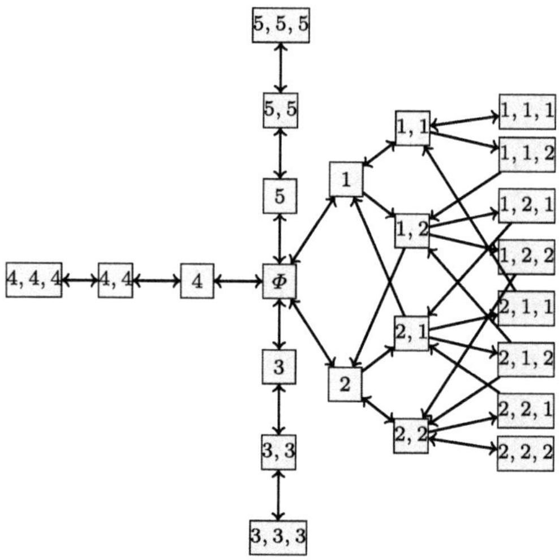

Fig. 2. CTMC for the second model, restricted to states with less than 4 items.

The Markov chain is not simple anymore (see Fig. 2) to have a closed form solution for its steady-state distribution. Following the approach we have used in [5], we have to lump the chain to obtain a simpler model. However, as mentioned previously the CTMC is infinite and not uniformizable while the classical theory about strong aggregation and lumpability has been derived for discrete time Markov chain or uniformizable CTMC. Therefore we have to check instead the conditions for strong lumpability of non uniformizable CTMC proved by Ball and Yeo in [3]. The following material comes from that reference.

Let W be a Markov chain on the set of states $\mathbb{W}$. We assume that the set of states in infinite denumerable. We consider $\mathcal{E}$ a partition $(B_1, B_2, ...)$ of $\mathbb{W}$ on $\mathbb{N}$. We define function h from $\mathbb{W}$ to $\mathbb{N}$ by $h(w) = j$ if and only if $w \in B_j$. Let $\{Y_t\} = \{h(X_t)\}$. Let ν be an initial probability vector for $\{X_t\}$.

Definition 4 (Strongly Lumpable) – *$\{X_t\}$ is lumpable with respect to $\mathcal{E}$ and ν if $\{Y_t\}$ is a CTMC given that $\{X_t\}$ has initial probability vector ν.*
– *$\{X_t\}$ is strongly lumpable with respect to $\mathcal{E}$, if it is lumpable with respect to any initial probability vector ν.*

Let Q the infinitesimal generator of $\{X_t\}$ with elements $q_{k,l}$. We define matrices $Q_{i,j}$ for i and j being indices of the macro-states in $\mathbb{N}$ by $Q_{i,j} = [q_{k,l}]_{k \in B_i, l \in B_j}$. Some conditions are imposed by Ball and Yeo on the process $\{X_t\}$ or Q.

Definition 5 (Conditions) *Ball et Yeo assume that the following conditions hold for the set of CTMC they considered:*

1. *Q is regular so a unique process exists..*
2. *$\{X_t\}$ is irreducible.*
3. *$\{X_t\}$ is positive recurrent.*
4. *for $i \in \mathbb{N}$, $Q_{i,i}^{-1}$ and $exp(Q_{i,i}t)$ are both well-defined.*

Note that the fourth condition is satisfied if the process is uniformizable and that ergodicity is required to check strong lumpability. Under these conditions Ball et al. proved the following result as a necessary and sufficient condition for strong lumpability.

Theorem 1 (Thm 2.4 [3]). *The process $\{X_t\}$ is strongly lumpable if and only if for all i,j there exist $\lambda_{i,j} \in \mathbb{R}$ such that*

$$Q_{i,j}1 = \lambda_{i,j}1,$$

where 1 is a column vector of ones of appropriate dimension.

First, we have to prove that the first three conditions on the processes are satisfied. Remark that condition 4 is based on the partition and we must define it first. We begin by some necessary definition and properties. The following material comes from Kijima [10].

Let J_n be the time just after the $n-th$ transition of $\{X_t\}$. And let Z_n be the embedded Markov chain associated with $\{X_t\}$.

Definition 6 *A continuous time Markov chain $\{X_t\}$ is called regular if* $\lim_{n \to \infty} J_n = \infty$ *with probability* 1.

We will use the following two results from [10]:

- Theorem 4.14 which states that $\{X_t\}$ is regular if Z_n is recurrent.
- Theorem 4.16 which states that $\{X_t\}$ is positive recurrent if Z_n is recurrent and its invariant distribution π is summable.

Therefore, the first step of the proof is to establish that Z_n is positive recurrent. We first describe the state space and the partition. We consider the following partition of the state space to prove both the lumpability (Lemma 4) and condition 4 used by Ball et Yeo (i.e. Lemma 3). This partition will be denoted as $\mathcal{E}$.

- States w with letters 1 and 2 in any particular order such that the length of w is k. They are grouped into macro state $B12_k$.

- Words containing only one type of items (or letters) distinct from 1 an 2 are not aggregated. Let Bi_x be this macro-state (for $i > 2$). It is a singleton which contains the state with x letters i.
- Similarly, the empty word remains in a singleton which is denoted as $B_\emptyset$.

Lemma 1. *The embedded Markov chain (i.e. Z_n) is positive recurrent.*

Proof. The proof is based on the following Liapounov function $V(X_t)$ which is the total number of items in the system at time t (i.e. for all x in $B12_k \cup (\bigcup_i Bi_k)$, $V(x) = k$).

The transitions of the embedded Markov chains are:

- increasing by one the number of item with probability $\lambda(x)/\Lambda(x)$.
- decreasing by one the number of items with probability $(\Lambda(x) - \lambda(x))/\Lambda(x)$.

And we have $\lambda(x) \leq \sum \alpha_i$ and $\Lambda(x) = \sum_i \alpha_i + k * \delta$. Therefore, the expected drift of V satisfies:

$$\mathbb{E}[V(X_{t+1}) - V(X_t) \mid X_t = Bi_k] \leq \frac{\sum_i \alpha_i - k\delta}{\sum_i \alpha_i + k\delta}.$$

Function $\frac{\sum_i \alpha_i - k\delta}{\sum_i \alpha_i + k\delta}$ is decreasing with k and its limit when k goes to infinity is -1. Thus, there exists a finite value of k such that this bound is strictly smaller than $-1/2$. These inequalities imply that the expected drift is uniformly negative outside a finite set. Hence, by the Foster-Lyapunov criterion (see [4]), Z_n is positive recurrent.

Lemma 2. *Conditions 1, 2 and* 3 *hold for process* $\{X_t\}$..

Proof. Condition 1 (Regularity): we proved in Lemma 1 that the embedded chain is recurrent. Therefore, due to Theorem 4.14 [10], process $\{X_t\}$ is regular.

Condition 2 (Irreducibility): Condition 2 is satisfied if $\alpha_i > 0$ and $\beta_i + n_i\delta > 0$. Every arrival type occurs with a positive rate, and any item may store or match. Therefore, from any non-empty state, there exists a finite sequence of transitions to the empty state. From the empty state, a sequence of arrivals can reach any state. Thus, the process is irreducible.

Condition 3 (Positive Recurrence): Lemma 1 proves that the embedded chain is positive recurrent. Therefore, the invariant distribution of Z_n is summable. Finally, due to Theorem 4.16 [10], process $\{X_t\}$ is positive recurrent.

Now the challenge lies in finding the appropriate partition and verifying the lumpability condition based on an abstract definition of the Markov chain (i.e., derived from the compatibility graph and the matching discipline).

Due to the compatibility graph, the state space of the Markov chain associated with the model is decomposed into:

- words containing letters 1 and 2 ordered according to their arrival instants,
- words containing only type of items (or letters) from 3 to n,

– empty word, denoted as $\emptyset$. There are no direct transitions between the first type of states and the second type of states.

Lemma 3. *Condition* 4 *holds for Process* $\{X_t\}$ *and partition* $\mathcal{E}$.

Proof. We have two cases for $Q_{i,i}$:

- Blocks $B_\emptyset$ and Bi_k (with $i > 2$) are singletons. Thus blocks $Q_{i,i}$ are matrices with size 1 which are the diagonal elements of matrix Q. Thus $Q_{i,i}[1,1] < 0$ (the indexing is local to block i) Thus clearly both $Q_{i,i}^{-}1$ and $exp(Q_{i,i}t)$ exist.
- Blocks $B12_k$. They always contain more than 2 elements. Let $w1$ and $w2$ be two distinct states of $B12_k$ (i.e. with the same k). Thus, by construction, the size of $w1$ is equal to the size of $w2$. Therefore there is no transitions from $w1$ to $w2$. Indeed in the matching model, the only allowed transitions increase or decrease by one be length of the word. The only non zero elements in $Q_{i,i}$ are the diagonal elements of $Q_{i,i}$ which contains the normalization of infinitesimal generator Q and these elements are non zero. Finally $Q_{i,i}$ is diagonal with all its elements non zero. Thus both $Q_{i,i}^{-}1$ and $exp(Q_{i,i}t)$ exist.

Lemma 4. *The chain is strongly aggregable for partition* $\mathcal{E}$*, and the lumped Markov chain is the chain associated with the compatibility graph* K_{n-1}.

Proof. As sets $B_\emptyset$ and Bi_x (for all i and x) are singletons, we just have to check the lumpability condition for sets $B12_k$. Let w_1 and w_2 be two words in $B12_k$. The transitions out of states in $B12_k$ are arrival of a non matching item, a arrival of matching item and an abandonment. We will look at the three cases:

- Arrival of a matching item (say z). Due to the compatibility graph, it means that z is not equal to 1 or 2. As the neighbors of 1 are also the neighbors of 2 in the compatibility graph, if z matches with 1 it also matches with 2. Therefore the arrival of z provokes one deletion in $w1$ and one deletion in $w2$ irrespective of the orders of items 1 and 2 in the words. The states we reach are both in $B12_{k-1}$ (or in $B_\emptyset$ if $k = 1$). In both cases, the arrival rate is $\sum_{i>2} \alpha_i = \beta$.
- Arrival of a non matching item. It must be an item of type 1 or 2. Therefore the states we reach are both in $B12_{k+1}$ and the transition rate is $\alpha_1 + \alpha_2$.
- Abandonment: as δ is not type dependent, the rate is $k\delta$ for all states in $B12_k$. The states after abandonment are both in $B12_{k-1}$ (or in $B_\emptyset$ if $k = 1$)

Hence, the lumpability condition holds for $B12_k$. Clearly the lumped chain is the CTMC associated to a compatibility graph K_{n-1} with Poisson processes with rate α' such that $\alpha'_i = \alpha_i$ for all $i > 2$ and arrival rate $\alpha'_1 = \alpha_1 + \alpha_2$ for items resulting to the aggregation of type 1 and 2 (Fig. 3).

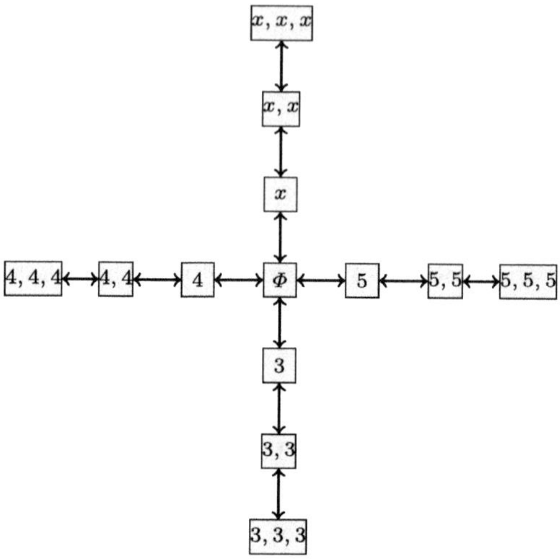

Fig. 3. Lumped version of the chain with compatibility graph $K_5 - (1,2)$ restricted to states with less than 4 items. x is a letter resulting from the aggregation of 1 and 2.

Corollary 1 *The expectation of the total number of items in the system with compatibility graph* $K_n - (1,2)$ *is* $\mathbb{E}[K_n - (1,2), \alpha] = \mathbb{E}[K_{n-1}, \alpha']$. *Thus,*

$$\mathbb{E}[K_n - (1,2), \alpha] = \sum_{m=1}^{\infty} m\ \pi_0' \prod_{k=1}^{m} \frac{\alpha_1 + \alpha_2}{\beta + k\delta} + \sum_{i=3}^{n} \sum_{m=1}^{\infty} m\ \pi_0' \prod_{k=1}^{m} \frac{\alpha_i}{\beta_i + k\delta}, \tag{12}$$

where π_0' *is the probability of the empty state in the second model.*

$$\pi_0' = \left(\sum_{m=1}^{\infty} \prod_{k=1}^{m} \frac{\alpha_1 + \alpha_2}{\beta + k\delta} + \sum_{i=3}^{n} \sum_{m=1}^{\infty} \prod_{k=1}^{m} \frac{\alpha_i}{\beta_i + k\delta} + 1 \right)^{-1}. \tag{13}$$

4 Paradox

The objective is to find some values for the arrival rate vectors α such that

$$\mathbb{E}[K_n - (1,2), \alpha] < \mathbb{E}[K_n, \alpha].$$

The main difficulties come from the infinite summations we have to compute to get both expectations. Unfortunately, to the best of our knowledge, no closed-form solutions for such infinite sum exists. Therefore, we compute bounds (upper and lower) with a finite complexity for both expectations. More precisely, we will derive $\underline{\mathbb{E}[K_n, \alpha]}$ and $\overline{\mathbb{E}[K_n - (1,2), \alpha]}$ such that

$$\mathbb{E}[K_n - (1,2), \alpha] < \overline{\mathbb{E}[K_n - (1,2), \alpha]}$$

and

$$\underline{\mathbb{E}[K_n, \alpha]} < \mathbb{E}[K_n, \alpha].$$

And we only have to find rates α_i and δ such that $\overline{\mathbb{E}[K_n - (1,2), \alpha]} < \underline{\mathbb{E}[K_n, \alpha]}$ to obtain a paradox by transitivity.

Note that as $\mathbb{E}[K_n - (1,2), \alpha] = \mathbb{E}[K_{n-1}, \alpha']$ we only have to derive bounds for the expectation for a complete compatibility graph.

4.1 Numerical Analysis and Bounds

In this section, we provide a method for numerically bound π_0 and the expected total number of items in the system. Remember that the normalizing constant π_0 is given by equation (8): $\pi_0 = \left(\sum_{i=1}^{n} \sum_{m=1}^{\infty} \prod_{k=1}^{m} \frac{\alpha_i}{\beta_i + k\delta} + 1\right)^{-1}$, where α_i, β_i and δ are defined in Subsect. 3.1. Define the partial sum for each type i as:

$$S_i = \sum_{m=1}^{\infty} \prod_{k=1}^{m} \frac{\alpha_i}{\beta_i + k\delta} = S_i(N_i) + R_i(N_i),$$

where $S_i(N_i)$ denotes the truncated sum up to $m = N_i$, and $R_i(N_i)$ is the residual. To control the total error in computing π_0, we require: $R_i(N_i) < \frac{\epsilon}{n}$, for a target error tolerance $\epsilon > 0$. Note that by construction $R_i(N_i) > 0$. We consider two cases for bounding $R_i(N_i)$.

Case 1: $\delta > \alpha_i$. As $\beta_i > 0$, we have:

$$R_i(N_i) = \sum_{m=N_i+1}^{\infty} \prod_{k=1}^{m} \frac{\alpha_i}{\beta_i + k\delta} < \sum_{m=N_i+1}^{\infty} \left(\frac{\alpha_i}{\delta}\right)^m \frac{1}{m!}$$

Since $\frac{\alpha_i}{\delta} < 1$, after some simple algebraic manipulations, we get:

$$R_i(N_i) < \frac{1}{(N_i - 1)!} \sum_{m=N_i+1}^{\infty} \frac{1}{(m-1)^2}.$$

As function $1/x^2$ is decreasing, we have $\frac{1}{p^2} < \int_p^{p+1} \frac{1}{x^2} dx$ for all p. Therefore

$$\int_{N_i}^{\infty} \frac{1}{x^2} dx = \frac{1}{N_i}, \quad \text{and } \mathrm{R_i(N_i)} < \frac{1}{(\mathrm{N_i})!}$$

Therefore it is sufficient to choose N_i such that $\frac{1}{N_i!} < \frac{\epsilon}{n}$.

Case 2: $\delta \leq \alpha_i$. Let P be the smallest integer such that $\alpha_i < P\delta$. We begin with a trivial decomposition, assuming that $N_i > P$.

$$\prod_{k=1}^{m} \frac{\alpha_i}{\beta_i + k\delta} = \prod_{k=1}^{P} \frac{\alpha_i}{\beta_i + k\delta} \prod_{k=P+1}^{m} \frac{\alpha_i}{\beta_i + k\delta}$$

Then, we bound the first term by using that $k \geq 1$ and the second term taking into acount that $\beta_i > 0$ and $k > P$.

$$R_i(N_i) = \sum_{m=N_i+1}^{\infty} \prod_{k=1}^{m} \frac{\alpha_i}{\beta_i + k\delta} < \left(\frac{\alpha_i}{\beta_i + \delta}\right)^P \sum_{m=N_i+1}^{\infty} \left(\frac{\alpha_i}{P\delta}\right)^{m-P}.$$

Therefore we get:

$$R_i(N_i) < \left(\frac{\alpha_i}{\beta_i + \delta}\right)^P \frac{\left(\frac{\alpha_i}{P\delta}\right)^{N_i - P}}{1 - \frac{\alpha_i}{P\delta}}$$

Note that the function on the r.h.s of the inequality is decreasing with N_i. Thus, finding the value of N_i is now easy. We have to find the smallest N_i such that:

$$\left(\frac{\alpha_i}{\beta_i + \delta}\right)^P \frac{\left(\frac{\alpha_i}{P\delta}\right)^{N_i - P}}{1 - \frac{\alpha_i}{P\delta}} < \frac{\epsilon}{n}.$$

Finally, we take $N = \max_i\{N_i \mid i = 1, \ldots, n\}$. And we have:

$$|S_i - S_i(N)| < \frac{\epsilon}{n} \quad \text{for } i = 1, 2, \ldots, n.$$

Let us turn now to the bounds on π_0. Let us consider $\overline{\pi_0}$ defined by $\frac{1}{\sum_{i=1}^{n} S_i(N)+1}$. Clearly it is an upper bound of π_O. Now,

$$\begin{aligned}
\overline{\pi_0} - \pi_0 &= \frac{1}{\sum_{i=1}^{n} S_i(N)+1} - \frac{1}{\sum_{i=1}^{n} S_i+1} \\
&= \frac{\sum_{i=1}^{n} S_i - \sum_{i=1}^{n} S_i(N)}{(\sum_{i=1}^{n} S_i+1)(\sum_{i=1}^{n} S_i(N)+1)} \qquad (14) \\
&< \sum_{i=1}^{n}(S_i - S_i(N)) < \epsilon.
\end{aligned}$$

Therefore, we can obtain an upper bound by truncation as closed as we need to the true solution π_0.

Furthermore, using a similar proof, one can state that $\underline{\pi_0}$ defined in Eq. 15 is a lower bound of π_0 such that $\pi_0 - \underline{\pi_0} < \epsilon$:

$$\underline{\pi_0} = \left(\sum_{i=1}^{n} \sum_{n=1}^{N} \prod_{k=1}^{m} \frac{\alpha_i}{\beta_i + k\delta} + \epsilon + 1 \right)^{-1}. \qquad (15)$$

Finally we have to combine these bounds to obtain upper and lower bounds for the expectations. By definition, the expected value is given by

$$\mathbb{E}[K_n] = \sum_{i=1}^{n} \sum_{m=1}^{\infty} \left(\prod_{k=1}^{m} \frac{\alpha_i}{\beta_i + k\delta} \right) m\pi_0. \qquad (16)$$

We decompose the infinite summations on m into a sum from 1 to $N+1$ (say $A(N)$) and a sum from $N+2$ to infinity (say $B(N)$):

$$\sum_{i=1}^{n}\sum_{m=1}^{N+1}\left(\prod_{k=1}^{m}\frac{\alpha_i}{\beta_i+k\delta}\right)m\pi_0+\sum_{i=1}^{n}\sum_{m=N+2}^{\infty}\left(\prod_{k=1}^{m}\frac{\alpha_i}{\beta_i+k\delta}\right)m\pi_0=A(N)+B(N),$$

We now derive a bound of $B(N)$ using the previous results. First observe that:

$$B(N)=\pi_0\sum_{i=1}^{n}\sum_{m=N+2}^{\infty}\left(\prod_{k=1}^{m}\frac{\alpha_i}{\beta_i+k\delta}\right)m\leq\frac{\alpha_i}{\delta}\sum_{i=1}^{n}\sum_{m=N+2}^{\infty}\left(\prod_{k=1}^{m-1}\frac{\alpha_i}{\beta_i+k\delta}\right) \tag{17}$$

This relation is clear, given that $\pi_0 \leq 1$ and $\frac{m\alpha_i}{\beta+m\delta}<\frac{\alpha_i}{\delta}$.

Now one can identify easily

$$\sum_{m=N+2}^{\infty}\left(\prod_{k=1}^{m-1}\frac{\alpha_i}{\beta_i+k\delta}\right)=\sum_{m=N+1}^{\infty}\left(\prod_{k=1}^{m}\frac{\alpha_i}{\beta_i+k\delta}\right)=R_i(N)$$

As we have formerly chosen N such that $R_i(N)<\epsilon/n$, we finally obtain:

$$B(N)<\frac{\epsilon}{n}\sum_{i=1}^{n}\frac{\alpha_i}{\delta}$$

Thus, the lower and upper bounds for the expected total population can be defined as

$$\underline{\mathbb{E}}[K_n]=\sum_{i=1}^{n}\sum_{m=1}^{N+2}m\underline{\pi_0}\prod_{k=1}^{m}\frac{\alpha_i}{\beta_i+k\delta}\quad\text{and}\quad\overline{\mathbb{E}}[K_n]=\sum_{i=1}^{n}\sum_{m=1}^{N+2}m\overline{\pi_0}\prod_{k=1}^{m}\frac{\alpha_i}{\beta_i+k\delta}+\frac{\epsilon}{n\delta},$$

thus providing bounds for the calculation of expected values.

4.2 Examples of Performance Paradox

To demonstrate the performance paradox in the presence of abandonment, we present some numerical instances drawn from a large-scale Monte Carlo search. All results and programs are documented in [11]. For all the examples presented in the following, the truncation error ϵ is equal to 0.00001 and the number of type of items (i.e. n) is 5. Types 1 and 2 having equal arrival rates. For the sake of readability in the presentation of the results, we write K_4 instead of $K_5-(1,2)$ as we have proved that the models are equivalent for the expectation.

Abandonment rate $\delta = 0.01$: we consider the following arrival rates: $\alpha_1 = \alpha_2 =$ 0.07198009646943532, $\alpha_3 = 0.1505252430731784$,
$\alpha_4 = 0.2139285951521536$ and $\alpha_5 = 0.49158596883579736$. Applying the certified truncation method from Sect. 4.1, we obtain the two bounds for the expected total number of items as $\underline{\mathbb{E}}[K_5] = 4.517062201492523$ and $\overline{\mathbb{E}}[K_4] =$ 4.507590806996654. Since $\underline{\mathbb{E}}[K_5] > \overline{\mathbb{E}}[K_4]$, this example certifies a paradox.

Abandonment rate $\delta = 0.02$: With the arrival rates: $\alpha_1 = \alpha_2 = 0.137987656$, $\alpha_3 = 0.162773315$, $\alpha_4 = 0.47490324$ and $\alpha_5 = 0.086348129$ we get the following bounds: $\underline{\mathbb{E}}[K_5] = 2.705018525$ and $\overline{\mathbb{E}}[K_4] = 2.686966814$. Again a performance paradox.

Abandonment rate $\delta = 0.05$: We consider the following arrival rates: $\alpha_1 = \alpha_2 = 0.070548153$, $\alpha_3 = 0.248317959$, $\alpha_4 = 0.116798768$ and $\alpha_5 = 0.493786968$. We algorithms provide the following bounds: $\underline{\mathbb{E}}[K_5] = 2.068573185$ and $\overline{\mathbb{E}}[K_4] = 2.066821283$. And we obtain a new paradox: $\underline{\mathbb{E}}[K_5] > \overline{\mathbb{E}}[K_4]$.

Abandonment rate $\delta = 0.07$: The following arrival rates: $\alpha_1 = \alpha_2 = 0.041846729$, $\alpha_3 = 0.286078133$, $\alpha_4 = 0.134189224$ and $\alpha_5 = 0.496039185$ lead to $\underline{\mathbb{E}}[K_5] = 1.777650699$ and $\overline{\mathbb{E}}[K_4] = 1.777497359$. Again a performance paradox as $\underline{\mathbb{E}}[K_5] > \overline{\mathbb{E}}[K_4]$.

5 Conclusions and Remarks

In this work, we extended the notion of performance paradoxes in matching models to settings with abandonment. We established a tractable framework for exact and approximate evaluation of stationary distributions and expected item populations in such models. We provided an analytical decomposition of the state space and proved strong aggregation results for special compatibility structures. To overcome the intractability of infinite sums, we proposed and rigorously justified a truncation method with explicit error bounds on the normalizing constant and expectations.

References

1. United network for organ sharing, living donation kidney paired (Online). https://unos.org/wp-content/uploads/unos/livingdonationkidneypaired.pdf
2. Ashlagi, I., Jaillet, P., Manshadi, V.H.: Kidney exchange in dynamic sparse heterogenous pools. In: Proceedings of the Fourteenth ACM Conference on Electronic Commerce, pp. 25–26. EC '13, Association for Computing Machinery, New York, NY, USA (2013). https://doi.org/10.1145/2492002.2482565
3. Ball, F., Yeo, G.F.: Lumpability and marginalisability for continuous-time markov chains. J. Appl. Probab. **30**(3), 518–528 (1993)
4. Brémaud, P.: Markov Chains: Gibbs fields. Springer-Verlag, Monte Carlo Simulation and Queues (1999)
5. Bušić, A., Cadas, A., Doncel, J., Fourneau, J.M.: Performance paradox of dynamic matching models under greedy policies. Queueing Syst. **107**(3–4), 257–293 (2024). https://doi.org/10.1007/s11134-024-09924-z
6. Busic, A., Fourneau, J.M., Lunven, A., Li, S.: Performance paradoxes in matching systems are not that rare. In: Proceedings of NetGCoop Conference, Springer LNCS (2025)
7. Bušić, A., Gupta, V., Mairesse, J.: Stability of the Bipartite Matching Model. Adv. Appl. Probab. **45**(2), 351–378 (2013). https://doi.org/10.1239/aap/1370870122

8. Cadas, A., Doncel, J., Fourneau, J.M., Bušić, A.: Flexibility can hurt dynamic matching system performance. SIGMETRICS Perform. Eval. Rev. **49**(3), 37–42 (2022). https://doi.org/10.1145/3529113.3529126
9. Kelly, F.P.: Reversibility and Stochastic Networks, J. Wiley (1987)
10. Markov Processes for Stochastic Modeling. Springer, Boston, MA (1997). https://doi.org/10.1007/978-1-4899-3132-0
11. Li, S.: Matching with abandonment (2025). https://doi.org/10.6084/m9.figshare.29391455, https://github.com/shuligraph/matching-abandonmet.git
12. Mairesse, J., Moyal, P.: Stability of the stochastic matching model. J. Appl. Probab. **53**(4), 1064–1077 (2016). https://doi.org/10.1017/jpr.2016.65
13. Moyal, P., Bušić, A., Mairesse, J.: A product form for the general stochastic matching model. J. Appl. Probab. **58**(2), 449–468 (2021). https://doi.org/10.1017/jpr.2020.100
14. Ünver, M.U.: Dynamic kidney exchange. Rev. Econ. Stud. **77**(1), 372–414 (2010). https://doi.org/10.1111/j.1467-937X.2009.00575.x

The Arnoldi Aggregation for Approximate Transient Distributions of Markov Chains

Patrick Sonnentag(✉), Fabian Michel, and Markus Siegle

University of the Bundeswehr Munich, Institute for Computer Engineering, Werner-Heisenberg-Weg 39, Neubiberg 85579, Germany
{patrick.sonnentag,fabian.michel,markus.siegle}@unibw.de

Abstract. The paper proposes a new aggregation method, based on the Arnoldi iteration, for computing approximate transient distributions of Markov chains. This aggregation is not partition-based, which means that an aggregate state may represent any portion of any original state, leading to a reduced system which is not a Markov chain. Results on exactness (in case the algorithm finds an invariant Krylov subspace) and minimality of the size of the Arnoldi aggregation are proven. For practical use, a heuristic is proposed for deciding when to stop expanding the state space once a certain accuracy has been reached. Apart from the theory, the paper also includes an extensive empirical section where the new aggregation algorithm is tested on several models and compared to a lumping-based state space reduction scheme.

Keywords: Aggregation · Arnoldi Iteration · Krylov Subspace Method · Markov Chains · State Space Reduction

1 Introduction and Motivation

Approximate solutions of Markov chains by means of state space reduction have received a lot of attention in the literature. One of the earliest works is that of Simon and Ando [19] on nearly decomposable Markov chains. These techniques were further developed and applied to models of computer systems by Courtois [8] which also led to iterative aggregation/disaggregation methods [13]. Most of these early works on state space aggregation focused on the stationary distribution, while Buchholz in his seminal paper on lumpability [6] also considered transient distributions. An overview of general transient solution methods is also given in the paper [18], where—among several others—a Krylov subspace based method is briefly described. It is, of course, important to control the error caused by aggregation/disaggregation; see, for instance, [7]. Recently, state space reduction techniques for obtaining approximate transient distributions of Markov chains with formal error bounds have been studied [1]. This has been generalized in [16], the latter work characterising exactness of Markov chain aggregations, which goes beyond the well-known concept of lumping.

A. Remke et al. (Eds.): Valuetools 2025, LNICST 691, pp. 104–119, 2027.
https://doi.org/10.1007/978-3-032-23901-3_7

To achieve a state space reduction of a Markov chain with transition matrix P, the primary question is how to aggregate the state space, i.e. how to construct the reduced system. More concretely, the question is how to choose the size and the transition matrix of the reduced system. Secondly, once a solution for the reduced system has been obtained, a strategy is needed for mapping this solution back onto the original chain, i.e. one needs to specify a disaggregation scheme, usually in the form of a disaggregation matrix A. The third question concerns the choice of the initial vector for the aggregated system.

Common approaches to state space reduction use a partitioning of the original state space, leading to one aggregated state per class, which means that every original state belongs to exactly one state of the reduced system. The reduced system is usually considered to be a Markov chain again, its transition matrix constructed as a stochastic matrix, and the initial vector of the reduced system a probability vector. In this paper, we consider more general state space reductions, where a reduced state can represent any portion of any original state.

The Arnoldi iteration [2] is a well-known algorithm for computing an orthonormal basis of the Krylov subspace of a vector v w.r.t. a matrix M, i.e. the space span$\{ v^{\mathsf{T}}, v^{\mathsf{T}}M, \dots, v^{\mathsf{T}}M^{j-1} \}$. We develop the Arnoldi aggregation for Markov chains, based on the Arnoldi iteration, where the initial vector is the initial distribution ($v = p_0$) and $M = P$ is the transition matrix of the DTMC. The vectors computed as the basis of this Krylov subspace are used as the rows of the disaggregation matrix A, and the step matrix of the reduced system is obtained from the multiplication factors appearing in the Gram-Schmidt orthonormalization part of the Arnoldi process. The step matrix thus obtained is not a stochastic matrix, i.e. the reduced system is not a Markov chain, and—in consequence—the vectors obtained may not be probability distributions. We show that Arnoldi aggregations are either exact with minimal state space size or have an error of zero for the first $j-1$ time steps (where j is the number of Arnoldi iterations performed) with minimal state space size. For transient time points larger than the number of Arnoldi iterations (which is the interesting case), the error can be estimated by a heuristic during the Arnoldi iteration, thus making it possible to dynamically control the size of the reduced system based on the desired error.

The key contributions of this paper, which is based on the thesis [20], are as follows: A new aggregation scheme for Markov chains is proposed and analysed from a theoretical point of view, leading to exactness and minimality results. In view of finite floating point precision, practically viable termination criteria for the iterative Arnoldi procedure in the aggregation setting are established. Empirical results are provided which confirm the theoretical findings and show that the Arnoldi aggregation can be superior to other approaches.

The remainder of the paper is structured as follows: Starting in Sect. 2, we explain basic notation and formally introduce the Arnoldi iteration. In Sect. 3, we introduce the Arnoldi aggregation and derive its main theoretical properties. We further consider how to work with Arnoldi aggregations in floating point arithmetic, introduce the final algorithm and analyse its runtime and memory complexity. Lastly, in Sect. 4, Arnoldi aggregations are evaluated and compared to Exlump aggregations from [16, Algorithm 3] on a range of different models. A summary and outlook for future work are given in Sect. 5.

2 Preliminaries

2.1 Notation

Let $u, v \in \mathbb{R}^n$ and $M \in \mathbb{R}^{n\times m}$. Then, $|v|$ and $|M|$ denote the vector and the matrix with the absolute value applied component-wise. Furthermore, denote with $\mathbf{0}_n$ and $\mathbf{1}_n$ the vectors in $\mathbb{R}^n$ with all entries zero or one, respectively. Let $e_j \in \mathbb{R}^j$ be the jth standard basis vector of $\mathbb{R}^j$, and $I_n \in \mathbb{R}^{n\times n}$ the identity matrix. Lastly, define $\langle u, v\rangle := u^\intercal v$, $\|v\|_1 := \langle |v|, \mathbf{1}_n\rangle$ and the matrix norm $\|M\|_\infty$ as the maximum absolute row sum of M.

Here, we are going to work with time-homogeneous discrete-time Markov chains with finite state spaces $S = \{1, \ldots, n\}$ solely. Furthermore, if X_k is the state of the Markov chain at time k, let $P \in \mathbb{R}^{n\times n}$ be the transition matrix of the Markov chain where $P(i, j) := \mathbb{P}(X_{k+1} = j \mid X_k = i)$. With an initial distribution $p_0 \in \mathbb{R}^n$, transient distributions are given by $p_k^\intercal = p_0^\intercal P^k$.

Next, we consider state space reductions through aggregations. In an aggregation of dimension $m \leq n$, the (arbitrary) *aggregated step matrix* $\Pi \in \mathbb{R}^{m\times m}$ shall approximate the dynamics of P. Let $\pi_0 \in \mathbb{R}^m$ be the (arbitrary) *initial aggregated vector* and $\pi_k^\intercal := \pi_0^\intercal \Pi^k$ the *transient aggregated vector*. To return to an n-dimensional space, we use the (arbitrary) *disaggregation matrix* $A \in \mathbb{R}^{m\times n}$ to define *approximated transient distributions* as $\tilde{p}_k^\intercal := \pi_k^\intercal A$. Finally, following [16, Def. 8], an aggregation is *dynamic-exact* if $\Pi A = AP$. If further $p_0 = \tilde{p}_0$ holds, it is *exact*. This is motivated by dynamic-exactness implying $\tilde{p}_k^\intercal = \tilde{p}_0^\intercal P^k$ and exactness even offering $p_k = \tilde{p}_k$. The kth *transient error vector* is given through $\mathrm{err}_k := \tilde{p}_k - p_k$ with $\|\mathrm{err}_k\|_1$ denoting the *transient error* after k steps.

2.2 Arnoldi Iteration

For a vector $v \in \mathbb{R}^n$ and a matrix $M \in \mathbb{R}^{n\times n}$, the Arnoldi iteration, as first introduced in [2], builds an orthonormal basis $q_1^\intercal, \ldots, q_j^\intercal$ of the Krylov subspace

$$\mathcal{K}^j(v, M) := \operatorname{span}\{ v^\intercal, v^\intercal M, \ldots, v^\intercal M^{j-1} \},$$

using the Gram-Schmidt procedure, as done in Algorithm 1.

There, we can see the Gram-Schmidt procedure in lines 2, 4–9 and 12; lines 3, 10 and 13 construct some matrices $H_j \in \mathbb{R}^{j\times j}$ and $Q_j \in \mathbb{R}^{j\times n}$, and line 11 provides the return value once some arbitrary termination criterion is met (suggestions for this will follow later). Usually, $h_{j,j+1} = 0$ is part of this criterion to avoid division by zero. The relation

$$H_j Q_j + h_{j,j+1} e_j q_{j+1}^\intercal = Q_j M \tag{1}$$

Algorithm 1. Arnoldi Iteration

Let $v \in \mathbb{R}^n$, $M \in \mathbb{R}^{n \times n}$.
$q_1 := \frac{v}{\|v\|_2}$
$Q_1 := \begin{pmatrix} - q_1^\mathsf{T} - \end{pmatrix}$
for $j = 1, 2, \dots$ **do**
  $r_1^\mathsf{T} := q_j^\mathsf{T} M$
  for all $i = 1, 2, \dots, j$ **do**
    $h_{j,i} := \langle r_i, q_i \rangle$
    $r_{i+1} := r_i - h_{j,i} q_i$
  $h_{j,j+1} := \|r_{j+1}\|_2$
  $H_j := \begin{cases} \begin{pmatrix} h_{1,1} \end{pmatrix} & \text{if } j = 1 \\ \begin{pmatrix} H_{j-1} & \begin{matrix} \mathbf{0}_{j-2} \\ h_{j-1,j} \end{matrix} \\ h_{j,1} \cdots & h_{j,j} \end{pmatrix} & \text{else} \end{cases}$
  if criterion is true **then return** H_j, Q_j
  $q_{j+1} := \frac{r_{j+1}}{h_{j,j+1}}$
  $Q_{j+1} := \begin{pmatrix} Q_j \\ - q_{j+1}^\mathsf{T} - \end{pmatrix}$

holds if $\mathcal{K}^j(v, M) \subsetneq \mathcal{K}^{j+1}(v, M)$ (with $e_j \in \mathbb{R}^j$). If $\mathcal{K}^j(v, M) = \mathcal{K}^{j+1}(v, M)$ holds, (i.e., the Krylov subspace is invariant under M), Eq. (1) reduces to

$$H_j Q_j = Q_j M. \tag{2}$$

While not hard to show, proving Eqs. (1) and (2) thoroughly requires lengthy calculations. Refer to [17, Sec. 6.2] for a proof. There, a slight variation of the Arnoldi iteration is used, with rearranged order of operations for the underlying Gram-Schmidt procedure.

3 Using the Arnoldi Iteration to Build Aggregations

Both Eqs (1) and (2), but especially Eq. (2), are reminiscent of the definition of dynamic-exact aggregations of Markov chains in Sect. 2.1. Using these as a basis while further guaranteeing $p_0 = \tilde{p}_0$ motivates:

Definition 1 (Arnoldi aggregation). *With $P \in \mathbb{R}^{n \times n}$ as the transition matrix of a Markov chain and $p_0 \in \mathbb{R}^n$ an initial distribution, the aggregation with $\Pi := H_j$, $A := Q_j$, resulting from the Arnoldi iteration with P and p_0, and $\pi_0 := (\|p_0\|_2, 0, \dots, 0)^\mathsf{T} \in \mathbb{R}^j$, is the* Arnoldi aggregation *of size j for P and p_0.*

3.1 Exact and Initially Exact Arnoldi Aggregations

We start by exploring some properties of Arnoldi aggregations and their connection to (initially) exact aggregations.

Lemma 1. *In an Arnoldi aggregation of size j, it holds that*

$$\pi_k = (\underbrace{\lambda_1, \ldots, \lambda_{k+1}}_{\text{all} \in \mathbb{R}}, \underbrace{0, \ldots, 0}_{(j-k-1)\times})^{\mathsf{T}} \quad \text{for } 1 \le k \le j-1 \text{ and for some real numbers } \lambda_i.$$

Proof. Follows by induction on k and the form of H_j.

Lemma 2. *In Arnoldi aggregations of size j after k steps, we have*

$$\pi_0^{\mathsf{T}} H_j^k Q_j + \sum_{i=0}^{k-1} \pi_0^{\mathsf{T}} H_j^i \left(h_{j,j+1} e_j q_{j+1}^{\mathsf{T}}\right) P^{k-1-i} = \pi_0^{\mathsf{T}} Q_j P^k$$

Proof. By induction on k. Clearly, $\pi_0^{\mathsf{T}} I_j Q_j + 0 = \pi_0^{\mathsf{T}} Q_j I_n$. Induction step:

$$\begin{aligned}
\pi_0^{\mathsf{T}} Q_j P^{k+1} &= \pi_0^{\mathsf{T}} H_j^k Q_j P + \sum_{i=0}^{k-1} \pi_0^{\mathsf{T}} H_j^i \left(h_{j,j+1} e_j q_{j+1}^{\mathsf{T}}\right) P^{k-i} \\
&\overset{1}{=} \pi_0^{\mathsf{T}} H_j^k \left(H_j Q_j + h_{j,j+1} e_j q_{j+1}^{\mathsf{T}}\right) + \sum_{i=0}^{k-1} \pi_0^{\mathsf{T}} H_j^i \left(h_{j,j+1} e_j q_{j+1}^{\mathsf{T}}\right) P^{k-i} \\
&= \pi_0^{\mathsf{T}} H_j^{k+1} Q_j + \sum_{i=0}^{k} \pi_0^{\mathsf{T}} H_j^i \left(h_{j,j+1} e_j q_{j+1}^{\mathsf{T}}\right) P^{k-i}.
\end{aligned}$$

Proposition 1. *An Arnoldi aggregation of size j has $p_k = \tilde{p}_k$ for $0 \le k \le j-1$.*

Proof. Combine Lemmas 1 and 2 to get

$$\begin{aligned}
p_k^{\mathsf{T}} = \pi_0^{\mathsf{T}} Q_j P^k &\overset{\text{Lem. 2}}{=} \pi_0^{\mathsf{T}} H_j^k Q_j + \sum_{i=0}^{k-1} \pi_0^{\mathsf{T}} H_j^i \left(h_{j,j+1} e_j q_{j+1}^{\mathsf{T}}\right) P^{k-1-i} \\
&\overset{\text{Lem. 1}}{=} \pi_0^{\mathsf{T}} H_j^k Q_j + \sum_{i=0}^{k-1} \mathbf{0}_n^{\mathsf{T}} P^{k-1-i} = \pi_0^{\mathsf{T}} H_j^k Q_j = \tilde{p}_k^{\mathsf{T}}.
\end{aligned}$$

Proposition 1 motivates our choice of π_0 as it not only guarantees a necessary condition for exactness, $\|\mathrm{err}_0\|_1 = 0$, but extends it to the first $j-1$ steps.

Definition 2 (Initial exactness). *We call an aggregation* initially exact, *or more precisely,* $(j-1)$-exact, *if $\|\mathrm{err}_k\|_1 = 0$ for $0 \le k \le j-1$.*

Remark 1. Lemma 2 and Proposition 1 imply

$$\|\mathrm{err}_k\|_1 = \left\| \sum_{i=j-1}^{k-1} \pi_0^{\mathsf{T}} H_j^i \left(h_{j,j+1} e_j q_{j+1}^{\mathsf{T}}\right) P^{k-1-i} \right\|_1,$$

providing a closed-form formula for $\|\mathrm{err}_k\|_1$ in Arnoldi aggregations.

Proposition 2. *An Arnoldi aggregation of size j with the Krylov subspace $\mathcal{K}^j(p_0, P)$ being invariant under P is exact.*

Proof. Dynamic-exactness follows by Eq. (2) with invariance of $\mathcal{K}^j(p_0, P)$, and $p_0 = \tilde{p}_0$ follows through Proposition 1.

Theorem 1. *An Arnoldi aggregation of size j is a smallest $(j-1)$-exact aggregation of P and p_0.*

Proof. Assume we are given $P \in \mathbb{R}^{n\times n}$, $p_0 \in \mathbb{R}^n$, and an arbitrary $(j-1)$-exact aggregation with disaggregation matrix A and aggregated transient vectors π_k. Let A_{arn} be the disaggregation matrix of the corresponding Arnoldi aggregation of size j with rows q_i. By initial exactness, we must have for $0 \le k \le j-1$ that $\pi_k^\top A = p_k^\top$. Thus,

$$\begin{aligned} &\operatorname{span}\{\, p_0^\top, \ldots, p_{j-1}^\top \,\} \subseteq \operatorname{rowsp}(A) \\ \Longrightarrow\ &\operatorname{span}\{\, q_1^\top, \ldots, q_j^\top \,\} = \operatorname{span}\{\, p_0^\top, \ldots, p_{j-1}^\top \,\} \subseteq \operatorname{rowsp}(A). \end{aligned}$$

As by definition $\operatorname{rowsp}(A_{\text{arn}}) = \operatorname{span}\{\, q_1^\top, \ldots, q_j^\top \,\}$, the Arnoldi aggregation of size j is indeed of minimal size because $q_1^\top, \ldots, q_j^\top$ are linearly independent.

Theorem 2. *An Arnoldi aggregation of size j with $\mathcal{K}^j(p_0, P)$ being invariant under P is a smallest exact aggregation of P and p_0.*

Proof. Follows analogous to Theorem 1. Given an exact aggregation of arbitrary size m with disaggregation matrix A, we know that $\operatorname{span}\{\, p_0^\top, p_1^\top, \ldots \} \subseteq \operatorname{rowsp}(A)$. As $q_1^\top, \ldots, q_j^\top$ is a basis of $\operatorname{span}\{\, p_0^\top, p_1^\top, \ldots \}$, the Arnoldi aggregation of size j with $q_1^\top, \ldots, q_j^\top$ as rows of the disaggregation matrix is minimal, i.e., $j \le m$.

3.2 Determining Convergence

Recall that in Algorithm 1, we have left the criterion for termination open. Naturally, with the definition of exactness requiring $\|H_j Q_j - Q_j P\|_\infty = 0$ and Eqs. (1) and (2), $\|H_j Q_j - Q_j P\|_\infty = 0$, $|h_{j,j+1}| = 0$, or $\|r_{j+1}\|_1 = 0$ offer themselves as intuitive measurements for detecting exactness.

Unfortunately, none of these approaches work in general, which we illustrate by looking at an example DTMC. The RSVP model is a stochastic process algebra model from [23]. It is composed of a lower channel submodel with capacity M, an upper channel submodel with capacity N, and some instances of mobile nodes making call requests at a constant rate. For $M = 7$, $N = 5$ and three mobile nodes, resulting in 842 states, symmetries among these nodes enable an exact aggregation with $j = 234$ for the DTMC resulting from uniformisation of the original CTMC with uniformisation rate 30.01 [16, Sec. 6.4]. Then, by Theorem 2, Algorithm 1 must find an exact Arnoldi aggregation at size $j = 234$ or lower.

Figure 1 shows the proposed naive termination criteria for $p_0 = (1, 0, \ldots, 0)^\top \in \mathbb{R}^{842}$, for which an exact aggregation as described exists. Note that $|h_{j,j+1}|$ is multiplied by 15 in Fig. 1 simply to match the size of the other two criteria. Since there is obviously no striking behaviour near $j = 234$, these

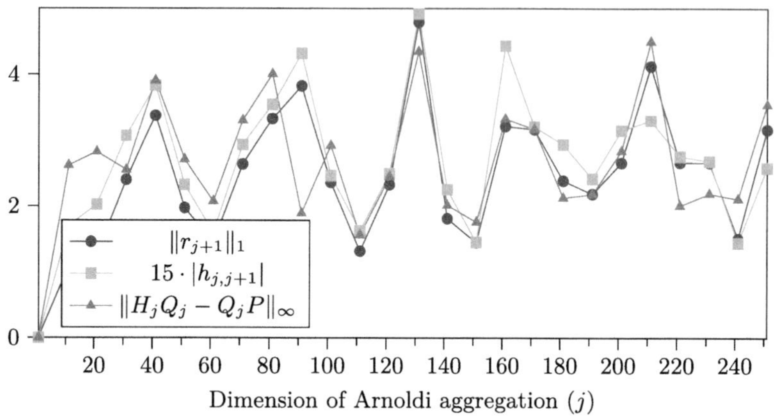

Fig. 1. Different values related to $\|H_jQ_j - Q_jP\|_\infty$ depending on the dimension of Arnoldi aggregations of the RSVP model.

three criteria are not suitable as termination criteria for Fig. 1. Therefore, we must take a different approach altogether.

By [16, Thm. 4 (i)] and Proposition 1, the error bound

$$\|\mathrm{err}_k\|_1 \leq \sum_{j=0}^{k-1} \langle |\pi_k|, |H_jQ_j - Q_jP| \cdot \mathbf{1}_n \rangle \tag{3}$$

holds for all Arnoldi aggregations. Note that, in general, Eq. (3) cannot be improved. Although Eq. (3) offers the tightest general bound, its computational cost is too high for a usable criterion to determine whether to stop the expansion of an Arnoldi aggregation.

For an exact aggregation, it must hold that $\langle |\pi_k|, |H_jQ_j - Q_jP| \cdot \mathbf{1}_n \rangle = 0$ for all k. Under the assumption that $(\pi_k)_{k \in \mathbb{N}}$ converges to an eigenvector π, it must then hold that $\langle |\pi|, |H_jQ_j - Q_jP| \cdot \mathbf{1}_n \rangle = 0$. Importantly, this is not an equivalence and the assumption about the convergence of $(\pi_k)_{k \in \mathbb{N}}$ does not have to hold either. Still, we propose to use $\langle |\pi|, |H_jQ_j - Q_jP| \cdot \mathbf{1}_n \rangle \leq \varepsilon$ for some given $\varepsilon \in \mathbb{R}_0^+$ as a stopping criterion since it appears to work well in practice.

Per [17, Sec. 6.7], the largest eigenvalues of H_j eventually yield very good approximations of the largest eigenvalues of P for large enough j. In this case, both H_j and P, as a transition matrix, will have largest eigenvalue one. Thus, we use the Krylov-Schur method presented in [22] to determine π with eigenvalue one. If there are multiple such π, we choose the one whose eigenvalue is numerically closest to one. If π has complex entries, hinting at improper convergence, we immediately further expand the aggregation. In practice, this happens only at j so small that the resulting aggregation is unusable.

This results in Fig. 2, where we either used random p_0 or initial distributions for which we know that there is an exact aggregation at $j = 234$. Furthermore, we used ten samples per data point and $\varepsilon_{\mathrm{mach}}$ is the IEEE 754 double precision

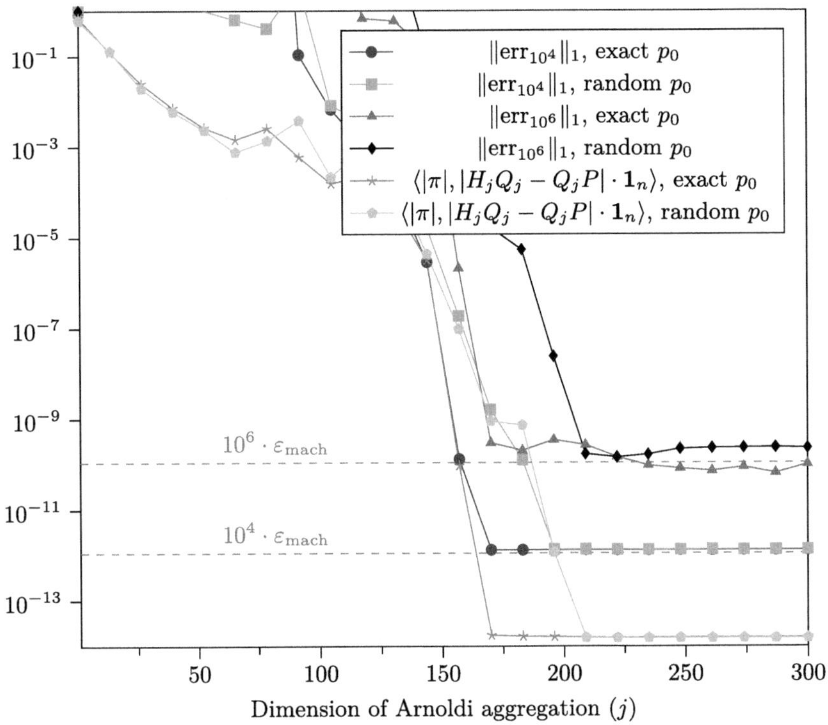

Fig. 2. Proposed convergence criterion and error after 10^4 and 10^6 steps in the RSVP model, depending on the dimension of the Arnoldi aggregation.

rounding machine epsilon. As such, there is a visible correlation between $\|\mathrm{err}_k\|_1$ and $\langle|\pi|, |H_jQ_j - Q_jP| \cdot \mathbf{1}_n\rangle$, although no formal proof or connection between these two is known. Still, over a range of models (see Sect. 4), we were not able to find a case where the general trend, as seen, does not hold.

The algorithm to compute Arnoldi aggregations with $p_k \approx \tilde{p}_k$ is the same as Algorithm 1 but with line 11 replaced, as seen in Algorithm 2. The convergence criterion is naively applied only every tenth expansion to reduce the runtime.

We can also easily analyse the runtime. If P is dense, the vector-matrix multiplication in line 5 is in $\mathcal{O}(n^2)$, if P is sparse, it is in $\mathcal{O}(n)$ instead. The outer for loop is, by definition, repeated j times and the inner one on average $\frac{j}{2}$ times. Furthermore, the inner product in the inner for loop takes $\mathcal{O}(n)$. Thus, without the convergence criterion, we are in $\mathcal{O}(n^2j+nj^2)$ for dense P or $\mathcal{O}(nj^2)$ for sparse P. In the computation needed for the convergence criterion, the calculation of π is the dominant factor. There, the Arnoldi iteration is applied to H_j a finite number of times (independent of H_j and j) with a random starting vector in our implementation. As H_j is dense, this is in $\mathcal{O}(j^2)$. Although further steps are taken to compute π, they all end up in constant time, even though with

Algorithm 2. Finding an Arnoldi aggregation with $\langle |\pi|, |H_j Q_j - Q_j P| \cdot \mathbf{1}_n \rangle \leq \varepsilon$

Let $\varepsilon \in \mathbb{R}_0^+$, $p_0 \in \mathbb{R}^n$, $P \in \mathbb{R}^{n \times n}$.
$q_1 := \frac{p_0}{\|p_0\|_2}$
$Q_1 := \left(- q_1^\mathsf{T} - \right)$
for $j = 1, 2, \ldots$ **do**
    $r_1^\mathsf{T} := q_j^\mathsf{T} P$
    $\ldots$ ▷ *Algorithm 1, lines 6–10*
    if $j \pmod{10} = 0$ **then**
        Compute dominant eigenvector π^T of H_j as in [22]
        $\pi = \frac{\pi}{\|\pi^\mathsf{T} Q_j\|_1}$
        if $\pi \in \mathbb{R}^j$ and $\langle |\pi|, |H_j Q_j - Q_j P| \cdot \mathbf{1}_n \rangle \leq \varepsilon$ **then**
            $\pi_0 := (\|p_0\|_2, 0, \ldots, 0)^\mathsf{T} \in \mathbb{R}^j$
            return H_j, Q_j, π_0, π
    $\ldots$ ▷ *Algorithm 1, lines 12 and 13*

a fairly large constant. Overall, we are in $\mathcal{O}(n^2 j + n j^2 + j^3)$ for dense P and $\mathcal{O}(n j^2 + j^3)$ for sparse P. The memory complexity is the same, asymptotically. In our experience, the bottleneck is the runtime and not the memory requirement.

4 Reviewing Arnoldi Aggregations

Now that we have devised Algorithm 2, evaluating its performance is of great interest. An implementation in Julia (see [4]) version 1.11.2, using the package KrylovKit [10] for the underlying Arnoldi iteration and for the Krylov-Schur method from [22], can be found at [21]. Using this implementation, we compare Algorithm 2 to the Exlump algorithm [16, Algorithm 3]. This algorithm works by forming an explicit partition of the original state space, such that for any two states within the same aggregate, their incoming probabilities are close in some way. We use a so-called uniform disaggregation matrix A in Exlump aggregations, where $A(i, j)$ is the reciprocal of the size of the ith aggregate [16, p. 14].

Apart from the already introduced RSVP model, we compare these two algorithms on a range of Markov chains. For one, we use a Lotka-Volterra model (see [9] for example) with a maximum population of 100, resulting in 10,201 states, which is uniformised at a rate of 2,078. We also look at a Markov chain with 15,540 states, modelling two workstation clusters with 20 workstations per cluster, where each workstation can fail and be repaired [11]. There, the uniformisation rate is 50.08. Finally, our largest Markov chain is given by a prokaryotic gene expression model [12] with a maximal population size of five and a state space of 43,957, uniformised at a rate of 16.78. Note that the Exlump algorithm was implemented in Python, whereas we compute Arnoldi aggregations by using Julia. Thus, runtimes cannot be compared directly between these two.

We compare transient errors of the RSVP model in Fig. 3, where we see that Exlump aggregations perform similarly to Arnoldi aggregations, with the first usable aggregations at $j \approx 130$.

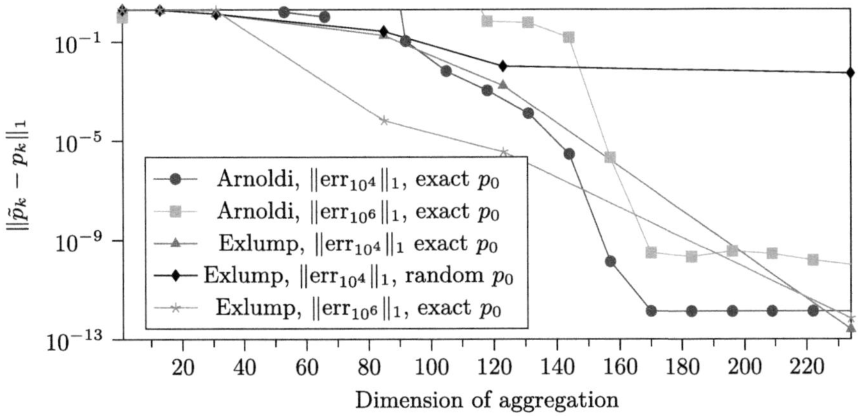

Fig. 3. $\|\mathrm{err}_{10^4}\|_1$ and $\|\mathrm{err}_{10^6}\|_1$ in the RSVP model for Arnoldi and Exlump aggregations, with different initial distributions, depending on the aggregation dimension.

The only exception occurs with random p_0 after 10^4 steps in Exlump aggregations. This is due to Exlump aggregations being formed independently of p_0, but with only specific p_0 enabling exact aggregations.

In contrast to the similar error performance, the runtime analysis in Fig. 4 shows significant differences. Note that the different line heights indicating the time needed to compute p_{10^5} without aggregation are caused by Exlump and Algorithms 1 and 2 being implemented in different programming languages. In Fig. 4 and the following figures, Algorithm 1 is run for some pre-specified number of iterations without any termination criterion. Exlump allows to compute $\tilde{p}_{10^5}$ consistently faster than computing p_{10^5} naively.

While the Exlump algorithm itself is, relatively speaking, faster and scales better for larger aggregation sizes than Algorithms 1 and 2, it also offers a more important advantage: the Π of Exlump aggregations retains the sparsity of P, whereas the H_j of an Arnoldi aggregation is dense by definition. Thus, computing approximated transient distributions is much faster for Exlump aggregations. In comparison, it accounts for around 85% of the total runtime needed to compute $\tilde{p}_{10^5}$ in Arnoldi aggregations. The criterion from Algorithm 2 takes around 12% of the total runtime with the remaining 3% needed for the actual underlying Arnoldi iteration.

We continue with the errors in the workstation cluster model in Fig. 5, where the behaviour is different.

Arnoldi aggregations have already reached their optimum at $j \approx 400$, beating Exlump aggregations by far until their exact aggregation at size 5,523. Notably, in Arnoldi aggregations we consistently have $k\varepsilon_{\mathrm{mach}} \approx \|\mathrm{err}_k\|_1$ for $j \gtrsim 400$, while Exlump aggregations can eventually achieve a lower error. This can be explained by $\tilde{p}_k$ converging toward the actual stationary distribution in Exlump aggregations (because the actual stationary distribution is compatible with the exact aggregation with 5,523 states, see [6, Theorem 3]), which is not guaran-

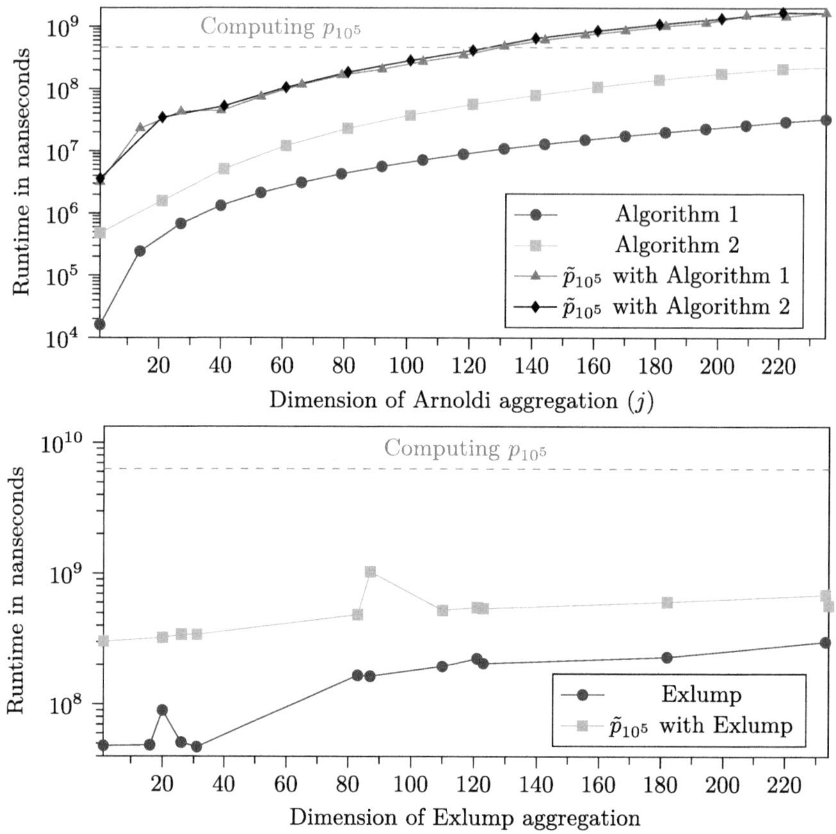

Fig. 4. Runtime of computing Arnoldi and Exlump aggregations of the RSVP model, both with and without computing $\tilde{p}_{10^5}$, depending on the dimension of the aggregations.

teed for Arnoldi aggregations of the size considered here. Generally speaking, random p_0 yield the same effect as shown here for those p_0 which enable an exact aggregation of dimension 5,523.

While computing $\tilde{p}_k$ still takes the most time for the workstation cluster model in Fig. 6 with the Arnoldi aggregation, its share went down to about 45% with the convergence criterion now needing roughly 40% of the total runtime. Still, the results are much better than in the RSVP model.

Exlump aggregations fail to consistently beat the naive approach for computing transient distributions, whereas Algorithm 2 is faster up to $j \approx 400$. An Arnoldi aggregation with $j \approx 300$ has $\|\text{err}_{10^5}\|_1 \approx 10^{-8}$, while being almost four times faster than computing p_{10^5}.

Errors for our largest model, the gene expression model, can be seen in Fig. 7.

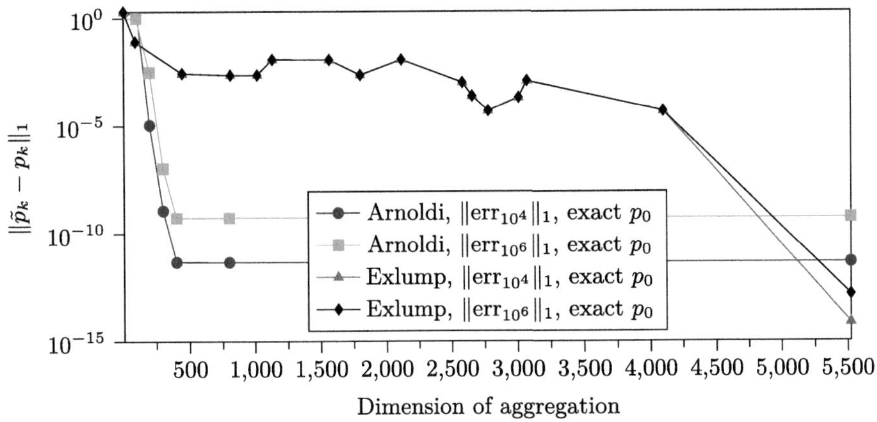

Fig. 5. $\|\mathrm{err}_{10^4}\|_1$ and $\|\mathrm{err}_{10^6}\|_1$ in the workstation cluster model for Arnoldi and Exlump aggregations, depending on the aggregation dimension.

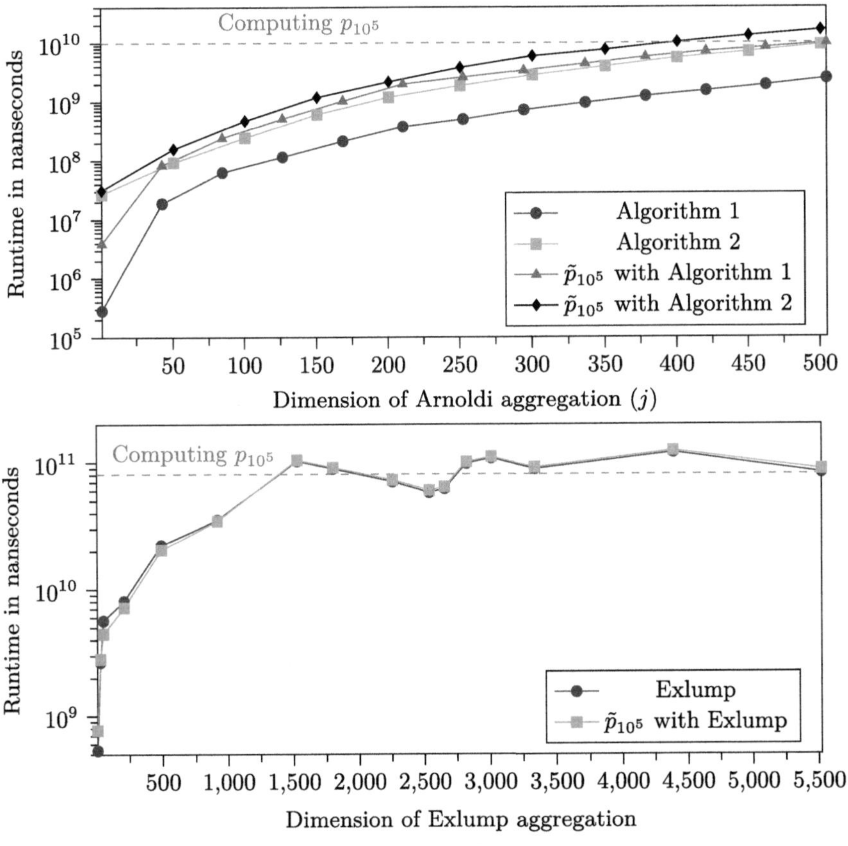

Fig. 6. Runtime of computing Arnoldi and Exlump aggregations of the workstation cluster model, both with and without computing $\tilde{p}_{10^5}$, depending on the dimension of the aggregations.

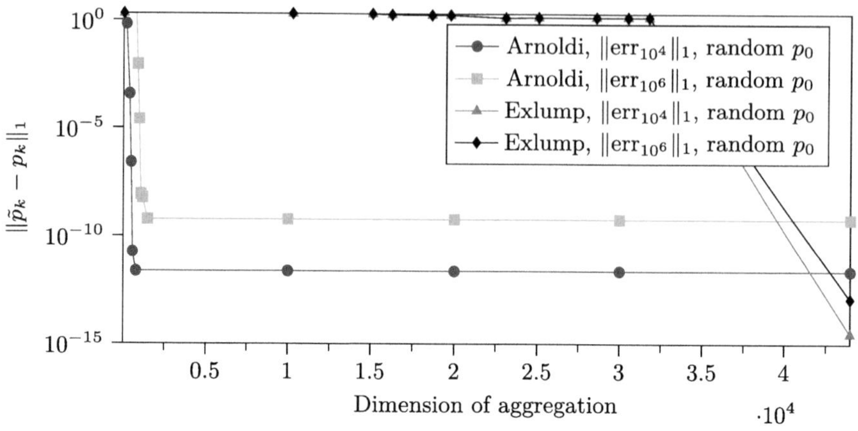

Fig. 7. $\|err_{10^4}\|_1$ and $\|err_{10^6}\|_1$ in the gene expression model for Arnoldi and Exlump aggregations, depending on the aggregation dimension.

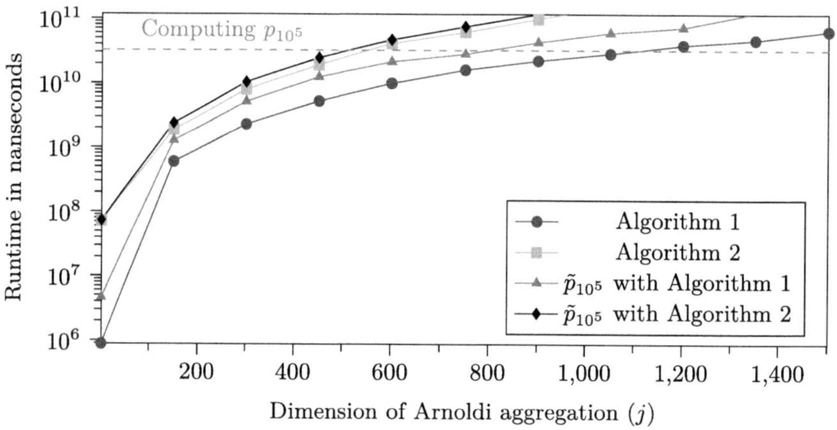

Fig. 8. Runtime of computing Arnoldi aggregations of the gene expression model, both with and without computing $\tilde{p}_{10^5}$, depending on the dimension of the aggregation.

The only usable Exlump aggregation is the one with $j = n$, thus disqualifying Exlump for this model, while Arnoldi aggregations quickly improve and reach their optimum at around $j \approx 1{,}100$, again limited by rounding errors.

The same holds if we look at the runtime needed to reduce the state space of the gene expression model, as in Fig. 8. We did not plot the runtime needed by Exlump aggregations, as they failed to produce any acceptable errors, as seen in Fig. 7.

With such a large model, the dense vector-matrix multiplication forced by a dense H_j in Arnoldi aggregations is no longer dominant. Instead, the convergence criterion takes up most of the runtime, around 75%. $j \approx 450$ is the last dimension of the Arnoldi aggregation where we see a speed-up. However, an error of $\|\mathrm{err}_{10^5}\|_1 \approx 10^{-1}$ at this size makes it irrelevant for practical use.

Lastly, although not plotted, we get to the Lotka-Volterra model. It mirrors the behaviour of the gene expression model at a smaller size, as Exlump again fails to find a usable aggregation except for the trivial aggregation of size n, while Arnoldi aggregations converge very soon, although still too late to be fast enough for practical applications.

5 Conclusion

Results. Definition 1 defines an Arnoldi iteration based aggregation of a DTMC that incorporates the initial distribution p_0. Theorems 1and 2 then show that, under exact arithmetic, any (initially) exact Arnoldi aggregation is of minimal size. In practice, however, numerical instability in the Arnoldi iteration (see Sect. 3.2) prevents exactness. Instead, we adopt the convergence criterion $\langle|\pi|, |H_jQ_j - Q_jP| \cdot \mathbf{1}_n\rangle \leq \varepsilon$, although choosing ε remains heuristic, since no direct bound links $\|\mathrm{err}_k\|_1$ to $\langle|\pi|, |H_jQ_j - Q_jP| \cdot \mathbf{1}_n\rangle$. Empirically, the relationship in Fig. 2 holds across all tested models.

In experiments, small Arnoldi aggregations suffer from dense H_j, such that computing $\tilde{p}_k$ has cost $\mathcal{O}(kj^2)$, whereas computing p_k costs only $\mathcal{O}(kn)$ for sparse P. As the model size grows, computing the eigenvector π of H_j eventually dominates the cost of the dense vector-matrix product. Overall, Algorithm 2 runs in $\mathcal{O}(n^2j + nj^2 + j^3)$ for dense P and in $\mathcal{O}(nj^2 + j^3)$ for sparse ones. Despite these costs, we observed substantial speed-ups at low error bounds for the workstation cluster model, outperforming Exlump aggregations in this case. Moreover, Arnoldi aggregations consistently produce non-trivial aggregations, whereas Exlump sometimes fails to do so.

Outlook. We see several avenues for future work. One is to evaluate our method against additional aggregation techniques (e.g., [1,5,7,16]) over a broader suite of models and a wider range of time points. A second is to speed up Algorithm 2 by dynamically tuning how often the convergence criterion $\langle|\pi|, |H_jQ_j - Q_jP| \cdot \mathbf{1}_n\rangle \leq \varepsilon$ is checked. Expanding on this, when the criterion is first satisfied at dimension $j + \ell$ but not at j, one can exploit the recursive structure of $H_{j+\ell}$ and $Q_{j+\ell}$ along with the Krylov-Schur approach of [22] to identify an intermediate aggregation dimension j' (with $j < j' \leq j + \ell$) that still meets the criterion at lower computational cost for $\tilde{p}_k$. Lastly, the Arnoldi iteration itself could be optimized via parallel or randomized Gram-Schmidt variants (e.g., [3,15]), improved memory management, or integration with high-performance libraries such as ARPACK [14].

References

1. Abate, A., Andriushchenko, R., Češka, M., Kwiatkowska, M.: Adaptive formal approximations of Markov chains. Perform. Eval. **148**, 102207 (2021). https://doi.org/10.1016/j.peva.2021.102207

2. Arnoldi, W.E.: The principle of minimized iterations in the solution of the matrix eigenvalue problem. Q. Appl. Math. **9**(1), 17–29 (1951). https://doi.org/10.1090/qam/42792
3. Balabanov, O., Grigori, L.: Randomized Gram-Schmidt process with application to GMRES. SIAM J. Sci. Comput. **44**(3), A1450–A1474 (2022). https://doi.org/10.1137/20M138870X
4. Bezanson, J., Edelman, A., Karpinski, S., Shah, V.B.: Julia: a fresh approach to numerical computing. SIAM Rev. **59**(1), 65–98 (2017). https://doi.org/10.1137/141000671
5. Bittracher, A., Schütte, C.: A probabilistic algorithm for aggregating vastly undersampled large Markov chains. Physica D: Nonlinear Phenomena **416**, 132799 (2021). https://doi.org/10.1016/j.physd.2020.132799
6. Buchholz, P.: Exact and ordinary lumpability in finite Markov chains. J. Appl. Probab. **31**(1), 59–75 (1994). https://doi.org/10.2307/3215235
7. Buchholz, P., Kriege, J.: Approximate aggregation of Markovian models using alternating least squares. Perform. Eval. **73**, 73–90 (2014). https://doi.org/10.1016/j.peva.2013.09.001
8. Courtois, P.J.: Decomposability: Queueing and Computer System Applications. Academic Press. ACM monograph series (1977). https://doi.org/10.1016/C2013-0-07302-1
9. Gillespie, D.T.: Exact stochastic simulation of coupled chemical reactions. J. Phys. Chem. **81**(25), 2340–2361 (1977). https://doi.org/10.1021/j100540a008
10. Haegeman, J.: KrylovKit (version 0.9.4) (2025). https://doi.org/10.5281/zenodo.14832110
11. Haverkort, B., Hermanns, H., Katoen, J.P.: On the use of model checking techniques for dependability evaluation. In: Proceedings 19th IEEE Symposium on Reliable Distributed Systems SRDS-2000, pp. 228–237 (2000). https://doi.org/10.1109/RELDI.2000.885410
12. Kierzek, A.M., Zaim, J., Zielenkiewicz, P.: The effect of transcription and translation initiation frequencies on the stochastic fluctuations in prokaryotic gene expression. J. Biol. Chem. **276**(11), 8165–8171 (2001). https://doi.org/10.1074/jbc.M006264200
13. Koury, J.R., McAllister, D.F., Stewart, W.J.: Iterative methods for computing stationary distributions of nearly completely decomposable Markov chains. SIAM J. Algebraic Disc. Methods **5**(2), 164–186 (1984). https://doi.org/10.1137/0605019
14. Lehoucq, R., Sorensen, D.C., Yang, C.: ARPACK Users' Guide. Society for Industrial and Applied Mathematics (1998). https://doi.org/10.1137/1.9780898719628
15. Lingen, F.J.: Efficient Gram-Schmidt orthonormalisation on parallel computers. Commun. Numer. Methods Eng. **16**(1), 57–66 (2000). https://doi.org/10.1002/(SICI)1099-0887(200001)16:1<57::AID-CNM320>3.0.CO;2-I
16. Michel, F., Siegle, M.: Formal error bounds for the state space reduction of Markov chains. Perform. Eval. **167**, 102464 (2025). https://doi.org/10.1016/j.peva.2024.102464
17. Saad, Y.: Krylov Subspace Methods, 2 edn., chap. 6, pp. 125–162. Society for Industrial and Applied Mathematics (2011). https://doi.org/10.1137/1.9781611970739.ch6
18. de Souza e Silva, E., Gail, H.R.: Transient Solutions for Markov Chains, pp. 43–79. Springer US, Boston (2000). https://doi.org/10.1007/978-1-4757-4828-4_3
19. Simon, H.A., Ando, A.: Aggregation of variables in dynamic systems. Econometrica **29**(2), 111–138 (1961). https://doi.org/10.2307/1909285

20. Sonnentag, P.: Finding the smallest possible exact aggregation of a Markov chain (2025). https://doi.org/10.48550/arXiv.2507.11157
21. Sonnentag, P.: MarkovChainAggregations (version 0.1.0) (2025). https://doi.org/10.5281/zenodo.16082617
22. Stewart, G.W.: A Krylov-Schur algorithm for large eigenproblems. SIAM J. Matrix Anal. Appl. **23**(3), 601–614 (2002). https://doi.org/10.1137/S0895479800371529
23. Wang, H., Laurenson, D.I., Hillston, J.: Evaluation of RSVP and mobility-aware RSVP using performance evaluation process algebra. In: 2008 IEEE International Conference on Communications, pp. 192–197 (2008). https://doi.org/10.1109/ICC.2008.43

Efficient Agent Based Simulation Exploiting the Model Structure

Marzio Pennisi[1], Giuliana Franceschinis[1(✉)], Davide Cerotti[1], Lorenzo Capra[2], and Massimiliano De Pierro[3]

[1] DISIT, Computer Science Institute, Università del Piemonte Orientale, Alessandria, Italy
{marzio.pennisi,giuliana.franceschinis,davide.cerotti}@uniupo.it
[2] Dipartimento di Informatica, Università degli Studi di Milano, Milano, Italy
lorenzo.capra@unimi.it
[3] Dipartimento di Informatica, Università di Torino, Torino, Italy
massimiliano.depierro@unito.it

Abstract. Agent Based Models (ABM) simulation supports the study of systems whose overall evolution emerges from the behavior of several interacting agents. In [6] a compositional method based on the meta-formalism Agent Based Extended Stochastic Symmetric Nets (AB-ESSN) has been proposed to build ABMs that are then simulated in continuous time according to a next event time advance algorithm. In [22] a structure-based approach has been proposed to improve ABM simulation efficiency, leveraging the possibility of exploiting structural properties of Symmetric Nets (SN) to identify the interdependencies among the agents' actions. The approach is now facilitated by the tool SNexpression and its recently added module [15,16] supporting the computation of all dependency relations on a SN. In this paper, the possibility of automatizing the ABM simulation optimization process, thanks to the new features of the SNexpression tool, is discussed through an example.

Keywords: Agent Based Modeling · Simulation · Structural Analysis · Symmetric Nets · NetLogo

1 Introduction

Agent Based Models (ABMs) enable the representation and simulation of systems where the overall behavior emerges from that of several similarly behaving agents. The possibility of describing the system from the point of view of agents allows us to capture information that could be lost if a more abstract representation is used.

An open issue related to the ABM languages and tools concerns the lack of formalization of the semantics guiding the simulation algorithm: most ABM simulation tools and frameworks assume discrete time and use a fixed interval time advance approach (FITA), but each simulation tool handles the order in which

A. Remke et al. (Eds.): Valuetools 2025, LNICST 691, pp. 120–139, 2027.
https://doi.org/10.1007/978-3-032-23901-3_8

the agents' actions and interactions occur at each time step differently, possibly introducing arbitrary rules when the model entails some non deterministic choice. A less common approach used in ABM simulation is the next event time advance (NETA) approach, assuming continuous time. This approach has been considered more appropriate in [27] and in [19], where the stochastic process underlying the ABM model is precisely defined and the choices are determined by the occurrence time of the scheduled events.

In [6], we presented an ABM formalism (called AB-ESSN, Agent Based-Extended Stochastic Symmetric Nets) and a NETA simulation approach that was shown to provide coherent results when compared to other more abstract models and simulation approaches [5]. The provided well-defined semantics for the models and the simulation algorithm ensure clarity, consistency, and verifiability of the models.

However, one Achilles' heel of this approach is the fact that as the number of agents grows, the simulation could pose efficiency problems. More specifically, the proposed simulation approach imposes the recalculation of all action rates after each state change, resulting in rather inefficient performance. This problem can be faced with different methods, for example trying to exploit specific properties of the model, as, e.g., in [21,24] and [20], or by exploiting parallelism, e.g. through FlameGPU as discussed in [18,23] and in [8].

The former approach has been applied in [24] to Agent-Based Models (ABMs) in the ML3 Domain Specific Language (DSL) [25]; this work uses a NETA approach in continuous time as in our case. In [21], an optimization taking into account dependencies between state transition rules was introduced dynamically in the MASON ABM framework using Aspect-Oriented Programming (AOP); while flexible and successful at exploiting locality, this incurs an overhead that reduces performance compared to manually optimized code. More recently an embedding of the ML3 DSL into Rust [20] allowed to obtain an improvement in simulation times while keeping the advantages of a DSL and the full power of the Rust programming language.

The approach that leverages parallelism exploits instead multi-core architectures to accelerate the execution of agents' actions. Most implementations in this domain utilize a FITA method, where all agents execute actions within predefined, discrete time steps. A prominent example is FlameGPU, which harnesses GPU computing to simulate the interactions and actions of millions of agents concurrently at each time-step. Agents in this framework are represented by X-machines (finite-state automata extended with message passing for communication/interaction). To facilitate model development within this ecosystem, Beccuti et al. [8] developed a graphical framework. Crucially, recent work has demonstrated the feasibility of implementing our NETA simulation algorithm, originally proposed in [5,6], atop the FlameGPU platform [23]. This integration provides a significant optimization: the computationally intensive re-computation of agent rates is efficiently parallelized by exploiting the massive processing capabilities of the GPU.

Other strategies that leverage the use of parallel simulation for NETA models have been presented in [7], where the authors showed how some synchronous optimistic synchronization approaches, closely related to the breathing time buckets algorithm [26], may efficiently exploit the processing power of CPUs and GPUs. It is worth noting that adopting such high-performance approaches necessitates the availability of specialized hardware and requires developers to master some specific languages and modeling frameworks.

Another approach that can be applied when the number of agents is very large, consists of approximating the discrete agents count with a continuous value, and expressing the possible state evolution of the agents through differential equations. The mean field method [10] focuses on a particular tagged entity, and replaces all the interactions with the other entities with an average interaction. Asymptotic results enable the analysis of systems where the number of entities approaches infinity and provide an approximation when the number of entities is large. In the case of Markovian Agent Model [11,17], each of these entity is represented by a finite-state Continuous Time Markov Chain over which a transition kernel is defined. Agents are located in a space and both their local properties and mutual interactions may depend on their positions. In this way, the individuality of each entity is modeled, but at the same time its interaction with the whole system. The temporal evolution of the average numbers of agent in a given state for every location is obtained with a mean field approximation.

The approach proposed in this paper is based on the observation that, typically, state changes in ABM involve only the agent selected for the next action and, at most, a limited number of other agents, usually those in its neighborhood. Thus, the execution of a single action leads to a state change in the system that is, in some sense, "local". To improve the simulation performance, we decided to exploit this "locality" property by applying structural analysis methods to the AB-ESSN model structure, in order to derive expressions representing the dependency relationships between agents' actions. The SNexpression tool implements the required structural analysis computation through algebraic manipulation of the functions appearing on the arcs of AB-ESSN models: in particular, recent developments of the tool [15] that automatize the calculation of all dependencies (expressed in a symbolic form) on the whole net allowed us to define a general procedure for the (semi-)automatic generation of optimized NetLogo code, going one step forward with respect to [22].

The rest of the paper includes: in Sect. 2 the informal definition of the AB-ESSN formalism and comprises an example model used also for the experiments; in Sect. 3 the definition of the structural dependencies allowing to detect the scope of the agents' actions influence, followed by a brief introduction on the SNexpression tool, with it recently implemented matrix calculus operating on the whole net, and an example of application of the implemented calculus on the example AB-ESSN model. Section 4 explains the translation of the AB-ESSN model into an optimized Netlogo simulation model. The results of the experiments illustrating the improvement of the simulation execution times due to the code optimization are reported in Sect. 5. Finally, conclusions and ideas for future work are presented in Sect. 6.

2 The AB-ESSN Formalism

We recall here some key concepts concerning ABMs, the AB-ESSN formalism, and the mapping of an AB-ESSN model and the corresponding ABM.

An ABM is defined as a set of agent types, which categorize the different kinds of agents in the model; a set of primitive types, representing basic data types like integers or strings that describe agent characteristics; a set of agent features (attributes), where each feature has a type from the primitive types and a specific set of features is linked to each agent type. The potential configurations of an agent are derived from the possible values that its associated features can take. The definition also includes a set of interaction/transition rules, which are split into those describing actions driven purely by an agent's internal state and those describing interactions between agents. Each rule is defined by two parts: a function that determines its occurrence probability or rate, which can depend on the agents' states and is zero if preconditions are not met, and a definition of the state changes that occur when the rule is executed, potentially even creating or removing agents. These changes are essentially functions that map the current states of the involved agents to their new states (or a 'null' state if an agent is removed). Finally, an initial subset of agents is defined, along with their internal configurations, to obtain the initial condition for the simulation.

The AB-ESSN formalism has been defined in [6] as an extension of ESSNs (an high level Stochastic Petri Net formalism, whose transition instances are timed, and the associated delay is an exponentially distributed random variable) to specify a set of agents and their behavior according to a compositional approach; added values of the AB-ESSN formalism are the graphical representation of the agents and their behavior, and its role as an intermediate description language that can be translated into an ABM programming language (such as Netlogo). Morover, its structure can be exploited to speed up the simulation, as we shall see in a later section. An example AB-ESSN model is presented in Sect. 2.1. The different agent types are described by labeled ESSN submodels that are then composed by merging labeled transitions which represent interactions between agents. The places in each submodel represent the possible states for the corresponding agent type, while the tuples associated with tokens in such places represent agents with a unique identity and other attributes (the places color domain, defined as Cartesian product of so called color classes, specify the type of each attribute). The transitions represent events responsible for state changes in one or more agents; transitions representing interactions involve more than one agent, in this case a leader agent is chosen. The complete AB-ESSN model is obtained by applying the unary conjugate composition of the submodels on labeled transitions [3].

The translation from an AB-ESSN model into a NetlogoABM works as follows: each color class that identifies agents of a specific type in the AB-ESSN becomes an agent type in the ABM. Other color classes become primitive types. The places whose color domains include an agent ID class correspond to a feature in the ABM that represents the agent's current state (which place it is in). The places themselves become the possible values for this state feature. Any other color classes within a place's color domain are translated into additional agent features. An agent's full configuration is then defined by its state (place) and these other features. Every transition in the ESSN is translated into an action in the ABM. The preconditions for a rule are determined by the transition's color domain, guard, and the expressions on its input arcs. Each transition instance requires specific sets of agents, identified by functions on input arcs, to be in particular states and have certain feature values that match the transition variables and guard conditions. The number and types of agents affected by a rule depend on the input and output arc expressions. If the same agent ID variable appears on both an input and an output arc of a transition, the rule will change that agent's internal state, i.e. the place where it is located, and/or the value of the other token color elements that represent additional attributes of the agent. Interaction transitions, which involve more than one agent, are central to inter-agent dynamics. An agent is typically designated as the leading participant responsible for executing the rule, while others are 'passive'. The guard conditions of these interaction transitions might reference variables from transitions with which they will be composed, and the agent identity variables must be distinct for the different agents involved. This algorithm is currently implemented in GreatSPN3 [4] and allows us to produce models that can be executed in Netlogo.

The simulation process of the ABM resulting from the translation makes use of a Next-Event-Time-Advance algorithm in continuous time and it is composed of two main steps. First, it calculates the individual (agent) rates at which rules could occur for each agent by checking preconditions and computing rates. Second, it selects the next agent and rule to be executed based on these rates (using a roulette-wheel method) and then applies the state changes defined by the chosen rule.

2.1 An Example: the SEIRS Epidemic Model

To show the proposed methodology for determining structural properties and their application in optimizing Agent-Based Model (ABM) simulation time, we refer to the SEIRS model illustrated in Fig. 1. This established epidemiological model, previously modeled using the AB-ESSN formalism in [6,9] represents the propagation of infections within a population. The model includes a single agent type that may be in one of four distinct states: Susceptible (`S`), Exposed (`E`), Infected (`I`), Recovered (`R`) and Dead (`D`). These states are formally encoded as places within the model. Each agent is represented by a token and has three discrete attributes: a unique identifier (id), age, and spatial position, encoded as colors A, B, and Z, respectively. The agent id attribute is limited to be unique across the entire model. Agents in the `S` state can move to a different random position via the `MoveS` transition, or change their state to `E` after the firing of transition `Infection`, modeling the interaction with an `I` agent located at the same position. Similarly, exposed agents can move towards a different random location by the `MoveE` transition, or progress to the `I` state upon completion of the incubation period, represented by the `EndIncubation` transition. Infected agents can move to a different random position via the `MoveI` transition, can die at different age-dependent rates by firing of transition `Death`, and recover from infection progressing to state `Recovered` (transition `Recovery`). Finally, recovered agents can revert to the `S` state through the `EndImmunity` transition due to a loss of immunity.

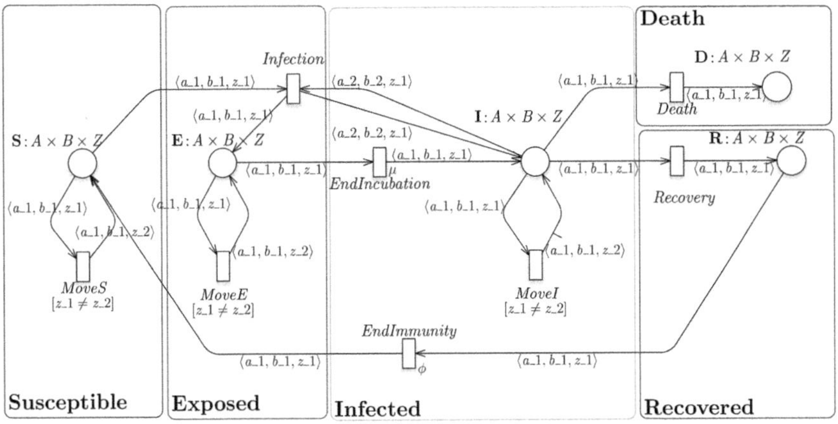

Fig. 1. The SEIRS infection model in the ESSN formalism.

The places represent the possible discrete states that an agent can occupy. Each distinct agent type possesses a unique and disjoint set of states. Furthermore, each agent type is associated with a specific color class, which serves to represent the unique identifiers of individual agents within that type. This color class is consequently incorporated into the color domain of all places associated with the corresponding agent type. The SEIRS example models a system with a single agent type hence there is only one color class of agent's unique identifiers: A. Transitions represent the actions executable by agents. Transitions are enabled according to their input arcs, and their firing removes colored tokens in their input places and puts them into their output places, according to the corresponding arc functions. Arc functions are denoted by expressions that take the form of tuples $\langle f_1, \dots f_k \rangle$ where the tuple elements f_i are class functions. The only type of class function present in the SEIRS example is *projection*, denoted by a transition variable v_i. For example, the input arc function of the `MoveS` transition is $\langle a\_1, b\_1, z\_1 \rangle$ and the output arc function is $\langle a\_1, b\_1, z\_2 \rangle$. Thus, the color domain of `MoveS` transition is $A \times B \times Z \times Z$ and a specific colored transition instance $\langle a\_1, b\_1, z\_1, z\_2 \rangle$ is enabled when in state `S` there is a colored token with id $a\_1 \in A$, age $b\_1 \in B$ at location $z\_1 \in Z$. The firing of such an instance puts a colored token $\langle a\_1, b\_1, z\_2 \rangle$ in place S, with $z\_1 \neq z\_2$ due to the guard $[z\_1 \neq z\_2]$ associated with the transition.

Transitions involving only a single agent are characterized by a color domain containing a single variable whose type is an agent id color class. These represent *internal actions* that an agent can directly execute without interactions with other agents. In contrast, transitions featuring multiple variables corresponding to distinct agent ids denote an *interaction among different agents*: for instance transition `Infection` representing the interaction between a susceptible and an infected agent, has two variables a_1 and a_2 of type A, and either can be the leader of the interaction. For every action or interaction, a designated leader agent is predetermined, which is responsible for calculating the action rate and executing the action upon selection. While the selection of a leader for multi-agent interactions is arbitrary, structural dependencies within the system may support the most appropriate choice. To complete the model one should specify the initial state of the agents: the only constraint on the state is that it is not possible to have the same agent identifier repeated in more than one place (it is possible to prove that if this is true in the initial state, it is true also in all the other reachable states).

3 Net-Wise Structural Dependencies Calculation

The specific syntax of Symmetric Nets (including AB-ESSNs) allows to exploit symmetry properties due to the similar behavior of the entities represented in these models by "colors". In the specific context of AB-ESSNs, the colors represent the agents' identities and their attributes.

The development of symbolic structural analysis for SNs has progressed over the past two decades. Theoretical foundations are based on [13], where a language is defined ($\mathfrak{L}$) as a minor extension of SN arc functions. The terms of $\mathfrak{L}$ resemble the functions that label the edges of SN, with the added functionality of employing guards as prefixes (called *filters*) and incorporating intersections of base color functions within tuples. An example of expression in $\mathfrak{L}$ with domain $C \times C$, where C is a color class partitioned into two or more sublcasses C_i, is[1] $[x_1 \neq x_2]\langle S, S_1 \cap (S - x_2), x_1 \rangle$, which maps a pair $(c_1, c_2) \in C \times C$ to a set of triplets $\{(c, c', c_1)\}$, where c' corresponds to any color of the subclass C_1 excluding c_2, and c denotes any color other than c' (due to the filter $[x_1 \neq x_2]$ on the left of the fuction-tuple, used to select from the result of the function-tuple only the triplets whose first two elements are different; hence the x_i symbols in the filter do not refer to the transition variables, but to the position of the elements of the triplets in the multiset returned by the function-tuple.). The results presented in [13] demonstrate the closure of $\mathfrak{L}$ under a fundamental set of functional operators (sum, difference, intersection, transpose, composition) used in structural analysis. With the aid of these operators, we can algebraically compute fundamental structural relationships in SNs, such as conflict, causality, and mutual exclusion,

[1] S/S_i is a constant function returning the whole set C/subset C_i.

eliminating the need for unfolding, and we can also verify symbolic (colored) invariants. The SNexpression software [14], which is a CLI based on a scalable Java library, facilitates the application of algebraic structural calculus for SN. For example, the (asymmetric) structural conflict between transition t and t' due to a shared input place p (in our example model, there are no inhibitor arcs so, for simplicity, we do not consider them) is obtained by calculating the following symbolic expression: $SC_p(t_1, t_2) : \mathcal{D}(t_2) \rightarrow 2^{\mathcal{D}(t_1)} = \overline{I(p, t_1) \ominus O(p, t_1)}' \circ \overline{I(p, t_2)}$, where $\mathcal{D}(.)$ denotes a color domain. Let us interpret it as follows:

- For a specific color instance of t_2, the expression $\overline{I(p, t_2)}$ yields the colors that should be in p for it to be enabled;
- For a specific instance of t_1, $\overline{I(p, t_1) \ominus O(p, t_1)}$ yields the colors it withdraws from p; its transpose (denoted by the operator $'$), given a color in p, identifies the instances of t_1 that withdraw it from p.

In the above expressions, the overline support operator is used to pass from a multiset expression to a set expression, both of which are compatible with SNexpression. The symbol $\ominus$ denotes the multiset difference (eliminating negative terms).

By summating $SC_p(t_1, t_2)$ in all input places in common between t_1 and t_2, we derive the formula for $SC(t_1, t_2)$. Using the SNexpression rewriting engine, this ultimately leads to a term in $\mathcal{L}$, offering an intuitive parametric representation of the set of t_1 instances that can potentially prevent the occurrence of any instance of t_2 in a marking. The SNexpression CLI provides predefined symbols to directly infer SC, SSC (causal connection), and SME (mutual exclusion) between transition pairs.

3.1 The SNexpression Tool

SNexpression [1,15] is an interactive tool for the structural analysis of SNs through a command-line interface (CLI). The software has a layered architecture whose foundations consist in an implementation of an algebraic calculus (LSC) for solving high level expressions used both in SN structural properties formulae and by structural analysis algorithms. The operands of these expressions are SN arc functions and the operators consist in a limited set of operators on functions. The solving engine of the LSC operates without *unfolding* the high level expressions into a scalar calculus, but by manipulating functions as symbols.

The top-most layer of the software is a CLI. It allows the user to solve any calculation based on SN functions, with their structured syntax, and a set of basic operators, namely, they are: the sum and difference (+, −) the composition (.), the support (<<.>>), the transposition ('), and the intersection (∩).

The mid-layers of the software, also accessible via CLI commands, provide higher level methods allowing to compute basic SN structural relations between SN transitions, namely they are: the conflict (SC), several forms of causal connection (SCC), and the mutual exclusion (SME). Let us here discuss SC and SCC, indirectly used in support of ABM simulation. $SC(t, t', p)$, with $t, t' \in T, p \in P$, is a function mapping a color instance (t', c) to the set of color instances of t whose firing could *disable* it, due to sharing of place p. For instance, in the SEIRS model, $SC(MoveE, EndIncubation, E)$ is a function providing the instances of $MoveE$ that disable a given instance of $EndIncubation$, due to a zone migration of an agent that is in state E. Using the CLI the user can compute the relationship with the built-in expression-solving command `solve` , applied to the formula `<<I(MoveE,E)-O(Move,E)>>'.<<I(EndIncubation,E)>>` , or directly with the built-in function `SC(MoveE,EndIncubation,E)` . The causal connection $SCC(t, t', p)$, instead, is a function mapping a color instance (t', c) to the set of color instances of t whose firing could *enable* it, due to sharing of place p. For instances, in the SEIRS model, when $MoveE$ fires for a given instance (modeling an agent that change zone) enables also given instance of $EndIncubation$. The following CLI command can be used to compute the relationship: `solve(<<O(MoveE,E)-I(Move,E)>>'.<<I(EndIncubation,E)>>)` , or directly with `SCC(MoveE,EndIncubation,E)` .

A comprehensive documentation of legacy functionalities can be found in the SNexpression's manual, also available on the dedicated web page [1].

SNexpression is implemented in Java and is freely distributed. The LSC is also distributed as a standalone jar file so that programmers can use it in other projects. The tool-set and the LSC API are available at [1]. The LSC sources are available at [2].

3.2 Matrix Calculus

A recent release [15] improved SNexpression by representing SN structural relationships throughout the model. Previously, the user could only compute relationships for pairs of transitions of interest. For this purpose, the algebraic structural calculus for SN has been broadened to operate at the matrix level. A *net relationship* R on the nodes of an SN is represented by a bidimensional matrix such that an element $R[i, j]$ is an expression that denotes the corresponding relationship between the color instances of node i-th and node j-th (nodes are identified by integer indexes). $R[i, j]$ is a mapping $\mathcal{D}(j) \rightarrow 2^{\mathcal{D}(i)}$. Let $\mathcal{R}$ be the set of net structural relationships in an SN model: Several operators are defined in $\mathcal{R}$, they are $\{+, -, \circ, ', *, s, \hat{}\}$, that is respectively, the union, the difference, the composition, the transposition, the transitive closure, the symmetric closure, and the power. Each operation in $\mathcal{R}$ is translated into one or more matrix operations.

The built-in net relationships belonging to $\mathcal{R}$ implemented in the current release are: I, O, and H, are the *supports* of the input, output and inhibition SN's arc functions, respectively, and are $|P| \times |T|$ matrices; SC (Structural Conflict), SSC (Symmetric SC), SCC (Structural Causal Connection), and SME (Structural Mutual Exclusion), are the basic form of structural relationships between transitions, and are $|T| \times |T|$ matrices; DP is a general form of dependency among transitions, and is again a $|T| \times |T|$ matrix; finally $\mathtt{1}_{|T| \times |T|}$ is the identity. By means of these operators, the user can define new structural relations starting from the built-in ones, and through symbol definition assign them a name.

To support ABM simulation two new built-in relations expressing local dependencies have been added, namely they are LD1 and LD2. Their semantics is discussed in the next section.

The theoretical background of the SN matrix calculus is given in [16].

3.3 Exploiting the Matrix Calculus in the AB-ESSN Model

In [22], we examined how ESSN structural analysis, particularly focused on relations SC and SCC, can improve the efficiency of simulating related ABMs by using the locality of state changes inherent in realistic models. The principle is to recompute rates (which significantly affects simulation times) only for agents within a certain "vicinity" of the agent that executed the most recent event. The concept of a neighborhood is precisely instantiated through the above-mentioned relations. An algorithm is proposed that includes this optimization based on SC and SCC in a semi-automated and somehow heuristic way.

In the following, we explain how the new facilities for matrix calculus recently included in SNexpression can significantly speed up the derivation of the structural dependencies needed in optimization (based on the transposing of the expressions SC and SCC and their composition with the input arc functions) and facilitate integration between tools.

We also discuss the ability to check the satisfaction of the constraints implicitly posed on the AB-ESSN model by invariant verification with SNexpression.

Structural Optimization of Simulation. To illustrate how the structural calculus provided in the SNexpression tool can be used in this context, let us look at the SEIRS. Considering that agent $\langle a_1, b_1, z_1\rangle$ is in place $\mathbf{E}$ (exposed), two events can occur that would change its state or its attributes: respectively, they are $EndIncubation$ and $MoveE$. If event $EndIncubation$ occurs, the agent's state changes to $\mathbf{I}$ (infected); moreover, in the new state event $MoveE$ can no longer occur to the agent, as well $EndIncubation$. The event list associated with agent $\langle a_1, b_1, z_1\rangle$ must be updated accordingly. Being more general, we can determine the instances of $MoveE$ influenced by the event $EndIncubation$ computing the set $A = \mathrm{SC}'(MoveE, EndIncubation, \mathbf{E})(\langle a_1, b_1, z_1\rangle)$, these are the instances of $MoveE$ whose rates must be recomputed. The agents in state $\mathbf{E}$ affected by these events are then obtained evaluating the input function on A: $\bar{\mathrm{I}}(\mathbf{E}, MoveE)(A)$. Formally, the following two structural relations (respectively for the SCC and SC forms of dependency) will provide the information needed to optimize the simulation.

$$\mathrm{LD1}_{p_i}(k,j) = \bar{\mathrm{I}}(p_i, t_k) \circ \mathrm{SC}'(t_k, t_j, p) \text{ for each } k, j \tag{1}$$

$$\mathrm{LD2}_{p_i}(k,j) = \bar{\mathrm{I}}(p_i, t_k) \circ \mathrm{SCC}'(t_k, t_j, p) \text{ for each } k, j \tag{2}$$

SNexpression has been extended with the two built-in matrix relations LD1 and LD2. They succinctly encapsulate all potential dependencies locally induced by the firing of a transition instance (representing an action by an agent).

According to the interpretation of the relation SC (SCC) and the transposition/composition of the matrices, the element $\text{LD1}_{p_i}[k, j]$ ($\text{LD2}_{p_i}[k, j]$), is a function that provides for a given color instance c of the transition t_j, the tokens in place p_i that are required by any transition t_k instance that is in conflict (causal connection) with (t_j, c). When (t_j, c) denotes the action of a leader agent, the aggregate of the two contributions delineates the potential set of agents (in place p_i) for which a recalculation of the firing rates is necessary after the execution of action (t_j, c).

Validation Through Invariants. Using the matrix composition (and the difference), we can verify symbolically invariant properties that hold on reachable markings. The simplest are (P-)semiflows[2]. Formally, a candidate semiflow PINV is a vector of size $|P|$ such that PINV$[i]$ is a function $\mathcal{D}(p_i) \to \text{Bag}(\mathcal{D}')$, where $\mathcal{D}'$ if built from color classes of place domains. A semiflow is a "positive" solution of the homogeneous system:

$$\text{PINV}_{1\times|P|} \cdot (\text{O} - \text{I})_{|P|\times|T|} = 0_{1\times|T|}$$

where in subscripts we have indicated the dimensions of the elements. Observe that the operations apply to "generalized" multisets, which allow the inclusion of negative terms. The definition of generalized composition is given in [12] and will eventually be incorporated into SNexpression.

In ABM-ESSN models, places represent the different states of an agent, and each agent type has its own distinct set of places. A color class is linked to each agent type (which represents the agents' unique identifiers) and is included in the color domain for every place related to that particular agent type. The SEIRS example is limited to a single agent type. These models implicitly require that agent identifiers must be distinct and that, across all reachable markings, each agent can appear as a token in only one place.

This implicit constraint matches the following potential semiflows, one for each agent type A_i and relative set P_i of places:

$$\text{PINV}_i[j] = \begin{cases} \langle a^i \rangle & if\ p_j \in P_i \\ 0 & if\ p_j \notin P_i \end{cases}$$

where the symbol a^i denotes the projection $\mathcal{D}(p_{i_j}) \to A_i$

In the context of the SEIRS model, where each place uniformly represents the same type of agent A, the superscript can be omitted for simplicity. It becomes apparent that PINV $= [a, \ldots, a]_{|P|}$ constitutes a semi-flow. The current version of SNexpression does not provide the capability to directly define a matrix of functions, so, at present, the multiplication in PINV.(O − I) is verified through a separate formula for each vector element.

Let us show the verification of PINV in column $Infection$. Let C be O − I, then $\text{C}[S, Infection] = -\langle a_1, b_1, z_1 \rangle$, $\text{C}[I, Infection] = \langle a_2, b_2, z_1 \rangle - \langle a_2, b_2, z_1 \rangle = 0$, $\text{C}[E, Infection] = \langle a_1, b_1, z_1 \rangle$, and $\text{C}[., Infection] = 0$ elsewhere. Since

[2] We can check more general invariants using the other operators.

PINV.C $= \langle a \rangle.C[S, Infection] + \langle a \rangle.C[E, Infection] = -\langle a_1 \rangle + \langle a_1 \rangle = 0$, the semiflow is verified for $Infection$. The same procedure must be repeated for each column (transition).

The reader can find at the SNexpression's webpage [1], section "Documentation and sample files", both the SEIRS model in the SNexpression format and a notebook reporting the commands here illustrated.

4 Discussion About Automatic Translation of Dependency Expressions Into Netlogo Code

To detail the proposed structural optimizations, we will first summarize the translation of an AB-ESSN into a NetLogo agent-based model. Each colored instance representing an agent's ID is defined as a new agent within the NetLogo model. The agent's state encapsulates the place where the agent instance currently resides, along with other variables describing its characteristics (e.g. in case of the SEIRS model the agent age and position) as defined in the AB-ESSN model. Agent's state is updated by firing rules, which can be local (involving only the agent itself) or interaction-based, where a 'leader' agent actively executes the rule and requests participation from other 'passive' agents. The simulation progresses iteratively: for each agent and its enabled rules, the corresponding rates are calculated and stored in an array called 'myrate'. A specific agent and rule are then chosen using a roulette-wheel selection, weighted by the computed rates. The chosen rule is executed, changing the internal states of the involved active and passive agents, and the current simulation time is updated with respect to the global rate of the enabled rules; more details can be found in [6].

In the original algorithm, at each iteration the rates of all rules were recomputed; however, exploiting the structural relations in Eq. 1 and 2, and keeping track in the 'myrate' array of the rules requiring rate recalculation, the complexity of the simulation can be reduced. For example, in the SEIRS model, such an array will include elements identifying all the possible actions (`Infection`, `EndIncubation`, `Recovery`, `EndImmunity`, `MoveS`, `MoveE`, `MoveI`, `Death`). Considering the place in which the agent currently resides, only some actions will be enabled, e.g., an agent in the `I` (infected) place will not be able to execute the EndImmunity transition that can be executed only by agents that are in the REC place. Thus, the array 'myrate' can be filled in the following way: If the item myrate(i) $= 0 \rightarrow$ the action cannot be executed by the agent in such place; If the item myrate(i) $=$ k $(> 0) \rightarrow$ the action can be potentially executed with rate k; Furthermore, we add here the possibility to have "myrate(i) $= -1$", meaning that the rate for the action i needs to be recalculated. In this way, at each iteration only agents that have some "-1" in their myrate array will re-calculate the rates for such actions. As a consequence of that, for each place describing an agent sub-state, and considering also its features, it is possible, exploiting the net structure, to define a template array (composed only by either 0 or -1) to reset the agents possible actions (whose rate needs to be recalculated) and incompatible actions. Such templates can be used to reset the myrate array when an agent moves from a place to another (meaning a state change, for instance, an exposed that becomes infected after the EndIncubation action) or at the beginning of the simulation to initialize the possible actions according to the place where agents are.

So, in NetLogo new global variables *Pi_template* have to be added and, at the end of the setup procedure, the following code must be inserted.

```
set Pi_template  (list   0 0 -1 -1 ...)

;; Here Pi identifies a given place Pi for which a template is
available. For this example the first two actions cannot be executed,
the third and the fourth need rate recalculation.
...
let allAgents  (turtle-set AgentFamily1,
AgentFamily2, AgentFamily3...)

;;We will select all the agent families

ask allAgents  with [place = Pi][set
myrate Pi_template   set totrate 0.0 ]

;; we initialize the myrate array for all the agents in the place P_i
according to the template and we also initialize the total agent rate
to 0. Note that the set and the ask statements should be repeated
for all available templates.
```

After the initialization phase, when the simulation starts, the information about all the leading agents that need rate recalculation on the transitions given by SCC or SC structural relations is used. Without losing generality, in the following examples we will include only two features in each agent, which will be useful for understanding how the translation works.

As stated in the previous section, the novel structural analysis procedure provided by SNexpression takes advantage of SC and SCC (and their transposed functions) to obtain, for each pair of transitions t_j and t_k of the input model (representing in our case two possible agent actions) the transition instances of t_k that are influenced by t_j, i.e. the instances of t_k that will either be disabled or require rate recalculation. Applying $\mathrm{LD1}_{p_i}[k,j]$ and $\mathrm{LD2}_{p_i}[k,j]$, we will obtain the potential set of leader agents (that are in place p_i, with p_i connected to both t_j and t_k) for which a recalculation of the firing rates is necessary if a specific instance of t_j fires.

From the point of view of the NetLogo translation, we will therefore add the necessary code lines to disable/enable the rate recalculation of all affected agents (in place p_i) and involved transitions, at the end of the code of the action t_j.

Thus, after the execution of action t_j, we consider $\mathbf{F_1} = \mathrm{LD1}_{p_i}[k,j]$ and $\mathbf{F_2} = \mathrm{LD2}_{p_i}[k,j]$ to obtain a list of pairs of the form $(t_k, \mathbf{F_1})$ and $(t_k, \mathbf{F_2})$, where t_k is the transition for which the leading agents currently in p_i need to recalculate the rate.

Note that the functions $\mathbf{F_1}$ and $\mathbf{F_2}$ can be interpreted as templates allowing to select specific agents in place p_i. In our example, the templates will have the form $\langle f, g, h\rangle[\phi]$, where, f, g, and h are either color variables or color (sub) sets used for identifying subsets of agents, and ϕ is a boolean expression (called guard), that expresses conditions on the instance of t_j that has just been executed, involving variables in f, g, and h. The terms of the boolean expression may include equality, inequality and membership in a static subclass.

In our case, we suppose here to identify with a_1 the variable that contains the id of a given agent ($a_2, a_3, ...$ will be used similarly, for identifying other involved agents) and $b_i, c_i, ...$ for identifying other features (i.e. position, state, age, etc.) of agent a_i. Note that agents belonging to different agent types may have a different set of features.

S_A will be used to identify the set that contains all the possible agent ids belonging to agents class A; So, $S_A - a_1$ will identify, for example, any agent except agent a_1. Similarly, $S_B, S_C, ..$ will identify the sets that contain all the possible values of features b and c, and $S_B - b_1, S_C - c_1$, will identify all the possible values for features b and c, except b_1 and c_1, respectively.

For a formula like $(t_k, \langle a_1, b_1, z_1\rangle)$, the agent identified by a_1, b_1, z_1 (in place p_i) will have to either disable the action t_k (for example if it leaves the current place) or its rate needs to be recalculated (in case of self loops that move the agent from t_j, to t_j, possibly changing its internal features).

For instance, in the SEIRS model we observe this situation when a given infected agent (place `I`) executes the action `Recovery` (t_j), with respect to action `Infection` (t_k) for which it is also leader. Here, only such agent, now recovered (place `R`), has to recalculate the `Infection` rate and, for this specific case, it will be 0 as this transition is no longer enabled.

In such a case, the related Netlogo template code to be placed inside the code for the firing of the action t_j will have the following form:

```
ask turtle a1 [
;; the turtle with id a1 is the leading agent
...
set myrate replace-item k myrate (-1)
;;in case of rate (re)calculations is needed or...
set myrate replace-item k myrate (0)
;; in case of action is disabled
]
```

This template also holds for formulas like $(t_k, \langle a_1, b_1, c_2\rangle[c_1! = c_2])$ appearing in LD2_{p_i}, as in such a case the formula is saying that agent a_1 changed its feature from c_1 to a value that is different (identified by c_2).

For instance, in the SEIRS model we observe this kind of situation when `MoveS` (t_j) fires for a given susceptible agent (place `S`), with respect to `Infection` (t_k), and in particular if susceptible agents are also leaders for the `Infection`. In such scenario, only the susceptible agent that moved to a new position has to recalculate its rate for the `Infection`, as in the new position there could be a different number of infected agents to interact with.

For formulas like $(t_k, \langle S_A, S_B, c_1\rangle)$, all agents ($S_A$), with any value for the second characteristic (S_B), but with the third equal to c_1 (that is, the value of the characteristic belonging to agent a_1) have to recompute their rates for the action t_k for which they are leaders; In this scenario, the template is slightly different, as the leading agent, which is in charge of executing the t_j action, will ask the other agents that satisfy the aforementioned conditions to recalculate the rate for t_k.

An example of this scenario can be observed in the SEIRS model by looking at the `EndIncubation` (t_j) action executed by an exposed agent that becomes infected (place `I`). Then, all the leaders of action `Infection` (t_k) (i.e., the susceptible agents) in the same position as the new infected have to recalculate their `Infection` rate, as there is a new agent with which they can potentially interact.

If we call p_l the place where such agents are (that is, one of the input places for transition t_k), we will have:

```
ask turtle a1 [
;; the turtle with id a1 is the leading agent
...
;;here with the term agents we identify the invoved agent family
ask agents with [c = c1 and place = p_l]
    [set myrate replace-item k myrate (0)]
;; in case of action is disabled, otherwise
ask agents with [c = c1 and place = p_l]
    [set myrate replace-item k myrate (-1)]
;; the rate needs to be recalculated
]
```

For formulas like $(t_k, \langle S_A, S_B, c_2\rangle[c_1! = c_2])$, the added information of $c_1! = c_2$ will be used to select all agents that are the leaders of the action t_k and have the third characteristic equal to c_2 because they have to recalculate the rates for t_k. The new value c_2 is determined during the execution of t_j and may be the consequence, for example, of a change in the value in one of the features of the leading agent from c_1 to a different value c_2. This last scenario can be observed within the SEIRS model by looking at the `MoveI` action executed by an infected agent that moves to a new position. In such a scenario, we have an SCC, and all the susceptible agents (leaders of the `Infection`) in the new position have to recalculate their rates. The template code is analogous to the previous one but, in this specific case, also the susceptible agents in the old position of the infected agent that just moved have to recalculate their rates.

5 Experimental Results

To evaluate the potential benefits of exploiting structural information, we first automatically generated the NetLogo model of the SEIRS network shown in

Fig. 1, using GreatSPN. The resulting naïve model was already configured to employ the NETA simulation algorithm introduced in [6]. We then incorporated the structural optimizations suggested by `SNexpression` into the naïve model.

For the infection transition—the only transition that requires a leader specification—we tested two scenarios: (i) the transition managed by susceptible agents and (ii) the transition managed by infected agents. This resulted in two distinct optimized models.

We performed simulations with all three NetLogo models (the one naïve and the two optimized versions), varying the initial population size. Specifically, we considered 100, 500, 1000 and 2000 agents, with a fixed susceptible-to-infected ratio of 9:1. The initial numbers of exposed and recovered agents were set to zero. The susceptible agents were uniformly distributed in 25 spatial positions, while all infected agents were placed at the same initial location. All simulations were stopped when the final time $T_{end} = 20$ was reached.

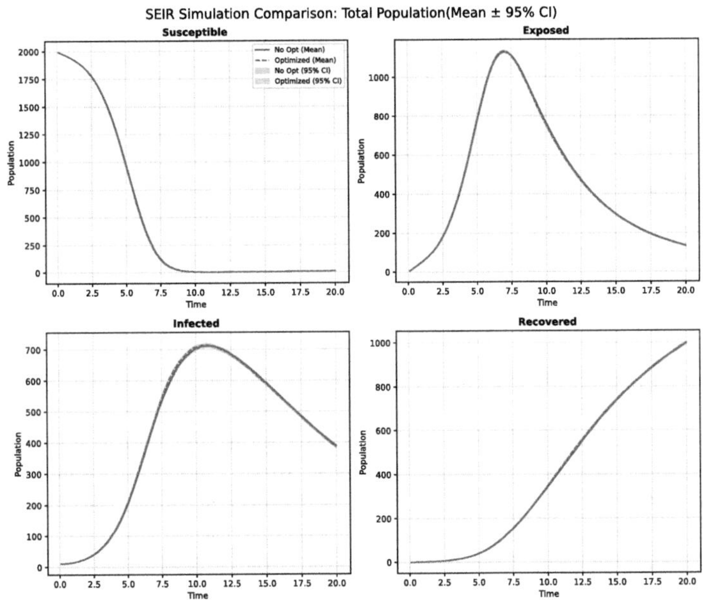

Fig. 2. Mean population behaviors ± 95% CI for simulation example with 2000 susceptible agents and 10 infected agents.

For each configuration, we performed 100 runs using NetLogo 6.4.0 with different random seeds. The experiments were carried out on an Apple Silicon M4 Pro CPU (10 performance cores), exploiting 10 parallel threads via the NetLogo BehaviorSpace feature. We note here that, over the 100 Monte-Carlo simulations, the variability of the estimates remained remarkably low, with SEM values consistently below 1% for large populations and generally within 2–4% for intermediate ones. Higher relative SEM values were observed only when the corresponding population sizes approached zero, a regime in which percentage-based measures are not informative. For the sake of clarity, we show in Fig. 2 the mean population behaviors ± 95% CI obtained for the non-optimized and for the optimized code versions, in a test scenario with an initial number of susceptible agents set to 2000 and 10 initially infected agents.

The mean execution times ± 95% confidence intervals are reported in Fig. 3. The results show a substantial reduction (approximately 1 order of magnitude)

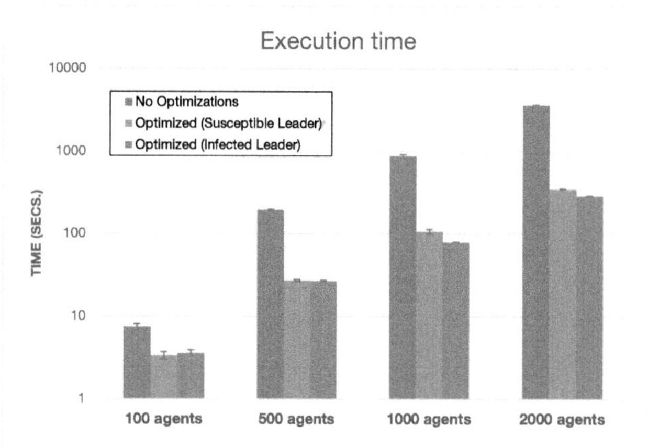

Fig. 3. Simulation times (log scale) for the three tested scenarios.

in the computation times for both optimized models compared to naïve one. The absolute performance gain increases with the initial population size. In addition, slight but statistically significant differences emerge between the two optimized versions as the number of agents increases. In particular, for simulations with 1000 and 2000 agents, the model where infected agents act as leaders for the infection transition outperforms the one where susceptible agents are leaders. This advantage is likely due to the initially smaller number of infected agents, which reduces the overhead for rate recalculations. Nevertheless, the difference remains limited, since as the simulation progresses the number of infected agents increases while the number of susceptible agents decreases, partially compensating for the initial imbalance.

6 Conclusions and Future Work

This paper successfully demonstrated a methodology for significantly improving the efficiency of AB-ESSN simulations by exploiting structural properties of the models. Leveraging recent advancements in the SNexpression tool, particularly its matrix calculus capabilities, the approach enables a more efficient and semi-automated optimization process for ABMs. The structural analysis focuses on identifying "local" state changes and dependency relationships, which are then used to optimize rate recalculations during simulation.

The effectiveness of this structural optimization was experimentally validated using the SEIRS epidemic model, with simulations automatically generated for NetLogo. The results showed a substantial reduction in computation times, approximately an order of magnitude, for the optimized models compared to the naïve one. The optimization by choosing infected agents as leaders for the infection transition proved slightly more efficient for larger populations due to the initially smaller number of infected agents, reducing overhead for rate recalculations.

For future work, we aim at integrating SNexpression into an automatic pipeline for the generation of AB-ESSN compliant models. More specifically, continued efforts will focus on defining the automatic translation of complex dependency expressions into optimized NetLogo code, aiming for more comprehensive and fully automated optimization. Furthermore, a more direct verification of invariant properties derived from P-semiflows, will be included to verify the consistency of AB-ESSN models, and in particular the uniqueness of agents. Finally, we plan to better evaluate the effectiveness of the methodology by applying it to a wider range of models.

References

1. SNexpression home page (2025). http://www.di.unito.it/~depierro/SNexpression
2. The Library for Symbolic Calculus (2025), https://github.com/lgcapra/SNlib-stable
3. Amparore, E.G., Donatelli, S.: The ins and outs of Petri net composition. In: Bernardinello, L., Petrucci, L. (eds.) Application and Theory of Petri Nets and Concurrency - 43rd Int. Conf., PETRI NETS 2022, Bergen, Norway, June 19-24, 2022, Proceedings. Lecture Notes in Computer Science, vol. 13288, pp. 278–299. Springer, Cham (2022)
4. Amparore, E.G., Balbo, G., Beccuti, M., Donatelli, S., Franceschinis, G.: 30 years of GreatSPN. In: Principles of Performance and Reliability Modeling and Evaluation, pp. 227–254. Springer, Cham (2016)
5. Amparore, E.G., Beccuti, M., Castagno, P., Franceschinis, G., Pennisi, M., Pernice, S.: Multiformalism modeling and simulation of immune system mechanisms. Proceedings - 2021 IEEE International Conference on Bioinformatics and Biomedicine, BIBM 2021, pp. 3259–3266 (2021)
6. Amparore, E.G., Beccuti, M., Castagno, P., Pernice, S., Franceschinis, G., Pennisi, M.: From compositional Petri net modeling to macro and micro simulation by means of stochastic simulation and agent-based models. ACM Trans. Model. Perform. Eval. Comput. Syst. **9**(1), 1:1–1:30 (2024). https://doi.org/10.1145/3617681
7. Andelfinger, P., Uhrmacher, A.M.: Synchronous speculative simulation of tightly coupled agents in continuous time on CPUs and GPUs. Simulation **100**(1), 5–21 (2023). https://doi.org/10.1177/00375497231158930

8. Baccega, D., et al.: Forge4Flame: an intuitive dashboard for designing GPU agent-based models to simulate infectious disease spread. Simul. Model. Pract. Theory, **145**(103205) (2025)
9. Beccuti, M., Castagno, P., Franceschinis, G., Pennisi, M., Pernice, S.: A Petri net formalism to study systems at different scales exploiting agent-based and stochastic simulations. In: Proceedings of 17th European Workshop, EPEW 2021, and 26th International Conference, ASMTA. LNCS, vol. 13104. Springer, Cham (2022)
10. Benaïm, M., Le Boudec, J.Y.: A class of mean field interaction models for computer and communication systems. Perform. Eval. **65**(11–12), 823–838 (2008). https://doi.org/10.1016/j.peva.2008.03.005
11. Bruneo, D., Scarpa, M., Bobbio, A., Cerotti, D., Gribaudo, M.: An intelligent swarm of markovian agents. In: Kacprzyk, J., Pedrycz, W. (eds.) Springer Handbook of Computational Intelligence, pp. 1345–1359. Springer, Heidelberg (2015). https://doi.org/10.1007/978-3-662-43505-2_69
12. Capra, L., De Pierro, M., Franceschinis, G.: General composition for symmetric net arc functions with applications. In: Proceedings of the International Workshop on Petri Nets and Software Engineering 2021. CEUR workshop proceedings, vol. 2907
13. Capra, L., De Pierro, M., Franceschinis, G.: A high level language for structural relations in stochastic well-formed nets. In: Applications and Theory of Petri Nets 2005, vol. 3536, pp. 168–187. Springer, Cham (2005). https://doi.org/10.1007/11494744_11
14. Capra, L., De Pierro, M., Franceschinis, G.: Snexpression: a symbolic calculator for symmetric net expressions. In: Proceedings of the 41st International Conference Petri Nets 2020. LNCS, vol. 12152, pp. 381–391. Springer, Cham (2020)
15. Capra, L., De Pierro, M., Franceschinis, G.: SNexpression: a new component for SN matrix-based structural analysis. In: Proceedings of the 45th International Conference on Formal Techniques for Distributed Objects, Components, and Systems - FORTE 2025. Lille, France (2025)
16. Capra, L., De Pierro, M., Franceschinis, G.: Symbolic dependency relations calculation in Symmetric Nets. Trans. Petri Nets Other Models Concurrency (2025). accepted for publication
17. Cerotti, D., Bobbio, A., Bruneo, D., Distefano, S., Scarpa, M., Gribaudo, M.: Assessing self-adapting routing algorithm in an industrial IoT environment. In: 2021 Annual Reliability and Maintainability Symposium (RAMS), pp. 1–7 (2021). https://doi.org/10.1109/RAMS48097.2021.9605660
18. Chimeh, M.K., Richmond, P.: Simulating heterogeneous behaviours in complex systems on GPUs. Simul. Model. Pract. Theory **83**, 3–17 (2018). https://www.sciencedirect.com/science/article/pii/S1569190X18300170. agent-based Modelling and Simulation
19. Figueredo, G.P., Siebers, P.O., Owen, M., Reps, J., Aickelin, U.: Comparing stochastic differential equations and agent-based modelling and simulation for early-stage cancer. PLoS ONE **9** (2014)
20. Köster, T., Reinhardt, O., Hinsch, M., Bijak, J., Uhrmacher, A.M.: A fast embedded language for continuous-time agent-based simulation. J. Artif. Soc. Soc. Simul. **27**(1) (2024)
21. Kreikemeyer, J.N., Köster, T., Uhrmacher, A.M., Warnke, T.: Inferring dependency graphs for agent-based models using aspect-oriented programming. In: 2021 Winter Simulation Conference (WSC), pp. 1–12 (2021)
22. Pennisi, M., Amparore, E.G., Franceschinis, G.: Exploiting structural dependency relations for efficient agent based model simulation. In: 19th European Workshop,

EPEW 2023, and 27th International Conference, ASMTA 2023, Florence, Italy, June 20-23, 2023, Proceedings. LNCS, vol. 14231, pp. 353–368. Springer, Cham (2023). https://doi.org/10.1007/978-3-031-43185-2_24
23. Pennisi, M., Franceschinis, G., Baccega, D., Pernice, S., Terrone, I.: Exploiting GPU computing for effective agent-based simulation: initial experiments. In: 33rd Euromicro Int. Conf. on Parallel, Distributed, and Network-Based Processing, PDP 2025, Turin, Italy, March 12-14, 2025, pp. 303–308. IEEE (2025)
24. Reinhardt, O., Uhrmacher, A.M.: An efficient simulation algorithm for continuous-time agent-based linked lives models. In: Proc. of the 50th Annual Simulation Symp. pp. 9:1–9:12. SCS International / ACM (2017)
25. Reinhardt, O., Warnke, T., Uhrmacher, A.M.: A language for agent-based discrete-event modeling and simulation of linked lives. ACM Trans. Model. Comput. Simul. (TOMACS) **32**(1), 1–26 (2022)
26. Steinman, J.: Speedes: synchronous parallel environment for emulation and discrete event simulation. In: Proceedings of SCS Western Multi-conference on Advances in Parallel and Discrete Simulation, vol. 23, pp. 1111–1115 (1991)
27. Warnke, T., Reinhardt, O., Uhrmacher, A.M.: Population-based CTMCS and agent-based models. In: Winter Simulation Conference, WSC 2016, Washington, DC, USA, December 11-14, 2016, pp. 1253–1264. IEEE (2016)

Efficient Guaranteed Controllers for Switched Dynamical Systems Using Probabilistic Approximations

Yahia Bahloul, Adrien Le Coënt(✉), Benoît Barbot, and Nihal Pekergin

Univ Paris Est Creteil, LACL, F-94010 Creteil, France
{adrien.le-coent,benoit.barbot}@u-pec.fr

Abstract. In this paper, we tackle the problem of computing guaranteed controllers for switched dynamical systems. We design a control procedure inspired from model predictive control, but instead of relying on a cost function that is evaluated by simulating the original system, we first build a formal discrete probabilistic approximation of the original system, and the cost function is evaluated using this approximation. This approximate model is essentially a Markov chain, and we store it in a compact way as a dynamic Bayesian network (DBN). The inference algorithms available for DBNs allow us to evaluate and minimize an approximate cost function in a very efficient manner. We compute guaranteed controllers thanks to the use of set-based reachability analysis for computing the transition probabilities of the approximate model. Moreover, the search space of the optimization procedure is reduced to the control modes that are guaranteed safe.

Keywords: Switched systems · Markov chains · Bayesian networks · Model Predictive Control

1 Introduction

Model Predictive Control (MPC) has become a cornerstone of modern control strategies, owing to its capacity to handle multi-variable systems and incorporate state and input constraints in a systematic manner. However, guaranteeing safety and correctness in the presence of model uncertainty remains a critical challenge, especially in applications where violations of constraints can lead to undesirable or unsafe behavior.

In this work, we introduce a formal MPC framework based on Dynamic Bayesian Network (DBN) approximations to compute correct-by-construction controllers for switched control systems. Our approach leverages the expressive power of DBNs to approximate system dynamics while enabling tractable, safety-aware control synthesis. By incorporating formal verification techniques within

This work is supported by ANR MAVeriQ (ANR-20-CE25-0012).

A. Remke et al. (Eds.): Valuetools 2025, LNICST 691, pp. 140–156, 2027.
https://doi.org/10.1007/978-3-032-23901-3_9

the MPC loop and DBN approximation, we obtain provable safety guarantees across a subset of modes and states of the switched system.

In this paper, we focus on systems with linear dynamics subject to bounded perturbations and measurement errors, where each mode of the switched system evolves according to a known linear model. This assumption allows for efficient synthesis and verification while capturing a wide range of practical behaviors. Nonetheless, the proposed framework is designed to be extensible, and future work will explore the incorporation of nonlinear dynamics, where richer and more realistic behaviors can be modeled, and for which more advanced reachability techniques must be used.

The primary application we consider is thermal regulation, a domain where switched linear models naturally arise, and where strict safety constraints must be enforced to prevent overheating or energy inefficiencies. Nevertheless, the proposed methodology is general and scalable, and is intended to support more complex case studies in the future, including hybrid systems with nonlinear dynamics.

The contributions of this paper are as follows: we present a formal abstraction of switched systems using Markov chains by using formal reachability analysis; Markov chains approximations are then efficiently stored as DBNs; we design an MPC-inspired synthesis procedure that uses DBNs as predictive models and ensures safety guarantees if the system starts in a safe state; we demonstrate the practical applicability of our approach through case studies in thermal regulation, with future extensions toward more complex, nonlinear systems. Our approach essentially leverages DBNs as guaranteed abstractions for switched systems, and applies MPC on DBN models to compute efficient and safe control sequences.

Related Work. Guaranteed control of switched and continuous systems typically relies on finite-state abstractions, where the state space is discretized and control synthesis is performed on the resulting automaton using techniques like Binary Decision Diagrams (BDDs). Methods such as PESSOA [20] and CoSyMA [23] construct approximately bisimilar models under strong assumptions like incremental stability [3,24], while SCOTS [28] introduces feedback refinement relations [27]. Tiling-based approaches [15,21] exploit system monotonicity, and SMT-based techniques [26] use Lyapunov-like functions for abstraction. In contrast, methods such as [8] compute abstractions of stochastic systems with the aim of performing simulation, verification and control synthesis. In this paper, we focus on abstractions of ODE based systems, and make use of Model Predictive Control (MPC). MPC, also called Receding Horizon Control, is an advanced control technique that relies on model-based prediction of future states and optimization to find the best control sequence for a given time window [2,10,14]. While efficient, few attempts have been made to use formal methods in the context of MPC. It has been tackled using tiling and validated simulation in [29]. Unlike these methods, our approach uses Dynamic Bayesian Networks to approximate system dynamics and integrates formal guarantees directly within the DBN model, which is used as the predictive model for the MPC framework.

DBNs and MPC have been used in [31] for controlling power grids but without formal verification. Using DBNs as safe abstractions, combined with MPC for control input computation, yields a method that is more scalable than competing formal approaches. This scalability stems both from the reduced abstraction size and from the ease of computing the controller on the compact model, all without relying on strong structural assumptions such as incremental stability or monotonicity.

An extended version of this paper which includes all the proofs, additional remarks and experiments is given in [7].

2 Problem Setting and Mathematical Tools

We are interested in continuous-time switched systems described by the set of linear ordinary differential equations:

$$\dot{\boldsymbol{x}} = f_u(\boldsymbol{x}, \boldsymbol{\varepsilon}), \tag{1}$$

where $\boldsymbol{x} \in \mathbb{R}^n$ is the state of the system, $\boldsymbol{\varepsilon} \in \mathbb{R}^m$ is a bounded perturbation, $u \in \Sigma$ is the mode of the system. The finite set $\Sigma = \{1, \ldots, N\}$ is the set of switching modes of the system. The functions $f_u : \mathbb{R}^n \times \mathbb{R}^m \longrightarrow \mathbb{R}^n$, with $u \in \Sigma$, are the vector fields describing the dynamics of each mode u of the system, in this paper, functions f_u are linear, of the form $f_u(\boldsymbol{x}) = A_u\boldsymbol{x} + \boldsymbol{b}_u + \boldsymbol{\varepsilon}$ with $A_u \in \mathbb{R}^{n \times n}$, $\boldsymbol{b}_u \in \mathbb{R}^n$, and $\boldsymbol{\varepsilon} \in \mathbb{R}^n$ for all $u \in \Sigma$. The system can be in only one mode at a time. We suppose that switchings occur periodically every δ time units.

Our goal is to compute a switching rule $\sigma(\cdot) : \mathbb{R}^n \longrightarrow \Sigma$, such that the state $\boldsymbol{x}$ verifies some desired properties, mainly, safety in a set $S \subset \mathbb{R}^n$, and following as closely as possible a time-varying target state $\boldsymbol{x}^t$ that evolves within S. Given a switching rule $\sigma(\cdot)$, we will denote by $\phi(t; t_0, \boldsymbol{x}_0, \boldsymbol{\varepsilon}, \sigma)$ the state reached by the system at time $t > t_0$, from the initial state $\boldsymbol{x}_0 \in \mathbb{R}^n$ at time $t_0 \geq 0$, and under control input σ and perturbation $\boldsymbol{\varepsilon}$ evolving in a bounded set D. The perturbation $\boldsymbol{\varepsilon}$ is omitted when there is no perturbation. Our objective is thus to find a switching rule $\sigma(\cdot)$ such that for all $t > 0$, $\boldsymbol{x}_0 \in S$, $\boldsymbol{\varepsilon} \in D$, $\phi(t; 0, \boldsymbol{x}_0, \sigma) \in S$ and $\|\phi(t; t_0, \boldsymbol{x}_0, \sigma) - \boldsymbol{x}^t\|$ is as small as possible. If $\boldsymbol{x}_0 \notin S$, our controllers return the modes for which the probability to reach S is the highest.

In the remainder of this section, we detail some mathematical results and objects that will be used throughout the rest of the paper.

2.1 Solutions of Linear ODEs

Being given a linear switched system satisfying

$$\dot{\boldsymbol{x}} = A_u\boldsymbol{x} + \boldsymbol{b}_u, \tag{2}$$

and an initial condition $\boldsymbol{x}_0 \in \mathbb{R}^n$ at time $t = 0$, if mode $u \in \Sigma$ is applied on $[0, \delta]$, then the solution at time $t = \delta$ is given by

$$\phi(t; 0, \boldsymbol{x}_0, u) = e^{A_u \delta}\boldsymbol{x}_0 + \int_0^\delta e^{A_u(t-s)}\boldsymbol{b}_u ds. \tag{3}$$

In the case where A_u is invertible, we furthermore have

$$\phi(t; 0, \boldsymbol{x}_0, u) = e^{A_u \delta}\boldsymbol{x}_0 + (e^{A_u \delta} - I_n)A_u^{-1}\boldsymbol{b}_u$$

where I_n is the identity matrix of size n. In both cases we have an affine transformation.

2.2 Polytopes

A polytope is a type of bounded convex set usually defined in $\mathbb{R}^n$ as being the convex hull of a finite set of points. We use instead the other classical definition that relies on half-spaces, referred to as the H-representation.

Definition 1. *A polytope $P \subset \mathbb{R}^n$ is said to be given in* half-space representation *(or* H-representation*) if it can be written as the solution set of a finite system of linear inequalities:*

$$P = \{\boldsymbol{x} \in \mathbb{R}^n \mid A\boldsymbol{x} \leq \boldsymbol{b}\}$$

where:

- *$A \in \mathbb{R}^{m\times n}$ is a real matrix,*
- *$\boldsymbol{b} \in \mathbb{R}^m$ is a real vector,*
- *and the inequality $Ax \leq b$ is interpreted componentwise, i.e., $(A\boldsymbol{x})_i \leq b_i$ for all $i = 1, \ldots, m$.*

In the remainder of the paper, we say that a polytope is full-dimensional if it is of dimension n. An affine transformation applied to a polytope is a polytope, and it can be computed exactly, as stated in the following Proposition.

Proposition 1. *Let $P \subset \mathbb{R}^n$ be a polytope given in H-representation:*

$$P = \{\boldsymbol{x} \in \mathbb{R}^n \mid A\boldsymbol{x} \leq \boldsymbol{b}\},$$

where $A \in \mathbb{R}^{m\times n}$, $b \in \mathbb{R}^m$, and suppose that $T : \mathbb{R}^n \to \mathbb{R}^n$ is an affine transformation of the form

$$T(\boldsymbol{x}) = M\boldsymbol{x} + \boldsymbol{c},$$

with $M \in \mathbb{R}^{n\times n}$ invertible and $c \in \mathbb{R}^n$. Then the image of P under T is also a polytope, and is given by

$$T(P) = \{\boldsymbol{y} \in \mathbb{R}^n \mid AM^{-1}\boldsymbol{y} \leq \boldsymbol{b} + AM^{-1}\boldsymbol{c}\}.$$

We introduced polytopes by their H-representation as this is how we use them in our implementation. Proposition 1 can be established using other representations.

2.3 Reachability Computation

Definition 2. *Let us denote by $Post_u(X)$ the successor set of a set $X \subset \mathbb{R}^n$ subject to the dynamics* (1) *when mode $u \in \Sigma$ is applied for a time horizon τ:*

$$Post_u(X) = \bigcup_{\boldsymbol{x} \in X} \phi(\tau; 0, \boldsymbol{x}, u) \tag{4}$$

If X is given as a product of intervals or a polytope with H-representation, and is subject to a linear dynamics (2), its successor set can be computed exactly using Proposition 1 and the affine transformation (3).

2.4 Reachability Computation with Small Perturbations

Assume that the system is subject to a small perturbation $\boldsymbol{\varepsilon} \in D = [-\varepsilon_1, \varepsilon_1] \times \cdots \times [-\varepsilon_n, \varepsilon_n]$:

$$\dot{\boldsymbol{x}} = A_u \boldsymbol{x} + \boldsymbol{b}_u + \boldsymbol{\varepsilon}. \tag{5}$$

Denote by γ the vector $(\varepsilon_1, \ldots, \varepsilon_n)$. Denote by $T_u(\boldsymbol{x}) = e^{A_u \tau} \boldsymbol{x} + (e^{A_u \tau} - I_n) A_u^{-1} \boldsymbol{b}_u = M\boldsymbol{x} + \boldsymbol{c}$ the affine transformation induced by dynamics (2) under mode u for a time horizon τ without perturbation. One can compute the successor set with perturbations using the following Proposition.

Proposition 2. *The successor set of a set $X \subset \mathbb{R}^n = \{\boldsymbol{x} \in \mathbb{R}^n | A\boldsymbol{x} \leq \boldsymbol{b}\}$, when mode $u \in \Sigma$ and small perturbation $\boldsymbol{\varepsilon} \in D$ are applied for a time horizon τ in the dynamics* (5), *is over-approximated [11,12] by the polytope*

$$Post_u(X, D) \subseteq \left\{ \boldsymbol{y} \in \mathbb{R}^n | AM^{-1}\boldsymbol{y} \leq \boldsymbol{b} + AM^{-1}\boldsymbol{c} + \tau\gamma \right\}.$$

In simple terms, the polytope image of the perturbed system is enlarged by a small value $\tau\varepsilon_i$ in each dimension i compared to the non perturbed system.

3 Probabilistic Approximations

3.1 Markov Chain Approximation

Consider a continuous system without perturbations. To approximate the continuous system by a discrete probabilistic system, we assume that the state x evolves within a bounded set $\mathcal{X}$ given as a product of intervals. This bounded set is divided in (products of) sub-intervals to obtain a discrete state abstraction. Out-of-bound states can be considered in the discrete model to circumvent the hypothesis that x stays in $\mathcal{X}$, but this is not necessary for our case studies. Since $\mathcal{X}$ is discretized in sub-intervals, the discrete state abstraction is an approximating Markov chain that gives the probability for the continuous state to transition from one product of sub-intervals to another product of sub-intervals.

Let us introduce some notations. Let $x_1, \ldots, x_n$ be our set of variables. Suppose that each variable evolves within an interval $\mathcal{X} = \mathcal{X}_1 \times \cdots \times \mathcal{X}_n = [x_1^{min}, x_1^{max}] \times \cdots \times [x_n^{min}, x_n^{max}]$. The set $S = S_1 \times \cdots \times S_n = [s_1^{min}, s_1^{max}] \times$

$\cdots \times [s_n^{min}, s_n^{max}]$ is the safety set in which a controller must guarantee that the state stays. One typically chooses $S \subseteq \mathcal{X}$. The controllers we compute will guarantee that if the state starts in S, it stays in S. Assume now that each interval $\mathcal{X}_i$ is discretized into L_i sub-intervals $I_{i,1}, I_{i,2}, \ldots, I_{i,L_i}$.

Suppose furthermore that time is discretized with time-step δ to specify an increasing sequence of time instants $(t_j)_{j=0}^{T}$, where $t_0 = 0$ and $\delta \cdot T = \tau$ is the observation horizon. The discretized state is given by a vector of discrete random variables:

$$\boldsymbol{X}^t = (X_1^t, X_2^t, \ldots, X_n^t)$$

where $X_i^t \in \{1, \ldots, L_i\}$ denotes the sub-interval (discrete state) of the ith variable at time t. The control mode being already discrete, we denote its value at discrete time t by U^t, the joint probability distribution of this random vector is computed as follows:

$$\begin{aligned} p(\boldsymbol{X}^{0:T}) &= p(\boldsymbol{X}^0)p(\boldsymbol{X}^1|\boldsymbol{X}^0, U^0)\cdots p(\boldsymbol{X}^T|\boldsymbol{X}^{T-1}, U^{T-1}) \\ &= p(\boldsymbol{X}^0)\prod_{t=1}^{T} p(\boldsymbol{X}^t|\boldsymbol{X}^{t-1}, U^{t-1}) \end{aligned}$$

This model is thus a DTMC. The transition probabilities of a DTMC are typically stored in a transition probability matrix, $\boldsymbol{P}$ such that

$$\boldsymbol{P}[\boldsymbol{i}, \boldsymbol{j}, u] = p(\boldsymbol{X}^t = \boldsymbol{j} \mid \boldsymbol{X}^{t-1} = \boldsymbol{i}, U^{t-1} = u) \tag{6}$$

where $\boldsymbol{i}, \boldsymbol{j}$ are any two (vector) states of the underlying stochastic process, and u is the switched mode at time $t-1$.

To estimate the transition probability matrix, one typically draws samples of the continuous system for various initial conditions and control modes, and then counts which discrete states are explored by the different trajectories. This is what was done in [18] with the final aim of estimating parameters of biochemical networks. In our case, we instead want to compute control modes to apply, and guarantee that the trajectories are kept within the safety set. To do so, we estimate the transition probabilities exactly by computing reachability sets of the products of sub-intervals instead of relying on samples that might miss some critical behaviors. Doing so, we guarantee with probability 1 that the state stays in the safety set. The transition probabilities are computed exactly using the following theorem. The proof is given in [7].

Theorem 1. *Let us consider system* (1)*, consider the continuous state x at time t, and suppose that its discretization belongs in a discrete state $\boldsymbol{l}^{pred} = (l_1^{pred}, \ldots, l_n^{pred}) \in \{1, \ldots, L_1\} \times \cdots \times \{1, \ldots, L_n\}$ at time t. Suppose a uniform distribution for the continuous state in $I^{pred} = I_{1,l_1^{pred}} \times \cdots \times I_{n,l_n^{pred}}$ at time t. Suppose mode $u \in \Sigma$ is applied between time t and $t+\delta$. The probability that the continuous variable reaches $I^{next} = I_{1,l_1^{next}} \times \cdots \times I_{n,l_n^{next}}$, corresponding to a discrete state $\boldsymbol{l}^{next} = (l_1^{next}, \ldots, l_n^{next}) \in \{1, \ldots, L_1\} \times \cdots \times \{1, \ldots, L_n\}$ at time $t+\delta$ when mode $u \in \Sigma$ is applied, is given by :*

$$P(\boldsymbol{X}^{t+1} = \boldsymbol{l}^{next} \mid \boldsymbol{X}^t = \boldsymbol{l}^{pred},\ U^t = u) = \frac{\lambda(I^{next} \cap Post_u(I^{pred}))}{\lambda(Post_u(I^{pred}))}$$

where λ denotes the Lebesgue measure of a set.

Remark 1. In our framework, sets are either products of intervals or full dimensional polytopes, their Lebesgue measure is thus equal to their volume.

Remark 2. We assume a uniform distribution for the continuous variable in $I_{1,l_1^{pred}} \times \cdots \times I_{n,l_n^{pred}}$, but to obtain safety guarantees, one could consider instead any distribution which is non uniform but always strictly positive on $I_{1,l_1^{pred}} \times \cdots \times I_{n,l_n^{pred}}$.

Perturbations and Measurement Noise. If the system is subject to small perturbations, all computations involving the $Post_u(X)$ operator for a set X should be replaced with $Post_u(X, D)$ where D is the set in which the perturbations evolve, as stated in Sect. 2.4. Doing so, all transitions enabled by perturbations are captured in the discrete model.

Bounded measurement noise can similarly be addressed by using overlapping sub-intervals instead of a partition in the state space discretization.

3.2 DBNs as Compact MCs

The size of the transition probability matrix grows exponentially with the number of variables. For large systems, its computation and storage become prohibitive. We thus make some conditional independence hypotheses for the discrete variables that allow us to store the transition matrix as a DBN, which is much more tractable.

A Bayesian network (BN) is essentially a graph that encodes the conditional dependencies between some random variables, and stores the conditional probability distributions of said variables. A dynamic Bayesian network (DBN) is a BN adapted to temporal models since it relies on a BN template that is repeated for a number of time steps. In our case, it allows to store a Markov chain in a compact way by assuming conditional independencies between some variables. In a few words, we suppose that a given variable does not depend on every variable in (6). Consequently, the joint probability can be computed with fewer parameters. The formal definition of a BN is the following.

Definition 3. *A Bayesian network is a pair $\mathcal{B} = (\mathcal{G}, P_B)$. $\mathcal{G}$ is a directed, acyclic graph (DAG) whose nodes are random variables $\boldsymbol{X} = X_1, \ldots, X_n$ and edges are labelled by mode in σ. The graph structure represents the dependency relations among random variables: there is an incoming arc to node X_i from node X_j labelled by u, if and only if the value of X_i depends on X_j in f_u. Let $Pa_u(X_i)$*

denote the set of parents of X_i *in* $\mathcal{G}$. *The distribution over* $\boldsymbol{X} = X_1, \ldots, X_n$ *can be factorized as a product:*

$$p(\boldsymbol{X}|u) = \prod_{i=1}^{n} p(X_i|Pa_u(X_i))$$

$p(X_i|Pa_u(X_i))$ *is called the Conditional Probability Distribution for node* X_i *specified as a Conditional Probability Table (CPT) at node* X_i. P_B *is the set of CPTs associated with* $\mathcal{G}$*'s nodes.*

In the following, we use a specific type of DBN for which the transition matrices are the same for each time step, this is a valid setting when each switched mode of the ODE (1) is time-homogeneous, as is indeed the case. The formal definition is the following.

Definition 4. *A 2-Time-slice Bayesian Network (2-TBN) for a process over* $\boldsymbol{X}$ *is a Bayesian network specifying the evolution of random variables at time* $t+1$, $\boldsymbol{X}^{t+1}$, *given the random variables at time* t, $\boldsymbol{X}^t$. $\boldsymbol{X}_I \subseteq \boldsymbol{X}$ *is a set of input variables having no parents in* $\mathcal{G}$. $\boldsymbol{X}'$ *is the set of output random variables. The transition model, for any time step* t, *is given by conditional probabilities* $p(\boldsymbol{X}' \mid \boldsymbol{X}_I)$. *Therefore, for each output random variable* X_i, *the CPT* $p(X_i|Pa_u(Xi))$ *is given once to specify the transition probabilities from* $\boldsymbol{X}^t$ *at time* t *to* $\boldsymbol{X}^{t+1}$ *at time* $t+1$ *with* $\boldsymbol{X}^t \subseteq \boldsymbol{X}_I$ *for all* t.

The Markov chain approximation of system (1) is fully represented by the 2-TBN with arcs connecting every left node to every right node, as illustrated in Fig. 1.

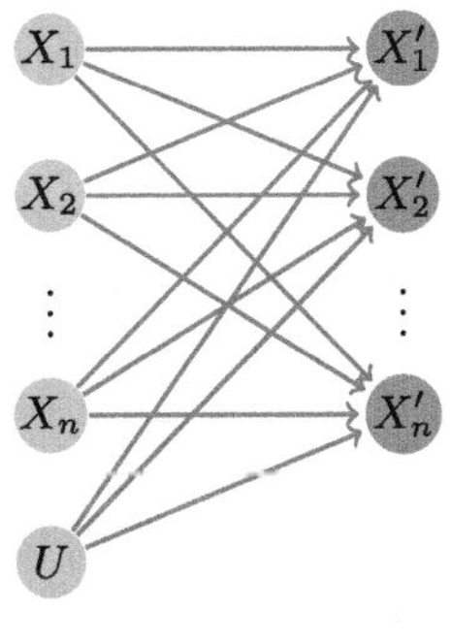

Fig. 1. The fully connected 2-TBN structure of a switched system.

To actually gain some storage space and DBN construction time, we suppose that each variable depends only on the ones that appear on the right hand side of the differential equation in (1), plus itself. This effectively breaks the exponential complexity which, for a DTMC approximation, is proportional to

NL^{2n} possible transitions if every dimension is divided in L sub-intervals, into a complexity proportional to NL^{f+1} where f, called the *maximum fan-in*, is the maximum number of variables on which a DBN node depends. This makes this approach much more scalable than classical state transition model abstractions. Often, and in our case studies, the real solution of the differential equation makes every variable depend on every variable, since, for example, in a thermal regulation example as in Sect. 5.2, the temperature of one room influences its neighboring room in the short-term, and its neighboring room will influence its next neighboring room in the slightly longer term, but in the differential equation, only the first neighboring room is seen by the first room (appears in the right-hand side of the ODE).

The hypothesis that a variable, say x_i, depends only on a subset of the other variables, namely x_{j_1} to x_{j_ℓ}, and not on all of them, implies that the remaining variables, x_{k_1} to $x_{k_{\bar{\ell}}}$, can independently take any value in the domain $\mathcal{X}_{k_1} \times \cdots \times \mathcal{X}_{k_{\bar{\ell}}}$ (or in $S_{k_1} \times \cdots \times S_{k_{\bar{\ell}}}$ if each variable is constrained to lie within its respective safety interval). We thus adapt the computation of the transition probabilities of the DBN by supposing that the non connected variables in the DBN graph take their values in their entire respective state space (interval $\mathcal{X}_{k_p}$). This is formalized as follows.

Let us recall that the set of variables is $x_1, \ldots, x_n$, and each variable x_i evolves in $\mathcal{X}_i = [x_i^{min}, x_i^{max}]$ which is discretized into L_i intervals $I_{i,1}, \ldots, I_{i,L_i}$. Suppose for the remainder of this section that $S = \mathcal{X}$. A safety controller ensures that x_i in S_i. Each discrete variable X_i depends only on a subset $\text{Pa}_u(X_i)$ of the variables. Similarly, let us denote by $\text{PaInd}_u(i)$ the set of indices corresponding to the variables of $\text{Pa}_u(X_i)$. Let π_i denote the projection on dimension $i \in \{1, \ldots, n\}$.

Definition 5. *Let $\boldsymbol{l}$ denote a vector of discrete states. Consider a variable x_i with $i \in \{1, \ldots, n\}$. Let $P(\boldsymbol{l}, i)$ be the full-dimensional polytope such that*

$$P(\boldsymbol{l}, i) = \left\{ \boldsymbol{x} \in \mathbb{R}^n \mid \begin{array}{ll} x_j \in I_{j,s_j}, \forall j \in PaInd_u(i) \\ x_{\bar{j}} \in S_{\bar{j}}, \quad \forall \bar{j} \in \{1, \cdots, n\} \backslash PaInd_u(i) \end{array} \right\}.$$

Let $W_u^{\boldsymbol{l},i} \subset \mathcal{X}_i$ be the DBN successor of $\boldsymbol{l}$ for variable i under mode u with bounded perturbations in D.[1] *Then the propagation of discrete state $\boldsymbol{l}$ for the parents of variable i with DBN-encoded independencies is computed as the successor of $P(\boldsymbol{l}, i)$ by mode u:*

$$W_u^{\boldsymbol{l},i} = \pi_i Post_u(P(\boldsymbol{l}, i), D)$$

The transition probabilities for the DBN CPTs are then computed as follows:

$$P\left(X_i^{t+1} = l_i^{next} \mid (\text{Pa}_u(X_i))^t = \boldsymbol{l},\ U^t = u\right) = \frac{\lambda(I_i^{next} \cap W_u^{\boldsymbol{l},i})}{\lambda(W_u^{\boldsymbol{l},i})}. \tag{7}$$

[1] The DBN successor of $\boldsymbol{l}$ for variable i means that $\boldsymbol{l}$ is restricted to the parents of variable i, the remaining variables being ignored by the graph-encoded dependencies, the successor state is computed without any knowledge on the discrete state of these remaining variables.

Finally, safety will be ensured using the following intermediate result, the proof is given in [7].

Theorem 2. *Consider a discrete state* $\boldsymbol{l} = (l_1, \ldots, l_n) \in \{1, \ldots, L_1\} \times \cdots \times \{1, \ldots, L_n\}$*, a perturbation set* D *and a mode* $u \in \Sigma$*. For all* $i \in \{1, \ldots, n\}$*, let* $W_u^{\boldsymbol{l},i}$ *be the propagation of discrete state* $\boldsymbol{l}$ *for the parents of variable* i*.*

If $I_{1,l_1} \times \cdots \times I_{n,l_n} \subset S$*, and if for all* $i \in \{1, \ldots, n\}$*,* $W_u^{\boldsymbol{l},i} \subset S_i$*, then* $Post_u(I_{1,l_1} \times \cdots \times I_{n,l_n}, D) \subset S$*.*

4 DBN Based MPC

Given a DBN, we perform a control procedure highly similar to standard model predictive control. Consider a time horizon T, a given control sequence $U^{0:T}$ and an initial condition $\boldsymbol{X^0} = (X_1^0, \ldots, X_n^0)$, the distribution of the state can be estimated over time by unrolling the DBN (computing the posterior $\boldsymbol{X}^{0:T}$):

$$p(\boldsymbol{X}^{0:T} | U^{0:T}, \boldsymbol{X^0}) \tag{8}$$

Our objective is to iteratively compute control sequences $U^{0:T}$ that

1. keep the state in the safety set S,
2. minimize a given cost.

When a sequence is computed, the first mode of the sequence is applied for the next time step, and, by the time the next time step ends, a new sequence is computed and is applied for the following time step.

Safety. First, to ensure safety (1), a pre-selection of the control modes that keep the state in S for the first time step is carried out. This is done by red flagging modes that lead out of the safety set with non zero probability for every possible discrete state. This can be done in two ways.

DBN-Based Pre-selection. We For each possible discrete state $\boldsymbol{l}$, for each variable i, let $W_u^{\boldsymbol{l},i}$ be the DBN successor of discrete state $\boldsymbol{l}$ for variable i. Let us define $\Theta : \boldsymbol{l} \rightarrow \mathcal{P}(\Sigma)$, the function that associates to a discrete state the set of modes which are not red flagged by the DBN i.e. $\Theta(\boldsymbol{l}) = \{u \in \Sigma, \forall i \in \{1, \ldots, n\}, W_u^{\boldsymbol{l},i} \cap S_i = W_u^{\boldsymbol{l},i}\}$. We call every mode u such that $u \notin \Theta(\boldsymbol{l})$ red flagged.

This is the most conservative approach, since an over-approximation of the actual discrete state image is used to verify that the system will be in S after the next time step. This is also the least computationally expensive approach since $W_u^{\boldsymbol{l},i}$ has already been computed for every $\boldsymbol{l}$, i and u to build the DBN approximation. It essentially means that if a mode yields a non null probability to go out of S for a given discrete state in the already computed DBN approximation, then the mode is red flagged for this discrete state. This is an under-approximation of the safe modes as the DBN is an over-approximation due to the independence of the variables. Safety using *DBN-based pre-selection* is ensured by the following theorem. The proof is given in [7].

Theorem 3. *Given an initial condition $\boldsymbol{x^0} = (x_1^0, \ldots, x_n^0)$, and a perturbation $\varepsilon \in D$, assume there is no safety deadlock; that is, for all discrete states $\boldsymbol{l} = (l_1, \ldots, l_n)$ such that $I_{j,l_j} \subseteq S_j$ for all j, the set of admissible modes $\Theta(\boldsymbol{l}) \neq \emptyset$.*

Let $(\boldsymbol{x}^k)_{k\geq 0}$ be a sequence of continuous states, $(\boldsymbol{l}^k)_{k\geq 0}$ the corresponding sequence of discrete states, and $(u^k)_{k\geq 0}$ a sequence of modes such that:

- $x_j^k \in I_{j,l_j^k}$ *for all j,*
- $u^k \in \Theta(\boldsymbol{l}^k)$,
- $\boldsymbol{x}^{k+1} = \phi(\delta; 0, \boldsymbol{x}^k, \varepsilon, u^k)$.

If $I_{j,l_j^0} \subseteq S_j$ for all j, then for all $k \geq 0$, $\boldsymbol{x}^k \in S$.

Full-State Pre-selection. It is possible to make the mode pre-selection by propagating every possible discrete state for every possible mode using the actual dynamics (2) instead of the DBN approximation, and red flag the modes that lead out of S. More precisely, for every discrete state $\boldsymbol{l}$, every mode u such that $Post_u(I_{1,l_1^k} \times \cdots \times I_{n,l_n^k}) \cap S \neq Post_u(I_{1,l_1^k} \times \cdots \times I_{n,l_n^k})$ is red flagged for $\boldsymbol{l}$. This requires an additional computation step that takes roughly the same amount of time as the DBN construction, but is worth doing when many dependencies are omitted in the graph, making the safety hard to ensure in practice. A theorem analog to Theorem 3 can be established for the *full-state pre-selection*, the proof is straightforward.

Perturbations and Measurement Noise. Once again, small perturbations can easily be handled by replacing every occurrence of the $Post_u(X)$ operator for a set X by $Post_u(X, D)$ where D is the perturbation set. Measurement noise is handled by enlarging the set X.

Cost Minimization. Then, to minimize a chosen cost function (2), the following optimization procedure is performed. Recall that the discrete state X_i is a discrete value associated to interval: $X_i = l$, $1 \leq l \leq L_i$ (see Subsect. 3.1). Let $\bar{x}_i^l$ denote the midpoint of interval $I_{i,l}$. For each time instant $j \in \{1, \ldots, T\}$, a real-valued estimate of the state of variable i is derived from the posterior distribution as follows:

$$\tilde{x}_i^j = \sum_{l \in \{1,\ldots,L_i\}} p(X_i^j = l \mid U^{0:j-1}, \boldsymbol{X^0}) \bar{x}_i^l. \tag{9}$$

The control sequence to apply for the next horizon is then estimated by minimizing the sum of squared errors:

$$\varepsilon(U^{0:T}) = \sum_{\{j=1,\ldots,T\}} (x^j - \tilde{x}^j)^2. \tag{10}$$

The search space for the optimal control sequence is thus reduced by eliminating the modes possibly leading out of S during the first time step. The optimization problem (10) is then solved with an *ad-hoc* direct search heuristic based on the Hooke and Jeeves procedure [22], but a more generic black box optimization algorithm such as NOMAD [4,5] could be used instead. Some further refinements are proposed in [7].

Distribution Reconstruction Heuristics. Suppose that the current (real valued) state is x_i on dimension $i \in \{1, \ldots, n\}$, which belongs to $\mathcal{X}_i = [x_i^{min}, x_i^{max}]$. Let us denote by $\bar{x}_i^l$ the midpoints of intervals $I_{i,l}$ for $l \in \{1, \ldots, L_i\}$. If $x_i \geq \bar{x}_i^1$ and $x_i < \bar{x}_i^{L_i}$, then there exists $k \in \{1, \ldots, L_i\}$ such that $\bar{x}_i^k \leq x_i < \bar{x}_i^{k+1}$. Let $\alpha \in [0, 1]$ such that $x_i = \alpha \bar{x}_i^k + (1 - \alpha)\bar{x}_i^{k+1}$. The initial distribution in (8) is chosen such that $p(X_i^0 = k) = \alpha$, and $p(X_i^0 = k+1) = 1 - \alpha$, and 0 everywhere else. If $x_i < \bar{x}_i^1$, all probabilities are 0 except for $p(X_i^0 = 1) = 1$. Similarly for $x_i \geq \bar{x}_i^{L_i}$, all probabilities are 0 except for : $p(X_i^0 = L_i) = 1$.

5 Applications

As can be expected, the choice of the sets $\mathcal{X}$ and S plays a crucial role in the ability to ensure safety guarantees. Selecting a broad safety set S, potentially equal to the full state space $\mathcal{X}$, combined with the *full-state pre-selection* strategy for mode selection (see Sect. 4), typically facilitates the synthesis of safe controllers but produces weak safety guarantee. In contrast, employing a narrower safety set $S \subset \mathcal{X}$, along with the *DBN-based pre-selection*, increases the safety guarantee at the risk of ending up in a safety deadlock *i.e.* $\Theta(\boldsymbol{l}) = \emptyset$ for the current discrete state $\boldsymbol{l}$. Another challenge resides in the initial state which may lie outside of the safety region. In this case several safety sets could be used, one to guarantee that each trace stays in $\mathcal{X}$, and a smaller one in which the trajectory stays once reached. Proving the reachability into this smaller set remains challenging and is left for future work.

Besides, it is worth noting that, in Definition 5, the set S is used to define the region in which the independent variables evolve when computing the DBN successor states. This construction is valid only when $S = \mathcal{X}$. In cases where $S \neq \mathcal{X}$, the set $\mathcal{X}$ must replace S in Definition 5, and the use of *full-state pre-selection* becomes necessary to maintain the validity of the safety guarantees.

In the following, we present some case studies that illustrate some possible choices for $\mathcal{X}$ and S. Furthermore, we would like to emphasize that even in cases where we end up in a safety deadlock, we can still return the modes that maximize the probability of reaching the target. This is a major strength compared to usual formal methods of control synthesis that typically do not return a controller in zones for which they did not manage to prove safety.

Implementation. The procedures described in this paper have been implemented and tested on a MacBook Pro 2022, with an Apple M2 chip (8-core CPU) and 8 GB of RAM. The present method is implemented in a Python prototype available at [6]. The DBN objects and inference algorithms are manipulated with the PyAgrum library [25]. The reachability computations that rely on polytopes are implemented with the Python package Polytope [1] which allows to compute the intersection of two polytopes, and the volume (Lebesgue measure) of a polytope.

5.1 Two-Room Apartment

This case study is based on a simple model of a two-room apartment adapted from [13], heated by one heater in one room, or two heaters (one in each room).

In this example, the objective is to control the temperature of both rooms. There is heat exchange between the two rooms and with the environment. The *continuous* dynamics of the system is given by the equation:

$$\begin{pmatrix} \dot{T}_1 \\ \dot{T}_2 \end{pmatrix} = \begin{pmatrix} -\alpha_{21} - \alpha_{e1} - \alpha_f u_1 & \alpha_{21} \\ \alpha_{12} & -\alpha_{12} - \alpha_{e2} - \alpha_f u_2 \end{pmatrix} \begin{pmatrix} T_1 \\ T_2 \end{pmatrix} + \begin{pmatrix} \alpha_{e1} T_e + \alpha_f T_f u_1 \\ \alpha_{e2} T_e + \alpha_f T_f u_2 \end{pmatrix}.$$

Here, T_1 and T_2 are the temperatures of the two rooms, and the state of the system corresponds to $T = (T_1, T_2)$. The control mode variable u_1 (respectively u_2) can take the values 0 or 1, depending on whether the heater in room 1 (respectively room 2) is switched off or on (hence $\Sigma_1 = \Sigma_2 = \{0, 1\}$). Hence, the dimension of the system is $n = 2$, and the number of switched modes is $N = 4$ if two heaters are considered. One of the heaters can be removed and its corresponding control input variable can be made equal to 0, the number of switched modes is then $N = 2$. Temperature T_e corresponds to the temperature of the environment, and T_f to the temperature of the heaters. The values of the different parameters are as follows: $\alpha_{12} = 5 \times 10^{-2}$, $\alpha_{21} = 5 \times 10^{-2}$, $\alpha_{e1} = 5 \times 10^{-3}$, $\alpha_{e2} = 5 \times 10^{-3}$, $\alpha_f = 8.3 \times 10^{-3}$, $T_e = 10$, $T_f = 35$, and the switching period is $\tau = 1$ seconds. When only one heater is used, $T_f = 50$.

A first experiment is realized with one heater to guarantee safety in the entire state space $\mathcal{X} = S = [13, 23]^2$ with no perturbations. The DBN construction time and *DBN-based pre-selection* take 0.1s when the state space is discretized in 5 sub-intervals for each dimension, and 0.7s for 10 sub-intervals. An MPC step takes about 0.15s for a horizon of length 3. In this case, regardless of the number of sub-intervals, the lowest sub-interval presents a deadlock since with only one heater, the temperature of the non heated room can go below the safety region for a brief time. Once higher intervals are reached, safety is proven without deadlocks. A second experiment is performed with one heater and a narrower safety set $S = [17, 21]^2$ with the state space $\mathcal{X} = [13, 23]^2$. Once the state reaches S, it is guaranteed to stay in S. Outside of S, the modes that yield the highest probability to track the target are returned. The results are plotted in Fig. 2 for different targets and safety sets. A third experiment is carried out with one heater, a broad safety set $\mathcal{X} = S = [13, 23]^2$ and an additional perturbation in $D = [-0.1, 0.1] \times [-0.1, 0.1]$. The results are plotted in Fig. 3 for different targets.

5.2 Eleven-Room House Floor Heating

This case study, proposed by the Danish company Seluxit, aims at controlling the temperature of an eleven room house, heated by geothermal energy. The *continuous* dynamics of the system is the following:

$$\dot{T}_i = \sum_{j=1}^{n} A^d_{i,j}(T_j - T_i) + B_i(T_{env} - T_i) + H^v_{i,j}.v_j. \tag{11}$$

The temperatures of the rooms are the T_i. The matrix A^d contains the heat transfer coefficients between the rooms, matrix B contains the heat transfer

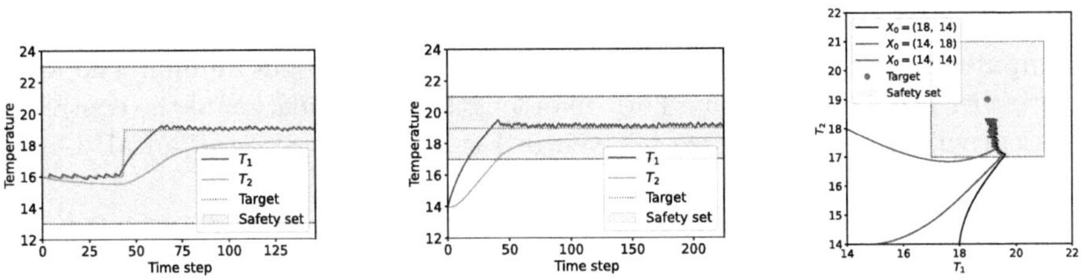

Fig. 2. Simulations of the MPC controlled two-room one-heater case study: (left) a time-varying target in a broad safety set, plotted within time; (middle) a constant target in a narrow safety set, plotted within time; (right) a constant target in a narrow safety set and three different initial conditions, plotted in the (T_1, T_2) plane.

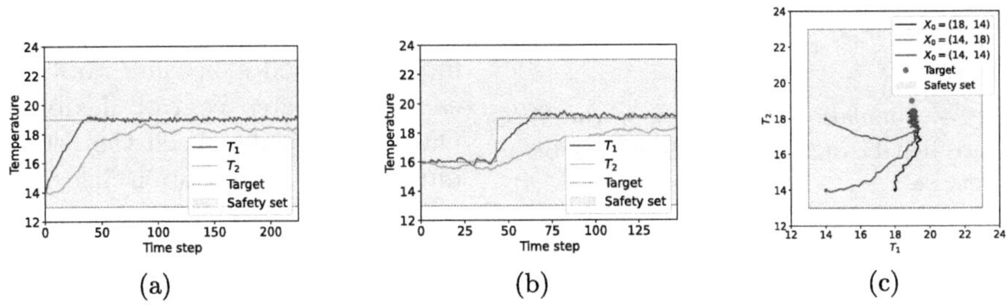

Fig. 3. Simulations of the MPC controlled two-room one-heater case study with perturbations for a broad safety set and: (a) a constant target, plotted within time; (b) a time-varying target, plotted within time; (c) a constant target and three different initial conditions, plotted in the (T_1, T_2) plane.

coefficients between the rooms and the external temperature T_{env} which can vary between some given bounds over time. The control matrix H^v contains the effects of the control on the room temperatures, and the control variable is here denoted by v_j. We have $v_j = 1$ (resp. $v_j = 0$) if the heater in room j is turned on (resp. turned off). We thus have $n = 11$ and $N = 2^{11} = 2048$ switching modes.

Note that the matrix A^d is parametrized by the open of closed state of the doors in the house. In our case, the average between closed and open matrices was taken for the computations. The exact values of the coefficients are given in [16]. The controller has to select which heater to turn on in the eleven rooms. Due to a limitation of the capacity supplied by the geothermal device, the 11 heaters cannot be turned on at the same time. In our case, we limit to 4 the number of heaters that can be on at the same time. We would like to emphasize that this case study is very challenging for formal methods because of the combinatorial explosion that is inherent to this switched model. Addressing such complexity typically requires the use of compositional techniques [17] or other tailored strategies.

For this case study, the DBN approximation was constructed with a broad safety set $S = \mathcal{X} = [11, 23]^{11}$ divided in 3 sub-intervals for each variable. The

DBN construction time took less than 1.5h. Note that each variable CPT can be computed in parallel. The *full-state pre-selection* took about 40 min. The MPC controller is computed with a horizon of length 3. A simulation of the controlled system with safety guarantee is given in Fig. 4. Computation of an MPC step takes less than a minute.

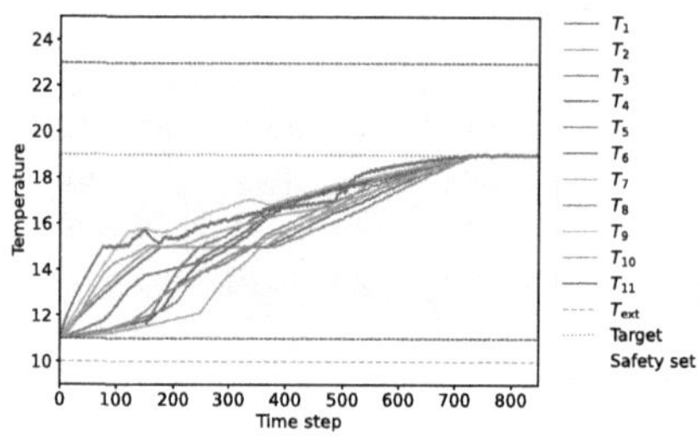

Fig. 4. Simulation within time of the MPC controlled 11-room case study with a broad safety set.

The experiment starts with all rooms at 11 °C, aiming for a target of 19 °C. The lowest temperature interval is very constrained: with only four heaters, a single control mode preserves system safety. As shown, this mode is used throughout the first 100 time steps. As variables move into higher intervals, more safe modes become available, enabling greater control flexibility. Once all variables reach the central interval, our optimization algorithm can be fully exploited. From time step 400 onward, trajectories become notably smoother and more efficient. Upon reaching the target temperature of 19 °C, the system stabilizes and maintains values closely aligned with our goal.

6 Conclusion

Throughout this paper, we have presented an MPC inspired control synthesis method that guarantees safety for linear switched control systems. We use a discrete probabilistic abstraction of the system which is a Markov chain, it is compactly stored as a DBN by making independence hypotheses between the different variables of the system. The transition probabilities and safety guarantees are computed with the help of exact polytope propagation. Our approach is more scalable than competing state-of-the-art formal methods, and we have an additional strength which is that our MPC approach returns efficient controllers even when safety cannot be guaranteed, making it applicable to more case studies.

In future work, we aim to apply our method to more challenging case studies, particularly those involving nonlinear systems. Currently, the exact propagation of polytopes is feasible due to the system's linearity. To extend our approach to the nonlinear setting, we plan to use formal over- and under-approximations of reachable sets [19,30] to estimate the transition probabilities of the discrete models. Additionally, we intend to refine our framework to handle more expressive specifications, for example by incorporating temporal logic constraints such as those defined in Linear Temporal Logic (LTL) [9].

References

1. Polytope 0.2.5. https://pypi.org/project/polytope/
2. Allgower, F., Findeisen, R., Nagy, Z.K., et al.: Nonlinear model predictive control: from theory to application. J.-Chin. Inst. Chem. Eng. **35**(3), 299–316 (2004)
3. Angeli, D.: A Lyapunov approach to incremental stability. In: Proceedings of IEEE Conference on Decision and Control, vol. 3, pp. 2947–2952 (2000)
4. Audet, C., Le Digabel, S., Rochon Montplaisir, V., Tribes, C.: Algorithm 1027: NOMAD version 4: nonlinear optimization with the MADS algorithm. ACM Trans. Math. Softw. **48**(3), 35:1–35:22 (2022). https://doi.org/10.1145/3544489
5. Audet, C., Dennis, J.E., Jr.: Mesh adaptive direct search algorithms for constrained optimization. SIAM J. Optim. **17**(1), 188–217 (2006)
6. Bahloul, Y.: DYNBACON: DYNamic BAyesian CONtrol (2025). https://git.lacl.fr/alecoent/dynbacon
7. Bahloul, Y., Le Coënt, A., Barbot, B., Pekergin, N.: Efficient Guaranteed Controllers for Switched Dynamical Systems Using Probabilistic Approximations (2025). https://hal.science/hal-05362437
8. Cauchi, N., Abate, A.: Stochy-automated verification and synthesis of stochastic processes. In: Proceedings of the 22nd ACM International Conference on Hybrid Systems: Computation and Control, pp. 258–259 (2019)
9. Davoren, J.M., Nerode, A.: Logics for hybrid systems. Proc. IEEE **88**(7), 985–1010 (2000)
10. Franz, R., Milam, M., Hauser, J.: Applied receding horizon control of the caltech ducted fan. In: Proceedings of the 2002 American Control Conference (IEEE Cat. No. CH37301), vol. 5, pp. 3735–3740. IEEE (2002)
11. Fribourg, L., Soulat, R.: Control of Switching Systems by Invariance Analysis: Application to Power Electronics. Wiley (2013)
12. Girard, A.: Reachability of uncertain linear systems using zonotopes. In: International Workshop on Hybrid Systems: Computation and Control, pp. 291–305. Springer (2005)
13. Girard, A.: Low-complexity switching controllers for safety using symbolic models. IFAC Proc. Vol. **45**(9), 82–87 (2012)
14. Jadbabaie, A., Yu, J., Hauser, J.: Stabilizing receding horizon control of nonlinear systems: a control lyapunov function approach. In: Proceedings of the 1999 American Control Conference (Cat. No. 99CH36251), vol. 3, pp. 1535–1539. IEEE (1999)
15. Kim, E.S., Arcak, M., Seshia, S.A.: Symbolic control design for monotone systems with directed specifications. Automatica **83**, 10–19 (2017). http://dx.doi.org/10.1016/j.automatica.2017.04.060. http://www.sciencedirect.com/science/article/pii/S0005109817302558
16. Larsen, K.G., Mikučionis, M., Muñiz, M., Srba, J., Taankvist, J.H.: Online and compositional learning of controllers with application to floor heating. In: Chechik, M., Raskin, J.-F. (eds.) TACAS 2016. LNCS, vol. 9636, pp. 244–259. Springer, Heidelberg (2016). https://doi.org/10.1007/978-3-662-49674-9_14
17. Le Coënt, A., Fribourg, L., Markey, N., De Vuyst, F., Chamoin, L.: Compositional synthesis of state-dependent switching control. Theoret. Comput. Sci. **750**, 53–68 (2018)
18. Le Coënt, A., Barbot, B., Pekergin, N.: Efficient probabilistic inference in biochemical networks. Comput. Biol. Med. **183**, 109280 (2024). https://doi.org/10.1016/j.compbiomed.2024.109280

19. Li, M., Mosaad, P.N., Fränzle, M., She, Z., Xue, B.: Safe over- and under-approximation of reachable sets for autonomous dynamical systems. In: Jansen, D.N., Prabhakar, P. (eds.) FORMATS 2018. LNCS, vol. 11022, pp. 252–270. Springer, Cham (2018). https://doi.org/10.1007/978-3-030-00151-3_15
20. Mazo, M., Davitian, A., Tabuada, P.: PESSOA: a tool for embedded controller synthesis. In: Touili, T., Cook, B., Jackson, P. (eds.) CAV 2010. LNCS, vol. 6174, pp. 566–569. Springer, Heidelberg (2010). https://doi.org/10.1007/978-3-642-14295-6_49
21. Meyer, P.J., Girard, A., Witrant, E.: Robust controlled invariance for monotone systems: application to ventilation regulation in buildings. Automatica **70**, 14–20 (2016)
22. Moser, I.: Hooke-Jeeves revisited. In: 2009 IEEE Congress on Evolutionary Computation, pp. 2670–2676. IEEE (2009)
23. Mouelhi, S., Girard, A., Gössler, G.: Cosyma: a tool for controller synthesis using multi-scale abstractions. In: Proceedings of the 16th International Conference on Hybrid Systems: Computation and Control, pp. 83–88. ACM (2013)
24. Pola, G., Girard, A., Tabuada, P.: Approximately bisimilar symbolic models for nonlinear control systems. Automatica **44**(10), 2508–2516 (2008)
25. agrum/pyagrum. https://agrum.gitlab.io/
26. Ravanbakhsh, H., Sankaranarayanan, S.: Robust controller synthesis of switched systems using counterexample guided framework. In: 2016 International Conference on Embedded Software (EMSOFT), pp. 1–10. IEEE (2016)
27. Reissig, G., Weber, A., Rungger, M.: Feedback refinement relations for the synthesis of symbolic controllers. arXiv preprint arXiv:1503.03715 (2015)
28. Rungger, M., Zamani, M.: SCOTS: a tool for the synthesis of symbolic controllers. In: Proceedings of the 19th International Conference on Hybrid Systems: Computation and Control, pp. 99–104. ACM (2016)
29. Alexandre dit Sandretto, J.: Reliable nonlinear model-predictive control via validated simulation. In: 2018 Annual American Control Conference (ACC). pp. 609–614 (2018). https://doi.org/10.23919/ACC.2018.8431304
30. Sandretto, J.A.D., Chapoutot, A.: Validated explicit and implicit Runge-Kutta methods. Reliable Computing electronic edition 22 (2016)
31. Wang, H., Huang, Q., Li, Z.S.: A dynamic Bayesian network control strategy for modeling grid-connected inverter stability. IEEE Trans. Reliab. **71**(1), 75–86 (2021)

Cyber attacks

Modeling Lateral Attack Containment via Honeypot Architectures in Virtualized Systems

Pierre Charreaux[1(✉)], Yezekael Hayel[2], Francesco De Pellegrini[2], Alexandre Reiffers-Masson[1], and Françoise Sailhan[1]

[1] Lab-STICC, IMT Atlantique, Brest, France
{pierre.charreaux,alexandre.reiffers-masson, francoise.sailhan}@imt-atlantique.fr

[2] Laboratoire Informatique d'Avignon, University of Avignon, Avignon, France
{yezekael.hayel,francesco.de-pellegrini}@univ-avignon.fr

Abstract. Cloud-hosted microservices enable scalable and flexible delivery of online services, but unfortunately, also introduce new attack surfaces. In particular, lateral movement attacks exploit interconnected microservice chains and compromise target service without defenders having time to discover and remediate the breach. In this paper, we explore ways to deploy honeypots as a deception-based defense against lateral movement attacks targeting a microservice oriented architecture. We consider a cost metric corresponding to the expected number of lateral movement steps to perform so that the attack succeed. Using a Markov model, we describe the performance of exploration strategies adopted by an attack to reach its target. The model describes two types of attackers, namely a naive attacker with no knowledge on the system, as well as an experienced attacker with partial information about the distance to travel to reach the target. We evaluate our framework and simulate an attack against a vulnerable microservices chain in a Kubernetes cluster. Evaluations confirm that the honeypot-based defense strategy significantly increases the average time involved to reach the target, providing a baseline for sizing honeypots deployment that effectively slows down attacks.

Keywords: Microservice chains · Honeypots · Cyberdeception · Stochastic processes · Hitting time

1 Introduction

Whilst driving the digital transformation, cloud is also opening up new attack opportunities [10,12] and security threats for the public and private organizations that rely on it. Cloud-hosted services grant a privileged access to the organization information system and thereby constitute a prominent target characterized by a new attack surface. One of the most critical threats [7] to a

A. Remke et al. (Eds.): Valuetools 2025, LNICST 691, pp. 159–175, 2027.
https://doi.org/10.1007/978-3-032-23901-3_10

cloud environment is lateral movement, an attack which is performed to explore and compromise the sub-systems (i.e., micro-services) of a cloud-hosted service. The lateral movement attack typically starts with a compromised cloud frontend service from which the attacker gradually reaches on-premise back-end service (i.e., the target). In practice, the attacker applies lateral movement(s): the attacker follows the chain of modular microservices, either deployed in Virtual Machines (VMs) or containers, that form a full-featured service. Defending the cloud against lateral movement attacks remains a challenge to address [2,14] because attacker takes advantage of the communication paths and trust relationship of the microservice chain [3]. Therefore, attackers move quickly and remain unnoticed.

In this work, we investigate the use of honeypots to lure attackers, divert their efforts, and ultimately isolate them from legitimate services. We study a performance metric that evaluates the efficiency of the deployed honeypots. Traditionally, honeypots serve as a tool to monitor, and support post-attack analysis [8]. However, honeypots can also serve as dynamic shields that protect microservice-based applications by misdirecting and containing adversaries. In our setting, a honeypot is a component (e.g., a microservice, pod, or a container) that corresponds to a decoy emulating a legitimate component, that the attacker cannot distinguish from a legitimate one. A honeypot is accessible from genuine microservices. In practice, the honeypot is configured to ensure that any outgoing traffic is redirected to itself or to another honeypot, effectively trapping the attacker within a deceptive environment. Despite their benefits, the deployment of honeypots at scale, is challenging due to their resource (CPU, storage, memory...) usage and associated operational costs.

Recent approaches [4–6,11,13] optimize the dynamic placement of honeypots to minimize resource consumption. Given a certain number of available honeypots, honeypots are placed so that the expected success chance of the attacker to reach the target is minimized. For instance, in [11] the honeypot placement is formulated as mixed-integer program (MIP), which is further solved via a clustering-based heuristic, suitable for large scale, dynamic graphs. In [4], the dynamic placement of honeypots is modeled as a partially observable stochastic game. Attacker sequentially chooses which hosts to attack and progresses towards the ultimate target, while the defender selects the hosts that act as honeypots and detect specific attacker's moves. The authors of [6] model the lateral movement attack as a time-expanded network with randomly appearing service links. They propose an optimal strategy to place honeypots dynamically on idle production servers, so as to proactively mitigate long-term risks. In [13], the authors model the attacker-defender interactions as a continuous-time Markov decision process where the defender detects and ejects the attacker, at any time, and finds an equilibrium between risks and information obtained from the attacker. In [5], the authors use a semi-Markov decision process to model the attacker's movements and the defender's actions. The defender changes the honeypots' interactivity configuration to optimize the attacker's sojourn time in a honeypot. Using reinforcement learning, they find policies to optimize information gains while reducing risks. In contrast to the above efforts, our model is intended to both (i) evaluate the number of honeypots necessary to slow down the attacker, and (ii) to place them, assuming that the attacker cannot distinguish honeypots from genuine services. Based on our model, a cloud administrator may carefully estimate and place the right number of honeypots to slow down the attacker so as to gain sufficient time to develop countermeasures, or even completely discourage the attacker. Depending on the number of honeypots, a cloud administrator estimates the associated overhead[1] (e.g., financial cost), which depends on e.g., the cloud system, its virtualisation/hardware components.

Our model assumes that the attacker cannot distinguish a genuine microservice from a honeypot and therefore chooses the next move at random: the next microservice to attack is selected, be it a genuine microservice or a honeypot. We assume that the attacker, which believes he/she is trapped in a honeypot, has no option but to start from the entry point (i.e., the frontend microservice). Recall that (i) the attacker does not distinguish honeypots from genuine microservices, and (ii) there is also no backtracking to a genuine microservice from a honeypot. Our model takes into account two types of attackers: a naive attacker (also called *myopic* attacker) that has no information about the cloud/application, and an *experienced* attacker that is capable of estimating the number of microservices between the frontend microservice and the target. Thus, when too many lateral movements have been performed without finding the target, the experienced attacker returns to the frontend microservice to perform another attempt. In contrast, a myopic attacker has no information about the system and randomly chooses when to return to the frontend microservice.

Overall, we provide two main contributions. First, we introduce a Markov model of a lateral movement attack performed on a microservices chain equipped with honeypots. The model accounts for generic attackers who do not distinguish honeypots from genuine microservices (Sect. 2). Specifically, we introduce two models that deal with myopic and experienced attackers. Second, we find a mathematical closed form for the mean number of lateral movements necessary to reach the target (Sect. 3). We validate our model numerically w.r.t. the number of attack steps to reach the target and describe the (optimal) behaviour of the myopic and experienced intruders (Sect. 4). Finally, the attack is studied under a real-world setting with a lateral movement attack performed on a microservice chain in a Kubernetes cluster. In addition, our real-world evaluation (Sect. 4.3) confirms that, even with a lightweight deployment, with i.e., one honeypot per microservice, the time for an attacker to reach the target becomes significant, namely at least 20 times longer than without the proposed deception strategy.

2 System Model

We consider a cloud environment (Fig. 1a) with a microservices chain in which the microservice at the frontend serves as an entry point for any user (including an attacker). The attacker aims at accessing the database at the

[1] Determining an overhead is out of scope of this paper.

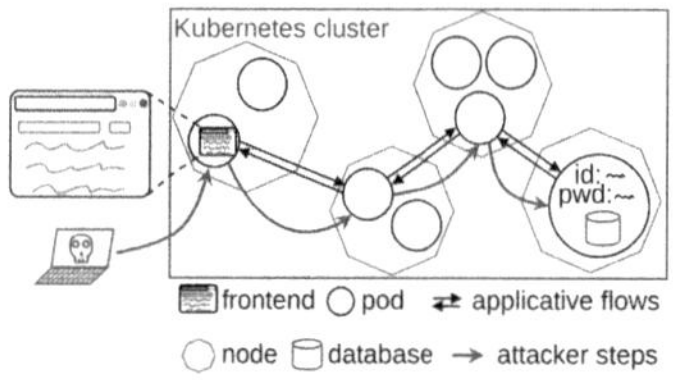

(a) Lateral movement attack on Kubernetes cluster: starting by attacking/poisonning the entry point, the attacker moves laterally exploiting the vulnerabilities on the encountered microservices.

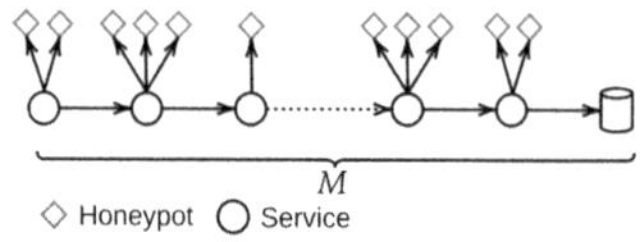

(b) System is represented as a graph composed of genuine microservices and honeypots.

Fig. 1. An application, composed of a microservices chain, is hosted in a Kubernetes cluster along with honeypots.

backend of the chain. The system is modeled (Fig. 1b) as a path composed of M nodes. Each node represents a genuine microservice, the first node is the frontend microservice, and the M-th node is the target, $M \geq 2$. Overall, the attacker performs $M-1$ moves along the microservice chain to reach the target. For each genuine node i (with $1 \leq i \leq M-1$), the defender creates a set containing $L_i - 1$ honeypots, which appear to the attacker as genuine neighbors of node i. Honeypots are connected to other honeypots. Thus, at step k (with $1 \leq k \leq M-1$) the attacker is offered L_k possible microservices to attack, which may refer to genuine microservice iff node k is a genuine node.

2.1 Lateral Movement Policy and Objective Function

At each step k of a lateral movement attack, the next microservice to attack is chosen uniformly at random among the L_k available microservices. We assume that an attacker is aware of the potential presence of honeypots and is willing to avoid getting trapped indefinitely. An attacker may henceforth stop the current attempt and may start a new one from the entry point. We call each of these attempts an *attack*.

The global cost perceived by the attacker depends on the Lateral Movement Policy (LMP), denoted by π. At each step k of the lateral movement, the attacker continues the attack with probability $\pi(k)$ or starts a new attack with probability $1-\pi(k)$. The probability depends on the number of explored nodes. Note that the number of steps of an attack may be greater than the number of genuine microservices M, in which case the current attack is trapped in a honeypot. We denote q_i the probability of reaching a honeypot once performing a lateral movement from a genuine node of index i; this probability depends on the placement of honeypots, i.e., L_i, in the microservice architecture. The total number of steps $\tau_M(\pi)$ necessary for the attacker to hit the target starting from the initial entry point and using the LMP π verifies:

$$\tau_M(\pi) = (M-1) + \sum_{k=1}^{N(\pi)-1} \tau_\pi(k), \tag{1}$$

with $N(\pi)$ the number of attacks and $\tau_\pi(k)$ the length of the k-th attack, i.e., the number of lateral movements they performed. The total cost $J(\pi)$ with discount factor $\gamma \in [0,1]$, for the attacker following the LMP π, satisfies:

$$J(\pi) = \mathbb{E}_\pi \left[\sum_{k=1}^{\tau_M(\pi)} \gamma^t \right] = \mathbb{E}_\pi \left[\frac{1-\gamma^{\tau_M(\pi)}}{1-\gamma} \right], \tag{2}$$

where the rightmost equality is true when $\gamma < 1$. The discount γ (with $\gamma \in [0,1]$) mimics the persistence of the attacker: the smaller γ, the more likely an attacker prolongs the current attack before starting another attack. With $\gamma = 1$, the total cost corresponds to the expected number of steps to reach the target. As shown in the following, for any LMP π, attacks are independent, and thus the lengths of attacks are i.i.d and independent of the number $N(\pi)$ of attacks.

2.2 Markov Model

We introduce a Markovian model to study the cost associated with a LMP performed by an attacker. The proofs of the theorems and propositions are provided in the Appendix, except for Theorem 2 for which a sketch of proof is provided because a formal proof requires using hitting time theory. Each attack is performed in discrete steps at $t = 0, 1, \ldots$, where the initial step ($t = 0$) is associated with the exploitation of the vulnerability at the entry point. At any step t, the system state is described by $S(t) = (X(t), Y(t))$ where $X(t) \in \{1, \ldots, M\}$ is the number of steps in genuine microservices and $Y(t) \in \{0, \ldots, \infty\}$ is the number of steps in honeypots, where the attacker only knows the overall number of steps $X(t) + Y(t)$. Recall that q_k is the probability that an attack gets trapped in a honeypot while performing a lateral movement from the k-th genuine microservice. The transition probabilities $\mathbb{P}(S(t+1)|S(t) = P((k',h'),(k,h))$ write

$$\begin{aligned}
&\mathbb{P}((k+1,0)|(k,0)) = (1-q_k)\pi(k), k = 1, \ldots, M-1,\\
&\mathbb{P}((k,1)|(k,0)) = q_k\pi(k), k = 1, \ldots, M-1,\\
&\mathbb{P}((k,h+1)|(k,h)) = \pi(k+h), \forall h \geq 1,\\
&\mathbb{P}((1,0)|(k,h)) = 1 - \pi(k+h), \forall k \neq M,\\
&\mathbb{P}((M,0)|(M,0)) = 1.
\end{aligned}$$

The attack starts at the entry node, which means that $\mathbb{P}(S(0) = (1,0)) = 1$. An attacker that reaches the target, stays there indefinitely with a zero transition cost. Overall, the total number of steps τ_M involved to hit the target satisfies:

$$\tau_M = \min\{t \in \mathbb{N} | X(t) = M\}.$$

The total number of steps depends on the number of attacks and their respective lengths, as described in (1). Let $\tau_b(k)$ be the length of the k-th time an attack starts, i.e., the attacker backs off to state $(1, 0)$. It verifies:

$$\tau_b(0) = 0 \text{ and } \tau_b(k) = \min\{t \in \mathbb{N} | t > \tau_b(k-1), S(t) = (1,0)\},\ k > 0.$$

Note that τ_b are the hitting times for state $S_0 = (1, 0)$. In order to avoid trivialities, we assume in the rest of the paper that the attacker is rational, i.e., the attacker is not trapped indefinitely in honeypot and therefore backs off with positive probability: formally, the LMPs are such that $\sum_{k=1}^{\infty}(1 - \pi(k)) = +\infty$, i.e., the state S_0 is positive recurrent once we remove the absorbing state $(M, 0)$ from the kernel of the original MDP. The length of an attack is $\tau(k) = \tau_b(k) - \tau_b(k-1)$. The number of attacks launched from the entry point is defined by:

$$N = \max\{k \in \mathbb{N}_+, \tau_M > \tau_b(k)\} + 1.$$

The next theorem provides the probability distribution of the number of attacks N.

Theorem 1. *Let* $\rho = \prod_{k=1}^{M-1}(1 - q_k)\pi(k)$. *Then:*
i. If $\rho = 0$, *then* $N = \infty$ *w.p.1., i.e., the attacker never reaches the target.*
ii. If $\rho > 0$, *then the number of attacks* N *that are necessary to reach the target follows a geometric distribution* $\mathbb{P}(N = h) = \rho(1 - \rho)^{h-1}, \quad h = 1, 2, \ldots$

Theorem 2. *i. The attack lengths* $\tau(1), \ldots \tau(N-1)$ *are independent.*
ii. The distribution of the length of failed attacks $\tau(h), h = 1, \ldots, N-1$ *writes*

$$\mathbb{P}(\tau(1) = k) = (1 - \pi(k)) \prod_{j=1}^{k-1} \pi(j),$$

The above theorem gives the distribution probability of the length of failed attacks. Incidentally, such length depends only on the impatience of the attacker. Finally, the following proposition gives a closed-form expression of the total cost for any LMP π.

Proposition 1. *Let* $\gamma < 1$, *and* ρ *be as in Theorem 1, then*

$$J(\pi) = \frac{\gamma}{1-\gamma} \frac{1 - G_{\tau(1)}(\gamma)(1 - \rho(1 - \gamma^{M-1}))}{G_{\tau(1)}(\gamma)\big(1 - (1-\rho)G_{\tau(1)}(\gamma)\big)}$$

where $G_{\tau(1)}(\gamma) = \sum_{k=1}^{+\infty} \gamma^k \mathbb{P}(\tau(1) = k)$.

While the attacker is interested in finding the optimal attack policy π^*, which is the one that minimizes its total cost, i.e., $\pi^* := \arg\min_\pi J(\pi)$, the attacker has a partial knowledge, which implies that the attacker cannot solve for the optimal policy. In the next section, we investigate the best attack strategies for a myopic attacker and a deterministic attacker.

3 Specific LMP

We model the Lateral Movement Policy associated with a myopic attacker and a deterministic one. The myopic attacker randomly decides at each step to continue the attack or to go back to the initial node (and launch another attack); the deterministic attacker takes into account the number of nodes already visited to decide whether to continue the attack.

The deployment of honeypots is assumed uniform, i.e., the defender deploys a constant number $L-1$ of honeypot nodes attached to each genuine microservice on the microservice chain. Hence the probability of falling into a honeypot from a genuine microservice at the k-the step of an attack is $q_k = 1 - L^{-1}$.

3.1 Myopic LMP

During each attack, we assume that the myopic attacker takes at least a first step to the next microservice or honeypot (i.e., $\pi(1) = 1$). Afterwards, the attacker performs a lateral movement with positive, constant probability $\pi(i) = 1 - p$, and start a new attack with constant probability $p = 1 - \pi(i)$. Thus, according to Theorem 1, the probability ρ to reach the target during an attack satisfies $\rho = \frac{(1-p)^{M-2}}{L^{M-1}}$. For $\gamma = 1$, the total cost function is the expected number of steps to reach the target:

$$J(p) = M - 1 + \mathbb{E}\left[\sum_{k=1}^{N-1} \tau(k)\right] = M - 1 + \mathbb{E}[\tau(1)]\mathbb{E}[N-1],$$

where we applied Wald's equation [15]. From Theorem 2 it follows that $\mathbb{E}[N] = \frac{1-\rho}{\rho}$. We can write explicitly $\mathbb{P}\left(\tau(1) = h\right) = p(1-p)^{h-2}$, $h = 2, 3, ...$, from which it holds that:

$$J(p) = (M-1) + \frac{1+p}{p}\left(\frac{1}{\frac{(1-p)^{M-2}}{L^{M-1}}} - 1\right) \tag{3}$$

Due to the lack of space, we do not provide derivations for $\gamma < 1$ that are similar to determine. Instead, we investigate in the following the worst case for a myopic attack.

Proposition 2. *i. There exists a unique optimal myopic attack policy with parameter* p^*.
ii. $p^* = \Theta(\frac{1}{M-1})$ *for large* L.

The previous proposition implies that, by increasing the number of honeypots for a given value of M, the optimal policy depends only on the number M of genuine microservices. In particular, in order to avoid being restrained in honeypots indefinitely, the optimal myopic attacker makes paths of average length M. Typically, an attacker ignores the value of M but may have knowledge of its distribution. This kind of Bayesian approach leads to the study of the deterministic threshold policies derived in the next section.

3.2 Threshold Policies

We consider an attack behavior in which the decision to continue the exploration of the microservices chain is deterministic. In practice, being unable to distinguish honeypots from genuine microservice nodes, the attacker explores a microservices chain of fixed length σ before going back to the initial entry point, i.e., the attacker goes back to the entry point whenever $X + Y = \sigma$. Formally, a threshold policy π_σ, for a given $\sigma > 0$, is a LMP defined as

$$\pi_\sigma(k) = \begin{cases} 1 & \text{if} \quad k = 1, \dots, \sigma - 1, \\ 0 & \text{if} \quad k \geq \sigma. \end{cases} \tag{4}$$

Note that if the attacker knows the exact number M of genuine nodes composing the microservice chain, then the optimal policy is the deterministic threshold policy π_M that consists of pursuing an attack of length $\sigma = M$. In general, we assume that the attacker may have just a conjectural distribution on the number of nodes M which compose the microservice chain, namely β. Hence, we determine the expected cost corresponding to a certain threshold policy π_σ. The attacker's cost function is $J(\pi_\sigma) = \mathbb{E}_{\pi_\sigma}\left[\frac{1-\gamma^{\tau_M(\pi_\sigma)}}{1-\gamma}\right]$, where $\tau_M(\pi_\sigma)$ is the total number of steps to hit the target under LMP π_σ.

Let us fix $M = m$ and define $J(\pi_\sigma, m)$ the cost under π_σ. We distinguish two cases:

$\sigma < m$: The attacker never hits the target, i.e., $\tau_M(\pi_\sigma) = +\infty$ w.p.1., so that $J(\pi_\sigma, m) = \frac{1}{1-\gamma}$.

$\sigma \geq m$: The attacker hits the target after a finite number of attacks $N(\pi_\sigma)$ w.p.1., where from Theorem 1, $N(\pi_\sigma)$ follows a geometric distribution with parameter $\rho = 1/L^{m-1}$.

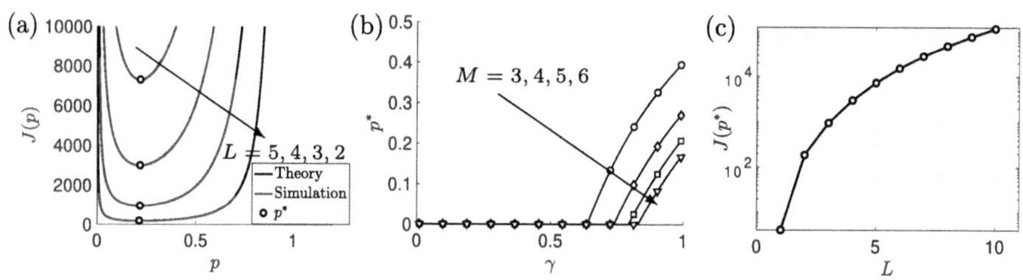

Fig. 2. (a) Equation (1) (black) and simulation curve (blue) for myopic attacker, for $M = 5$ and $L = 5, 4, 3, 2$; the round marker indicates the optimal myopic policy p^*. (b) Impact of the discount factor γ on the optimal myopic policy, for $M = 3, 4, 5, 6$ and $L = 3$. (c) Minimum number of steps to reach target for a myopic attacker as a function of L.

$$J(\pi_\sigma, m) = \rho \sum_{j=0}^{+\infty} (1-\rho)^j \left(\frac{1 - \gamma^{j\sigma + m - 1}}{1 - \gamma}\right) = \frac{1}{1-\gamma}\left(1 - \frac{\rho\gamma^{m-1}}{1 - (1-\rho)\gamma^\sigma}\right) \tag{5}$$

Finally, given a conjectural distribution β for the attacker about the number of genuine microservices in the architecture, the attacker will choose the LMP π_σ that minimizes the following expected cost:

$$J(\pi_\sigma) = \sum_{m=1}^{\infty} J(\pi_\sigma, m)\beta(m) = \frac{1}{1-\gamma}\left(1 - \sum_{m=1}^{\sigma} \frac{L^{-(m-1)}\gamma^{m-1}}{1-(1-L^{-(m-1)})\gamma^{\sigma}}\beta(m)\right).$$

Note that the latter function depends on σ, so that the optimal threshold for an apriori distribution β can be computed, as shown later in the numerical section.

4 Numerical Illustration and Empirical Experimentation

We perform numerical evaluations for the case of an attacker adopting either the myopic policy (Sect. 4.1) or the deterministic threshold policy (Sect. 4.2). We complement evaluation (Sect. 4.2) with a set of real experiments performed on a cloud emulation platform. We consider a microservice architecture where users access the web page of a target service. The server hosting the web page is forwarding the users' requests to a gateway, which is in charge of routing such requests to the actual service. The service is composed of several microservices, chained together and executed in cascade according to the given chain order. The last microservice extracts data available in a database and forwarding it to the previous microservices. We detail the setup of our microservice architecture and of the lateral movement attack.

4.1 Numerical Illustrations of a Myopic Policy Attack

Expected Time to Reach the Target: In Fig. 2a, we consider the average number of movements of an attacker to hit the target for different probabilities of restarting an attack ($p = 1 - \pi$). We consider a number of microservices $M = 5$ and a different number of honeypots per node. The theoretical curve, given by equation (1), in black, matches the simulation results, in blue. As expected from Prop. 2, the optimal probability p^* for a naive attacker to reach the target depends on M and it is upper bounded by $\frac{1}{M-1}$.

Attacker Persistence: We can consider a discount factor on the myopic intruders to characterize their persistence when performing an attack. In our model, it indicates whether attackers take into account the future when planning their steps. An impatient attacker takes into account the whole future and is wary of traps: this corresponds to a large value of γ. Conversely, a small value of γ corresponds to a persistent attacker.

In Fig. 2b, we plot the optimal probability p^* to start back at front-end for $L = 3$ and different values of M. We observe the presence of a critical threshold value γ^c for which $p^*(\gamma) = 0$ for all $\gamma < \gamma^c$. In particular, $\gamma^c = 0.64$, 0.74, 0.8 and 0.83 for $M = 3, 4, 5, 6$, respectively. For attackers with higher discount factors (e.g., for $\gamma \geq 0.83$ when $M = 6$), the optimal probability to restart the current attack grows mildly super-linearly.

Comparing Fig. 2a and Fig. 2b, the worst attackers from the point of view of an administrator are impatient. Their probability is set to reduce the number of steps as γ tends to one. Actually, for low values of γ, an attacker may not even return to the front-end service, as visible for $\gamma \leq 0.5$.

Impact of the Number of Honeypots: to illustrate the impact of the number of honeypots in slowing down attackers, we reported in Fig. 2c the value of $J(p^*)$ for $M = 5$ and increasing L. From (3), it can be seen that the mean number of steps increases polynomially with L. We see that an optimal myopic attack would require around 200 steps on average when deploying one honeypot per genuine microservice ($L = 2$), and around 10^5 steps when we deploy 9. With this graph, we obtain an indication on how many honeypots are needed to shield the microservice chain. Indeed, if the attack needs to be slowed down to at least 10^3 steps on average, then 2 honeypots per microservices are enough. However, if the attacker needs to be slowed for no less than 5000 steps on average, we would need 4 honeypots per microservices. Overall, as the number of honeypots is $(M-1) \times (L-1)$, 4 decoy honeypots per microservice would require to deploy 16 honeypots along a microservice chain with 5 nodes.

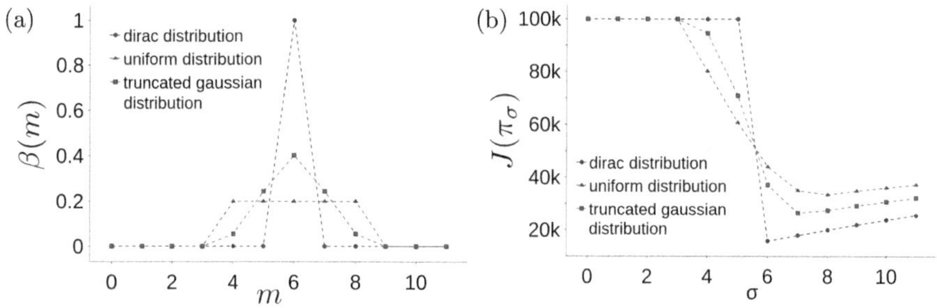

Fig. 3. Threshold attack policies for various β distributions. (a) Attacker's knowledge of the length of the microservices chain $\beta(m)$. In blue (with circles), perfect knowledge, in green (with triangles) uniform possibilities, and in red (with squares) gaussian possibilities, all with mean $M = 6$. (b) Attackers chooses the optimal σ as the one that returns the least average amount of steps, for a given distribution. In blue (with circles), perfect knowledge, in green (with triangles) uniform possibilities, and in red (with squares) gaussian possibilities, all with mean $M = 6$.

4.2 Numerical Illustrations of a Threshold Policy Attack

We consider three distributions representing the possible knowledge on M of an experienced attacker (Fig. 3). In Fig. 3b, we plot the cost $J(\pi_\sigma)$ that a persistent attacker ($\gamma \to 1$) undergoes by choosing threshold policy σ. As γ is close to 1, the cost is as large as 10^5 (actually, $\gamma = 1$ would mean infinite average cost). When the attacker knows the exact microservice chain length M, their optimal strategy is $\sigma^* = M$ (Fig. 3b, blue curve with circle markers). It is interesting to notice that when instead the attacker hesitates uniformly between several possible values of M (Fig. 3b, green curve with triangle markers), their optimal strategy σ^* is to explore up to the highest possible value, i.e., $\sigma^* = 8$. However, in the truncated gaussian case (Fig. 3b, red curve with square markers), where higher values correspond to a smaller tail of the distribution, the optimal threshold σ^* is smaller than the highest possible value. In this case, in fact, the event that $\{M = 8\}$ has a very low probability, and the optimal choice for the attacker is $\sigma^* = 7$. We observe that a more precise apriori knowledge on M – a skewed distribution mimics a more precise apriori knowledge than a uniform one – leads also to a reduction of the minimum expected cost for the attacker.

4.3 Empirical Experimentation in a Virtualized Environment

Table 1. Efficiency of myopic and threshold policy with honeypots compared to baseline policy without honeypots for $M = 6$.

Policy	L	# Experiments	Avg. time to success	$\hat{\tau_M}$	Avg. attack duration	$\hat{\tau}$	$\hat{N}$
Myopic: $p^* = 0.175$	3	9	16851 s	935	116.5 s	6.9 (var = 24)	142.2 (var = 5182)
Threshold: $\sigma^* = 6$	3	10	13023 s	690	92.4 s	5 (var = 0)	138 (var = 8225)
Myopic: $p^* = 0.173$	2	10	3309 s	221	92 s	6.3 (var = 21)	35.2 (var = 1181)
Threshold: $\sigma^* = 6$	2	10	1644 s	75	107.7 s	5 (var = 0)	15 (var = 192)
Baseline	1	44	70.9 s	5	70.9 s	5 (var = 0)	1 (var = 0)

Using kubeadm, we setup and manage a Kubernetes cluster made of 3 master nodes that control the cluster and 2 workers that run the service. We use the Calico framework to configure secure networking and enforce advanced policies for cloud-native microservices/applications. Using this framework, we deploy vulnerable microservices, and then we attack the cluster through a lateral movement strategy. We setup 5 genuine microservices, each with two pods, and a single backend microservice, resulting in a total of $M = 6$ microservices. Each microservice corresponds to a Python web server with a vulnerability: the attacker may execute any user-submitted data as a system command. As illustration, the frontend microservice allows the execution of arbitrary commands submitted through a webpage while the backend microservice reachable from the previous vulnerable microservice, returns a success flag. Additionally, we deploy honeypots mimicking a genuine microservices but with no possibility to reach another genuine microservice: this is prevented by the calico network rules. Similarly, Calico network rules enforce lateral movement between consecutive microservices.

The attacker relies on the Netcat tool, which creates TCP connections between machines and enables remote system commands execution. In practice, the attacker first gets a reverse shell on the front-end microservice with a terminal capable of executing remote commands. Then, the attacker listens for connections to the front-end machine, and uses the vulnerability of the next microservice to obtain another reverse shell. Repeating these steps, the attacker reaches the backend service. To automate the attack, a Python script sends HTTP calls to the vulnerable microservices, associated with a specific Netcat command, to initialize reverse shells. The script listens for connections, and once a reverse shell is established, the script deploys other scripts for lateral movement and scanning. This process repeats until either the attacker reaches the backend or, depending on the LMP, it starts another attack on the front-end.

Results - To evaluate the efficiency of the honeypots strategy, we consider several metrics related to lateral movement attacks:

1. The average time to success—the time it takes for an attacker to reach the target microservice or database;
2. The average number of steps to reach the target $\hat{\tau}_M$;
3. The average duration of an attack;
4. The average number of steps per attack $\hat{\tau}$;
5. The average number of attacks to reach the target $\hat{N}$.

We compare the results for the myopic and threshold policies with a honeypot reachable from each microservice, against a baseline policy with no honeypots, where the attacker always succeeds in one attack (Table 1). Experiments were conducted on a chain of 6 microservices. The optimal myopic policy was found using the theoretical curve (Eq. (1)), and the best threshold policy is when $\sigma^* = 6$ is exactly the number of microservices to reach the target. For myopic and threshold policies, with honeypots, the attack (until success) was executed 10 times. The attack was executed 44 times without honeypots, as a baseline. In the baseline setup, the first attack always succeeds as no honeypot can deceive and trap the attacker. The attack then takes an average of 71 seconds to reach the target, or exactly 5 lateral movement steps. However, with one honeypot reachable per microservice, or a total of five honeypots, the attacker can get stuck in honeypots and now needs to start new attacks with no knowledge over which microservice is genuine or not.

Table 1 shows the effectiveness of adding honeypots. The optimal myopic policy $p^* = 0.173$ takes an average time to success of 3309 seconds and an average of 221 total steps, about 45 times the average time to success of the baseline. The optimal threshold policy with $\sigma^* = 6$ also performs worse than the baseline, taking an average time to success of 1644 seconds and an average of 75 steps. This represents 23 times the average time to success of the baseline, and about 15 times the number of steps. In practice, the threshold policy is used by experienced attackers that gather intelligence on the system. Interestingly, the only way for the attacker to follow the optimal myopic policy is to know the chain length, meaning that the myopic policy is used only when no information on the system is known, as the threshold policy may have no chance of reaching the target.

5 Conclusion

Lateral movement attacks are a critical threat in cloud environments since they allow attackers to explore and compromise various internal cloud sub-systems. Honeypots are traditionally used to deceive attackers and collect attack information. As shown in this paper, they can also serve as a dynamic shield against lateral movement attacks. However, while honeypots deter attackers from reaching their target, honeypots are expensive to deploy and maintain. In this regards, our analysis supports reference performance to dimension the number of honeypots that are deployed for effective defense. We measured the practical impact of the scheme by executing lateral movement attacks in a Kubernetes environment. By adding just 5 honeypots on a 6 microservices chain, the attack average time increases significantly: about 45 times for naive attackers, and 25 times for experienced attackers.

Our model can be extended on the attacker side and defender side. On the attacker side, the model may take into account the attacker's expertise, i.e., the ability to distinguish genuine microservices from honeypots, which translates into a probability α that equals to 1 for a skilled attacker and 0 for a naive attacker. During each lateral movement, the attacker determines if the microservice corresponds to a genuine microservice (in which case the attacker continues the attack) or a honeypot, in which case the attacker starts a new attack. The transition probabilities $\mathbb{P}(S(t+1)|S(t))$ corresponds to:

$$\mathbb{P}((k,h+1)|(k,h)) = (1-\alpha)\pi(k+h), \forall h > 0, \forall k \neq M,$$
$$\mathbb{P}((1,0)|(k,h)) = 1 - \pi(k+h) + \alpha\pi(k+h), \forall h > 0, \forall k \neq M.$$

Note that the average number of attacks does not change and the average length of attacks depends on the probability of detection α.

On the defender's side, rather than assuming a uniform repartition of honeypots (i.e. $q_k = 1 - \frac{1}{L}$), we suppose that the closer we get to the target, the more honeypots are deployed. Thus, a defender makes it increasingly difficult for each attacker's step to succeed. An extreme case refers to an exponentially distributed number of honeypots.

Finally, the microservice architecture can be extended to deal with a directed acyclic graph rather than a chain. In such a case, the system is modeled as a Markov chain with one absorbing state (corresponding to the ultimate target), and, the time to reach the absorbing state follows a phase-type distribution (Sect. 2.5 in [9]).

Acknowledgement. Research was sponsored by the Army and was accomplished under Grant Number W911NF-24-0149. The views and conclusions contained in this document are those of the authors and should not be interpreted as representing the official policies, either expressed or implied, of the U.S. Army or the U.S. Government. The U.S. Government is authorized to reproduce and distribute reprints for Government purposes notwithstanding any copyright notation herein.

The research of F. De Pellegrini and F. Sailhan has been sponsored by the French National Research Agency (ANR) within the framework of the PARFAIT project (ANR-21-CE25-0013).

Proof of Theorem 1

Proof. Let $f = \mathbb{P}(\tau_b(1) < \infty | S(0) = S_0)$. In particular, as the attacker is rational, $f = 1 - \mathbb{P}(X(M-1) = M)$ so that

$$1 - f = \mathbb{P}(S(t) = (t, 0), t = 2, \ldots, M | S(0) = (1, 0)) = \prod_{k=1}^{M-1} (1 - q_k)\pi(k)$$

Case i. is trivial. In order to prove case ii., we observe that $N = N_{S_0} + 1$, where N_{S_0} is the number of returns to state $S_0 = (1, 0)$, i.e., $N_{S_0} = \sum_{t>0} \mathbb{1}\{S(t) = S_0)\}$. In our case, the number of returns to a given state has probability distribution $\mathbb{P}(N_{S_0} = h | S(0) = S_0) = (1-f)f^h$ for $h \geq 0$ [1][Thm. 7.2, pp. 86]. By identifying $\rho = 1 - f$, this concludes the proof.

Sketch of proof of Theorem 2

Proof. i. In order to prove that the attack lengths are independent, observe that, by definition, $\{\tau_b\}$ are the successive return times to $S(0)$. As such, they are stopping times for the process $S(t)$. Hence, from the Strong Markov Property, [1][Thm. 7.1, pp. 85], $\tau(k)$ is independent of any $\tau(h)$, $h > k$. Also, because the Markov chain is homogeneous, they are identically distributed, thus we just study the probability distribution of $\tau(1)$.

ii. We provide a sketch of proof. The formal proof requires to introduce hitting time theory and related derivations, which are out of the scope of the present work. The distribution of a finite return time $\mathbb{P}(\tau(1) = h)$ is obtained by conditioning on the fact that the target is never reached. Thus, the length of a failed attack only depends on the event of continuing the attack for $h - 1$ steps and then terminating the attack at step h. In turn, this depends just on the policy π. Taking previous remark into account, we have:

$$\begin{aligned}
\mathbb{P}(\tau(1) = h) &= \mathbb{P}(X(h) = 1, \bigcap_{t=1}^{h-1} \{X(t) \notin \{1, M\}\} | S(0) = S_0, X(t) \neq M\}) \\
&= \mathbb{P}(X(h) = 1, X(h-1) \notin \{1, M\} | X(t) \neq M) \\
&\times \prod_{t=1}^{h-2} \mathbb{P}(X(t+1) \notin \{1, M\} | X(t) \notin \{1, M\}) \\
&\times P(X(1) \notin \{1, M\} | S(0) = S_0, X(t) \neq M)
\end{aligned}$$

from which the result follows.

Proof of Proposition 1

Proof. We first recall basic facts about probability generating functions. Let $W = \sum_{j=1}^{N} X_j$, where $\{X_j\}$ are i.i.d. integer nonnegative random variables and N is a random natural number, then $G_W(z) = G_N(G_X(z))$, so that $G_{W-1}(z) = \frac{G_N(G_X(z))}{G_X(z)}$. The proof is based on a different rewriting of (2) using an alternative expression of (1) as

$$J(\pi) = \mathbb{E}_\pi\left[\sum_{m=1}^{M-1} \gamma^{\sum_{j=1}^{N-1}\tau(j)} \gamma^m + \sum_{k=1}^{N-1}\sum_{i=1}^{\tau(k)} \gamma^{\sum_{j=1}^{k-1}\tau(j)} \gamma^i\right] = J_1(\pi) + J_2(\pi)$$

The first term $J_1(\pi)$ writes as $J_1(\pi) = \frac{\gamma-\gamma^M}{1-\gamma}\mathbb{E}_\pi\left[\gamma^{\sum_{j=1}^{N-1}\tau(j)}\right] = \frac{1-\gamma^M}{1-\gamma}\frac{G_N(G_{\tau(1)}(\gamma))}{G_{\tau(1)}(\gamma)}$.

Similarly, we obtain

$$
\begin{aligned}
J_2(\pi) &= \mathbb{E}_\pi\left[\sum_{k=1}^{N-1} \mathbb{E}\left[\gamma^{\sum_{j=1}^{k-1}\tau(j)} \mid N\right] \mathbb{E}\left[\sum_{i=1}^{\tau(k)} \gamma^i \mid N\right]\right] \\
&= \gamma\mathbb{E}_N\left[\sum_{k=1}^{N-1} \mathbb{E}\left[\frac{1-\gamma^{\tau(k)}}{1-\gamma} \mid N\right] \prod_{j=1}^{k-1} \mathbb{E}\left[\gamma^{\tau(j)} \mid N\right]\right] \\
&= \gamma\frac{1-G_{\tau(1)}(\gamma)}{1-\gamma}\mathbb{E}\left[\sum_{k=1}^{N-1} G_{\tau(1)}^{k-1}(\gamma)\right] = \gamma\frac{1-G_{\tau(1)}(\gamma)}{1-\gamma}\mathbb{E}\left[\frac{1-G_{\tau(1)}^{N-1}(\gamma)}{1-G_{\tau(1)}(\gamma)}\right] \\
&= \frac{\gamma}{1-\gamma}\frac{1-G_N(G_{\tau(1)}(\gamma))}{G_{\tau(1)}(\gamma)}
\end{aligned}
$$

Now, replacing the expression $G_N(z) = \frac{z\rho}{1-(1-\rho)z}$, the statement follows.

Proof of Proposition 2

Proof. i. For $M = 2$ the statement is obvious. For $M > 2$, the optimal policy solves the equation $\frac{d}{dp}J(p) = 0$, which writes $f(p) = g(p)$, where

$$f(p) = L^{M-1} - (1-p)^{M-2} \text{ and } g(p) = \frac{p(1+p)}{1-p}L^{M-1}(M-2)$$

In particular, f is a increasing concave, whereas g is an increasing convex. Since $f(0) = L^{M-1} - 1$ and $f(1) = L^{M-1}$ and $g(0) = 0$ and $g(1) = +\infty$, it is easy to see that the solution in $(0,1)$ exists and is unique.

ii. We now observe that, for $M > 2$, the solution $p^* \in [p_{min}, p_{max}]$, where p_{min} solves for $g(p_{min}) = L^{M-1} - 1 = f(0)$ and p_{max} solves for $g(p_{max}) =$

$L^{M-1} = f(1)$. For the sake of notation, we can express both p_{min} and p_{max} as the solutions of

$$L^{M-1} - \chi = \frac{p(1-p)}{1-p} L^{M-1}(M-2) \tag{6}$$

where $\chi = 1$ to determine p_{max} and $\chi = 0$ for p_{min}. If we define $A := \frac{L^{M-1}-\chi}{(M-2)L^{M-1}}$ then (6) becomes $\frac{p(1+p)}{1-p} = A$. For p_{max}, we can write

$$\frac{1}{M-2} = \frac{p_{max}(1+p_{max})}{1-p_{max}} \geq \frac{p_{max}}{1-p_{max}}$$

from which $p_{max} \leq \frac{1}{M-1}$. For p_{min}, from (6),

$$p = \frac{A+1}{2}\Big(-1 + \sqrt{1 + \frac{4A}{(A+1)^2}}\Big) \tag{7}$$

By leveraging the series expansion $(1+x)^{\alpha} = \sum_{n=0}^{+\infty} x^k$, we obtain $p_{min} = \frac{A}{A+1} + o(4A/(A+1)^2)$, where $4A/(A+1)^2 < 1$. Observe that $\frac{A}{A+1} \xrightarrow{L} \frac{1}{M-1}$, so that $p_{min} = \Omega(\frac{1}{M-1})$, which concludes the proof.

References

1. Brémaud, P.: Markov Chains: Gibbs Fields, Monte Carlo Simulation, and Queues. Springer, Heidelberg (1999)
2. Chowdhary, A., Sengupta, S., Huang, D., et al.: Markov game modeling of moving target defense for strategic detection of threats in cloud networks. In: Workshop on Artificial Intelligence for Cyber Security (2019)
3. Fraunholz, D., Schneider, D., Zemitis, J., et al.: Hack my company: an empirical assessment of post-exploitation behavior and lateral movement in cloud environments. In: Central European Cybersecurity Conference (2018)
4. Horák, K., Bošanský, B., et al., P.T.: Optimizing honeypot strategies against dynamic lateral movement using partially observable stochastic games. Comput. Secur. **87** (2019)
5. Huang, L., Zhu, Q.: Adaptive honeypot engagement through reinforcement learning of semi-Markov decision processes. In: International Conference on Decision and Game Theory for Security (2019)
6. Huang, L., Zhu, Q.: Farsighted risk mitigation of lateral movement using dynamic cognitive honeypots. In: International Conference on Decision and Game Theory for Security (2020)
7. Iqbal, S., Kiah, M.L.M., Dhaghighi, B., et al.: On cloud security attacks: a taxonomy and intrusion detection and prevention as a service. J. Netw. Comput. Appl. **74** (2016)
8. Kuwatly, I., Sraj, M., Al Masri, Z., et al.: A dynamic honeypot design for intrusion detection. In: IEEE/ACS International Conference on Pervasive Services (2004)
9. Latouche, G., Ramaswami, V.: Introduction to matrix analytic methods in stochastic modeling. Soc. Ind. Appl. Math. (1999)

10. MITRE: MITRE ATTACK Framework (2025). https://attack.mitre.org
11. Ngo, H.Q., Guo, M., Nguyen, H.: Catch me if you can: effective honeypot placement in dynamic ad attack graphs. In: IEEE Conference on Computer Communications (2024)
12. OWASP Foundation: OWASP: Common Attack Types (2025). https://owasp.org/www-community/attacks
13. Pawlick, J., Nguyen, T.T.H., Colbert, E., et al.: Optimal timing in dynamic and robust attacker engagement during advanced persistent threats. In: IEEE International Symposium on Modeling and Optimization in Mobile, Ad Hoc, and Wireless Networks (2019)
14. Poeng, K., Schumacher, L.: Lateral movement identification in cross-cloud deployment. In: IEEE International Conference on Network and Service Management (2024)
15. Ross, S.M.: Stochastic Processes, 2nd edn. Wiley, Hoboken (1995)

Multidomain Cyber Deception: A Multigraph Centrality Game Approach

Arthur Ngoufo[1,3](✉), Willie Kouam[2], Franklin Tchakounte[1], Yezekael Hayel[3], and Charles Kamhoua[4]

[1] University of Ngoundéré, Ngaoundéré, Cameroon
[2] LIT Secure and Correct Systems Lab, Johannes Kepler University Linz, Linz, Austria
arnold.kouam_kounchou@jku.at
[3] CERI/LIA, University of Avignon, Avignon, France
arthur-farel.ngoufo-mboho@alumni.univ-avignon.fr, yezekael.hayel@univ-avignon.fr
[4] DEVCOM Army Research Laboratory, Adelphi, Maryland, USA
charles.a.kamhoua.civ@army.mil

Abstract. The growing interdependence between cyber and physical infrastructures, together with increasingly sophisticated techniques for compromising network architectures, raises significant security challenges, especially for military and critical systems. In this work, we introduce a game-theoretic framework that models attacker–defender interactions over bi-layer networks, where cyber nodes influence physical defence components. The model captures cascading effects triggered by cyber compromises and quantifies their impact using centrality metrics across layers. Unlike traditional approaches based on fixed strategies on static or single-layer networks, our framework formulates a dynamic parametric game on a multigraph in which both agents search for the centrality measure that maximizes their respective objectives. To account for asymmetric real-world cyber conflicts, we develop a heterogeneous game structure and integrate a deception mechanism based on honeypot deployment. Centrality optimization is performed using Simultaneous Perturbation Stochastic Approximation ($SPSA$), allowing scalability without explicit gradients. Numerical experiments show the convergence of the algorithm, compare the optimal centrality to classical measures and show its effectiveness in limiting lateral movement, while also highlighting the critical role of inter-layer topology in shaping vulnerabilities.

Keywords: Centrality game · Optimization · Multidomain · Cyber deception

1 Introduction

The management of critical infrastructures (e.g., homes, airports, bridges) has evolved beyond purely physical considerations [1]. With the proliferation of

A. Remke et al. (Eds.): Valuetools 2025, LNICST 691, pp. 176–196, 2027.
https://doi.org/10.1007/978-3-032-23901-3_11

interconnected systems, cybersecurity threats have become both pervasive and increasingly complex to manage. This is particularly critical in military settings, where the protection of sensitive zones relies heavily on cyber-controlled vehicles and systems [2]. To address cyber-physical threats, researchers have extensively modeled the problem as a strategic interaction between attackers and defenders, leading to the formulation of various game-theoretic frameworks. Several studies have employed such models to investigate adversarial dynamics. For instance, [3] introduced a Boolean game framework that integrates cyber and physical domains into a unified analytical space. However, their model assumes full network observability, a simplification that limits its applicability in realistic scenarios. In contrast, [4] proposed a more realistic approach by modeling the infrastructure as a multilayer network and formulating the interaction as an asymmetric Stackelberg game, thereby capturing the advantage attackers often possess in terms of system knowledge. To align with conventional military strategies such as deception, the notion of *cyber deception* has emerged as a viable defense mechanism [5]. At the core of cyber deception lies the proactive shift from traditional defense mechanisms toward more adaptive, stealthy, and resilient security strategies [6]. In cybersecurity, this method complicates the attacker's environment, making it more confusing and challenging, thereby increasing the cost and difficulty of executing malicious actions. Such an approach not only supports early threat detection but also strengthens the overall security resilience of the system [7]. This technique seeks to mislead adversaries by directing them towards decoy components thereby limiting their capacity for lateral movement [8].

Despite these advancements, much of the existing literature predominantly emphasizes the cyber dimension while underrepresenting the physical consequences of such threats. Modeling cybersecurity challenges, especially when cyber deception is involved, shows that single-domain game-theoretic approaches are insufficient for capturing the intricate dynamics present in multi-domain environments. These approaches overlook the essential interaction between cyber and physical environments, a relationship critical to fully understanding both vulnerabilities and defense strategies. To overcome this limitation, it is necessary to adopt a multi-domain modeling approach that differentiates between two interconnected layers: the cyber layer and the physical infrastructure. By incorporating both dimensions, this framework allows for more nuanced and realistic models, enabling security professionals to design and test more sophisticated deception and mitigation systems. The shift toward multi-domain representations marks a significant step forward in the evolution of integrated cybersecurity defense mechanisms, and recent work has begun to bridge this gap. For instance, [9] underscored the relevance of multi-domain deception strategies in future combat scenarios. Building on this perspective, [10] developed a cyber-physical game model using a two-layer graph, incorporating both cyber interactions and deception strategies across layers. Nevertheless, their reliance on the Double Oracle algorithm presents notable scalability challenges. These computational limitations have been partially addressed by [11] through the development of centrality-based heuristics. In their work, a suite of centrality metrics was introduced to enhance the tractability of game-theoretic models, while [13] proposed *centrality-based games* that reduce complexity by focusing on node influence. However, these models remain constrained to the cyber layer and do not definitively identify an optimal centrality measure. Moreover, the authors of [14] introduced a novel centrality expressed as a linear combination of classical metrics in a lateral movement context, yet its performance within multilayer and non-cooperative game frameworks has not been rigorously validated. In our paper, we propose a multi-domain game, focusing exclusively on the cyber layer, where node failures can induce cascading effects. The physical implications are captured implicitly through this layer. We formulate the problem as a two-player game that incorporates centrality measures, attacker lateral movement costs, and edge protection costs. Unlike previous symmetric formulations, our model introduces asymmetry and is solved in two stages. The main contributions of the paper are as follows:

- We propose a novel modeling framework that integrates both cyber and physical components within a unified representation. The system is captured as a bi-layer network, where one layer corresponds to the cyber infrastructure and the other to the physical layer. The interdependencies specifically, the control exerted by the cyber layer over the physical layer are encoded through directed inter-layer connections, linking the two graphs.
- By leveraging the centrality game approach to overcome scalability limitations, we focus on the cyber domain, with a dedicated analysis of its influence on the physical layer via the Fiedler value computation.
- Unlike existing models that assume static centrality measures, our approach treats centrality as a decision variable that is jointly optimized with players' strategies.
- Given that the optimization problem constitutes a black-box setting due to the absence of analytical closed-form expressions for the objective functions, we employ the Simultaneous Perturbation Stochastic Approximation (SPSA) algorithm to numerically estimate the gradients and compute the corresponding optimal centrality values.
- We compare the computed optimal centralities against classical centrality metrics commonly used in the literature.

2 Problem Description

2.1 Context and Motivation

The increasing cyber-dependence in the management of critical infrastructures introduces a new vulnerability: if the cyber network controlling a defense system is compromised by a malicious actor, the physical infrastructures it protects may become exposed to direct attacks (e.g., sabotage, destruction). This results in a cascading failure across multiple security domains. Consequently, infrastructure managers and cybersecurity teams must fortify the cyber systems controlling physical defense assets, ensuring resilience against multi-domain security threats. From there, we present in this article an attack-defense framework operating in a multi-domain environment comprising both physical and cyber domains. The physical domain includes various equipment targeted by the attacker, which we model using a graph structure that captures how the compromise of one unit affects neighboring equipment (grid networks, interconnected power plants, ...). To defend these physical assets, a set of physical defenses such as Remote Weapon Stations, are positioned across different locations based on their operational range and the coverage requirements of specific areas, which may overlap. The control of these physical defense resources is handled remotely via controllers residing in the cyber domain, which is also represented as a graph. Nodes in this cyber graph include computers, servers, and other networked devices, while edges denote communication links. The attacker can operate in both domains and may attempt to directly breach the physical layer. Securing these controllers is critical, as their compromise can disrupt the operation of the physical defense resources they manage. Consequently, any equipment in the area under this affected physical defense becomes vulnerable unless it is covered by another physical defense. To enhance the security of the cyber domain and specifically the precious controller nodes, the defender employs a cyber deception approach, notably the deployment of honeypots, which are designed to mislead, detect, and mitigate cyber threats. The defender's objective is to construct a resilient defense that minimizes the adversary's success rate while maximizing the protection of critical assets, where an asset's importance is quantified by its centrality value. The following subsection details the strategies adopted by agents and provides an in-depth description of the architecture and mechanisms within each domain.

2.2 Model Description

Physical Domain: The physical domain is modeled as a non oriented weighted graph $G_1 = (V_1, E_1)$, where nodes V_1 represent locations requiring protection. Each node $v \in V_1$ has a weight $\phi(v)$, we assume to be equal to 1. N agents $\{v_1, v_2, \cdots, v_N\}$ are deployed at selected physical areas $\{A_1, A_2, \cdots, A_N\}$ such that $A_1 \cup \cdots \cup A_N = V_1$, to protect each of them. When an attack targets $v \in A_i$, the agent v_i who protects the area A_i has the ability to defend it. The area A_i is defined as a set of nodes of the graph G_1 connected to the node v_i.

Cyber Domain: The cyber domain is modeled as a non oriented graph $G_2 = (V_2, E_2)$, where nodes V_2 represent cyber entities (e.g., servers, computers) and edges E_2 denote communication links. Within the cyber domain, there are three categories of nodes: entry nodes V_e of vertices already compromised by the adversary, the target nodes V_t (controller nodes) controlling the N physical agents, and the intermediate nodes V_{int} serving as a gateway for the attacker to reach targets. In our model, each cyber target $t_i \in V_t$ controls only one physical agent, as illustrated in Fig. 1.

As previously stated, when a target cyber node is compromised, the physical defense agent it controls becomes inactive, rendering it incapable of defending

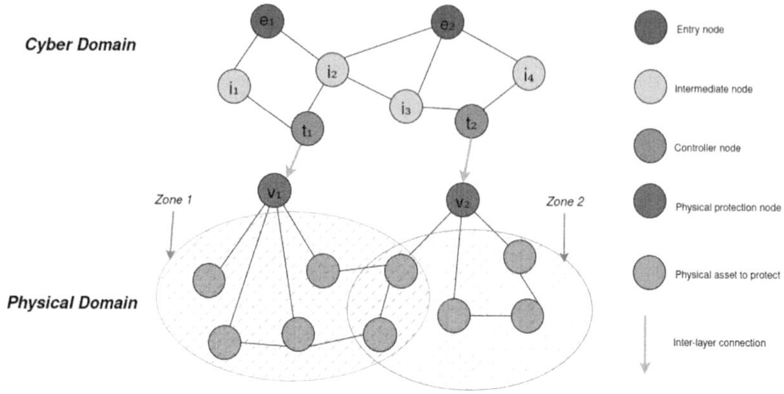

Fig. 1. Multilayer graph of the cyber physical problem.

the entire physical area under its protection against direct attacks made by the adversary. The attacker thus gains full advantage over this zone's assets, previously safeguarded solely by that agent. In other words, if a node v belongs to $A_i \cap A_j$, and if the agent v_i is successfully attacked and the agent v_j is still active, then the node v is protected by the agent v_j. Moreover, the importance of a cyber intermediate node increases with its proximity to a controller node. Here, proximity is not merely geographic or topological but is quantified through centrality values. These centrality values reflect the relative importance of intermediary cyber nodes from both the attacker's and defender's perspectives. They serve to evaluate the value of compromising or protecting these nodes during the confrontation in the cyber domain. Without loss of generality, the problem analysis can be restricted to the cyber network. i.e. only the failure of a cyber node can induce a change in the physical system. Moreover, such a transition in the physical domain has no impact on future cyber movements in the current model. The gain associated with a successful attack on a physical node depends on his weight and is incorporated into a global metric, defined over the set of physical nodes affected by a cyber cascade. This metric is then attributed to the success of the attack on the corresponding cyber control node. More specifically, let $G = (G_1, G_2, \mathcal{E})$ be a two-layered graph, where G_1 represents the physical layer and G_2 denotes the cyber layer (not oriented in our study). The set $\mathcal{E}$ consists of inter-layer (oriented) connections linking cyber control nodes to physical protective agents. These connections are typically modeled using a *super-adjacency matrix*, as introduced in [20]. The compromise of a controller node induces a structural disconnection in graph G, modifying the topology of the physical layer G_1. This disruption leads to the removal of edges linking the physical defense agent to the nodes it safeguards. The impact of this disruption is quantified by the change in the Fiedler value λ_2 of the Laplacian matrix $\mathcal{L}(G_1)$ [15]. Let $\lambda_2^{(0)}$ and $\lambda_2^{(i)}$ be the Fiedler values before and after compromising a target v_i, respectively, the influence of v_i from an agents' point of view, or the centrality value of v_i is defined as $C_{v_i} = \lambda_2^{(i)} - \lambda_2^{(0)}$. To mitigate threats within the cyber network, the defender adopts a cyber deception strategy by deploying honeypots on a selected subset of edges. These honeypots serve as protective barriers, preventing any attempt by an attacker to propagate infections through the secured connections. However, due to limited resources, the defender cannot place honeypots throughout the entire network. Consequently, he must devise a placement strategy that accounts for the limited number of honeypots while prioritizing the protection of nodes based on their influence, reflecting their strategic importance from the attacker's perspective. In this context, nodes with higher centrality values are more likely to be protected, as they represent key intermediaries in the network. Nevertheless, no node is guaranteed protection with certainty, since there is no prior assurance that the attacker will traverse a given path. This uncertainty highlights a fundamental challenge: how to assess the importance of each intermediate node in a way that maximizes the probability of detecting the attacker through optimal honeypot placement. To address this, we assume that the optimal centrality measure is not known a priori and instead propose a *parametric game framework*, where the parameter represents the centrality metric to be identified.

3 Dynamic Parametric Game

The game models the strategic interaction between an attacker and a defender on a multi-layer network $G = (G_1, G_2, \mathcal{E})$. The attacker seeks to maximize physical intrusion success by navigating the cyber layer to reach target nodes, using a strategy that balances stealth and speed. In response, the defender employs cyber deception to disrupt and delay the attacker's movement while minimizing costs. The infection process follows a *Susceptible-Infected-Susceptible (SIS)* model: entry and intermediate nodes may revert to susceptible upon detection, but target nodes, once infected, are *permanently compromised.* At time $t = 0$, only the entry nodes are infected. Determining optimal paths for the attacker while avoiding potential defender traps that could reveal their presence is computationally expensive. As a result, we advocate solving small stage games sequentially, and optimizing the global strategy through a centrality-based approach. We formulate a non-zero-sum game where both players share the same node *centrality assessment*, and propose a precise analysis of optimal attack lateral movement and efficient defense deployment in a dynamic cyber-physical environment.

3.1 The Non-zero Sum Centrality Game Formulation

The dynamic parameterized game integrating the centrality measure as parameter is defined as $\mathcal{G} = \big(G, C, N_G, Z, b^0, \mathcal{A} = \mathcal{A}_1 \times \mathcal{A}_2, \mathcal{R} = (\mathcal{R}_d, \mathcal{R}_a)\big)$ where,

- $C = (C_{u_i})_{i=1}^{|V_2|}$ is defined over the cyber layer nodes, is considered to be common knowledge and jointly used by both players. This assumption reflects a strategic dynamic in which one player determines the centrality structure, and the other gradually aligns with it via adaptive learning.

- N_G is the set of players, the defender and the attacker.
- Z is the set of cyber node states; a state $z \in Z$ is defined for each node $u_i \in V_2$ as: $z_{u_i} = \begin{cases} S, & \text{if node } u_i \text{ is susceptible,} \\ I, & \text{if node } u_i \text{ is infected.} \end{cases}$
- The defender's initial belief over the system state, denoted b^0, is progressively revised using Bayes' rule as new observations become available [12].
- $\mathcal{A}_1$ is the defender's actions set, consists in selecting h edges in the *stake zone* $\$ = \{(u_i, u_j), (u_j, u_i) \mid (u_i, u_j) \in E_2\}$, to protect using intrusion prevention systems (IPS). Since the size of $\$$ can be very large and due to uncertainty about the exact network state, the defender focuses its efforts on the set $\$_{b^t} = \bigcup_{z \in \text{supp}(b^t)} \$_z$, with $\$_z = (I^z \times S^z) \cap \$$, where I^z and S^z are the infected and susceptible node sets in state z, and $\text{supp}(b^t) = \{z \in Z \mid b^t(z) \neq 0\}$ is the support of the defender's belief at time t. To avoid redundancy on undirected edges (since the intelligent and rational defender will not place more than one IPS on an edge), we define $\$_{b^t}^{\text{Und}} = \{(u_x, u_y) \mid (u_x, u_y) \in \$_{b^t} \text{ or } (u_y, u_x) \in \$_{b^t}\}$. Then the defender's action space at a given time t is:
$$\mathcal{A}_1(t) = \begin{cases} \left\{a_1 \in \binom{\$_{b^t}}{h} \mid \forall (u_i, u_j) \in a_1, (u_j, u_i) \notin a_1\right\}, & \text{if } |\$_{b^t}^{\text{Und}}| > h, \\ \left\{a_1 \subseteq \$_{b^t} \mid |a_1| = |\$_{b^t}^{\text{Und}}|, (u_j, u_i) \notin a_1 \text{ if } (u_i, u_j) \in a_1\right\}, & \text{otherwise} \end{cases}$$
- $\mathcal{A}_2(z)$ is the attacker's action set at state z. From each infected node $u_i \in I^z$, the attacker targets a disjoint subset of susceptible neighbors, i.e., $a_2 \in (\mathcal{N}(u_i))_{u_i \in I^z}$ where $\mathcal{N}(u_i) = \{u_j \in S^z \mid \{u_i, u_j\} \in E_2\}$. The attacker's actions must therefore satisfy $\begin{cases} (u_i, u_j) \in \$_z, & \forall u_j \in \mathcal{N}(u_i), \\ \mathcal{N}(u_k) \cap \mathcal{N}(u_l) = \emptyset, & \text{for } u_k \neq u_l \in I^z. \end{cases}$
- $\mathcal{R}_d$ and $\mathcal{R}_a$ are the defender's and attacker's rewards, respectively. The defender incurs a cost D_c per protected edge, and the attacker pays a cost A_c per vulnerability edge exploited. To reflect the strategic importance of different nodes, the node-specific reward C_{u_j}, which quantifies the potential gain or loss from actions involving the node u_j. This value typically captures the role of centrality (for intermediate nodes) or physical consequence following a successful cyber intrusion (for target nodes). Thus, the higher the centrality of a node, the more valuable it becomes for the attacker to compromise it, and the more critical it is for the defender to protect it. The reward matrix on edge (u_i, u_j) under joint action (a_1, a_2) is given in Table 1.
Exploiting the Table 1, the players' reward for an action profile (a_1, a_2) is,
$$\mathcal{R}_d(z, a_1, a_2) = \sum_{(u_i,u_j) \in \$_1} (-D_c + C_{u_j}) + \sum_{(u_i,u_j) \in \$_2} (-C_{u_j}) + \sum_{(u_i,u_j) \in \$_3} (-D_c).$$

Table 1. Expected reward resulting from a joint action (a_1, a_2) on edge (u_i, u_j).

		Attacker Propagate $u_i \to u_j$?	
		Propagate $((u_i, u_j) \in a_2)$	No propagate $((u_i, u_j) \notin a_2)$
Defender	Protect $((u_i, u_j) \in a_1)$	$-D_c + C_{u_j}, -A_c$	$-D_c$, 0
$(u_i, u_j) \in a_1$?	Not Protect $((u_i, u_j) \notin a_1)$	$-C_{u_j}, -A_c + C_{u_j}$	0, 0

$$\mathcal{R}_a(z, a_1, a_2) = \sum_{(u_i,u_j)\in \mathbb{S}_1} (-A_c) + \sum_{(u_i,u_j)\in \mathbb{S}_2} (-A_c + C_{u_j}), \qquad \text{with}$$

$$\mathbb{S}_1 = \{(u_i, u_j) \in \mathbb{S} \mid (u_i, u_j) \in a_1 \cap a_2\}, \quad \mathbb{S}_4 = \{(u_i, u_j) \in \mathbb{S} \mid (u_i, u_j) \notin a_1 \cup a_2\}$$
$$\mathbb{S}_2 = \{(u_i, u_j) \in \mathbb{S} \mid (u_i, u_j) \notin a_1 \wedge (u_i, u_j) \in a_2\},$$
$$\mathbb{S}_3 = \{(u_i, u_j) \in \mathbb{S} \mid (u_i, u_j) \in a_1 \wedge (u_i, u_j) \notin a_2\}$$

Remark 1. We initially treat the centrality parameter C as fixed and analyze the resulting game accordingly. In the Sect. 4, we will leverage this solution to determine the optimal centrality measure for both the defender and the attacker.

3.2 Players' Reward Associated With a Strategy Profile

Defender's Reward: The expected reward for the defender, given the strategy profile $\pi = (\pi_d, \pi_a)$ and the belief b^t is $\mathcal{R}_d(\pi_d, \pi_a|b^t) = \sum_{z\in Z} b^t(z)\mathcal{R}_d(\pi_d, \pi_a|z)$.

We define the marginal probabilities $\pi_a(u_i, u_j|b^t) = \sum_{z\in Z} \pi_a(u_i, u_j|z)\, b^t(z)$ and $\pi_d(u_i, u_j|b^t) = \pi_d(u_i, u_j)$ and rewrite the defender's reward as:

$$\mathcal{R}_d\left(\pi_d, \pi_a \left|b^t\right.\right) = \sum_{(u_i,u_j)\in \mathbb{S}} \left[\pi_d(u_i, u_j)\, \Phi_d\left(u_i, u_j\left|b^t, \pi_a\right.\right) + \Psi_d\left(u_i, u_j\left|b^t, \pi_a\right.\right)\right]$$

$$\text{where}: \begin{cases} \Phi_d\left(u_i, u_j\left|b^t, \pi_a\right.\right) = 2\pi_a\left(u_i, u_j\left|b^t\right.\right) C_{u_j} - D_c \\ \Psi_d\left(u_i, u_j\left|b^t, \pi_a\right.\right) = -\pi_a\left(u_i, u_j\left|b^t\right.\right) C_{u_j} \end{cases}$$

Attacker's Reward: Similarly, the attacker's expected reward is expressed as,

$$\mathcal{R}_a\left(\pi_d, \pi_a\left|b^t\right.\right) = \sum_{z\in Z} b^t(z)\mathcal{R}_a(\pi_d, \pi_a|z) \text{ with}$$

$$\begin{cases} \mathcal{R}_a\left(\pi_d, \pi_a\left|b^t\right.\right) = \sum_{(u_i,u_j)\in \mathbb{S}} \pi_a\left(u_i, u_j\left|b^t\right.\right) \Phi_a\left(u_i, u_j\left|b^t, \pi_d\right.\right) \\ \Phi_a\left(u_i, u_j\left|b^t, \pi_d\right.\right) = -A_c + C_{u_j} - \pi_d(u_i, u_j)\, C_{u_j} \end{cases}$$

3.3 Players Best Response Strategy

Defender's Best Response: Assuming the attacker follows a strategy π_a, the defender's optimal counter-strategy is π_d, maximizing the expected payoff $\mathcal{R}_d(\pi \mid b^t) = \sum_{(u_i,u_j)\in\$} \pi_d(u_i,u_j)\,\Phi_d(u_i,u_j \mid b^t,\pi_a) + \sum_{(u_i,u_j)\in\$} \Psi_d(u_i,u_j \mid b^t,\pi_a)$. To make it, the defender should focus on the top h edges of $\$_b$ based on their rank value $\rho(u_i,u_j \mid b,\pi_a)$ and set $\pi_d(u_i,u_j)$ to 0 for the remaining edges. This rank value is expressed as $\rho(u_i,u_j \mid b,\pi_a) := 1 + |\{(u_x,u_y) \in \$_b : \Phi_d(u_x,u_y \mid b,\pi_a) > \Phi_d(u_i,u_j \mid b,\pi_a)\}|$. Given the attacker's strategy π_a, the values of $\Phi_d(u_i,u_j \mid b,\pi_a)$ and $\Psi_d(u_i,u_j \mid b,\pi_a)$ are determined for every edge $(u_i,u_j) \in \$$. The defender maximizes $\mathcal{R}_d(\pi_d,\pi_a|b)$ by focusing on $\mathcal{C}_d(\pi_a) := \{(u_x,u_y) \in \$_b, \rho(u_x,u_y \mid b,\pi_a) \leqslant h\}$ known as the critical defence subset, containing edges the defender should prioritize to optimally counter the attack. Thus, the best defensive response satisfies: $\pi_d(u_i,u_j) = 0,\ \forall (u_i,u_j) \notin \mathcal{C}_d(\pi_a)$.

Attacker's Best Response Analogously, given a defender's strategy $\pi_d \in \Pi_d$, the attacker's best response $\pi_a \in \Pi_a$ is the one maximizing the attacker's reward $\mathcal{R}_a(\pi \mid b^t) = \sum_{(u_i,u_j)\in\$}\sum_{z\in Z} \pi_a(u_i,u_j|z)\, b^t(z)\, \Phi_a(u_i,u_j \mid \pi_d)$. For a given defender's strategy π_d, with fixed coefficients $\Phi_a(u_i,u_j \mid b^t,\pi_d)$, the maximum reward for the attacker is achieved when $\pi_a(u_i,u_j|z) = 0,\quad \forall (u_i,u_j) \notin \mathcal{C}_a(\pi_d)$. Here, the set $\mathcal{C}_a(\pi_d) := \{(u_x,u_y) \in \$_{b^t} \mid \forall (u_p,u_q) \in \$_b, \Phi_a(u_x,u_y|b^t,\pi_d) \geqslant \Phi_a(u_p,u_q|b^t,\pi_d)\}$ is known as the critical attack subset, representing the edges where launching an attack maximizes impact while minimizing defender interference.

Assuming both players have implemented their optimal response strategy $\pi^* = (\pi_d^*, \pi_a^*)$ at NE, the following propositions hold regarding the critical subsets of players corresponding to their best responses as defined above.

Proposition 1. *Assume that* $\mathcal{C}_a(\pi_d^*) \neq \$$. *Then, the defender's shortlist is necessarily a subset of the attacker's shortlist, that is* $\mathcal{C}_d(\pi_a^*) \subseteq \mathcal{C}_a(\pi_d^*)$.
In other words and obviously, unless the defender intends to monitor every edge in the graph, he may safely ignore edges that are not valuable to the attacker.

Proposition 2. *Using the definition of the attacker's shortlist* $\mathcal{C}_a(\pi_d^*)$, *and denoting by* $s_C = \max_{(u_i,u_j)\in\$_{b^t}} \Phi_a(u_i,u_j \mid b^t,\pi_d^*)$ *the maximum value of* Φ_a *at the NE, we characterize the defender's optimal strategy over the graph's edges. Specifically, the defender should select edges leading to the nodes targeted for protection, accounting for the following:*

1. *For all pairs* $(u_k,u_l),(u_{k'},u_{l'}) \in \mathcal{C}_a(\pi_d^*) \setminus \mathcal{C}_d(\pi_a^*)$, *it holds* $C_{u_l} = C_{u_{l'}}$.
2. *For all* $(u_i,u_j) \in \mathcal{C}_d(\pi_a^*)$, $(u_k,u_l) \in \mathcal{C}_a(\pi_d^*)\setminus\mathcal{C}_d(\pi_a^*)$, *and* $(u_x,u_y) \in \$\setminus\mathcal{C}_a(\pi_d^*)$, *it holds* $\begin{cases} C_{u_j} \geqslant C_{u_l} > C_{u_y}, \\ C_{u_j} > C_{u_l} \iff \pi_d^*(u_i,u_j) > 0. \end{cases}$

Theorem 1 (Threshold-Based Characterization of Equilibrium Strategies). *Define for* $p \in \{a, d\}$, $\theta_p := \min_{(u,v)\in\mathcal{C}_p(\pi^*_{-p})} C_v$. *The following assertions hold.*

1. $\theta_a \leqslant \theta_d$; *and the attacker and defender shortlists are respectively defined as*
$$\mathcal{C}_d(\pi^*_a) = \{(u_i, u_j) \in \$_{b^t} \mid C_{u_j} \geqslant \theta_d\}, \quad \mathcal{C}_a(\pi^*_d) = \{(u_i, u_j) \in \$ \mid C_{u_j} \geqslant \theta_a\};$$
2. *If* $\theta_a < \theta_d$, *then no value of centrality of the form* C_{u_j} *with* $(u_i, u_j) \in \$$ *lies in the open interval* (θ_a, θ_d).

3.4 Optimal Strategy of the Defender

At a Nash equilibrium (NE), the defender's strategy consists of protecting nodes whose centrality exceeds a threshold θ_d, while the attacker targets nodes with centrality not below another threshold θ_a. These thresholds depend on the specific centrality measure adopted by both players.

Proposition 3. *For every pair* $(u_i, u_j) \in \$$,

1. *If* $C_{u_j} = 0$ *then,* $\pi^*_d(u_i, u_j) = 0$, *otherwise the defender's optimal strategy is*
$$\begin{cases} (u_i, u_j) \in \mathcal{C}_a(\pi^*_d) \iff \Phi_a(u_i, u_j \mid \pi^*_d) = s_C \\ \text{and in that case, } \pi^*_d(u_i, u_j) = \dfrac{-s_C - A_c}{C_{u_j}} + 1 \quad \text{if } C_{u_j} \neq 0 \\ (u_i, u_j) \notin \mathcal{C}_a(\pi^*_d) \Rightarrow \Phi_a(u_i, u_j \mid \pi^*_d) < s_C, \quad \pi^*_d(u_i, u_j) = 0 \end{cases}$$
2. *The defender's probability distribution verifies* $\sum_{\substack{(u_i,u_j)\in\$_b \\ C_{u_j}\geqslant\theta_d}} \pi^*_d(u_i, u_j) = h$, *where* h *is the number of available defensive resources.*
3. *The attacker's threshold payoff* s_C *satisfies* $s_C = \dfrac{\sum_{(u_i,u_j)\in\$|C_{u_j}\geqslant\theta_d} 1 - h}{\sum_{(u_i,u_j)\in\$|C_{u_j}\geqslant\theta_d} \dfrac{1}{C_{u_j}}} - A_c.$
4. *The threshold pair* (θ_d, θ_a) *satisfies* $\sum_{(u_i,u_j)\in\$|C_{u_j}\geqslant\theta_d} \left(1 - \dfrac{\theta_d}{C_{u_j}}\right) \leqslant h.$

   If $\theta_d > \theta_a$, $\sum_{(u_i,u_j)\in\$_b|C_{u_j}\geqslant\theta_d} \left(1 - \dfrac{\theta_a}{C_{u_j}}\right) = \sum_{(u_i,u_j)\in\$_b|C_{u_j}\geqslant\theta_a} \left(1 - \dfrac{\theta_a}{C_{u_j}}\right) = h.$
5. *a) If* $s_C \leqslant 0$, *then the defender threshold is minimal, i.e.,* $\theta_d = \min_{(u_i,u_j)\in\$_b} C_{u_j}$.

   b) If $s_C > 0$, *the attacker targets nodes* u_j *such that* $\exists u_i$ *with* $\Phi_a(u_i, u_j \mid \pi^*_d) = s_C$.

3.5 Optimal Strategy of the Attacker

The attacker aims to maximize her reward, expressed as:

$$\mathcal{R}_a\left(\pi^*\left|b^t\right.\right) = \sum_{\substack{(u_i,u_j)\in\mathbb{S} \\ \Phi_a(u_i,u_j|\pi_d^*) \texttt{ is maximal}}} \pi_a^*\left(u_i,u_j\left|b^t\right.\right)\Phi_a\left(u_i,u_j\left|\pi_d^*\right.\right).$$

This implies that when $s_C > 0$, the attacker's optimal strategy at time t consists in targeting all susceptible nodes $u_j \in S^z$ such that $C_{u_j} \geqslant \theta_a$, ensuring that $\pi_a^*(.,u_j \mid z) = 1$. In other words, each such node u_j must be infected from a single source in the infected set I^z, and the attacker distributes probability mass over possible sources to ensure this constraint is met. However, a crucial constraint exists: a susceptible node cannot be infected by multiple sources simultaneously. Therefore, for each targeted node u_j, the attacker must select a single source $u_i \in I^z$ from which the infection is attempted.

To formalize this, define for every $z \in Z$ and $u_j \in S^z$ satisfying $C_{u_j} \geqslant \theta_a$, the set $\mathbb{H}_{u_j} = \{(u_i,u_j) \in \mathcal{C}_a(\pi_d^*) \mid u_i \in I^z\}$ Since the attacker aims to ensure that $\pi_a^*(.,u_j \mid z) = \sum_{(u_i,u_j)\in\mathbb{H}_{u_j}} \pi_a^*(u_i,u_j \mid z) = 1$, an optimal strategy π_a^* consists in adopting a uniform distribution over the set $\mathbb{H}_{u_j}$. This entails infecting node u_j by selecting uniformly at random a source $u_i \in I^z$ such that $(u_i,u_j) \in \mathbb{H}_{u_j}$. In other words, this leads to $\pi_a^*(u_i,u_j \mid z) = \frac{1}{|\mathbb{H}_{u_j}|}, \quad \forall\,(u_i,u_j) \in \mathbb{H}_{u_j}$.

4 Optimal Centrality Computation

4.1 Problem Formulation

The objective is to identify the optimal centrality measure C that maximizes the long-term strategic rewards of each player, depending on their role in the game hierarchy. Specifically, when the attacker acts as the leader, the goal is to optimize C such that the attacker maximizes its cumulative reward. Conversely, when the attacker is the follower, the defender seeks to choose C that maximizes their own long-term benefit. Let $\mathcal{R}_d^C\left(\pi_d^*,\pi_a^*\left|b^t\right.\right)$ and $\mathcal{R}_a^C\left(\pi_d^*,\pi_a^*\left|b^t\right.\right)$ denote the expected rewards of the defender and the attacker, respectively, at time t under centrality C. Given that the equilibrium strategies (π_d^*,π_a^*) are known for any fixed centrality, finding the optimal centrality reduces to solving the following optimization problems:

$$\begin{cases}\text{Find } C^* \in \text{Sol}\\ C^* \in \arg\max\limits_{C\in\text{Sol}} F_d(C)\end{cases} \quad (1) \qquad \begin{cases}\text{Find } C^* \in \text{Sol}\\ C^* \in \arg\max\limits_{C\in\text{Sol}} F_a(C)\end{cases} \quad (2)$$

– $$F_d(C) = \begin{cases}\sum\limits_{t=0}^{\infty}\gamma^t\mathcal{R}_d^C(\pi_d^*,\pi_a^* \mid b^t), & \text{if } C > 0\\ 0, & \text{if } C_{u_j} = 0,\ \forall u_j \in V_2 \setminus V_t\end{cases}, \gamma \in (0,1)$$

- $F_a(C) = \begin{cases} \sum_{t=0}^{\infty} \gamma^t \mathcal{R}_a^C(\pi_d^*, \pi_a^* \mid b^t), & \text{if } C > 0 \\ 0, & \text{if } C_{u_j} = 0,\ \forall u_j \in V_2 \setminus V_t \end{cases}, \gamma \in (0,1)$
- $\text{Sol} = \left\{ C = (C_{u_i})_{u_i \in V_2} \in \mathbb{R}_+^{|V_2|} \mid C_{u_i} \text{ fixed } \forall u_i \in V_t,\ C_{u_i} \leqslant 1\ \forall u_i \in V_2 \setminus V_t \right\}.$

Thus, the goal is to identify a centrality profile that optimally balances or maximizes one player's long-term reward.

4.2 Existence of Solutions

We investigate the mathematical conditions under which the defender's and attacker's optimization problems admit at least one solution. We begin by establishing the well-definedness of the expected reward functions and proceed to characterize the behavior of the objective function over a restricted set of feasible centrality vectors. These results allow us to demonstrate the existence of optimal strategies within a compact and regular subset of the decision space, ensuring the tractability and robustness of the proposed game-theoretic framework.

Remark 2. Since $\gamma < 1$, the geometric series $\sum_{t=0}^{\infty} \gamma^t$ is convergent. Hence, both $F_d(C)$ and $F_a(C)$ are well-defined for any $C \in \text{Sol}$.

Proposition 4. *The null centrality $C = 0$ is optimal for the defender, while it is strictly suboptimal for the attacker. Under this centrality, neither attacks nor defenses are performed, and the expected rewards are $\mathcal{R}_d^0 = \mathcal{R}_a^0 = 0$.*

For the remainder of this section, we assume that all centralities are strictly positive: for each node u_j, $C_{u_j} \geqslant \alpha$ for some fixed $\alpha > 0$, restricting the feasible set to $Sol^* = \{(C_{u_j}) \in Sol : C_{u_j} \geqslant \alpha\}$.

Lemma 1. *The mapping $C \mapsto \mathcal{R}_a^C(\pi_d^*, \pi_a^* \mid b^t)$ is piecewise continuous over the set Sol^*.*

Proposition 5. *The sequence $\left(\mathcal{R}_a^C(\pi_d^*, \pi_a^* \mid b^t)\right)_{t \geqslant 0}$ defines a series that converges uniformly over the compact set Sol^*. Consequently, $F_a(C)$ is piecewise continuous, and the optimization problem* (2) *admits at least one solution.*

Remark 3. The uniqueness of the optimal centrality depends on the cyber network's topology. For example, if a node is isolated or unreachable from any entry point, its centrality can be arbitrary, making the optimal vector non-unique.

4.3 Resolution of the Attacker's Problem

The existence of a solution to Problem (2) has been established. We now introduce a descent-based method to compute the optimal centrality vector. As the objective function is black-box and lacks a closed-form expression, we adopt the gradient-free *Simultaneous Perturbation Stochastic Approximation (SPSA)* algorithm [19], which approximates gradients using random perturbations and adaptive step sizes.

Each SPSA iteration requires two evaluations of the objective function at perturbed points. Since the search space has dimension $d = |V_2| - |V_t|$, the evaluation complexity is $O(d)$. Calculating physical disconnections uses Lanczos or Arnoldi methods with quadratic cost, and Nash equilibrium computation for fixed centrality is also quadratic. Overall, the algorithm has complexity $O(d^3 + l^2)$, where $l = |V_1|$. The full procedure is shown in Algorithm 1.

Algorithm 1. SPSA Optimization for the Centrality Vector

Input: Graph G, Target nodes TN, number of iterations K, initial vector C
parameters: a, c, α, γ_0, A, A_c, D_c, h, initial belief b^0, number of steps n
Output: Optimized centrality vector C_{opt}
for $k = 1$ to K **do**
    Identify infected nodes and construct the stake zone $\mathbb{S}_z$
    Compute gain sequences: $a_k = \dfrac{a}{(k+A)^{\alpha}}, \quad c_k = \dfrac{c}{k^{\gamma_0}}$
    Generate perturbation vector Δ with entries ± 1
    Compute perturbed vectors: $C^+ = C + c_k \cdot \Delta, \quad C^- = C - c_k \cdot \Delta$
    Compute constant values: $C^+[i] = C^-[i] =$ fixed for all $i \in TN$
    Evaluate the rewards: $y^+ = F_a(C^+)$, $y^- = F_a(C^-)$
    Estimate the gradient and update C
    for each dimension i **do**
        $g_k = \dfrac{y^+ - y^-}{2c_k\, \Delta[i]}$
        $C[i] = C[i] + a_k \cdot g_k$
    end for
    Enforce constraints (e.g., fix specific values of C if needed)
end for
return C_{opt}

5 Numerical Illustrations

We considered a complete information setting in which both players have full knowledge of the network state and developed a custom Python-based simulator to evaluate our proposed methodology. To capture the impact of network structure on agent trajectories, we analyzed two specific graph configurations, depicted in Figs. 2a and 2c, to underscore the role of physical network topology in our approach. The cyber layer is modeled as a graph with 20 nodes and 30 edges, where four nodes are initially infected. The physical layer consists of 20 nodes, four of which act as critical protectors: the compromise of these nodes results in the loss of their connections to the others. Aiming to simulate models that realistically approximate interconnected networks, we adopted another multidomain scenario: the cyber layer was modeled using a Watts–Strogatz (WS) graph, commonly employed to represent scale-free and small-world structures such as social networks [21], while the physical layer was represented by an Erdős–Rényi graph. The defender is equipped with two IPS units. Theses values have been randomly selected to create a balanced testing environment under diverse network conditions. For the numerical evaluation, we consider the following parameters in Table 2.

Table 2. Parameter settings used in the SPSA optimization algorithm.

Parameter	γ_0	c	a	α	A	A_c	D_c	K	h	γ	Initial vector C
Value	0.2	0.1	0.01	0.6	10	0.01	0.02	2500	2	0.9	random vector

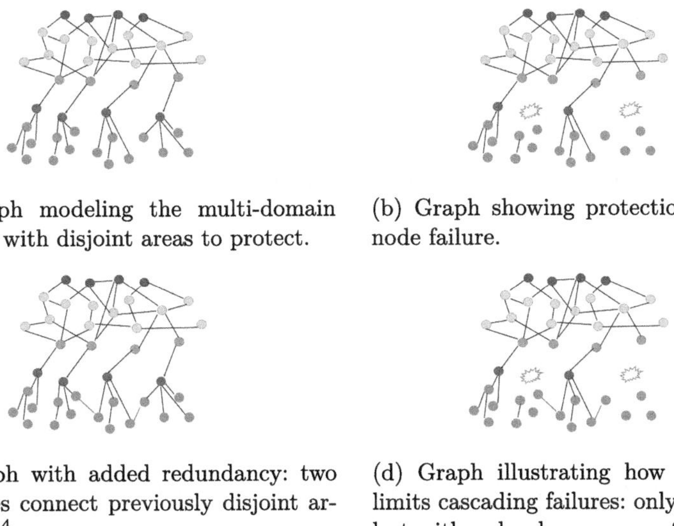

(a) Graph modeling the multi-domain problem with disjoint areas to protect.

(b) Graph showing protection loss after node failure.

(c) Graph with added redundancy: two red edges connect previously disjoint areas $\{A_i\}_{i=1}^4$.

(d) Graph illustrating how redundancy limits cascading failures: only 6 edges are lost with redundancy versus 8 without.

Fig. 2. Cyber-physical graphs before and after attacks, highlighting the benefits of redundancy.

The objectives of the following experiments are as follows:

1. **Convergence of the algorithm**: The SPSA algorithm shows clear convergence and satisfactory performance, as illustrated by the blue curves in

Fig. 3a and Fig. 3b. These curves represent the reward evolution across iterations during the computation of optimal centralities, gradually stabilizing into an horizontal line as convergence is achieved.

2. **Compare the optimal reward with outcomes under the following scenarios:**
   (a) *Optimal centrality with non-optimal mixed strategies:* In this case, the attacker exploits the optimal centrality computed via SPSA but follows suboptimal mixed strategies that disregard centrality thresholds. This highlights the need to optimize strategies prior to centrality computation. As illustrated by the red curve in Fig. 3a and Fig. 3b, suboptimal strategies lead to noticeably lower rewards, even with optimal centrality. In other words, this represents rewards computed at each iteration using the SPSA-derived centrality combined with suboptimal strategies.
   (b) *Non-optimal centrality with non-optimal mixed strategies:* In this scenario, both the centrality and mixed strategies are suboptimal. This case is represented by the green line in Figs. 3a and 3b. The reward corresponding to this curve is computed using the centrality obtained from SPSA and randomly selected strategies. Among all configurations, this setup yields the lowest performance, highlighting the significant impact of non-optimal decisions on the attacker's reward.
3. **Highlight the influence of graph topology on the attacker's optimal reward:** As seen in Fig. 3b for example, the optimal reward decreases under the redundant topology. The added physical connections enhance robustness by reducing the attacker's effectiveness. This highlights the importance of the physical network topology in determining the system's resilience.
4. **Compare the outcomes obtained using classical centrality measures with the one derived from the computed optimal centrality:** Table 3 presents the rewards obtained when the attacker uses classical centrality measures on the studied graphs, and the agents adopt the recommended optimal strategies. Except for betweenness centrality, all other classical centralities yield lower rewards on the redundant topology. Furthermore, these rewards are significantly lower than the optimal reward obtained through SPSA, highlighting the benefit of computing an optimized centrality rather than relying on predefined classical ones.

Table 3. Reward values based on classical centrality measures

Centrality	Closeness	Betweenness	Clustering	Degree	Eigenvector
Graph 2a	3.39	1.23	−0.14	1.64	2.47
Graph 2c	1.84	1.28	−1.19	1.63	2.2
Bigraph WS-ER	5.56	0.02	−0.19	0.23	1.36

Previous illustrations were conducted on a random graph. In the following, the analysis is extended to a bigraph structure by leveraging graph models com-

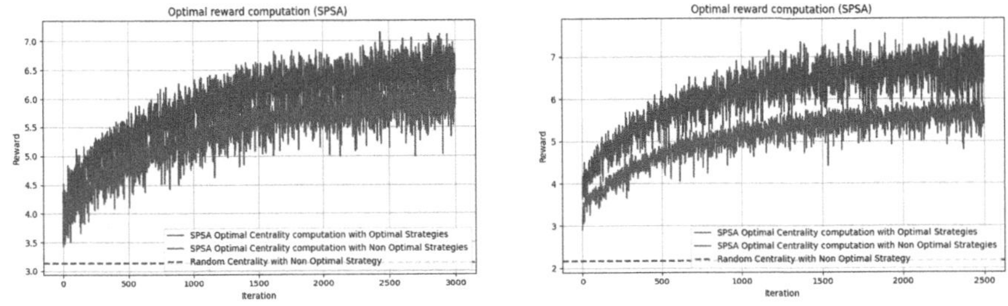

(a) **Optimal centrality computation using the topology of Figure 2a:** *The blue curve represents the optimal configuration, while the red curve corresponds to the scenario described in objective 2a, where the centrality is optimal but the mixed strategies are not. The green line shows the reward associated with the scenario in objective 2b, where both centrality and strategies are suboptimal. As expected, the attacker benefits from adopting the recommended optimal strategies once the SPSA algorithm has been applied to compute the optimal centrality vector.*

(b) **Optimal centrality computation using the topology of Figure 2c:** *we recompute the approximate optimal centrality via SPSA. Two additional edges provide redundancy, so a node remains protected even if its initial defender is compromised. The same scenarios as in Figure 3a are considered, yielding similar trends, optimal strategies, demonstrating better results than other methods. However, the optimal rewards are noticeably lower (6.87) compared to the previous case (6.5), highlighting the critical role of redundancy in enhancing performance.*

Fig. 3. Approximate optimal centrality vectors computed via SPSA under two distinct network topologies, with a comparative analysis between the optimal strategies and selected heuristic approaches

monly found in the literature. Specifically, the physical layer of the bigraph is modeled as an Erdős–Rényi (ER) graph, while the cyber layer is represented using a Watts–Strogatz (WS) graph. Both layers consist of 200 nodes, with the ER graph containing 3596 edges and the WS graph comprising 400 edges. The resulting structure is illustrated in Fig. 4.

Moreover, the graphs considered in this study exhibit relatively low connectivity, which may cause classical centrality measures to produce very small values and lead to potentially misleading interpretations. Our goal is to identify an optimal centrality measure that accurately reflects the relative importance of nodes. To evaluate the agreement between each candidate centrality measure and the optimal one, we use ordinal correlation analysis, specifically Spearman's rank correlation. This analysis is not applied to the random graph due to its symmetry and the potential occurrence of ties. Instead, it is performed on the realistic bi-graph, yielding the following results (Table 4).

6 Conclusion

This paper introduces a novel framework for modeling interactions in cyber-physical systems through the notion of *centrality-based games*. We formulate a

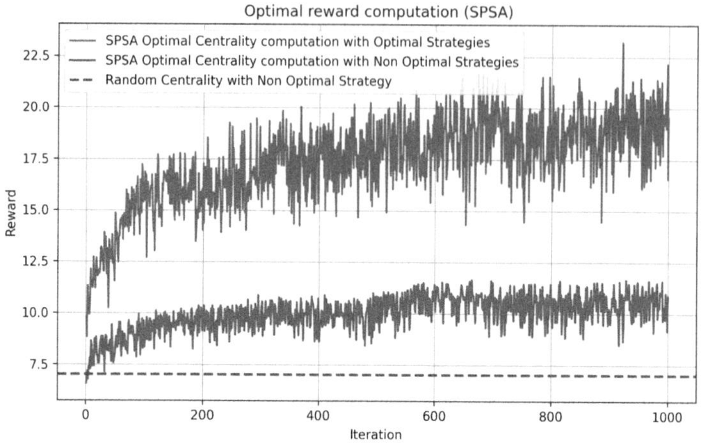

Fig. 4. Computation based on a realistic bi-graph (Watts–Strogatz and Erdős–Rényi): *The optimal centrality is computed using a more realistic bi-graph structure, combining a Watts–Strogatz model for the cyber layer and an Erdős–Rényi model for the physical layer. In this setup,* 4 *nodes are designated as entry points and another* 4 *as target nodes. The results obtained across different scenarios confirm the same trends observed in previous experiments.*

Table 4. Spearman's correlation coefficient between optimal centrality and classical centralities

Centrality	Closeness	Betweenness	Clustering	Degree	Eigenvector
Correlation	0.08	−0.07	−0.01	0.11	0.15

dynamic parametric game that captures the strategic behavior of an attacker and a defender over a bi-layer network. Our approach explicitly integrates the physical domain by redefining node centralities based on the physical network's topology, specifically, through changes in the Fiedler value of the physical graph's Laplacian matrix. We subsequently optimized the centrality assignments by treating them not as fixed values, but as decision variables to be adjusted to align with the objective function. Using the SPSA algorithm, we compute an *approximate optimal centrality* that significantly inhibits lateral movement within the cyber layer, with cascading impacts on the physical system captured in the reward structure. Through numerical simulations, we compare this optimized centrality with several classical centrality measures and observe that while closeness centrality achieves the highest attacker reward among them, it remains well below that of the optimized centrality. Even the assessment of the ordinal relationship using Spearman's correlation coefficient confirms the significant gap, highlighting the limits of traditional metrics in a such adversarial settings. Furthermore, we shown that physical topology changes such as redundant defense paths reduce attacker rewards while preserving classical rankings, underscoring the robustness of our approach. Moreover, we observe that the optimal centrality configuration differs markedly between the attacker and the defender. This asymmetry raises a strategic dilemma: can a unified centrality measure serve both agents optimally, or should each agent adopt a distinct configuration tailored to its goals? Our findings suggest the latter, motivating future work on dual-agent optimization in multi-domain systems.

Acknowledgments. Research was sponsored by the DEVCOM Army Research Laboratory and was accomplished under Grant Number W911NF-24-1-0250. The views and conclusions contained in this document are those of the authors and should not be interpreted as representing the official policies, either expressed or implied, of the DEVCOM Army Research Laboratory or the U.S. Government. The U.S. Government is authorized to reproduce and distribute reprints for Government purposes, notwithstanding any copyright notation herein.

A Appendix

Proof (of Proposition 1). Suppose that $\mathcal{C}_a(\pi_d^*) \neq \mathbb{S}$ and let us show that $\mathcal{C}_d(\pi_a^*) \subseteq \mathcal{C}_a(\pi_d^*)$. Consider an edge $(u_i, u_j) \notin \mathcal{C}_a(\pi_d^*)$. Then, for every $z \in Z$, we have $\pi_a^*(u_i, u_j \mid z) = 0$. Consequently, the defender's expected utility for this edge becomes
$\Phi_d(u_i, u_j|b^t, \pi_a^*) = 2\pi_a^*(u_i, u_j|b^t)C_{u_j} - D_c = 2\sum_{z\in Z} \pi_a^*(u_i, u_j|z)b^t(z)C_{u_j} - D_c = -D_c$. This shows that (u_i, u_j) has the minimal possible value in the ranking induced by $\Phi_d(\cdot \mid b^t, \pi_a^*)$, since for all $(u, v) \in \mathbb{S}$, $\Phi_d(u, v \mid b^t, \pi_a^*) \geqslant -D_c$. Moreover, since $\mathcal{C}_d(\pi_a^*) \neq \mathbb{S}$, there exists at least one edge $(u_x, u_y) \in \mathbb{S}$ that is not among the top h according to $\Phi_d(\cdot \mid b^t, \pi_a^*)$. As $\Phi_d(u_x, u_y \mid b^t, \pi_a^*) \geqslant -D_c$, it follows that (u_i, u_j) cannot belong to $\mathcal{C}_d(\pi_a^*)$, which concludes the proof. □

Proof (of Proposition 2).

1. Since $(u_k, u_l), (u_{k'}, u_{l'}) \notin \mathcal{C}_d(\pi_a^*)$, we have $\pi_d^*(u_k, u_l) = \pi_d^*(u_{k'}, u_{l'}) = 0$. Moreover, as both pairs belong to $\mathcal{C}_a(\pi_d^*)$, their attacker utility values are $\Phi_a(u_k, u_l \mid b^t, \pi_d^*) = -A_c + C_{u_l}$, $\Phi_a(u_{k'}, u_{l'} \mid b^t, \pi_d^*) = -A_c + C_{u_{l'}}$. Since these values are maximal by definition of the shortlist, they must be equal, and hence $C_{u_l} = C_{u_{l'}}$.
2. Let $(u_i, u_j) \in \mathcal{C}_d(\pi_a^*)$ and $(u_k, u_l) \in \mathcal{C}_a(\pi_d^*) \setminus \mathcal{C}_d(\pi_a^*)$. Then, $\pi_d^*(u_k, u_l) = 0$, and since both edges belong to $\mathcal{C}_a(\pi_d^*)$, we have $\Phi_a(u_i, u_j \mid b^t, \pi_d^*) = \Phi_a(u_k, u_l \mid b^t, \pi_d^*)$. That is $C_{u_l} = C_{u_j} - \pi_d^*(u_i, u_j)C_{u_j} \leqslant C_{u_j}$. If $\pi_d^*(u_i, u_j) > 0$, then the inequality is strict, i.e., $C_{u_l} < C_{u_j}$.
   Now, for $(u_x, u_y) \in \mathbb{S} \setminus \mathcal{C}_a(\pi_d^*)$, by definition of the attacker's shortlist, we have $\Phi_a(u_x, u_y \mid b^t, \pi_d^*) < s_C = \Phi_a(u_k, u_l \mid b^t, \pi_d^*)$. Since $\pi_d^*(u_k, u_l) = 0$, we know that $\Phi_a(u_k, u_l \mid b^t, \pi_d^*) = -A_c + C_{u_l}$, and similarly, $\Phi_a(u_x, u_y \mid b^t, \pi_d^*) = -A_c + C_{u_y}$, so $C_{u_y} < C_{u_l}$, concluding the proof. □

Proof (of Theorem 1).

1. Since $\mathcal{C}_d(\pi_a^*) \subseteq \mathcal{C}_a(\pi_d^*)$, it follows from the monotonicity of the min operator that $\theta_a \leqslant \theta_d$. Moreover, by definition of θ_p, we have for all $(u,v) \in \mathcal{C}_p(\pi_{-p}^*)$, $C_v \geqslant \theta_p$.
   Conversely, suppose $(u,v) \in \mathbb{S}$ with $C_v \geqslant \theta_a$. Let $(u',v') \in \mathcal{C}_a(\pi_d^*)$ be such that $C_{v'} = \theta_a$. Then, $C_v \geqslant C_{v'}$, and by Proposition 2, it follows that $(u,v) \in \mathcal{C}_a(\pi_d^*)$. Similarly, if $(u,v) \in \mathbb{S}_{b^t}$ and $C_v \geqslant \theta_d$, then there exists $(u',v') \in \mathcal{C}_d(\pi_a^*)$ with $C_{v'} = \theta_d$. Thus, $C_v \geqslant C_{v'}$, and once more by Proposition 2, $(u,v) \in \mathcal{C}_d(\pi_a^*)$.
2. Suppose, for contradiction, that there exists $(u,v) \in \mathbb{S}$ such that $C_v \in]\theta_a, \theta_d[$. Since $C_v > \theta_a$, by exploiting the point 1, we have $(u,v) \in \mathcal{C}_a(\pi_d^*)$. If $(u,v) \notin \mathcal{C}_d(\pi_a^*)$, then $(u,v) \in \mathcal{C}_a(\pi_d^*) \setminus \mathcal{C}_d(\pi_a^*)$. By Proposition 2.1, all such centralities must equal θ_a, contradicting $C_v \in (\theta_a, \theta_d)$. □

Proof (proof of Proposition 3).

1. By definition, $s_C = \max_{(u_i,u_j)\in\mathbb{S}_b} \Phi_a(u_i,u_j \mid \pi_d^*)$, so $(u_i,u_j) \in \mathcal{C}_a(\pi_d^*)$ iff $\Phi_a(u_i,u_j \mid \pi_d^*) = s_C$. Given $\Phi_a(u_i,u_j \mid \pi_d^*) = -A_c + C_{u_j}(1 - \pi_d^*(u_i,u_j))$, solving for $\pi_d^*(u_i,u_j)$ yields the stated formula.
2. This follows directly from the constraint that h units of defense are distributed.
3. Plug the expression for π_d^* into the total constraint:

$$h = \sum_{\substack{(u_i,u_j)\in\mathbb{S}_b \\ C_{u_j}\geqslant\theta_d}} \left(\frac{-s_C - A_c}{C_{u_j}} + 1\right) = (-s_C - A_c) \sum_{\substack{(u_i,u_j)\in\mathbb{S}_b \\ C_{u_j}\geqslant\theta_d}} \frac{1}{C_{u_j}} + \sum_{\substack{(u_i,u_j)\in\mathbb{S}_b \\ C_{u_j}\geqslant\theta_d}} 1,$$

   which rearranges to give the value of s_C.
4. a) Non-negativity of defense probabilities and the definition of threshold θ_d provide the result.
   b) If $\theta_d > \theta_a$, the intervals $[0, \theta_a]$ and $[\theta_d, \infty)$ are disjoint.
5. For $s_C \leqslant 0$, from $\Phi_a(u_i,u_j \mid \pi_d^*) = -A_c + C_{u_j}(1 - \pi_d^*(u_i,u_j)) \leqslant 0$, we deduce $\pi_d^*(u_i,u_j) \geqslant \frac{C_{u_j} - A_c}{C_{u_j}} > 0 \Rightarrow C_{u_j} \geqslant \theta_d = \min C_{u_j}$.
   For $s_C > 0$, the attacker's optimal strategy allocates positive probability only to edges maximizing Φ_a, hence only to edges in $\mathcal{C}_a(\pi_d^*)$. □

Proof (of Proposition 4). When $C = 0_{\mathbb{R}^{|V_2|}}$, the defender's reward becomes:

$$\begin{aligned}\mathcal{R}_d(\pi_d, \pi_a \mid z) = &\sum_{(u_i,u_j)\in\mathbb{S}} \pi_d(u_i,u_j)\left(2\pi_a(u_i,u_j \mid z)C_{u_j} - D_c\right) \\ &+ \sum_{(u_i,u_j)\in\mathbb{S}} \pi_a(u_i,u_j \mid z)(-C_{u_j}) = -\sum_{(u_i,u_j)\in\mathbb{S}} D_c,\end{aligned}$$

since $C_{u_j} = 0$ for all u_j, and both reward terms vanish except for the fixed defense cost. This sum is minimized, so the defender prefers this choice. On the other hand, the attacker receives no positive reward from any attack, making this centrality strictly suboptimal for her. □

Proof (of Lemma 1). For each edge (u_i, u_j), the function $C \mapsto \pi_a(u_i, u_j \mid z)$ is a step function due to threshold-based strategies, while $C \mapsto s_C$ is continuous over Sol^*. The product of a step function and a continuous function is piecewise continuous. Hence, the composed function is piecewise continuous. By properties of function spaces [17], the space of such functions is closed under linear combinations, preserving piecewise continuity. □

Proof (of the Proposition 5). We estimate the partial sums:

$$\sum_{t=0}^{n} \left|\gamma^t \mathcal{R}_a^C(\pi_d^*, \pi_a^* \mid b^t)\right| \leqslant \sum_{t=0}^{n} \gamma^t \sum_{(u_i,u_j)\in\mathbb{S}} \sum_{z\in Z} |\pi_a^*(u_i, u_j \mid z)| \left|b^t(z)\right| |s_C|$$
$$\leqslant \sum_{t=0}^{n} \gamma^t \cdot 2^{|V_2|} \cdot |A_c - 1| \cdot |E_2| = C_0 \sum_{t=0}^{n} \gamma^t,$$

where $C_0 = 2^{|V_2|} \cdot |A_c - 1| \cdot |E_2|$ is a constant. Since the geometric series converges, the sequence is uniformly bounded and normally convergent. By the Weierstrass M-test [16], uniform convergence implies that the limit function $F_a(C)$ is continuous on each continuity segment. Since Sol^* is compact and F_a is piecewise continuous, F_a achieves a maximum on Sol^*. □

References

1. Garcia, M.L.: Design and Evaluation of Physical Protection Systems. Elsevier (2007)
2. Munasinghe, I., Perera, A., Deo, R.C.: A comprehensive review of UAV-UGV collaboration: advancements and challenges. J. Sens. Actuator Netw. **13**(6), 81 (2024)
3. Ma, C.Y.T., Rao, N.S.V., Yau, D.K.Y.: A game-theoretic study of attack and defense in cyber-physical systems. In: INFOCOM Workshops, pp. 708–713 (2011)
4. Liu, B., Sun, J.: Stackelberg game under asymmetric information in UAV swarm active deception defense. In: BDIDM 2021, pp. 75–79
5. Sayed, M.A., Kiekintveld, C.: A survey of solving imperfect information game and their applications in defensive deception (2023)
6. Roy, S., Sharmin, N., Acosta, J.C., Kiekintveld, C., Laszka, A.: Survey and taxonomy of adversarial reconnaissance techniques. ACM Comput. Surv. **55**(6), 1–38 (2022)
7. Zhu, M., Anwar, A.H., Wan, Z., Cho, J.H., Kamhoua, C.A., Singh, M.P.: A survey of defensive deception: approaches using game theory and machine learning. IEEE Commun. Surv. Tutorials **23**(4), 2460–2493 (2021)
8. Park, J., Mohaisen, A., Kamhoua, C.A., Weisman, M.J., Leslie, N.O., Njilla, L.: Cyber deception in the internet of battlefield things: techniques, instances, and assessments. In: You, I. (ed.) WISA 2019. LNCS, vol. 11897, pp. 299–312. Springer, Cham (2020). https://doi.org/10.1007/978-3-030-39303-8_23
9. Pikner, S.: Leveraging multi-domain military deception to expose the enemy in 2035. Mil. Rev. (2021)
10. Asghar, A.B., Hemida, A., Kamhoua, C., Kleinberg, J.: A scalable double-oracle algorithm for multi-domain deception game. In: IEEE CNS 2024, pp. 1–9

11. Kouam, W., Hayel, Y., Deugoue, G., Kamhoua, C., Tsemogne, O.: A network centrality game based on a compact representation of defender's belief for epidemic control. J. Dyn. Games (2024)
12. Stone, J.V.: Bayes' Rule: A Tutorial Introduction to Bayesian Analysis. Sebtel Press (2013)
13. Kouam, W., Hayel, Y., Deugoué, G., Kamhoua, C.: Exploring centrality dynamics for epidemic control in complex networks. Dyn. Games Appl. 1–33 (2024)
14. Kouam, W., Hayel, Y., Deugoué, G., Kamhoua, C.: A novel centrality measure for analyzing lateral movement in complex networks. XXPhys. A **658**, 130255 (2025)
15. Reiffers-Masson, A., Chonavel, T., Hayel, Y.: Estimating fiedler value on large networks based on random walk observations. In: ICASSP 2021-2021 IEEE International Conference on Acoustics, Speech and Signal Processing (ICASSP), pp. 5504–5508. IEEE (2021)
16. Rudin, W.: Principles of Mathematical Analysis. McGraw-Hill Education, 3rd edition, Theorem 7.10, p. 148 (2021)
17. Gillibert, J.: Chapitre 5: Intégration. Cours de mathématiques, Université Toulouse II (2010). https://www.math.univ-toulouse.fr/~jgillibe/enseignement/MHT204_chap5.pdf
18. Feng, X., et al.: A stackelberg game and Markov modeling of moving target defense. In: Decision and Game Theory for Security: 8th International Conference, GameSec 2017, Vienna, Austria, October 23–25, 2017, Proceedings
19. Spall, J.C.: A one-measurement form of simultaneous perturbation stochastic approximation. Automatica **33**(1), 109–112 (1997)
20. Ding, H., Zhao, Q.: Multilayer network modeling and stability analysis of Internet of Battlefield Things. In: Proceedings of the 2022 IEEE International Systems Conference (SysCon), pp. 1–6. IEEE (2022)
21. Newman, M.E.: The structure and function of complex networks. SIAM Rev. **45**(2), 167–256 (2003)

Tools

OOPredictor: Predicting Object-Oriented Accesses Using Static Analysis

Hassan Arafat[1(✉)], David Bremner[1], Kenneth B. Kent[1], and Julian Wang[2]

[1] University of New Brunswick, Fredericton, Canada
harafat@unb.ca
[2] IBM Canada, Toronto, Canada

Abstract. Object-oriented Programming has become one of the most dominant design paradigms as the separation of concerns and adaptability of design reduce development and maintenance costs. However, the convenience is not without cost. The added indirection inherent in such designs causes excessive pointer chasing, negatively affecting locality, which in turn degrades the performance of cache structures. Furthermore, modern hardware prefetchers are mostly stride prefetchers that are ill-equipped to handle the unpredictability of access patterns generated by pointer chasing. Most software approaches that seek to address this problem resort to profiling the program as it runs, which comes with a significant run-time overhead or requires data from previous runs. In this paper, we propose the use of compile-time static analysis to predict the most common access patterns displayed by a program during run time. Since Java is one of the most popular object-oriented languages, we implement our prototype within the OpenJ9 JVM, inside the OMR optimizer infrastructure. The outputs of our proposed predictor are Markov chains that model the expected behavior of the program. The effectiveness of the proposed predictor is evaluated by comparing the model with the actual run-time behavior of the program measured using an instrumented interpreter. Our experiments show that the proposed predictor exhibits good accuracy and can be used to inform minimally intrusive load stall mitigation strategies, e.g. informing copying GCs on more locality-friendly copying orders.

Keywords: Managed Runtimes · Markov chains · Compilers · Object-oriented Programming

This research was conducted within the Centre for Advanced Studies-Atlantic Faculty of Computer Science, University of New Brunswick. The authors are grateful for the colleagues and facilities of CAS-Atlantic in supporting our research. The authors would like to acknowledge the funding support of the Natural Sciences and Engineering Research Council of Canada (NSERC), 536287-18. Furthermore, we would also like to thank the New Brunswick Innovation Foundation for contributing to this project.

A. Remke et al. (Eds.): Valuetools 2025, LNICST 691, pp. 199–214, 2027.
https://doi.org/10.1007/978-3-032-23901-3_12

1 Introduction

In modern computers, the main memory is much slower than the processing unit. This gap in performance causes the memory to often be a performance bottleneck, the effect is often referred to as the *memory wall*. In order to help bridge the gap, computing systems utilize a hierarchy of progressively faster and smaller memories that are used to retain copies of active memory locations, those memories are often referred to as *caches*. Despite their small size compared to the main memory, caches alleviate the impact of the memory wall significantly. Their efficacy is driven by the fact that most programs' memory access patterns are not truly random; they display some degree of temporal and spatial *locality*.

To further improve the effectiveness of caches, data can be loaded from the memory before they are needed, in what is known as *prefetching*. Most high-end modern processors have dedicated hardware units to perform prefetching. Those *hardware prefetchers* analyze the access pattern of the processor and prefetch data from the memory when they detect simple stride patterns. While hardware prefetchers are effective at reducing cache misses from constant-stride accesses to arrays, they struggle with more complex access patterns, especially when the accessed addresses depend on values in memory.

A common memory access pattern that hardware prefetchers struggle with is called *pointer chasing*. Pointer chasing happens when the program has to retrieve the address of an object from memory by dereferencing a chain of pointers. This negatively impacts cache performance as most production hardware prefetchers are not designed to handle pointer chasing. The fact that the address to be accessed next is dependent on values in memory means that the hardware prefetcher does not know the address to be loaded until it finishes loading from memory. This results in a higher number of impactful load stalls and thus decreased performance [9]. Prior knowledge of the program's access pattern could allow us to explore different mitigation strategies.

Pointer chasing patterns appear often in machine code generated from *Object-Oriented Programming* (OOP) languages. OOP has become one of the most prevalent programming paradigms, especially for enterprise solutions. The division of code into manageable classes reduces development and maintenance costs. This, however, comes at a performance cost as the abstraction requires added levels of indirection. The added levels of indirection introduce extra pointer chasing.

In this paper we present a static analysis approach for predicting the pattern of object-oriented memory accesses in programs written in Java. The work investigates the feasibility, capabilities and limitations of such a system in a modern production runtime. We also present a preliminary analysis on a possible use of the generated Markov chains to construct affinity graphs.

The rest of this paper is structured as follows: we first discuss essential background concepts and elucidate related work, then we describe our predictor, followed by the methodology and experimental setup used to evaluate the predictor, next we show data gathered from our experiment and our analyses and finally we discuss our conclusions and future work.

2 Background

Programming is usually a challenging task, especially when the programmer has to manage memory. Modern programming languages, like Java, offer a multitude of tools to help the programmer and reduce development costs.

Those languages can also be run on complex runtimes that—in addition to garbage collection—include powerful tools to enhance performance, collect information and provide interoperability.

2.1 Managed Runtimes

Managing memory is a tedious and error-prone process. In order to simplify the job of a programmer, managed languages unburden the programmer by automatically managing the memory; they remove unused objects in what is known as *garbage collection*. While it does make the job of a programmer easier, garbage collection introduces overhead that can degrade performance [1].

Another one of the tools commonly available in modern runtimes is known as the *Just In Time* (JIT) compiler. It automatically and selectively compiles code on the run, targeting the local hardware. JIT compilers produce more optimal code—when compared to an interpreter—but they can also degrade performance if used haphazardly, since they run during the execution of the program. Virtual machines use complex policies to decide when and how to compile methods [13], in addition to a myriad of other cost reduction techniques, e.g. Ahead-of-Time compilation [12] and disaggregated JIT servers [11].

2.2 Static Analysis

To help improve performance, optimizing compilers analyze the code to find opportunities for optimizations. The analysis of the code itself before running is referred to as *Static Analysis*. On average, the more optimizations are enabled, the better-performing the resulting code and the longer the compilation time. The trade-off between compilation time and code performance is addressed by having multiple levels of optimization, e.g. warm, hot, very-hot and scorching. In a JIT environment, methods recompile with progressively higher levels of optimization as they are invoked more frequently.

2.3 Profiling

Gathering data about the behavior of a program as it runs can be very helpful in guiding powerful optimizations. This can be done in one of two approaches: the data can be gathered by *instrumenting* the program, i.e., adding snippets of code into the program that collect statistics, or by *sampling* it with a different thread or process, i.e., interrupting the execution of the program periodically and collecting information. While the data gathered from these approaches can be useful, the gathering of the data itself often incurs performance penalties. Many approaches have been proposed to reduce this impact, including running the profiler only for short bursts of time [8].

2.4 OpenJ9

Java is a general purpose, object-oriented programming language. Java source code is compiled into *bytecode* that can be run on any machine with a Java Virtual Machine installed. JVMs hide the complexities of the underlying machine and can run bytecode regardless of what type of machine produced it.

Eclipse OpenJ9 [6] is an open source JVM implementation that utilizes Eclipse OMR's language-agnostic components [5]. Those tools include garbage collectors, and many compilation tools.

3 Related Work

A recent study into the sources of hardware stalls in x86 architectures showed that object-oriented accesses are still a major source of load stalls in JVM workloads [15]. There are many proposed optimizations that can use information about object access patterns of a program to help mitigate this issue and those optimizations attempt to do that using a myriad of approaches.

Some approaches change the order of objects in memory, while leaving their internal structure intact. A main draw of such approaches is that they don't require any changes to the mutator. Chen et al. [2] propose a locality improving GC that can be triggered proactively to improve the cache performance of a program. The locality improving GC uses profile information collected using read barriers and access sampling to identify hot objects. During GC, those hot objects are copied first before processing the rest of the heap. Another approach discussed by Serrano and Zhuang [18] uses the GC itself to build *partial data context trees* (PDCT), those trees are then combined with cache miss information—collected by sampling hardware counters—to model the object access pattern of a program. They then use that information during copying in generational GC to better place objects in memory. An innovative approach by Yang et al. [21] makes heavy use of access barriers in a region based GC to copy small objects in the order that the mutators access them.

Other approaches change the structure of the objects themselves. Chilimbi, Davidson and Larus [3] introduce a tool that can recommend better structure definitions for C programs. The tool utilized both *structure splitting*—splitting the hot fields of structure so they can be collocated in a single cache line—and *field reordering*—changing the order of fields in structures such that fields that have high temporal affinity are placed next to each other in memory, using both dynamic information from a previous runs as well as static analysis of the program. An approach proposed by Eimouri, Kent and Micic [4] used *object splitting* at allocation time in the JVM. They use information collected using profiling to determine cold fields in objects, the collected data is then used to allocate cold fields in separate regions of the *balanced GC* policy in the OpenJ9 JVM.

The previous approaches all used performance profiling during the run or required profiling data from previous runs. The overhead of profiling as well as the impracticality of retaining profiling data were often a big factor in limiting the impact of those approaches.

Jeon, Shin and Han [10] introduce the idea of using static analysis to predict accesses patterns and then using that information to restructure the way objects in memory are allocated in C++. Their predictions are rather simplistic and are represented as regular expressions, which limits the amount of information the prediction provides.

Garbatov and Cachopo [7] present an analysis of different prediction models of database accesses of object-oriented applications, they discuss *Bayesian inference*, *importance analysis* and *Markov Chains*. Their results show that *Markov chains* is the model that shows least fluctuations. However, the building and updating of their models is done using profiling data.

4 Object-Oriented Access Predictor

Our aim is to model the object-oriented behavior of the running program, but without the overhead of fine-grain profiling or retaining previous profiles. We thus propose a technique that uses *static analysis* to build *Markov chains* that model the object-oriented behavior of a program; a novel static analysis-powered Object-Oriented access Predictor (OOPredictor). OOPredictor can also be enhanced with branch bias information if they are available at compile time, e.g., in a JIT environment.

The OOPredictor is implemented as an optimization within the OMR infrastructure used by the OpenJ9 JVM. Considering OMR is language agnostic, it makes extending this work to other languages easier. This is especially true for languages that have existing implementations that use OMR. Another advantage of implementing our predictor as an optimization is that it allows us to easily reuse the Control Flow Graph (CFG) that the compiler creates for other optimizations. The JIT compiler works with the *Intermediate Representation* (IR) of the instructions used by OMR, known as *TestaRossa Intermediate Language* (TRIL).

4.1 Objective

The predictor focuses mainly on making predictions about pointer-chasing patterns, ones specifically stemming from the dereferencing object fields that are themselves object addresses. The data gathered is class based, informing us about the order that reference fields in an object of a specific class are likely to be accessed. The fact that we "reuse" the CFG reduces the performance impact on compile time, which allows for the predictor to be used in a JIT environment. JIT compilation, however, does restrict the type of analysis that we can do to only intra-procedural analysis, as more expensive analyses risk significantly increasing compilation time.

Those predictions, constructed without the use of profiling, can be used to guide many optimizations that traditionally rely on profiling, eliminating the costs associated with profiling.

4.2 Output Format

The output of the predictor can be described as a compressed Markov Chain, where accesses that have 1.0 probability to be accessed in order are combined into one state. We build nodes, each containing a list of fields that are expected to be accessed in-order. Each node has a collection of outgoing edges to other nodes; the weight of each edge represents the probability that the execution will transition to the destination node after finishing the current one.

4.3 Building the Output

To build the output Markov Chain we traverse the CFG. For each *basic block* (a portion of the code that has no branches and no branch targets) we assume that accesses within are guaranteed to happen in-order—barring an interrupt, and as such form the list of accesses in a single node. This is assumed to hold since there cannot be any flow control within a *basic block* —by definition. Each node can be thought of as a series of states that have a 100% chance of transitioning from one to the next.

The fact we implement our approach in a JIT environment allows us access to some extra information, e.g., statistics about branch biases as well some extra type information when polymorphism is present. We can utilize the information to better inform our model without incurring extra profiling costs as the information is collected irrespective of our optimization. As a method is compiled to higher levels of optimization, multiple optimizations might cause changes to the resulting CFG and Markov chain.

In the case that such information is not available, e.g., *Ahead Of Time* (AOT) compilation, we can set static probabilities to be given to forward and back branches.

Our main interest are IR instructions that are indirect accesses, for each indirect access, we record the following:

1. class: the class of the accessed field.
2. field: the field within the object that is accessed.
3. type: the class of the object that field references.

The general outline of the algorithm is show in Algorithm 1. The two loops in the beginning were implemented as one—with handling for yet to be constructed state, but are separated into two distinct traversals in the pseudocode for clarity.

Transitions from a given block define which nodes are likely to be accessed next. Since many blocks do not contain accesses that are of interest to us, our resulting graph is full of empty nodes, with only a few nodes that have any accesses at all. Those empty nodes maintain only control flow information, we want to retain that information but reduce the size of the output. To do that, we *bypass* all empty nodes except the nodes representing entry and exit blocks.

We traverse the graph and we *bypass* nodes that are empty. The operation *bypass* removes the node and reconnects its parents to the children while retaining the probabilities that each node is reached. Self-loops, which can result from previous *bypass* operations, are removed and their probabilities distributed proportionally to outgoing edges. This is possible because we only care about the control flow information in empty nodes. Once the transitions are updated, the bypassed node is removed Algorithm 2.

```
input : CFG: The CFG of the method getting compiled
output: markovchain: A markov chain of OO Accesses

// Logic split into two loops for clarity
foreach block in breadthFirstTraverse(CFG) do
    newstate ←markovchain.newState(block.number)
    foreach instruction in block.instructions do
        if isOOAccess(instruction) then
            newstate.addAccess(toOOAccess(instruction))
foreach block in breadthFirstTraverse(CFG) do
    newstate ←findState(block.number)
    foreach successor in block.successors do
        // Use profiling values if available otherwise use defaults
        if sucessor.frequecny is available then
            weight ← successor.frequency
        else
            // static values depending on whether it is a forward edge
               or a backward edge
            weight ← static values
    newstate.addTransition(findState(successor.target.number),weight)

// Call bypass on empty states
foreach state in markovchain do
    if state is empty and state is neither an initial nor final state then
        markovchain.bypass(state)
```

Algorithm 1: Building Markov chain from CFG

5 Methodology

Validating the output requires measuring the behavior of the JVM and comparing it with our models. The instrumentation necessary for measuring is for evaluation purposes only and is not to be included in an actual production environment.

5.1 Java Interpreter Instrumentation

Our proposed predictor focuses solely on object-oriented accesses, this precludes the use of a low-level profiler as it would not be aware of object information in the JVM, e.g., class names, field names, field types. Consequently, we have decided to instrument the Java interpreter itself; the interpreter can access object and

```
input: state: The Markov chain state being bypassed
foreach edgein in state.incoming do
    // If it is a self-loop, redistribute probability equally
    if edgein in state.outgoing then
        weight ←edgein.weight/(state.outgoing.size − 1)
        deleteTransition(edgein)
        foreach edgeout in state.outgoing do
            edgeout.weight = edgeout.weight+weight
    else
        foreach edgeout in state.outgoing do
            // add transition will just add to weight of existing
               transition if such a transition exists
            edgein.source.addTransition(edgeout.target,
             edgein.weight × edgeout.weight)
```

Algorithm 2: Bypassing an empty state

class information easily, and is relatively straight forward to instrument. There are two relevant Java bytecodes that we will call *object-oriented accesses*:

1. getfield: retrieves the value of a field within an object.
2. putfield: updates the value of a field within an object.

For each object-oriented access we record the type and name of the field, as well as the name of the class to which the field belongs. We also save call sites to be able to identify the method model to compare against.

This approach has its challenges: in order to record every access, the programs had to be run in interpreter-only mode, with option *-Xint*. For modern workloads, interpreter-only execution time is—on average—15 times longer than execution time with JIT enabled on the HotSpot JVM [14]. Similar results can be expected from the OpenJ9 JVM as neither machine is optimized for interpreted performance. The slowdown is even greater when we take into account the instrumentation overhead.

Another problem is the size of the access logs as they can get very large for bigger benchmarks. Even with compression, processing those files proved to be prohibitively expensive. We consequently limited the size of the logs to 2×10^9 accesses. This translates to multiple hours of runtime on average in our experiments, giving the JVM more than ample time to reach a steady state.

It is important to note that while the instrumentation overhead would be prohibitively large in a production environment, the instrumentation is only intended for the evaluation of the OOPredictor. It is not part of the OOPredictor nor is it required by the OOPredictor to operate.

5.2 Experimental Setup

Every benchmark was run twice: once with the JIT enabled to build the prediction model, and once in interpreter-only mode to measure accesses. Since we are measuring the behavior of the Virtual Machine (VM) itself, not the underlying hardware, there is negligible relevant variation between the two runs. The measured accesses are compared to the model using a Python script, the model is simulated like a non-deterministic state machine. In order to maximize the amount of data, we therefore add the predictor optimization to all optimization policies.

During the JIT run, the predictor is instructed to output the prediction model as a set of JSON files. The files are then processed by the Python script and a list of symbol names for the relevant methods is saved. The recorded accesses from the interpreter run are then processed and the call sites of the relevant methods are saved. For each relevant method, we iterate through its call sites and run the model against the recorded accesses. For methods with more than 100 call sites, we select a random sample of 100 call sites. Our reliance on the JIT compiler to make the models means that we only get models for the most executed methods. Due to the limitation of the predictor to intra-procedural analysis, we have to accommodate some "gaps" of accesses that are not predicted by our models.

For each method, we record the number of accesses that were matched, the number of accesses that were skipped and the number of calls where the predicted model finished execution in a final state, i.e., one that represents an exit block in the CFG input. We reiterate that the interpreter-only run and the offline processing here are only for this validation experiment, and would not be part of a production use of the predictor.

We conclude the experiments with a brief case study of using the predictor to build affinity graphs for the chi-square benchmark from the Renaissance suite. We built those affinity graphs by defining accesses that are within two blocks from each other as affine. We compare those affinity graphs to those built more traditionally, using a sliding a window of accesses recorded, during an instrumented interpreter. The list of relevant class names—those which the compiler generated an affinity graph for—is passed to interpreter.

As both set of graphs have the same nodes, their adjacency matrices are of the same size and are then vectorized and compared directly. It is important to note that since the affinity graph edges can only have positive values, the resulting vectors are guaranteed to be in the positive orthant. We use two metrics for measuring the similarity of the two generated graphs: cosine similarity and Spearman's correlation coefficient. Cosine similarity is a common way of quantifying the symmetry between vectors, while we opt to use the Spearman's correlation coefficient as a way of measuring how the relative orders of edge weights compare. We made that choice since the relative weight of edges is a major determining factor in many optimizations that use affinity graphs.

5.3 Benchmarks

We use the Renaissance benchmark suite [16] to evaluate our predictor. The Renaissance benchmark suite covers a wide range of JVM workloads, and has become one of the most ubiquitous modern suites. We use all of the benchmark groups except the benchmarks in *concurrent*, as they failed to run in interpreter-only mode because of timeouts.

We use *SPECjbb2015* and *SPECjbb2005* benchmarks to evaluate our predictor's performance on business workloads. Although *SPECjbb2005* has been retired, its object access pattern is significantly different to that of its successor and our co-author informed us that it displays intriguing results in previous encounters. SPECjbb2005 emulates server-side Java commonly used by businesses, with clients and database replaced by driver threads and object binary trees, respectively [19]. SPECjbb2015 models the infrastructure of a worldwide supermarket company that handles point-of-sale requests, online purchases and data mining [20].

6 Results

Since our approach is intra-procedural, we expect many of the accesses we can not match with our predictor to be a result of function calls. So we allow for "gaps", during which accesses that are a result of another function are taking place and are thus not predicted by our Markov chains. The accesses in those gaps are counted, but they will not cause the Markov chain to fail. For each method we measure the percentage of calls that ended with the model in a final state—with allowance for gaps—we refer to that metric as the *termination rate.* To account for the impact of those gaps, we also measure the percentage of object-oriented accesses that were correctly predicted by the model, we refer to this metric as the *OO match rate.* The *termination rate* is intended as a measure of how often an access sequence predicted by our model is observed during runtime. On the other hand the *OO match rate* is intended as a measure of how many of the object-oriented accesses that are measured were predicted by OOPredictor.

We also note the number of bytecodes within a method as *method size* and the number of OO accesses in the model as *number of accesses*

We will use violin plots to visualize the data. Violin plots show the arithmetic mean, median as well as the first and third quartiles. They also show a Kernel Density Estimation (KDE) of the underlying data. The KDE is built using a Gaussian kernel function and Scott's rule of thumb to select bandwidth [17].

Since our data is non-parametric we use *Spearman's rank correlation coefficient* to measure the following correlations:

- **cot:** *OO match rate* and *termination rate.*
- **ctn:** *Termination rate* and *number of accesses*
- **con:** *OO match rate* and *number of accesses*
- **cts:** *Termination rate* and *method size*
- **cos:** *OO match rate* and *method size*

6.1 SPECJBB

The mean *termination rate* for both *SPECjbb2005* and *SPECjbb2015* is around 0.7 as shown in Fig. 1a. The KDE shape indicates the data is bimodal, with one peak around 1.0 and another around 0.0. The median and 3rd quartiles overlap at 1.0 indicating more than 50% of the methods terminated on 100% of the sampled sites. The KDE of the *OO match rate*, while showing the same bimodality, shows larger spread of the values with some density in the interval 0.2–0.8 (Fig. 1b).

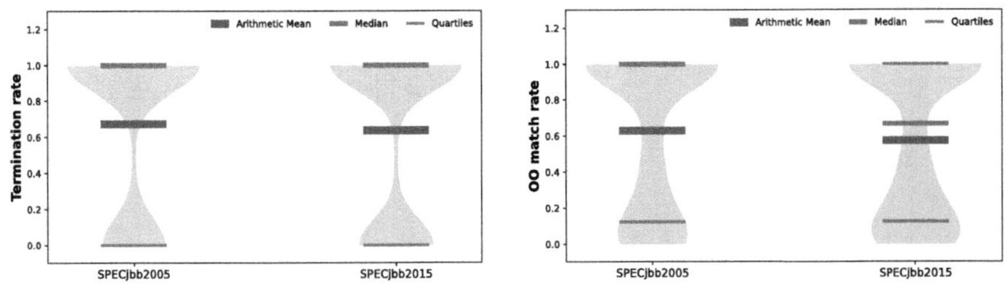

(a) *Termination rate* of SPECjbb workloads; the data is very top-heavy, this is clearly illustrated by the median and 3rd quartile overlapping.

(b) *OO match rate* of SPECjbb workloads; the upper quartile is at the maximum as a quarter of the methods consistently achieve a value of almost 1.

Fig. 1. Violin plots for data collected from the SPECjbb workloads

6.2 Renaissance

Renaissance is a massive benchmark suite, and as such we will address it in groups. Benchmarks in the *Concurrency* group could not be run, as timeout exceptions kept occurring when running in interpreter-only mode.

Apache Spark. This group contains benchmarks that are compute-bound, data-parallel and focus on machine learning. If we look at the *Termination Rate*, shown in Fig. 2a, we see that the data is extremely polarized. The predictor reaches a final state in more than 80% of the processed call sites for some methods, while only doing so 20% of time or less for others. It is important to note that over 50% of the methods in benchmarks of this group have a *termination rate* near 1.0, causing the arithmetic mean and the 3rd quartile to overlap at the 1.0. While 25% of the methods have a Termination rate near 0.0, causing the 1st quartile to be at the minimum.

The *OO match rate* for the same group shows the same bimodal distribution, but with more spread (Fig. 2b). The medians for *chi-square* and *gauss-mix* are above 0.9, meaning that 50% of the methods in those benchmarks had a 90% or more *OO match rate*.

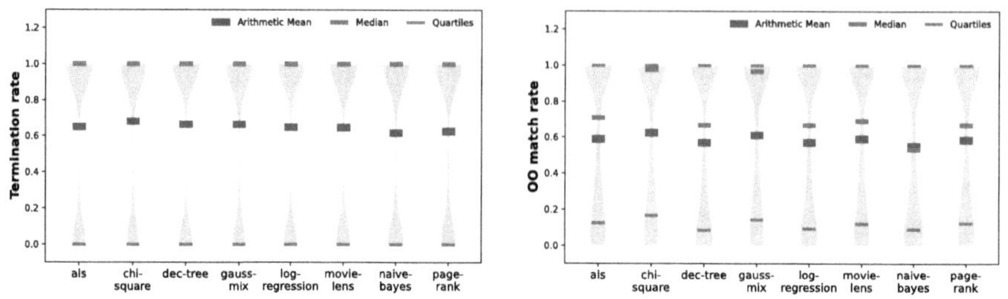

(a) *Termination rate* in the apache-spark group, the data is top heavy with the median and 3rd quartile overlapping.

(b) *OO match rate* in the apache-spark group, the upper quartile is at the maximum as a quarter of the methods consistently achieve a value of almost 1.

Fig. 2. Violin plots of data collected from the apache-spark group in the Renaissance suite

Method level correlations, shown in Table 1, show only weak correlation between *termination rate* and *OO match rate*. *Termination rate* and *OO match rate* are more strongly negatively-correlated with the *number of accesses* than raw *method size*.

Database. We only use the *db-shootout* benchmark, as the *neo4j-analytics* benchmark is not supported for JVM 11. *db-shootout* is a Java in-memory database benchmark that focuses on data structures and query-processing. The data from *db-shootout* shows more spread, even for the *termination rate* metric. The arithmetic mean of both *Termination rate* and *OO match rate* were in the 0.5–0.6 range.

Web. This group contains two benchmarks: *finagle-chirper* and *finagle-http*. Both benchmarks simulate web servers with a focus on futures, atomics and message-passing. The *termination rate* data displays strong bimodality with the arithmetic mean in the 0.7–0.8 range for the *Termination rate* and in the 0.5–0.6 range for *OO match rate*.

Functional. This group contains benchmarks that are task-parallel, memory-bound and have high contention. Looking at the *Termination Rate* graph, we see that the arithmetic mean and 3rd quartile overlap at 1.0, this indicates that more than 50% of the models from methods in these workloads always reached a final state (Fig. 3a).

The *OO match rate* graph shows that the data is less polarized, with the KDEs getting wider near the center (Fig. 3b). The arithmetic means are also slightly lower than those in the *apache-spark* group (Fig. 2b). At the method level, benchmarks in this group have a lower number of compiled methods and generally lower correlations across the board (Table 2).

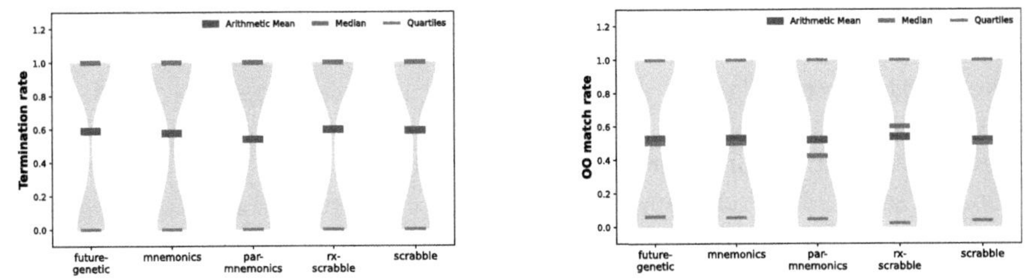

(a) *Termination rate* in the functional group, the data is top heavy with the median and 3rd quartile overlapping.

(b) *OO match rate* in the functional group, the upper quartile is at the maximum as a quarter of the methods consistently achieve a value of almost 1

Fig. 3. Violin plots of data collected from the functional group in the Renaissance suite

Scala. This group features a collection of Scala benchmarks that use Software Transactional Memory (STM) or Scala collections. The arithmetic means in this group are generally high, in the 0.6–0.8 interval. This group has the highest arithmetic means out of any other group. The patterns were very similar to benchmarks in the *functional* group.

Table 1. Table of the number of compiled methods and Spearman's rank correlation coefficients for workloads in the apache-spark group.

	methods	cot	ctn	con	cts	cos
als	813	0.48	−0.45	−0.59	−0.35	−0.47
chi-square	542	0.39	−0.40	−0.53	−0.32	−0.42
dec-tree	1360	0.42	−0.43	−0.60	−0.36	−0.50
gauss-mix	525	0.39	−0.42	−0.54	−0.34	−0.38
log-regression	1126	0.42	−0.43	−0.59	−0.34	−0.48
movie-lens	796	0.39	−0.41	−0.57	−0.32	−0.42
naive-bayes	749	0.43	−0.44	−0.58	−0.34	−0.46
page-rank	612	0.40	−0.42	−0.56	−0.32	−0.43

Table 2. Table of the number of compiled methods and Spearman's rank correlation coefficients for workloads in the functional group.

	methods	cot	ctn	con	cts	cos
future-genetic	198	0.40	−0.47	−0.57	−0.27	−0.44
mnemonics	89	0.39	−0.43	−0.48	−0.34	−0.34
par-mnemonics	94	0.54	−0.52	−0.46	−0.42	−0.35
rx-scrabble	173	0.38	−0.41	−0.34	−0.25	−0.24
scrabble	105	0.30	−0.45	−0.44	−0.33	−0.23

Summary. The bimodal nature of the collected data was consistent across benchmarks, regardless of size of benchmark or nature of workload. While the details of the distribution varied by workload, the arithmetic mean values of both the *termination rate* and *OO match rate* remained consistently above 0.5. The same can be said regarding the median, with the sole exception of the *par-mnemonics* benchmark in the *Renaissance* suite. Furthermore, 25% of the models for every benchmark had a match rate of 100% on both metrics.

Models that consistently have a high *termination rate* do not necessarily have a high *OO match rate*, as the correlation coefficient between them is consistently less than 0.5. Indicating that how often a predicted sequence appeared in-order had weak correlation to how many of the accesses that appeared were predicted. Although the absolute value of the correlation coefficients remained under 0.65, the size of the method as well as the number of object-oriented accesses in it were good indicators of lower predictor accuracy, with the number of accesses showing a stronger correlation. This was consistent across all benchmark groups, including those whose correlation data was omitted for brevity.

6.3 Affinity Graphs

Affinity graphs are used to guide many of the optimizations mentioned in Sect. 3, but they are traditionally built using profiling. We show a preliminary analysis of the accuracy of an affinity graph built from the chi-square benchmark of the Renaissance suite. Two histograms show the *cosine similarity* and *Spearman's correlation coefficient* between the class affinity graphs built using models produced from the OOPredictor and those produced traditionally using an instrumented interpreter.

For Spearman's correlation, we only consider classes where the Spearman's correlation test that meet our significance level requirement, i.e., $p{-}value \leq 0.05$. The distribution of the cosine results is skewed sharply to the right. The highest number of classes is in the 0.9–1.0 range, and the second highest in the 0.7–0.8 range, with the rest of the domain having values distributed roughly evenly (Fig. 4a). Furthermore, the Spearman's coefficient results show that the relative order of edges is strongly correlated for over a third of the classes, with a similar number of classes showing weak correlation (Fig. 4b).

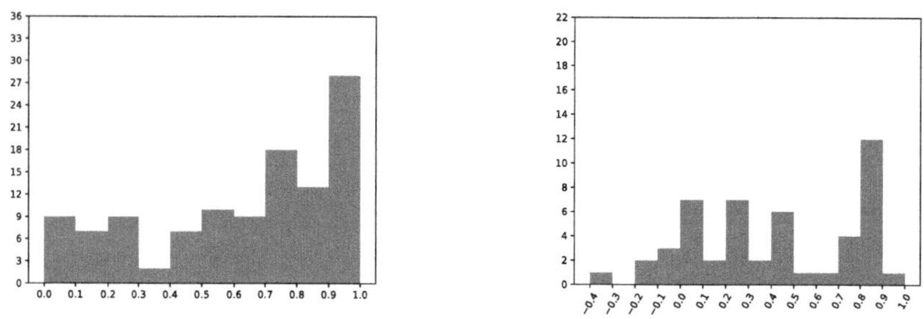

(a) Histogram of *cosine similarity* between the affinity graphs generated using *OOPredictor* and the ones built via profiling.

(b) Histogram of *Spearman's coefficient* between the affinity graphs generated using *OOPredictor* and the ones built via profiling.

Fig. 4. Similarity metrics between affinity graphs from the chi-square benchmark

7 Conclusion

The proposed predictor is consistently accurate for certain methods while frequently failing to make accurate predictions for others. The size of the resulting model is a better indicator of predictor accuracy than plain method size, which would encourage us, in situations where we would like to limit our predictor to "easily predictable" methods, to at least preliminarily determine the number of OO accesses in a method before deciding if we should use the predictor.

It is important to note that since the predictor models fail to predict the object-oriented access patterns of some functions, it is best to use this information to guide non-intrusive and low risk optimization strategies to improve the layout of objects in memory and thus the spatial locality of the programs.

We believe the results show that the proposed predictor can provide useful information about the runtime object-oriented access pattern of a program at the compilation time of its methods. Without having to incur the cost of extra runtime profiling. The models can be used to extract class affinity information about the program at compile time which can then be used by optimization strategies either in the compiler or the GC to improve performance. Our preliminary affinity graph analyses show the approach has promise. As for future work, further study into the feasibility of expanding this approach to inter-procedural analysis and how it affects both cost and accuracy of the predictor remains to be done. The affinity graph analysis needs to be expanded to other benchmarks, as well as improved metrics and sensitivity analyses. Affinity graphs built at compile time can be used to inform field layout optimizations at object allocation time, as well as object layout optimizations.

References

1. Carpen-Amarie, M., Marlier, P., Felber, P., Thomas, G.: A performance study of Java garbage collectors on multicore architectures. In: Proceedings of the Sixth International Workshop on Programming Models and Applications for Multicores and Manycores, PMAM 2015, pp. 20–29. Association for Computing Machinery, New York (2015)
2. Chen, W.K., Bhansali, S., Chilimbi, T., Gao, X., Chuang, W.: Profile-guided proactive garbage collection for locality optimization. SIGPLAN Not. **41**(6), 332–340 (2006)
3. Chilimbi, T.M., Davidson, B., Larus, J.R.: Cache-conscious structure definition. SIGPLAN Not. **34**(5), 13–24 (1999)
4. Eimouri, T., Kent, K.B., Micic, A.: Optimizing the JVM object model using object splitting. In: Proceedings of the 27th Annual International Conference on Computer Science and Software Engineering, CASCON 2017, pp. 170–179. IBM Corp., USA (2017). Event-place: Markham, Ontario, Canada
5. Foundation, Eclipse: Eclipse OMR (2024). www.eclipse.org/omr/
6. Foundation, Eclipse: Eclipse openj9 (2024). www.eclipse.org/openj9/
7. Garbatov, S., Cachopo, J.: Data access pattern analysis and prediction for object-oriented applications. INFOCOMP J. Comput. Sci. **10**(4), 1–14 (2011)

8. Hirzel, M., Chilimbi, T.: Bursty tracing: a framework for low-overhead temporal profiling. In: 4th ACM Workshop on Feedback-Directed and Dynamic Optimization (FDDO-4), pp. 117–126. Citeseer, ACM, New York (2001)
9. Inoue, H., Nakatani, T.: Identifying the sources of cache misses in Java programs without relying on hardware counters. In: Proceedings of the 2012 international symposium on Memory Management, ISMM 2012, pp. 133–142. Association for Computing Machinery, New York (2012)
10. Jeon, J., Shin, K., Han, H.: Layout transformations for heap objects using static access patterns. In: Krishnamurthi, S., Odersky, M. (eds.) CC 2007. LNCS, vol. 4420, pp. 187–201. Springer, Heidelberg (2007). https://doi.org/10.1007/978-3-540-71229-9_13
11. Khrabrov, A., Pirvu, M., Sundaresan, V., de Lara, E.: JITServer: Disaggregated caching JIT compiler for the JVM in the cloud. In: 2022 USENIX Annual Technical Conference (USENIX ATC 22), pp. 869–884. USENIX Association, Carlsbad (2022)
12. Krylov, G., et al.: Ahead-of-time compilation in eclipse OMR on example of WebAssembly. In: Proceedings of the 31st Annual International Conference on Computer Science and Software Engineering, CASCON 2021, pp. 237–243. IBM Corp., USA (2021)
13. Kulkarni, P.A.: JIT compilation policy for modern machines. In: Proceedings of the 2011 ACM international conference on Object oriented programming systems languages and applications, OOPSLA 2011, pp. 773–788. Association for Computing Machinery, New York (2011)
14. Lambert, J., Casey, K., Monahan, R.: Repositioning tiered hotspot execution performance relative to the interpreter. arXiv:2304.06460 [cs] (2023)
15. Li, Z., Arafat, H., Wang, J., Bremner, D., Kent, K.: Stalls in java applications on x86 platforms. In: Gribaudo, M., Iacono, M., Sedigh Sarvestani, S. (eds) Performance Evaluation Methodologies and Tools. Valuetools 2024. Lecture Notes of the Institute for Computer Sciences, Social Informatics and Telecommunications Engineering, vol. 663, pp. 391–404. Springer Cham (2024). https://doi.org/10.1007/978-3-032-06818-7_20
16. Prokopec, A., et al.: Renaissance: benchmarking suite for parallel applications on the JVM. In: Proceedings of the 40th ACM SIGPLAN Conference on Programming Language Design and Implementation, PLDI 2019, pp. 31–47. Association for Computing Machinery, New York (2019)
17. Scott, D.W.: Multivariate Density Estimation: Theory, Practice, and Visualization. Wiley, Newark (2015). Equation 6.44
18. Serrano, M.J., Zhuang, X.: Placement optimization using data context collected during garbage collection. In: Proceedings of the 2009 International Symposium on Memory Management, ISMM 2009, pp. 69–78. Association for Computing Machinery, New York (2009)
19. SPEC: Specjbb2005 (2006). https://www.spec.org/jbb2005/
20. SPEC: Specjbb2015 (2016). https://www.spec.org/jbb2015/
21. Yang, A.M., Österlund, E., Wrigstad, T.: Improving program locality in the gc using hotness. In: Proceedings of the 41st ACM SIGPLAN Conference on Programming Language Design and Implementation, PLDI 2020, pp. 301–313. Association for Computing Machinery, New York (2020)

Enhancing the PEPA Eclipse Plug-in

Alberto Casagrande[1], Carla Piazza[1], Riccardo Romanello[2(✉)], and Sabina Rossi[2]

[1] DMIF, University of Udine, Udine, Italy
{alberto.casagrande,carla.piazza}@uniud.it
[2] DAIS, University Ca' Foscari, Venice, Italy
{riccardo.romanello,sabina.rossi}@unive.it

Abstract. The Performance Evaluation Process Algebra (PEPA) is a formal language for the compositional modelling and analysis of concurrent systems, based on Markovian semantics. The PEPA Eclipse Plug-in provides an integrated environment for specifying, analyzing, and verifying PEPA models within Eclipse. In this work, we present several enhancements to the plug-in that extend its modelling and verification capabilities. First, we introduce new syntax and semantics to distinguish between high- and low-level actions and to evaluate behavioural equivalences such as low level and proportional lumpabilities. These extensions enable the automatic verification of security properties like Persistent Stochastic Non-Interference (PSNI). Then, recalling that a PEPA process is compiled into a Markov process, we integrate a static control mechanism for detecting Markov chain time reversibility. Finally, we add a set of syntactical rules for the direct specification of structurally causal reversible processes, facilitating the modelling of systems in which actions can be naturally undone. These enhancements significantly expand the expressiveness of the PEPA Eclipse Plug-in. The Plug-in is available at https://github.com/RiccardoRomanello/Valuetools_Pepa together with a set of examples showcasing the usefulness of the extensions.

Keywords: PEPA Eclipse Plug-in · PSNI · Reversibility · Lumpability

1 Introduction

PEPA (Performance Evaluation Process Algebra) [8] is an algebraic calculus enhanced with stochastic timing information which can be used both to calculate performance measures and to prove functional system properties. This formalism is particularly attractive in performance evaluation since it allows one to model complex systems compositionally and to study their internal behaviour. Among

The work described in this paper has been partially supported by PRIN project NiRvAna—Noninterference and Reversibility Analysis in Private Blockchains" (20202FCJMH, CUP G23C22000400005), by PNRR project SERICS—Security and Rights in the CyberSpace (CUP H73C22000890001), and by INdAM-GNCS project "MARQ: Modelli e Analisi per sistemi Reversibili e Quantistici".

A. Remke et al. (Eds.): Valuetools 2025, LNICST 691, pp. 215–227, 2027.
https://doi.org/10.1007/978-3-032-23901-3_13

the operators in its grammar, the cooperation operator $\bowtie_L$ plays a central role: two or more PEPA *processes* can be defined independently and then synchronized on a set of actions L. This makes the definition of large modular systems easier.

Underlying any PEPA process P there is a Continuous Time Markov Chain (CTMC), obtained via the notions of *derivation graph* and *apparent rate*. This bridge between PEPA and CTMCs enables the transfer of classical Markov-chain analysis techniques to the study of PEPA processes [8]. In particular, behavioural equivalences have been intensively studied: relations that allow us to determine whether two processes are *indistinguishable* with respect to some performance measure [6,10]. The connection between PEPA and CTMCs further allows the investigation of more advanced properties. An example is *Persistent Stochastic Non-Interference* (PSNI) [9], a security property which captures the absence of information leaks from *high*-level to *low*-level agents. In this sense, the partitioning of actions into high and low provides a formal way of distinguishing between observable and unobservable behaviour. Another classical property inherited from the Markovian world is *reversibility*, which can be interpreted in two different ways: *time reversibility*, i.e., invariance under temporal inversion, and *causal reversibility*, where each executed action can in principle be undone.

While PEPA provides an elegant and powerful framework, a major obstacle remains: because of cooperation, the induced CTMC often suffers from state-space explosion, making manual analysis infeasible. To overcome this issue, the PEPA Eclipse Plug-in was introduced in [18], providing automatic construction of CTMCs from PEPA models and relieving the user from cumbersome calculations. The open-source nature of this tool makes it suitable for extension with new modelling and analysis features.

In this paper, we present four new extensions of the PEPA Eclipse Plug-in:

- *Proportional Lumpability.* We integrate a polynomial-time algorithm [13] for computing proportional lumpability [10], enriching the existing set of equivalences and allowing model reduction by compressing the CTMC while preserving quantitative properties.
- *Persistent Stochastic Non-Interference (PSNI).* Following the three equivalent characterizations given in [9], we provide syntactic rules for defining high- and low-level actions and implement the verification of PSNI for PEPA models, with applications in areas such as smart contracts [7] and stochastically timed reversible systems [5].
- *Time Reversibility.* We adapt a DFS-based algorithm [15] to check whether the CTMC underlying a PEPA process is reversible. When the renaming function ρ is the identity, the algorithm detects standard time reversibility.
- *Causal Reversibility.* Inspired by [4], we extend the syntax to support *reversible actions*. By construction, any process reached through such an action can only be reached in that way, ensuring that reversible actions can always be undone without loss of behavioural information.

These enhancements significantly extend the expressiveness of the plug-in, enabling both performance and security analysis, while supporting advanced

Markovian properties such as lumpability and reversibility, in the spirit of the NiRvAna project–Noninterference and Reversibility Analysis in Private Blockchains [1]–where both reversibility and non-interference have been applied in the study of blockchains.

Structure of the Paper. The rest of the paper is organized as follows. Section 2 briefly recalls the PEPA calculus and the theoretical background behind the new extensions to the tool. Section 3 describes their integration into the PEPA Eclipse Plug-in. Finally, Sect. 4 concludes and outlines directions for future work.

2 PEPA Calculus

PEPA (Performance Evaluation Process Algebra) [8] is an algebraic calculus enhanced with stochastic timing information which may be used to calculate performance measures as well as prove functional system properties.

The basic elements of PEPA are *components* and *activities*. Each activity is a pair (α, r) where α is a label, or *action type*, and r is its *activity rate*, that is the parameter of a negative exponential distribution determining its duration. We assume that there is a countable set, $\mathcal{A}$, of possible action types, including a distinguished type, τ, which is the *unobservable* type. Activity rates may be any positive real number, or the distinguished symbol $\top$ which should be read as *unspecified*. The syntax for PEPA terms is defined by the grammar:

$$N ::= (\alpha, r).N \mid N + N \qquad P ::= N \mid P/A \mid P \underset{A}{\bowtie} P \tag{1}$$

where N denotes a *sequential component*, $A \subseteq \mathscr{A} \setminus \{\tau\}$ is a set of actions, and P denotes a *model component*. We write $\mathcal{C}$ for the set of all possible components.

In order to simplify component specification, a countable set of constants $\mathscr{X}$ may be defined and the syntax is extended as follows:

$$\begin{array}{ll} G ::= (\alpha, r).N \mid G + G & N ::= G \mid U \\ U ::= U + N \mid N + U \mid X & P ::= N \mid P/A \mid P \underset{A}{\bowtie} P \end{array} \tag{2}$$

where G and U represent *guarded* and *unguarded sequential components*, respectively, and X is a constant component in $\mathscr{X}$.

Every constant X must be defined by one and only one equation like $X \stackrel{def}{=} G$. Thus, in order to complete the syntax of a PEPA model component specification S, we need to add the following two rules to the syntax reported in Eq. 2:

$$Y ::= X \stackrel{def}{=} G; \qquad S ::= Y * \; P \tag{3}$$

where Y is a definition for the constant X and "$Y*$" is the Klenee's closure of Y.

The table defining the semantics of PEPA can be found in related articles (e.g., [8,9]). We now shortly present the main components of PEPA grammar.

A component $(\alpha, r).N$ performs activity (α, r) (type α, rate r), then behaves as N; shorthand $a.N$ when $a = (\alpha, r)$. Choice $M + Q$ enables all activities of M

and Q, with the first completed deciding the continuation, discarding the other. A constant X is defined by $X \stackrel{def}{=} G$. Hiding P/A replaces all activities in A by the unobservable type τ.

Cooperation $P \bowtie_{A} Q$ requires synchronization on action types in $A \subseteq \mathcal{A}!\backslash!\tau$: types not in A proceed independently, while types in A are shared and enabled only when both P and Q can perform them, with the shared rate given by the slower participant [8].

The *apparent rate* of action type α in process P, denoted $r_\alpha(P)$, is the sum of the rates of the α activities enabled in P. We refer the reader to [8] for a formal definition of the system's behaviour when operations involving $\top$ are concerned.

PEPA semantics is defined by labelled *multi-transition systems*, where arc multiplicities are significant. Each syntactic term (a *derivative*) is a state, with arcs representing activities that evolve one derivative into another [16].

We denote by $\mathcal{A}(P)$ the set of all the *current action types* of P, i.e., the set of action types which the component P may next engage in. We denote by $\mathcal{A}ct(P)$ the multiset of all the *current activities* of P. For any component P, the *exit rate* from P will be the sum of the activity rates of all the activities enabled in P, i.e., $q(P) = \sum_{a \in \mathcal{A}ct(P)} r_a$, with r_a being the rate of activity a. If P enables more than one activity, $|\mathcal{A}ct(P)| > 1$, then the dynamic behaviour of the model is determined by a race condition. As proved in [8] this associates to each finite PEPA model a CTMC.

The *transition rate* between two components P_i and P_j, is denoted with $q(P_i, P_j) = \sum_{a \in \mathcal{A}ct(P_i|P_j)} r_a$ where $P_i \neq P_j$ and $\mathcal{A}ct(P_i|P_j) = \{\!| a \in \mathcal{A}ct(P_i) | P_i \xrightarrow{a} P_j |\!\}$. The infinitesimal generator matrix of such CTMC is $q(P_i, P_j) = q_{ij}$ while $q_{ii} = -q(P_i)$, where $q(P_i) = \sum_{j \neq i} q(P_i, P_j)$. For any finite and irreducible PEPA model P, the steady-state distribution $\pi(\cdot)$ exists and it may be found by solving the normalization equation and the global balance equations.

The *conditional transition rate* from P_i to P_j via an action type α is denoted $q(P_i, P_j, \alpha)$. It is the rate at which a system behaving as component P_i evolves to behaving as component P_j as the result of completing a type α activity. The *total conditional transition rate* from P to $S \subseteq \mathscr{C}$ is defined as $q[P, S, \alpha] = \sum_{P' \in S} q(P, P', \alpha)$. Moreover, we define $q[P, a] = \sum_{P' \in \mathscr{C}} q(P, P', \alpha)$ as the sum of the total outgoing rates from state P to any component of the system.

For further explanations on PEPA and CTMCs we refer the reader to [8,12].

2.1 Observational Equivalence

Actions represent the observable behaviours of systems defined by process algebras. As a matter of the fact, two components are considered *equivalent under observation*, if they can apparently perform the same actions. *Lumpable bisimulation* [9] is an observational equivalence for PEPA components. Two PEPA components, P and Q, are *lumpably bisimilar* if there exists an equivalence relation such that, for any action type $\alpha \in \mathscr{A} \setminus \{\tau\}$, the total conditional transition rates from P and Q to any equivalence class through α are the same.

Definition 1 (Lumpable bisimulation). *An equivalence relation over PEPA components* $\mathcal{R} \subseteq \mathcal{C} \times \mathcal{C}$ *is a* lumpable bisimulation *if*

$$q[P, S, \alpha] = q[Q, S, \alpha]$$

for any $(P, Q) \in \mathcal{R}$, *for any* $\alpha \in \mathscr{A}$, *and for any class* S *in the equivalence partition* $\mathcal{C}/\mathcal{R}$ *such that either* $\alpha \neq \tau$ *or* $\alpha = \tau$ *and* $P, Q \notin S$

As for classical bisimulation, we are not interested in a generic lumpable bisimulation, but in the largest one. Two PEPA components P and Q are *lumpably bisimilar*, denoted as $P \approx_l Q$, if there exists a lumpable bisimulation $\mathcal{R}$ such that $(P, Q) \in \mathcal{R}$, where $\approx_l$ is the *lumpable bisimilarity*. The relation $\approx_l$ is a congruence for the evaluation contexts [9].

2.2 Proportional Lumpability

Lumpable bisimulation, as introduced above, is not the only observable equivalence introduced in the literature. Among the many, we focus on Proportional Lumpability, introduced in [10] and further investigated in [11]. As the name suggests, this lumpability introduces the notion of proportionality as condition aggregation. This ingredient extends the original definition of Strong—Ordinary—Lumpability in the way quasi-lumpability [6] does, but on the other hand, it also allows to exactly solve the original chain by working on the aggregated one.

Definition 2 (Proportional Lumpability). *Let* $\mathcal{X}(t)$ *be a CTMC with state space* $\mathcal{S}$ *and let* $\sim$ *be an equivalence relation over* $\mathcal{S}$. *We say that* $\mathcal{X}(t)$ *is* proportionally lumpable *with respect to* $\sim$*—in the same way,* $\sim$ *is a* proportional lumping *for* $\mathcal{X}(t)$*—if there exists a function* $\kappa : \mathcal{S} \to \mathbb{R}$ *such that* $\sim$ *induces a partition on the state space* $\mathcal{S}$ *such that for any equivalence classes* $S_i, S_j \in \mathcal{S}/\sim$, *with* $i \neq j$, *and for each pair* $s, s' \in S_i$, *the following holds:*

$$\frac{\sum_{\overline{s} \in S_j} q_{s,\overline{s}}}{\kappa(s)} = \frac{\sum_{\overline{s} \in S_j} q_{s',\overline{s}}}{\kappa(s')}$$

In [10] the authors describe how the proportionally lumped Markov Process $\tilde{\mathcal{X}}(t)$ is obtained from its original version $\mathcal{X}(t)$, $\sim$, and κ.

We now describe how the proportionally lumped Markov Process $\tilde{\mathcal{X}}(t)$ is obtained starting from its original version $\mathcal{X}(t)$, the equivalence $\sim$, and the function κ. In [11], authors also provided a relation between $\pi(s)$ and $\tilde{\pi}(s)$ the steady state distributions of $\mathcal{X}(t)$ and $\tilde{\mathcal{X}}(t)$, respectively. In particular:

$$\pi(s) = \frac{\tilde{\pi}(s)}{K\kappa(s)}, \text{ where } K = \sum_{s \in \mathcal{S}} \tilde{\pi}(s)/\kappa(s)$$

2.3 Security Through Persistent Stochastic Non-interference

Security community distinguishes low and high confidentiality levels. Low level data are public information that can be shared between any kind of agents or components, even the untrusted ones. Instead, high level pieces of information are sensitive data and should exclusively be transferred between reliable and trusted entities. Behind this, the distinction between low and high actions can also be used to model the effect of an unfriendly environment (high actions) on the evolution of an ethic agent (low actions), such as in the case of an untrusted OS requesting a undue money transfer to a payment application.

Persistent Stochastic Non-Interference (*PSNI*) is a security property [9] that excludes high level information leaks to low level PEPA components.

In order to formally define it, we need to partition $\mathscr{A} \setminus \{\tau\}$ into low ($\mathscr{L}$) and high ($\mathscr{H}$) action types, i.e., $\mathscr{L} \cup \mathscr{H} = \mathscr{A} \setminus \{\tau\}$ and $\mathscr{L} \cap \mathscr{H} = \emptyset$. A high level PEPA component H is a PEPA component such that each of its derivative has only high level actions. The set of all high level PEPA components is denoted by $\mathcal{C}_H$. The secured version of a PEPA component P as a copy of P that cannot perform any high level action. Hence, PSNI is as follows.

Definition 3 (PSNI). *The PEPA component P satisfies* PSNI, *denoted as $P \in$ PSNI, if $P' \setminus \mathscr{H} \approx_l (P' \underset{\mathscr{H}}{\bowtie} H)/\mathscr{H}$.*

PSNI can be characterised by means of a lumpable bisimulation that exclusively focus on high level actions: the *lumpable bisimilarity up to $\mathscr{H}$* [9].

Definition 4 (Lumpable bisimulation up to $\mathscr{H}$). *An equivalence relation over PEPA components $\mathcal{R} \subseteq \mathcal{C} \times \mathcal{C}$ is a* lumpable bisimulation up to $\mathscr{H}$ *if $q[P, S, \alpha] = q[Q, S, \alpha]$ for any $(P, Q) \in \mathcal{R}$, for any $\alpha \in \mathscr{A}$, and for any class S in the equivalence partition $\mathcal{C}/\mathcal{R}$ such that either $\alpha \notin \mathscr{H} \cup \{\tau\}$ or $\alpha \in \mathscr{H} \cup \{\tau\}$ and $P, Q \notin S$.*

Two PEPA components P and Q are *lumpably bisimilar*, denoted as $P \approx_l^{\mathscr{H}} Q$, if there exists a lumpable bisimulation up to $\mathscr{H}$, $\mathcal{R}$, such that $(P, Q) \in \mathcal{R}$, and $\approx_l^{\mathscr{H}}$ is the *lumpable bisimilarity up to $\mathscr{H}$*. It was proved that a component satisfies PSNI if and only if it is lumpably bisimilar up to $\mathscr{H}$ to its secured version.

2.4 Time Reversibility and ρ-Reversibility for Markov Processes

Previously we showed that the process $X(t)$ underlying any finite, complete PEPA model P is a CTMC with properties that guarantee the existence of a steady-state distribution π. Given an ergodic CTMC $X(t)$ with $t \in \mathbb{R}^+$, we define its *reversed process* as $X^R(t) := X(T - t)$. The reversed process $X^R(t)$ is itself a CTMC. The CTMC $X(t)$ is called *reversible* if it is stochastically equivalent to its reversed process $X^R(t)$. Reversibility can be characterized through the detailed balance equations, requiring that for all states i, j with $i \neq j$, $\pi_i q_{i,j} = \pi_j q_{j,i}$. Let ρ be a bijection over the state space. Given a CTMC $X(t)$, we define the renamed process $\rho(X)(t)$ as the process obtained from $X(t)$ by relabelling states according to ρ. We say that $X(t)$ is *ρ-reversible* if it is stochastically equivalent to $\rho(X^R)(t)$. The ρ-reversible analogue of the detailed balance equations follow by requiring equivalence between $X^R(t)$ and $\rho(X^R)(t)$. The notion of ρ-reversibility was introduced in [15]. Two main questions were investigated therein: (i) Given a process $X(t)$, does there exist a renaming ρ such that $X(t)$ is ρ-reversible? (ii) Given a fixed renaming ρ, can we efficiently decide whether $X(t)$ is ρ-reversible? For the second problem, the authors presented a polynomial time algorithm.

2.5 Causal Reversibility in Process Algebras

While in the previous section we investigated notions of time reversibility, we now move our focus towards causal reversibility [2,3]. Such notion boils down to the capability of undoing each step of a derivation—any *forward* operation can be correctly *undone* while following a backward path.

Recalling Equation (1), it is straightforward to see that there is no syntactic—and, therefore, semantic—rule that deals with the notion of reversibility in PEPA processes. In particular, whenever the rule $N ::= (\alpha, r).N$ is applied, no precaution or *history-preserving* action is taken in order to remember that the action α was executed. To achieve such endeavour, we took inspiration from what was done in [4] where authors enhanced the grammar for the symbol N by adding the following production, where a is said to be a *reversible action*:

$$N ::= (a^\dagger, r).N$$

3 PEPA Plug-in for Eclipse

Eclipse is an integrated development environment (IDE) [17]. It contains a base workspace and an extensible plug-in system for customising the environment. A PEPA plug-in for Eclipse was presented in [18] and it is available at https://www.dcs.ed.ac.uk/pepa/tools/plugin/. It is an environment to describe PEPA components and supports steady-state and performance analysis and simulations. The plug-in accepts "A <a_1,..., a_n> B", "X = G", and "tau" as specifications of "$A \underset{\{a_1,\ldots,a_n\}}{\bowtie} B$", "$X \overset{def}{=} G$", and "$\tau$", respectively.

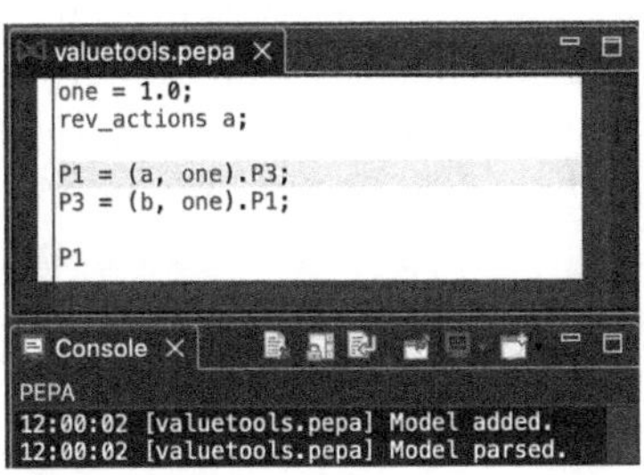

Fig. 1. The PEPA Plug-in for Eclipse.

3.1 Proportional Lumpability

In [13], authors proposed a polynomial algorithm to compute the proportionally lumped version of CTMCs. We implemented such procedure in the PEPA Eclipse Plug-in, to further enrich the set of lumpabilities available, which already contained contextual, exact, and strong ones.

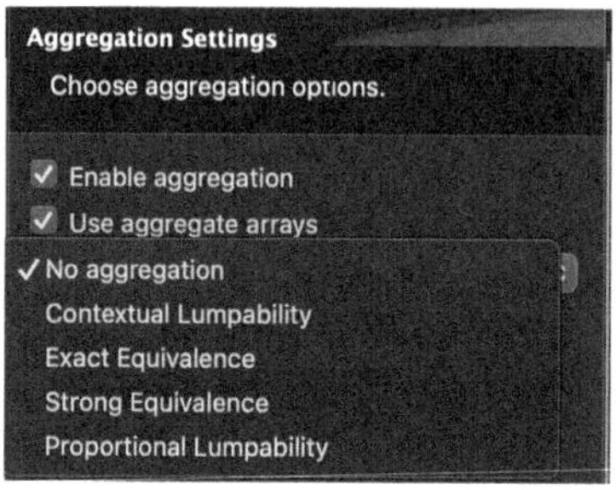

Fig. 2. The Plug-in aggregation menu.

Figure 2 is the menu shown to the user when selecting the aggregation method.

A process describing a blockchain mining activity is provided at https://github.com/RiccardoRomanello/Valuetools_Pepa/tree/main/Examples/ProportionalLumpability as an example that can be aggregated only through proportional lumpability.

The example considers a system composed of three fair miners, each of which can either *mine* or *verify* a block. When one miner successfully mines a block, the remaining two switch to the verification stage. The corresponding state-transition graph consists of four nodes: node 0 represents the state in which no block has been mined, while nodes 1, 2, and 3 represent the cases where miner i has mined a block and the other two are verifying it. The graph is *rooted* at node 0, with bidirectional connections between node 0 and each of nodes 1, 2, and 3.

As shown in [13], this process can be *proportionally lumped*, resulting in a reduced model with only two states. One state corresponds to node 0, and the other aggregates nodes 1, 2, and 3. Such a reduction cannot be achieved using strong, exact, or contextual equivalence. The same result is obtained using the PEPA Eclipse plug-in when aggregation through *Proportional Lumpability* is applied, thereby reducing the model to just two nodes.

3.2 Security Through Persistent Stochastic Non-interference

We extended the plug-in and implemented analysis of PEPA models via PSNI.

We have enriched PEPA syntax to label action types as high or low levels. The new syntax includes the rules in Eq.(2) and replaces those in Eq.(3) with:

$$\begin{array}{ll} Y ::= X \stackrel{def}{=} G; & D ::= \texttt{set\_default\_level}\ (\texttt{low} \mid \texttt{high}); \\ I ::= X \mid X\texttt{,}\ I & S ::= Y*\ (D\ L*)?\ P \\ L ::= (\texttt{low} \mid \texttt{high})\ I; & \end{array} \tag{4}$$

where "N?" is the optional closure of N, i.e., it requires one occurrence of N at most. By using the syntax introduced in Eq. (4), we can, for instance, label the actions of the PEPA model component depicted in Fig. 1 as follows in Listing 1.

```
1 set_default_level low;
2
3 high a, b;
4
5 %% rest of the code
```

Listing 1. Labeling action types by confidentiality level. This PEPA model component has 3 action types, i.e., `a`, `b`, and `c`. Line 3 labels `a` and `b` as high level, while `c` is not mentioned. The action type `c` is set to be low level because of line 1, which sets all action types different from τ to be low level.

We added a menu entry in the PEPA plug-in GUI to verify PSNI by using the lumpable bisimilarity up to $\mathscr{H}$ characterization (see Fig. 3).

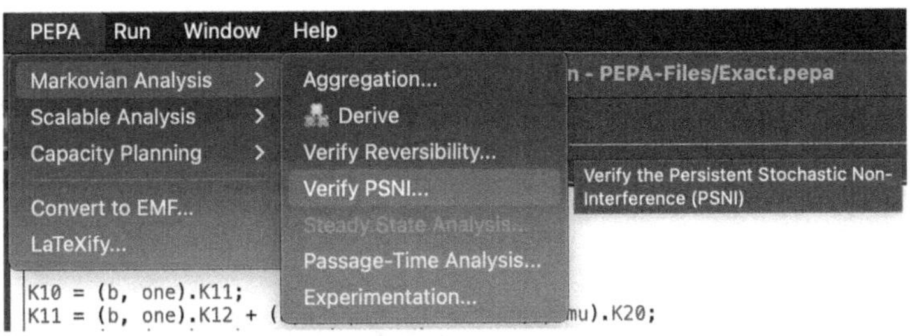

Fig. 3. Testing PSNI from the PEPA plug-in GUI.

In order to test the PSNI verification, we considered an example from [14]. In Ethereum, miners who discover a block earn 2 ETH plus transaction fees, while validators receive only the base fee. Fair miners alternate between mining (M_i) and validating (V_i), whereas an unfair miner avoids validation and stays in M_*. Starting with three fair miners, we study the case where one becomes unfair: if miner i finds a block (m_i), it returns to M_i; fair peers switch to V_i, while the unfair miner remains in M_*. After validation (v_i), validators resume mining.

The resulting *labelled transition system* (LTS), split in two blocks, is depicted in Fig. 4. One block models the 3-fair-miners systems; the other one describes a system with 2 fair and 1 unfair miners. A malicious environment tries to replace the fair miner with an unfair one by using the high action h.

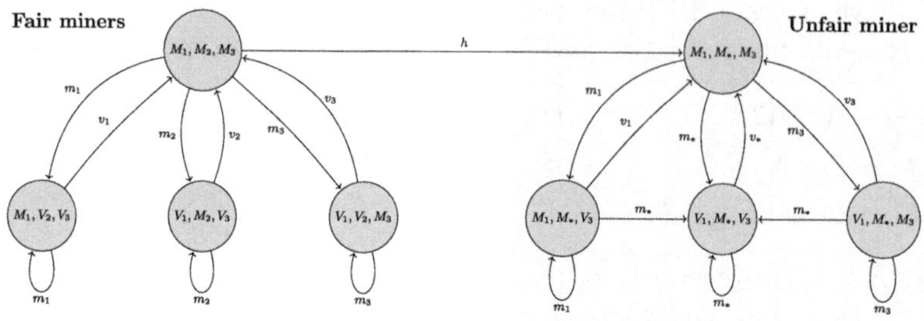

Fig. 4. Fair and unfair miners LTS.

The PEPA plugin instantaneously verifies that the model does not satisfy PSNI. In particular, it highlights that the states of the fair-miners block are not bisimilar to the corresponding states in its secured version.

The PEPA model of this example can be found at https://github.com/RiccardoRomanello/Valuetools_Pepa/tree/main/Examples/PSNI together with a Python script to generate models having k miners.

3.3 Time Reversibility and ρ-Reversibility for Markov Processes

Within the PEPA Eclipse Plug-in, every PEPA model is eventually translated into a labelled transition system (LTS). This structural transformation allows us to apply algorithms defined for CTMCs directly to the underlying semantics of PEPA models. On this basis, we implemented the algorithm presented in [15] in order to algorithmically verify whether the CTMC underlying a given PEPA process is time reversible. The procedure thus provides an automated method for checking time reversibility properties of PEPA models within the Eclipse Plug-in environment.

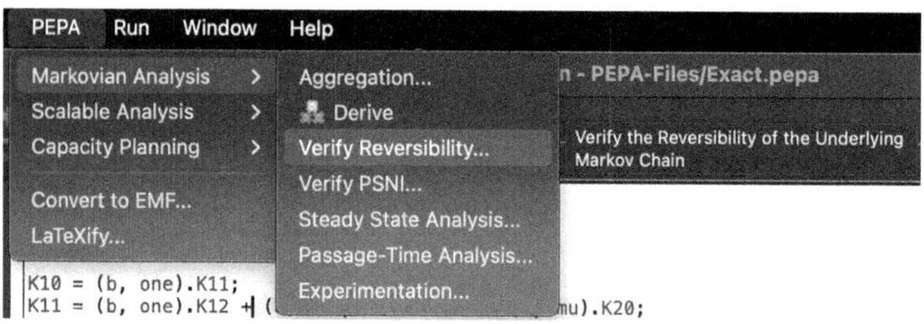

Fig. 5. Time Reversibility checking in PEPA Plug-in.

In Fig. 5 steps to trigger the time reversibility verification. The result of the control is shown through a pop-up window.

Some examples about reversibility can be found at https://github.com/RiccardoRomanello/Valuetools_Pepa/tree/main/Examples/TimeReversibility.

3.4 Causal Reversibility in Process Algebras

Inspired by the work done in [4], we implemented a mechanism to build causal reversible *by construction* processes in PEPA.

The action labels are split between reversible and non-reversible. Through the following syntax:

```
rev_actions $a, b, c$
```

the user marks the labels a, b, and c as reversible.

The effect of such definition is the following. If a process P_1 is reached from P via a reversible action, then P_1 cannot be reached by any other action—either reversible or not. The idea is that by imposing this constraint, we can always *undo* any reversible action since whenever we sit on P_1—generally speaking, a process reached via a reversible action—only a single action can be reverted.

The constraint on the number of incoming edges is verified at compile time.

Once the parsing phase has completed correctly, we tweak the LTS in order to reflect the *reversibility* we want to obtain. As before, assume P_2 is reached via one single reversible action a, with rate r, that originates from P_1. The LTS is modified with an edge (a, r) from P_2 to P_1. The *backward* edge is equivalent to $a^{\dagger}$ introduced in [4].

A graphical representation of the underlying workings is given in Fig. 6. If a process reached through a reversible action can also be reached by any other type of action (reversible or not), it is flagged at compile time as an incorrect process. This approach guarantees causal reversibility, since once a process is reached via a reversible action, the only action that can be undone is that one.

```
one = 1.0;

rev_actions a;

P1 = (a, one).P2;

P1
```

(a) A PEPA model.

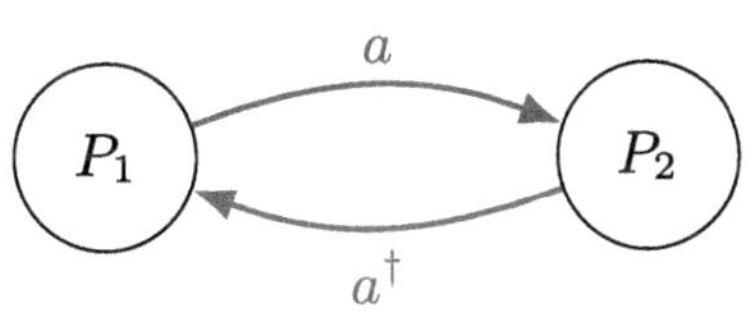

(b) The LTS with the backward (green) edge.

Fig. 6. Handling reversible actions in PEPA.

Comprehensive examples can be retrieved at https://github.com/RiccardoRomanello/Valuetools_Pepa/tree/main/Examples/CausalReversibility.

4 Conclusions

PEPA is a formalism that combines algebraic compositionality with stochastic timing, enabling both performance evaluation and verification of properties of concurrent systems. The PEPA Eclipse Plug-in provides a user-friendly integrated environment, where models can be specified, simulated, and analyzed.

In this work, we extended the plug-in with four significant add-ons that enrich both its syntax and its analytical capabilities. First, a polynomial time proportional lumpability aggregation algorithm allows for model reduction while preserving exact analysis. Second, the support for PSNI introduces security verification against information leakage. Third, a DFS-based time reversibility checker enables automated verification of whether the underlying CTMC satisfies detailed balance properties. Finally, causal reversibility enhances the syntax to support reversible actions. Together, these extensions broaden the expressive power of the plug-in, supporting performance and security analyses which have been crucial in the project NiRvAna [1].

As future work, we plan to both incorporate additional aggregation techniques on top of proportional lumpability and to extend security guarantees beyond PSNI.

References

1. NiRvAna project website (2025). http://www.sti.uniurb.it/nirvana/. Accessed 10 September 2025
2. Bernardo, M., Lanese, I., Marin, A., Mezzina, C.A., Rossi, S., Sacerdoti Coen, C.: Causal reversibility implies time reversibility. In: Jansen, N., Tribastone, M. (eds.) QEST 2023. LNCS, vol. 14287. Springer, Cham (2023). https://doi.org/10.1007/978-3-031-43835-6_19
3. Bernardo, M., Mezzina, C.A.: Bridging causal reversibility and time reversibility: a stochastic process algebraic approach. Logical Methods Comput. Sci. (2023)
4. Bernardo, M., Rossi, S., et al.: Reverse bisimilarity vs. forward bisimilarity. In: FoSSaCS, pp. 265–284 (2023)
5. Esposito, A., Aldini, A., Bernardo, M.: Noninterference analysis of stochastically timed reversible systems. In: Formal Techniques for Distributed Objects, Components, and Systems (2025)
6. Franceschinis, G., Muntz, R.R.: Bounds for quasi-Lumpable Markov chains. Perform. Eval. **20**(1), 223–243 (1994)
7. Guesmi, S., Piazza, C., Rossi, S., et al.: Noninterference analysis for smart contracts: would you bet on it. In: Distributed Ledger Technology Workshop (2024)
8. Hillston, J.: A Compositional Approach to Performance Modelling, vol. 348. Cambridge University Press Cambridge (1996). https://doi.org/10.1017/CBO9780511569951
9. Hillston, J., Marin, A., Piazza, C., Rossi, S.: Persistent stochastic non-interference. Fundam. Inform. **181** (2021). https://doi.org/10.3233/FI-2021-2049
10. Marin, A., Piazza, C., Rossi, S.: Proportional lumpability. In: André, É., Stoelinga, M. (eds.) FORMATS 2019. LNCS, vol. 11750, pp. 265–281. Springer, Cham (2019). https://doi.org/10.1007/978-3-030-29662-9_16
11. Marin, A., Piazza, C., Rossi, S.: Proportional lumpability and proportional bisimilarity. Acta Inform. **59** (2021). https://doi.org/10.1007/s00236-021-00404-y
12. Marin, A., Rossi, S.: On the relations between lumpability and reversibility. In: 2014 IEEE 22nd International Symposium on Modelling, Analysis and Simulation of Computer and Telecommunication Systems, pp. 427–432 (2014). https://doi.org/10.1109/MASCOTS.2014.59

13. Piazza, C., Rossi, S., Smuseva, D.: Efficient algorithm for proportional lumpability and its application to selfish mining in public blockchains. Algorithms **17**(4) (2024). https://doi.org/10.3390/a17040159
14. Smuseva, D., Malakhov, I., Marin, A., van Moorsel, A., Rossi, S.: Verifier's dilemma in ethereum blockchain: a quantitative analysis. In: Ábrahám, E., Paolieri, M. (eds.) QEST 2022. LNCS, vol. 13479, pp. 317–336. Springer, Cham (2022). https://doi.org/10.1007/978-3-031-16336-4_16
15. Sottana, M., Piazza, C., Albarelli, A.: Efficient computation of renaming functions for ρ-reversible discrete and continuous time Markov chains, pp. 52–59 (2017). https://doi.org/10.1145/3150928.3150942
16. Taubner, D.A.: Finite Representations of CCS and TCSP Programs by Automata and Petri Nets. LNCS, vol. 369. Springer, Cham (1989)
17. The Eclipse Foundation: Eclipse IDE for Java Developers (2025). https://www.eclipse.org. Version 2025-06 R. Accessed 13 Aug 2025
18. Tribastone, M., Duguid, A., Gilmore, S.: The PEPA eclipse plugin. Perform. Eval. Rev. **36**(4), 28–33 (2009). https://doi.org/10.1145/1530873.1530880

DrawNET 4: A Suite to Create Graph-Based Modeling Tools

Marco Gribaudo(✉)

Politecnico di Milano, Milan, Italy
marco.gribaudo@polimi.it
https://gribaudo.faculty.polimi.it/

Abstract. DrawNET is a suite for creating the graphical user interface for tools that can be used to define graph-based performance models. In particular, it allows the user to define a modeling formalism composed of a set of arcs and nodes. Nodes and arcs have their own visual characteristics and have a set of properties that can be defined and changed by the user. DrawNET allows to define models in the selected formalism, to set their parameters, to configure their primitives, and to send the specification to a solution tool that produces results from the given description.

Keywords: Performance Modeling Tools · Graphical User Interface · Graph-based Formalisms

1 Introduction

One of the main problems that researchers in Performance Evaluation have to face is the diffusion of their results to final users, which generally are researchers in specific applicative fields aiming at devising clever solution characterized by a high level of efficiency and reliability. Tools can usually bridge this gap, by offering a guided interface to the theoretical results: in this context, graphical users interfaces (GUIs) can further enhance the experience by adding visual elements to the description of the target systems. However, developing GUIs is an extremely demanding task, thus limiting their use to few generic and not easily customizable tools. The main goal of DrawNET is simplifying this aspect.

DrawNET started in 2002 [7], and had three main editions, with DrawNET III dated around 2006 [14]. The early versions were written in JAVA, and used XML to describe both formalisms and models. DrawNET IV was slowly developed in background, and now it has reached the maturity for it release. Unlike its predecessors, it is written in JavaScript, and it is enclosed inside an HTML5 web page, exploiting canvases to handle the visual interaction. It also uses JSON files to describe both formalisms and models. These enhancements caused a complete re-definition of the meta-modeling architecture of the tool, making it no longer compatible with the previous versions. This is not considered to be a problem, since version IV targets a slightly different audience: users seeking to create a

A. Remke et al. (Eds.): Valuetools 2025, LNICST 691, pp. 228–238, 2027.
https://doi.org/10.1007/978-3-032-23901-3_14

Java application can still use version III of the tool, while version VI is suited for web-based applications that leverage popular data analysis and modeling frameworks created for the Web and Python ecosystems. The tool is open-source, and the latest version can be downloaded from http://www.draw-net.com. The page also contains a minimal documentation on writing a new formalisms and a live version of the tool which, thanks to its JavaScript engine, can be run inside any modern web browser to try its main features. A screenshot of the tool is shown in Fig. 1.

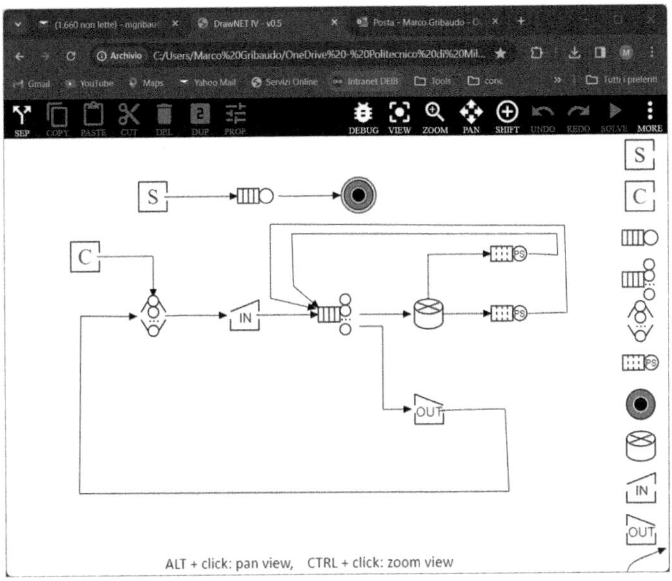

Fig. 1. A screenshot of the main user interface of the DrawNET IV tool.

2 Background

DrawNET IV, can be though as a *Platform-as-a-Service* cloud environment, in the sense that it mainly targets Performance Evaluation experts, who create tools that implement their research, but do not have time to develop a full-fledge GUI. Final users will exploit DrawNET to create, solve, and study the models of the systems they are interested in.

Although DrawNET does not focus on the computation of performance indices, it has been developed as an important component of the SYMthesis modeling framework (see [11,12] and [1]). The connection of DrawNET with multiformalism models [10] has been considered since its earliest version (see [8]). When the project started, DrawNET was related to other configurable multiformalism solution tools, such as Mobius [6,15], Abstract Petri Net Notation [3], SMART [5], Sharpe [16], Atom3 [13] and TimeNet [9]. A tool that has always been considered as a comparison, which has recently included the support for multiformalism models [2] is JMT - the Java Modeling Tool [4], since it has been partially developed in parallel with DrawNET IV.

3 Tool Presentation

DrawNET IV has been developed with several goals in mind. First, it is meant to function with a single button mouse, or with a touch screen (to support mobile devices), without the requirement of pressing meta-keys (i.e. Shift or Ctrl) with the pointer. However, it has been developed to exploit both secondary mouse key and meta-keys when available. The number of menu options has been reduced to the essential, and grouped into different bars, so that more frequently used commands are immediately available, while more complex functions require two or three levels of navigation. Arcs have been implemented using fully configurable spline curves; there is also the possibility of breaking an arc into several parts.

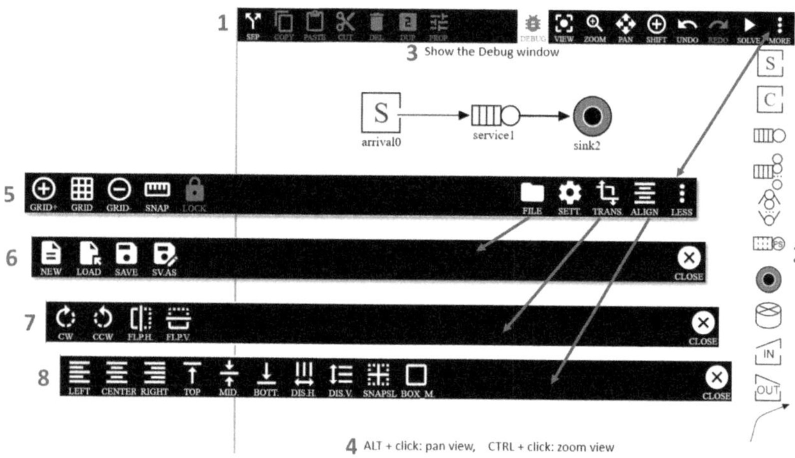

Fig. 2. The canvas structure and menu organization of the DrawNET IV tool.

Figure 2 shows the main menu bar (1 in the figure) of the tool, which contains the main editing functions, and the possibility of calling a solver to evaluate the model. Elements that can be used to draw a model are shown in the vertical panel at the right border of the canvas (2). The content of this panel changes according to the selected modeling formalism. The current action performed by pressing the mouse button, or the description of the primitive that can be selected, is shown in the message area just below the menu (3). Another help area that describes the effect of the meta-keys is shown at the bottom of the screen (4). The *Secondary Options* menu (5) allows to show and snap to a grid, as well to access extra functionalities, such as: the *File* menu (6), the *Quick Transform* menu (7- containing the command to mirror and rotate a node), and the *Alignments Panel* which contains functions to properly place and distribute the graph nodes.

Figure 3 shows the selection of a modeling formalism. When the *New* button is pressed, the list of the available formalisms is shown: for each formalism, several different start-up templates can be selected. Figure 3 shows how the right panel changes, depending on the chosen formalism.

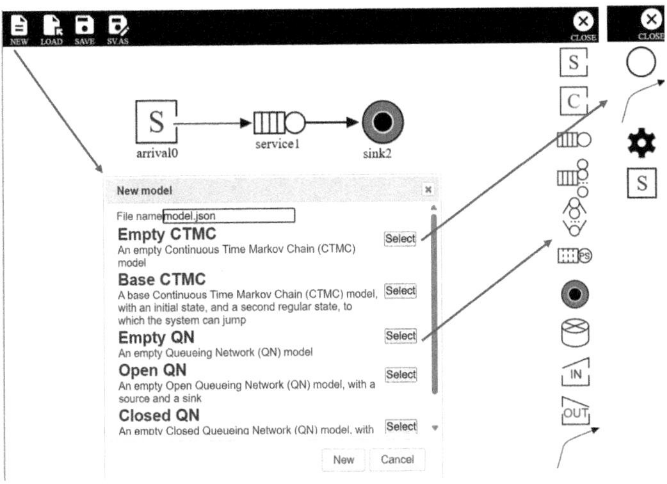

Fig. 3. The creation of a New Model.

4 Formalism Definition

The models that can be defined with DrawNET IV are *graphs*, where their basic primitives correspond to different types of nodes and arcs. All edges are *directed* and the user can specify the type of graphical representation used. Undirected graphs can then be drawn by excluding the arrow heads from the. The visual representation of the nodes can be defined depending on their type, as described in Sect. 4.1. Figure 4 shows the different elements of the GUI that are used when adding a primitive to a model. Beside their position and appearance, elements are characterized by properties and performance indices, which will be detailed in Sects. 4.2 and 4.3.

4.1 Graphical Description of the Formalism Elements

The appearance of a node can be defined by composing a set of basic shapes and configuring them through a set of properties. Moreover, the tool allows

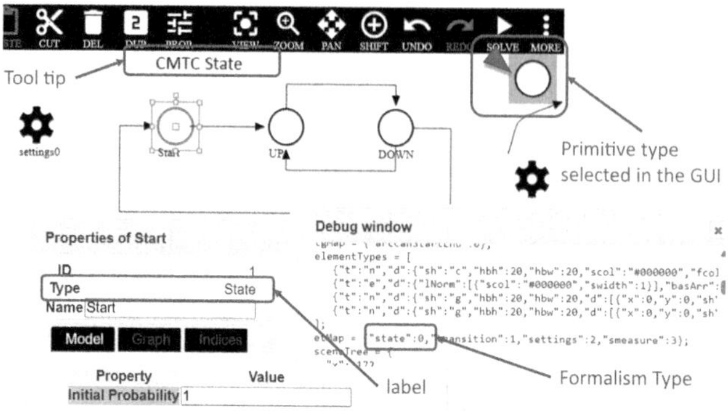

Fig. 4. How the *Formalism Type* of a modeling primitive is used in the GUI of the tool

for importing custom images and inserting text to give the user a rich set of primitives for defining the visual appearance of the modeling elements for the formalism being defined. Edges are composed by redrawing the same line several times (called *strokes*), each time with different graphical settings. Different types of arrow heads can then be added at the beginning and at the end of a line.

4.2 The DrawNET Type System

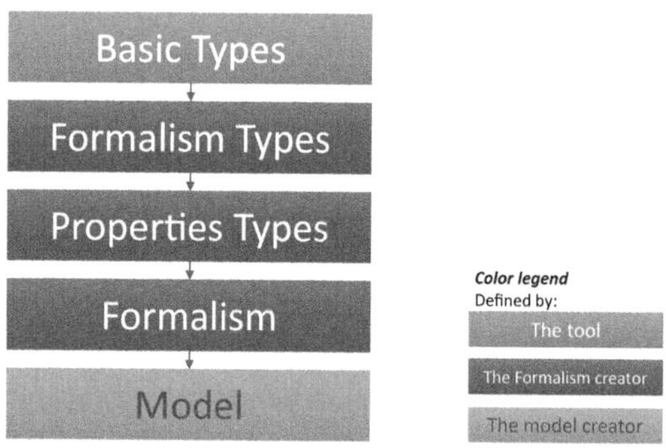

Fig. 5. The DrawNET IV Type System

Models are essentially a collection of entities with similar parameters, as defined by the formalism. A *type system* defines which entities can be used, what parameters can be assigned, and which constraints should be fulfilled. The type system is based on five levels, as shown in Fig. 5. The motivations for this organization are the following: i) the tool must be capable of copying and pasting values of the same type, regardless of what they represent. For example, we should be able to copy an inter-arrival time distribution of the source in a Queuing Network, into the service time of a queue, as shown in Fig. 6, since they are both probability distributions of a duration, even if they represent very different events. Every formalism, however, has its own values like probabilities, weights, labels, distributions, priorities, and so on, which need to be specified. The domain of these values can be defined starting from some basic type, by combining or restricting them. ii) Frequently a formalism allows the user to define different types of primitives, which have similar features and semantic, which can be potentially interchanged. For example, a queue in a Queuing Network can be replaced with a delay station, as shown in Fig. 7: in this case, the tool should be able to keep the data that have both the same type, and the same semantic (i.e. the service time distribution, and the routing policy specification).

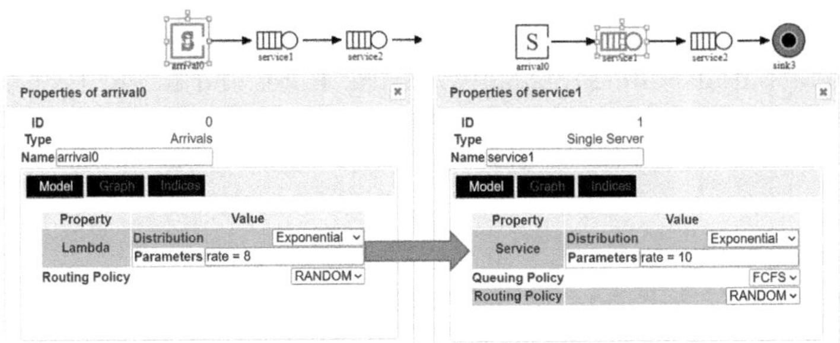

Fig. 6. Exchanging values between identical property types, in different context, such as copying an inter-arrival time distribution into a service time distribution

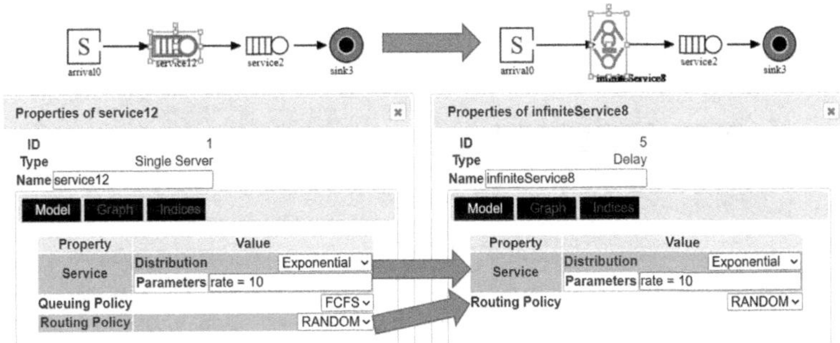

Fig. 7. Exchanging a modelling primitive with a compatible one, while maintaining the equivalent values

The first level of the *DrawNET IV Type System* (DN4TS) contains a few *Basic Types*. Currently, they include integers, floating point values, strings, booleans, structures (similar to C `struct`), enumerations and arrays. They are the foundation for creating more advanced types.

The second level of the DN4TS defines the *Formalism Types*, which combine and restrict the Basic Types to define the values used by the modeling primitives. Examples of Formalism Types include: Temporal Duration Distributions, Event Rates, Element Probabilities, enumeration of constants used, for example, to define the available Routing or Queuing Policies. The idea that supports this level is that the primitives of a model can have different attributes characterized by the same type of values, even if with totally different meanings. For example, as already briefly introduced, the service time distribution of a queuing station is something completely different, from a modeling point of view, with respect to the inter-arrival time distribution of a node representing arrivals to the system. However, both values are of the same kind: they are both descriptions of a probability distribution.

The third level of the DN4TS defines the *Property Types*, which are the attributes that can be associated to modeling primitives. Some examples are the following: Service Time Distribution, Inter-arrival Time Distribution, Routing probability, Initial State Probability, Arrival Rate, and so on. Property types also have associated labels that can be used in the GUI: for instance, Fig. 8 shows how they are used to help the user.

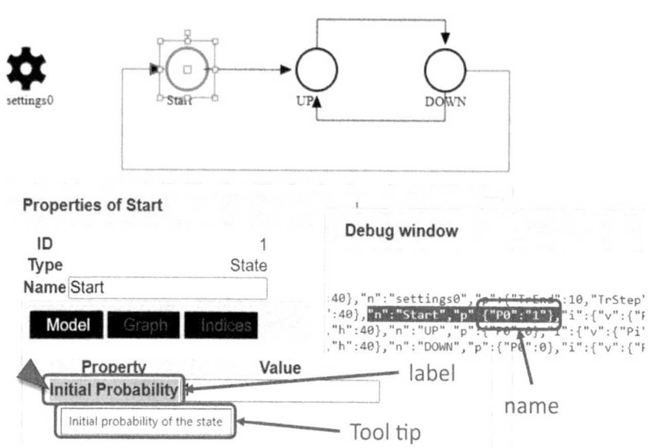

Fig. 8. How attributes are used in the GUI of the tool

The fourth level of the DN4TS is the *Formalism*. It defines the modeling primitives that can be used, as described in Sect. 4. For example, formalism elements can be: Queues, Arrivals, Departures, Routers, connections in Queueing Networks; Places, Transitions, Normal and Inhibiting arcs in Petri Nets; States and Transition arcs in CTMCs.

Finally, the Model is the last level of the DN4TS, and defines the input to the solution tool. For example, it can be a model to evaluate the performances of a scheduling algorithm of a Data Center, or an e-commerce system. It will be described in detail in Sect. 5.

4.3 Performance Indices

Performance indices are special properties associated to the elements of a model. The main difference from the property types is that they are meant to be computed by a *solver*, and not be filled directly by the user. Moreover, since the solution complexity of a model may depend on the number of performance indices that need to be computed, the user must be able to select which one should be considered and which one can be ignored in a specific scenario. Finally, the value computed during an execution should be saved together with the model, so that the user can easily retrieve the values computed in a previous session.

Performance indices are defined by *Property Types* (level three of the DN4TS), exactly as regular properties. In this way, for example, the user can copy a value computed in a Performance Index inside a regular property.

5 Model Definition

Models, which are the top-most level of the DN4TS, are defined as a set of instances of formalism elements. Model elements have a *Name*, that uniquely identifies them, and a *Type*, which associates it to the corresponding type in the considered formalism: for example, whether this entity represents a Place, a Transition, a connection Arc, or an Inhibitor Arc in a Petri Net.

Each element of a model assigns a value to each of its properties according to its type, as specified in the Formalism level of the DN4TS. The performance indices are defined in a similar way: in this case the user can select to compute or skip them, and their value is calculated by the solver.

5.1 Solution

The GUI, which is written in JavaScript, can be easily connected to external solution components in many ways. Together with the tool, there is a simple implementation that behaves as a web application, as shown in Fig. 9. The GUI sends a JSON encoding of the model to the web server, which then invokes the solver. The latter returns a set of commands that are used by the GUI to fill the values of the performance indices attributes of the elements in the model. In particular, the simple implementation uses the `flask` Python-based web server to enclose both the GUI and the solvers. Using a JSON encoding, the solution component can easily filter the model: for example, Fig. 10 shows how to extract the list of states and transitions defined in a CTMC model that allows the user to specify states and transitions.

The model solution is executed by pressing the *Solve* button. When a response is received, the results are first shown in a report contained in a window. Performance indices are also assigned to each primitive, where they can be accessed, as shown in Fig. 11.

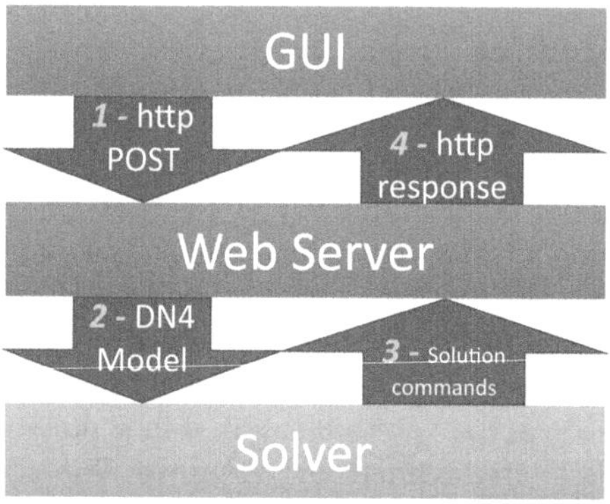

Fig. 9. The interface with the solution components.

```
def solve(model, etMap):
    states      = list(filter(lambda x: x['t'] == etMap['state'], model))
    Nst         = len(states)
    transitions = list(filter(lambda x: x['t'] == etMap['transition'], model))
```

Fig. 10. An example of a Python script to query the *States* and the *Transitions* in a CTMC model.

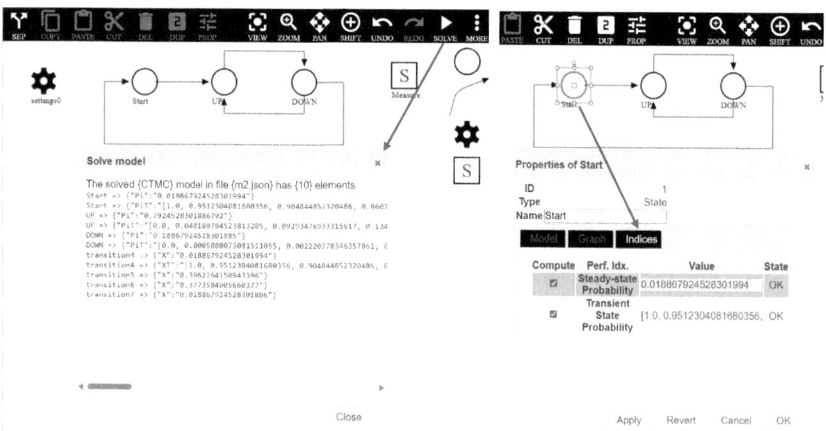

Fig. 11. Showing the solution results in the GUI.

6 Conclusions

DrawNET 4, is currently at a stage in which it is ready to be included in a project to speed-up the creation of GUI for a specific tool supporting a specific modeling language. For example, the creation of GUI to define separable queueing networks based on DrawNET IV took less than a day. Being tailored for Graph-based formalisms, it can be used for many classical modeling paradigms and extensions, as well as for Domain Specific Languages.

Future extensions will include new types, such as a "Union" type that will combine the enumeration with the group property features, to allow the user to specify different parameters depending on the value chosen in the enumeration, and a "Pointer" type, to allow the user to select one element of the model as a value for the corresponding property. A better support for the visualization of results and the introduction of tools to annotate a model will also be developed.

References

1. Barbierato, E., Gribaudo, M., Iacono, M.: Defining formalisms for performance evaluation with SIMTHESys. Electr. Notes Theor. Comput. Sci. **275**, 37–51 (2011)
2. Barbierato, E., Gribaudo, M., Serazzi, G.: Multi-formalism models for performance engineering. Future Internet **12**(3) (2020). https://doi.org/10.3390/fi12030050
3. Bause, F., Buchholz, P., Kemper, P.: A toolbox for functional and quantitative analysis of DEDS. In: Puigjaner, R., Savino, N.N., Serra, B. (eds.) TOOLS 1998. LNCS, vol. 1469, pp. 356–359. Springer, Heidelberg (1998). https://doi.org/10.1007/3-540-68061-6_32
4. Bertoli, M., Casale, G., Serazzi, G.: JMT: performance engineering tools for system modeling. SIGMETRICS Perform. Eval. Rev. **36**(4), 10–15 (2009). https://doi.org/10.1145/1530873.1530877
5. Ciardo, G., Miner, A.S.: SMART: the stochastic model checking analyzer for reliability and timing. In: International Conference on Quantitative Evaluation of Systems, pp. 338–339 (2004)
6. Deavours, D.D., et al.: The Möbius framework and its implementation (2002)
7. Franceschinis, G., Gribaudo, M., Iacono, M., Vittorini, V., Bertoncello, C.: DrawNet++: a flexible framework for building dependability models, p. 540 (2002). https://doi.org/10.1109/DSN.2002.1028961
8. Franceschinis, G., Gribaudo, M., Iacono, M., Mazzocca, N., Vittorini, V.: DrawNET++: model objects to support performance analysis and simulation of systems. In: Field, T., Harrison, P.G., Bradley, J., Harder, U. (eds.) TOOLS 2002. LNCS, vol. 2324, pp. 233–238. Springer, Heidelberg (2002). https://doi.org/10.1007/3-540-46029-2_18
9. German, R., Kelling, C., Zimmermann, A., Hommel, G.: TimeNet: a toolkit for evaluating non-Markovian stochastic petri nets. Perform. Eval. **24**(1-2), 69 – 87 (1995). https://doi.org/10.1016/0166-5316(95)00010-U
10. Gribaudo, M., Iacono, M.: Theory and application of multi-formalism modeling (2013). https://doi.org/10.4018/978-1-4666-4659-9
11. Iacono, M., Barbierato, E., Gribaudo, M.: The SIMTHESys multiformalism modeling framework. Comput. Math. Appl. **64**, 3828–3839 (2012). https://doi.org/10.1016/j.camwa.2012.03.009

12. Iacono, M., Gribaudo, M.: Element based semantics in multi formalism performance models, pp. 413–416 (2010). https://doi.org/10.1109/MASCOTS.2010.54
13. Lara, J., Vangheluwe, H.: AToM^3: a tool for multi-formalism and meta-modelling. In: Kutsche, R.-D., Weber, H. (eds.) FASE 2002. LNCS, vol. 2306, pp. 174–188. Springer, Heidelberg (2002). https://doi.org/10.1007/3-540-45923-5_12
14. Marco, G., Francesco, M., Mazzocca, N., Vittorini, V.: Multisolution of complex performability models in the OsMoSys/DrawNET framework, vol. 2005, pp. 85–94 (2005). https://doi.org/10.1109/QEST.2005.22
15. Sanders, W.: Integrated frameworks for multi-level and multi-formalism modeling. In: Proceedings of the 8th International Workshop on Petri Nets and Performance Models, pp. 2–9 (1999). https://doi.org/10.1109/PNPM.1999.796527
16. Trivedi, K.S.: Sharpe 2002: Symbolic hierarchical automated reliability and performance evaluator. In: DSN 2002: Proceedings of the 2002 International Conference on Dependable Systems and Networks, p. 544. IEEE Computer Society, Washington, DC (2002)

Networks and Routing

Impact of Packetization on Network Calculus Analysis

Yuming Jiang(✉)

Norwegian University of Science and Technology, Trondheim, Norway
yuming.jiang@ntnu.no

Abstract. For packet-switched networks, when the packetization effect is overlooked, network calculus analysis can produce faulty results. To exemplify, network calculus analysis is applied in this paper to two basic systems that are fundamental or default settings in Time-Sensitive Networking (TSN) and Deterministic Networking (DetNet). Through counterexamples, it is revealed that for the two fundamental settings, some widely adopted, network calculus-based service characterization results, known as service curves, which ignore packetization, are faulty. In addition, for performance bounds derived from the faulty service curves, it is shown that the validity of the bounds can be arguable. In particular, the output bound, backlog bound and concatenation service curve results are shown to be also faulty: counterexamples can be constructed. By factoring the packetization effect directly into the service models, corrected service curves and performance bounds are derived for the two basic systems. These results remind that special care is needed when applying network calculus analysis to packet-switched networks.

Keywords: Network Calculus · Service curve · Output bound · Backlog bound · Delay bound · Packetization · Time-Sensitive Networking (TSN) · Deterministic Networking (DetNet)

1 Introduction

Network calculus (NC) is a theory for performance guarantee analysis of communication networks [1–4]. A key idea of network calculus is to model traffic and service processes using some bounding functions and base the analysis on them. Among the various network calculus models, service curve models play a central role, based on which various performance bounds can be derived [1–4]. Since its introduction in the early 1990s [5,6], the network calculus has been extended and applied to various types of communication networks that are packet-switched. In particular, for IEEE 802.1 Time-Sensitive Networking (TSN) networks [7] and for IETF Deterministic Networking (DetNet) networks [8], the theory has been extensively utilized to construct service models and compute performance bounds. Representative results include [9–12]. A comprehensive review can be found in [13], and more recent results include [14,15]. All these results are based

A. Remke et al. (Eds.): Valuetools 2025, LNICST 691, pp. 241–254, 2027.
https://doi.org/10.1007/978-3-032-23901-3_15

on the service curve models of the transmission selection schemes studied, among which the constant bit rate link and strict priority scheduling are the most fundamental or default settings [7,8].

However, the investigation in this paper reveals that the widely adopted service curve characterization results, e.g. [9–12,14], and [15], for the two fundamental settings are faulty. In particular, counterexamples can be constructed, which disapproves the results of the adopted service curves. A closer look shows that the packetization effect is overlooked in them. The investigation is extended to examine the validity of the performance bounds derived from the faulty service curves. Counterexamples can also be constructed for output and backlog bounds as well as for the characterisation of the service curve of a concatenation system. This indicates that there is a need to update the service curve models and consequently also the performance bounds. To meet this need, corrected service curves and performance bounds for the two fundamental settings are derived, based on the idea of factoring the packetization effect directly into the service model. These results remind the necessity of taking the packetization effect into account when applying network calculus analysis.

The rest is organized as follows. In the next section, the system model and network calculus basics are introduced. In Sect. 3, it is shown with counterexamples that the widely adopted service curves for the two fundamental settings are faulty due to ignoring the packetization effect. Then, a study on the impact of using such faulty service curves on performance bounds is conducted. At the end of Sect. 3, discussion on related results from the network calculus theory is provided, which reveals that adjustments suggested by the theory for packetization have been overlooked by the faulty service curve results. In Sect. 4, corrected service curves and performance bounds are proved. Finally, conclusions are drawn in Sect. 5.

2 System Model and Network Calculus Basics

2.1 System Model

We consider systems in a packet-switched network. In particular, we focus on data traffic transmission over a constant bit rate link and through a priority queue that competes transmission over such a link with other priority queues. By convention, in such a system, *a packet is said to have arrived (respectively, been served) when and only when its last bit has arrived (respectively, departed)* [7]. When a packet arrives, the packet may be queued and the buffer size for the queue is assumed to be large enough, ensuring no packet loss. The queue is FIFO and initially empty.

The system is modeled by an input traffic process $A(t)$, a service process S, and an output traffic process $A^*(t)$ as illustrated in Fig. 1. Specifically, $A(t)$ denotes the cumulative amount of traffic from the input flow entering the system and $A^*(t)$ the cumulative amount of traffic from the flow leaving the system, up to time t (excluded). By convention, we adopt $A(0) = A^*(0) = 0$. In addition, we define $A(s,t) \equiv A(t) - A(s)$ and $A^*(s,t) \equiv A^*(t) - A^*(s)$, which respectively denote the amount of input traffic and the amount of output traffic in period $[s, t)$. Since traffic at t is excluded, $A(t, t) = 0$ by convention and so is $A^*(t, t) = 0$.

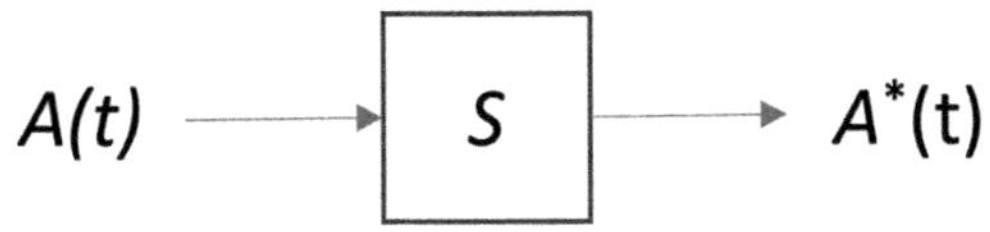

Fig. 1. System model

In addition, we can also model the input and output processes of the flow using marked-point processes, where packetization of traffic is explicitly taken into account [1]. Specifically, for the input, the marked point process $(\overrightarrow{a}, \overrightarrow{l})$ consists of two sequences of variables $\overrightarrow{a} = \{a(n), n = 0, 1, 2, ...\}$ and $\overrightarrow{l} = \{l(n), n = 0, 1, 2, ...\}$, where $a(n)$ denotes the arrival time of packet n and $l(n)$ its length. For the output, a similar marked point process is defined which is $(\overrightarrow{d}, \overrightarrow{l})$ with $\overrightarrow{d} = \{d(n), n = 0, 1, 2, ...\}$, where $d(n)$ denotes the departure time of the n-th packet from the system. Here, the packet 0 is a virtual packet, and by convention $a(0) = 0$, $l(0) = 0$ and $d(0) = 0$.

The backlog at time t, denoted as $B(t)$, is:

$$B(t) = A(t) - A^*(t). \tag{1}$$

The delay of packet $n(\geq 1)$, denoted by $D(n)$, is:

$$D(n) = d(n) - a(n). \tag{2}$$

In network calculus, a related delay concept, called virtual delay, has been adopted. Specifically, the virtual delay at time $t(> 0)$, denoted as $D(t)$, is defined as [1–4]:

$$D(t) = \inf\{\tau \geq 0 : A(t) \leq A^*(t + \tau)\}. \tag{3}$$

2.2 Network Calculus Basics

Let $\mathcal{F}$ denote the set of nonnegative nondecreasing functions, and $\mathcal{F}_0$ its subset with $f(0) = 0$. By their definitions, $A(\cdot)$ and $A^*(\cdot)$ are both in $\mathcal{F}_0$.

Definition 1. *A flow A is said to have an arrival curve $\alpha \in \mathcal{F}$, if for all $0 \leq s \leq t$, the traffic $A(s, t)$ is upper-constrained by [2]:*

$$A(s, t) \leq \alpha(t - s). \tag{4}$$

Definition 2. *A system is said to provide a service curve $\beta \in \mathcal{F}_0$, if for any time $t \geq 0$, there exists some time $s \in [0, t]$ such that $A^*(t) \geq A(s) + \beta(t - s)$ or equivalently, there holds for all $t \geq 0$ [2],*

$$A^*(t) \geq A \otimes \beta(t) \equiv \inf_{0 \leq s \leq t} \{A(s) + \beta(t - s)\}.$$

Theorem 1. *If the input flow has an arrival curve α and the system provides to the input flow a service curve β, there hold [2]:*

(i) the output has an arrival curve $\alpha^*(t) \equiv \sup_{u\geq 0}\{\alpha(u+t)-\beta(u)\}$, i.e. $\forall s,t \geq 0$,

$$A^*(s, s+t) \leq \alpha^*(t); \tag{5}$$

(ii) the backlog $B(t)$ is upper-bounded by, $\forall t \geq 0$,

$$B(t) \leq \sup_{t\geq 0}\{\alpha(t) - \beta(t)\}; \tag{6}$$

(iii) the virtual delay $D(t)$ is upper-bounded by, $\forall t \geq 0$:

$$D(t) \leq \sup_{t\geq 0} \inf\{\tau \geq 0 : \alpha(t) \leq \beta(t+\tau)\}. \tag{7}$$

As an example, suppose that the input flow is constrained by a token bucket with token generating rate ρ and bucket size σ [5] or has an arrival curve $\alpha(t) = \rho t + \sigma$. In addition, the system provides to the input a latency-rate service curve $\beta(t) = R(t-T)^+$, where R is called the rate term and T the latency term. If $\rho \leq R$, the bounds from Theorem 1 can be written as

$$\alpha^*(t) = \rho t + (\sigma + \rho T) \tag{8}$$

$$B(t) \leq \sigma + \rho T \tag{9}$$

$$D(t) \leq \frac{\sigma}{R} + T \tag{10}$$

In network calculus analysis, an important technique for finding the service curve characterization of a system makes use of the concept of strict service curve and its relation with the service curve model as summarized below.

Definition 3. *A system is said to provide a strict service curve $\beta \in \mathcal{F}_0$, if during any backlogged period of length t, the output satisfies [2] $A^*(t) \geq \beta(t)$.*

Proposition 1. *If $\beta(\in \mathcal{F}_0)$ is a strict service curve of a system, it is also a service curve of the system [2].*

For a concatenation system, the following result is important for finding its service curve characterization.

Theorem 2. *Consider a flow that traverses two systems S_1 and S_2 in sequence. If each system $S_i, (i = 1, 2)$ offers a service curve of β_i to its input, then the concatenated system offers a service curve of $\beta_1 \otimes \beta_2$ to the flow [2].*

3 Impact of Packetization on Network Calculus Analysis

In this paper, we focus on two fundamental transmission selection settings in a packet-switched network. One is a (work-conserving) constant bit rate link, and the other is a strict priority queue for packet transmission on such a link. The former is the foundation of any other transmission selection algorithm, while the latter is commonly implemented, e.g. as the default setting for time-sensitive networking [7]. For the two fundamental cases, the following service curve results have been widely applied, e.g. in [9–15]:

- A (work-conserving) link with constant bit rate c provides a (strict) service curve ct.
- When (non-preemptive) strict priority is applied on the link, the highest priority queue receives a (strict) service curve $c(t-\frac{l^{M_l}}{c})^+$, where l^{M_l} denotes the maximum packet length of all lower priority queues and $(x)^+ \equiv \max\{x, 0\}$.

Unfortunately, as shown in the following Sect. 3.1, both are faulty.

3.1 Faulty Service Curves

The Constant Bit Rate Case: The intuition behind using ct as a (strict) service curve of the system is as follows. Since the link is work-conserving, during any backlogged period, the link outputs traffic (in bits) at a rate c and hence has a strict service curve ct, with which ct as a service curve can also be concluded from Proposition 1. While this sounds straightforward, the following example and discussion highlight that special care is needed when packetization effect needs to be taken into account.

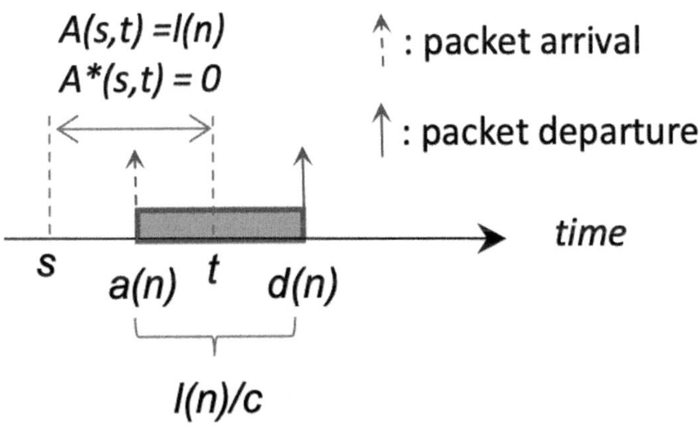

Fig. 2. Impact of packetization on the service of a constant bit rate link

Consider the transmission of a packet n on the link as illustrated in Fig. 2. Without considering the packetization effect, we would have $A(s,t) = A^*(s,t) = c(t-a(n))$ (in bits). However, under the packet model, taking packetization into account, we actually have $A(s,t) = l(n)$ while $A^*(s,t) = 0$. The former is because at time $a(n)$ which is within $[s,t)$, the (last bit of the) packet has arrived so that transmission can start. In contrast, for $A^*(s,t)$, $d(n)$ is not within the period, which means that the last bit of the packet has not finished transmission, so the packet is not considered to have been transmitted or served in the considered period $[s,t)$. Because $0 \le c(t-a(n)) \le l(n)$, we have $A^*(s,t) \le c(t-s)$, which contracts the definition of strict service curve if ct were used as a strict service curve.

The discussion above disapproves the validity of using ct as a strict service curve. However, the question of whether ct is a valid service curve remains. For this, we construct a case where $A^*(t) \ge A \otimes \beta(t)$ does not hold for $\beta(t) = ct$.

Consider the first packet. Let $a(1)$ be its arrival time and $l(1)(>0)$ its length. Then, for any time $t \in [a(1), a(1)+\frac{l(1)}{c})$, the period $(a(1),t)$ is backlogged because the packet has arrived but has not left. In addition, we have:

$$\begin{aligned} A \otimes \beta(t) &= \inf_{0\le s\le t}\{A(s)+c(t-s)\} \\ &= \min\left\{\inf_{0\le s<a(1)}\{A(s)+c(t-s)\}, \inf_{a(1)\le s\le t}\{A(s)+c(t-s)\}\right\} \\ &= \min\{c(t-a(1)), l(1)\} \\ &= c(t-a(1)) > 0 \end{aligned} \tag{11}$$

Note that $A^*(t) = 0$ because a packet is considered to have been served only when its last bit has left, the first packet has not left at $t(< a(1)+\frac{l(1)}{c})$ and therefore the packet cannot be counted in $A^*(t)$. In other words, for any $t \in [a(1), a(1)+\frac{l(1)}{c})$, $A \otimes \beta(t) > A^*(t)$, which contradicts the requirement of $A^*(t) \ge A \otimes \beta(t), \forall t \ge 0$ for β to be a service curve. Proposition 2 is now concluded.

Proposition 2. *For a system with constant bit rate c (in bps), ct is neither a strict service curve nor a service curve.*

The Strict Priority Case: For the (non-preemptive) strict priority case, the intuition behind using $c(t-\frac{l^{M_l}}{c})^+$ as a (strict) service curve is as follows. In the formulation, $\frac{l^{M_l}}{c}$ factors in the non-preemption effect, which is, upon arrival, a highest priority packet will have to wait for the packet under transmission to complete even though the packet under transmission is from a lower priority queue. However, as discussed for Proposition 2, when packetization is taken into account, ct is not a (strict) service curve for the link. In particular, factoring the non-preemption effect and adding $\frac{l^{M_l}}{c}$ at $a(n)$ in Fig. 2, the same analysis taking packetization into account can be conducted for the highest priority queue, from which we can consequently conclude Proposition 3.

Proposition 3. *For the highest priority queue on a link with constant bit rate* c, $c(t - \frac{l^{M_l}}{c})^+$ *is neither a strict service curve nor a service curve.*

Implications: The impact of packetization on the service curve characterization results as investigated above and summarized in Propositions 2 and 3 has two immediate implications:

- The various performance bounds derived from the faulty service curves, such as output arrival curve, backlog and delay bounds, must be re-examined for their validity and possibly updated.
- For any complex setting that builds on the two fundamental cases, if its service curve result implies a faulty service curve for either of the two fundamental cases as indicated in Propositions 2 and 3, the service curve result for the complex setting as well as the correspondingly derived performance bounds will need to be re-examined and possibly updated.

As a remark, for the latter, since a fundamental case is a special case of the complex setting, if the result for the special case is faulty, the result for the complex setting cannot hold either. In addition, it is worth highlighting that the constant bit rate case is implied in the strict priority case (SP). Specifically, it is a special case of SP with a single queue in the system.

3.2 Impact on Performance Bounds

In this subsection, we investigate the impact of a faulty service curve on the correspondingly obtained performance bound results. By constructing counterexamples, we show that the faulty service can lead to faulty output bound, faulty backlog bound and faulty concatenation service curve, while for delay bound the same conclusion cannot be made. We focus on the constant bit rate case. Because it is the most fundamental setting and is a special case of SP, the related conclusion on the invalidity of a bound is also applicable to the SP case.

Faulty Output Bound: To ease discussion, a simple input case is considered. Specifically, the input flow sends packets periodically to the system. Let τ denote the interval between two adjacent packets. All, except packet 1, have the same length l, while the length of packet 1 is $\sigma(> l)$. For stability, assume $\frac{l}{\tau} < c$. For this input case, it can be verified that it has an arrival curve $\alpha(t) = \frac{l}{\tau}t + \sigma$. An illustration of $A(t)$ and $\alpha(t)$ is presented in Fig. 3, where the output $A^*(t)$ and an output arrival curve $\alpha^*(t)$ that uses the same slope as α are also illustrated. (Remark: For α and α^*, they correspond to intervals starting from $a(1)$ and $d(1)$ respectively.) For the output, applying $\beta(t) = ct$ as a service curve to Theorem 1 would give $A^*(s, s+t) \leq \frac{l}{\tau}t + \sigma = \alpha(t)$, $\forall s, t \geq 0$, or in other words $\alpha^* = \alpha$. However, as illustrated in Fig. 3, $\alpha^*(t)$ needs to have a higher σ^* than the initial σ. In other words, the output is not constrained by $\alpha(t)$ and therefore using α as an upper bound on the output, based on derivation from the faulty service curve, is wrong.

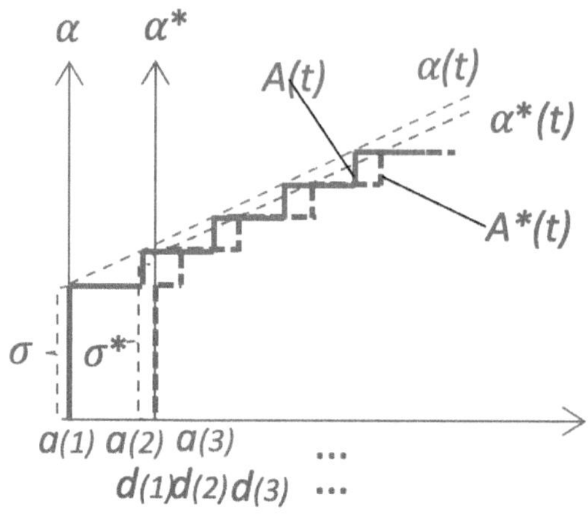

Fig. 3. Input-output: Input-related in blue and output-related in red (Color figure online)

Faulty Backlog Bound: For backlog, applying $\beta(t) = ct$ as service curve to Theorem 1 gives $B(t) \le \sigma$, $\forall t \ge 0$. However, this backlog bound σ is incorrect. Consider the same case as illustrated in Fig. 3. In particular, before packet 1 finishes, packet 2 has arrived. Hence, $B(t)$ for $t = d(1)_-$, i.e. the time just before packet 1 has finished its transmission, the backlog in the system is $\sigma + l$ where σ is the size of packet 1 and l is that of packet 2. Since $\sigma + l > \sigma$, the backlog bound σ from the faulty service curve is therefore incorrect.

Delay Bound: For delay, applying $\beta(t) = ct$ as service curve to Theorem 1 gives $D(t) \le \frac{\sigma}{c}$, $\forall t \ge 0$. Surprisingly, unlike that the output bound and backlog bound derived from the faulty service curve are also faulty, no similar conclusion can be made for the delay bound. This is because $\frac{\sigma}{c}$ is actually a valid delay bound, which has been proved but using another service-modeling technique [16]. More remarks related to this are provided in Sect. 3.3.

Faulty Concatenation Service Curve: Assume a flow traverses two switches S_1 and S_2 in sequence where the corresponding output links have constant bit rate c_1 and c_2 respectively. Let $\beta_i(t) = c_i t, (i = 1, 2)$. If they were correct service curves for S_1 and S_2 respectively, we would have $\beta_1 \otimes \beta_2(t) = \min\{c_1, c_2\}t$ to be a service curve for the concatenation system. Then, if the input has an arrival curve of $\rho t + \sigma$ with $\rho \le \min\{c_1, c_2\}$, the delay of any packet would be upper-bounded by $\frac{\sigma}{\min\{c_1, c_2\}}$, for which, however, counter examples can be constructed. Specifically, for simplicity, consider the case where all packets have the same length l, $\sigma = l$ and $c_1 = c_2 \equiv c$. Then we have $\frac{\sigma}{\min\{c_1, c_2\}} = \frac{l}{c}$. Furthermore, it is easily verified that for any packet, its delay is at least $2 \times \frac{l}{c}$

due to its transmission time of $\frac{l}{c}$ on both systems, which is larger than $\frac{l}{c}$. This implies that concatenation of faulty service curves leads to a faulty concatenation service curve for the concatenated system.

3.3 Remarks

It is worth highlighting that the service curves in the same forms for similar systems have been introduced in the network calculus theory but under different contexts.

- In [1], discrete time is adopted and *the service rate c is in the number of packets per unit time.* Under these assumptions, ct is proved to be a service curve, called an f-server in [1], for the constant rate server and for the highest priority queue.
- In [2,4], the analysis and results do not depend on whether the time model is discrete or continuous, which is also the case in the present paper. In [2,4], by defining *the amount of service counted at the bit level*, ct is shown to be a strict service curve for the constant bit rate case and so is $c(t - \frac{l^{M_l}}{c})^+$ for the highest priority queue on such a link (cf. Proposition 1.3.4 in [2] and Sect. 1.2 in [4]).

To account for the effect of packetization, particularly that a flow is composed of a sequence of (variable-length) packets and that the scheduling algorithm is at the packet level while not at the bit level, a novel concept called *packetizer* is introduced in [1] and also adopted in [2,4]. Its idea is to treat the system as the concatenation of two conceptual subsystems, as shown in Fig. 4. One is the bit-by-bit system, which is the part of the system before packetization is taken effect, and the other is a packetizer that assembles output traffic from the previous subsystem into packets.

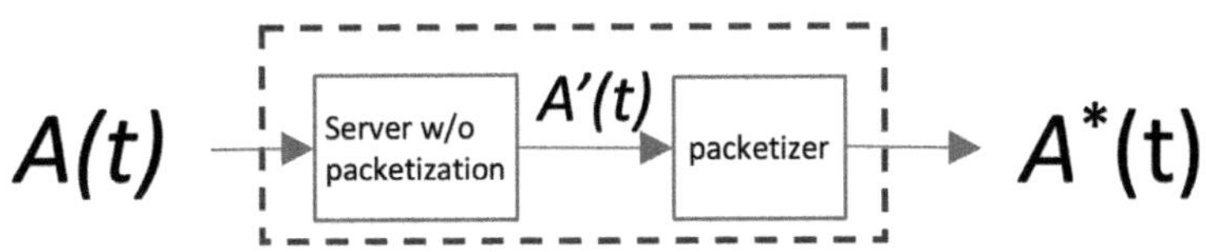

Fig. 4. System model: Packetizer

With the packetizer concept, it is highlighted in [1,2,4] that additional terms may need to be added to the service curve and performance bound results. In particular, the service curve, the backlog bound, and the concatenation service curve must be adjusted, although the packetizer is shown to not increase the maximum packet delay [1,2,4]. Unfortunately, this seems to have been largely overlooked in the recent application of network calculus analysis, e.g., in [9–12]

[13–15], where the faulty service curves are directly adopted without considering the packetization effect.

Unlike relying on the concept of packetizer to account for the packetization effect in [1,2], and [4], we take packetization into direct consideration when modeling the arrival and service processes. More specifically, as introduced in Sect. 2, we adopt the convention that *a packet is said to have arrived (respectively, been served) when and only when its last bit has arrived (respectively, departed)* and hence model the arrival and departure processes as marked point processes. Based on this idea, we conduct network calculus analysis and present corrected service curves and performance bounds for the two fundamental cases in the next Sect. 4.

4 Corrected Service Curves and Performance Bounds

4.1 The Constant Bit Rate Case

For the constant bit rate case, corrected service curves are presented in Proposition 4.

Proposition 4. *A system with constant bit rate c offers a strict service curve and a service curve $c(t - \frac{l^M}{c})^+$, where l^M denotes the maximum packet length in the system.*

Proof. Consider any backlogged period $(s, t]$ as shown in Fig. 5, and let n_0 denote the packet whose arrival starts the backlogged period. Clearly, we have $s \geq a(n_0)$. Without loss of generality, suppose that packet m is the first packet that leaves after time s, and n the first packet that departs after time t. By their definitions, we must have $d(m-1) < s \leq d(m)$ and $d(n-1) \leq t < d(n)$. Since the system is backlogged during $(s, t]$, it must also be so during (i) $(s, d(m)]$, (ii) $(d(m), d(n-1)]$ and (iii) $(d(n-1), t]$. Because the system has a constant bit rate c, during any backlogged period of duration τ, the amount of traffic it serves/transmits is $c\tau$ (in bits). We hence have $c(d(m) - s) \leq l(m)$, $c[d(n-1) - d(m)] = \sum_{k=m+1}^{n-1} l(k)$, and $c[t - d(n-1)] \leq l(n) \leq l^M$. Since $A^*(s,t) = \sum_{k=m}^{n-1} l(k)$ as illustrated by Fig. 5, we have

$$\begin{aligned} A^*(s,t) &= l(m) + c[d(n-1) - d(m)] \\ &\geq c[d(n-1) - s] \geq c(t - s - \frac{l^M}{c}) \end{aligned} \tag{12}$$

which, together with the fact that $A^*(s,t) \geq 0$, ends the proof.

With Proposition 4, various performance bounds can immediately be derived from Theorem 1. As a specific example where the input is constrained by a token-bucket arrival curve, they are summarized in Corollary 1.

Corollary 1. *Consider a traffic flow transmitting over a link that has a constant bit rate c. If the traffic has a token-bucket arrival curve $\alpha(t) = \rho t + \sigma$ with $\rho \leq c$, there hold:*

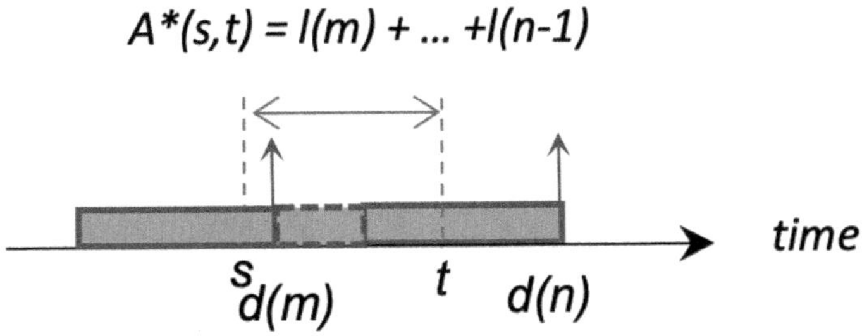

Fig. 5. Service of a link during a backlogged period.

(i) the output has an arrival curve $\rho t + \sigma + \rho\frac{l^M}{c}$, *i.e.* $\forall s, t \geq 0$,

$$A^*(s, s+t) \leq \rho t + \sigma + \frac{\rho}{c} l^M; \tag{13}$$

(ii) the backlog $B(t)$ *is upper-bounded by,* $\forall t \geq 0$,

$$B(t) \leq \sigma + \frac{\rho}{c} l^M; \tag{14}$$

(iii) the virtual delay $D(t)$ *is upper-bounded by,* $\forall t \geq 0$:

$$D(t) \leq \frac{\sigma + l^M}{c}. \tag{15}$$

In addition, with Proposition 4 and Theorem 2, a corrected concatenation service curve can be found for the counterexample case discussed in Sect. 3.2.

Corollary 2. *Consider a flow that traverses two switches in sequence. The corresponding output links have constant bit rate* $c_i, (i = 1, 2)$ *respectively. The concatenation system offers to the flow a service curve of* $\min\{c_1, c_2\}(t - \frac{l^M}{c_1} - \frac{l^M}{c_2})^+$.

4.2 The Strict Priority Case

For the strict priority case, a corrected strict service curve, which is also a service curve, is presented in Proposition 5. For the proof, it is similar to that of Proposition 4. The key difference is that s may be within the transmission period of a lower priority packet that has started its transmission and cannot be preempted by the arrival of the highest priority packet n_0. In such a scenario, we have $c(s - d(n_0)) \leq l(n_0) + l^{M_l}$, $c(d(n-1) - d(n_0)) = \sum_{k=n_0+1}^{n-1} l(k)$, and $c[t - d(n-1)] \leq l(n) \leq l^M$. From these, we obtain

$$A^*(s,t) = \sum_{k=n_0}^{n-1} l(k) \geq c[d(n-1) - s - \frac{l^{M_l}}{c}] \geq c(t - s - \frac{l^M}{c} - \frac{l^{M_l}}{c}) \tag{16}$$

where l^M and l^{M_l} respectively denote the maximum packet length of the considered highest priority queue and the maximum packet length of all lower priority queues. For other scenarios, where the arrival of the highest priority packet n_0 does not see any ongoing transmission of a lower priority packet, they are the same as in the proof of Proposition 4 and hence $A^*(s,t) \geq c(t-s-\frac{l^M}{c})$. Combining all scenarios and the fact that $A^*(s,t) \geq 0$, Proposition 5 can be concluded.

Proposition 5. *For the highest priority queue in a system with constant service rate c (in bps), $c(t-\frac{l^M}{c}-\frac{l^{M_l}}{c})^+$ is both a strict service curve and a service curve.*

Similarly, with Proposition 5, various performance bounds can also be derived from Theorem 1. Specifically, if the input is constrained by a token-bucket arrival curve, the corresponding bounds are summarized in Corollary 3.

Corollary 3. *Consider a traffic flow competing with other flows to transmit on a link that has a constant bit rate c, and the considered flow is given the highest priority. If the traffic of the highest priority flow has a token-bucket arrival curve $\alpha(t) = \rho t + \sigma$ with $\rho \leq c$, there hold:*

(i) the output has an arrival curve $\rho t + \sigma + \rho\frac{l^M + l^{M_l}}{c}$, i.e. $\forall s, t \geq 0$,

$$A^*(s, s+t) \leq \rho t + \sigma + \frac{\rho}{c}(l^M + l^{M_l}); \tag{17}$$

(ii) the backlog $B(t)$ is upper-bounded by, $\forall t \geq 0$,

$$B(t) \leq \sigma + \frac{\rho}{c}(l^M + l^{M_l}); \tag{18}$$

(iii) the virtual delay $D(t)$ is upper-bounded by, $\forall t \geq 0$:

$$D(t) \leq \frac{\sigma + l^M + l^{M_l}}{c}. \tag{19}$$

Similarly, with Proposition 5 and Theorem 2, a service curve can be found for the concatenation of two priority systems.

Corollary 4. *Consider a flow that traverses two systems in sequence. Both systems adopt strict priority scheduling to share among flows the service rate (in bps) $c_i, (i = 1, 2)$, which is constant. The flow is given highest priority at both systems. Then, the concatenation system offers the flow a service curve of $\min\{c_1, c_2\}(t - \frac{l^M+l^{M_l}}{c_1} - \frac{l^M+l^{M_l}}{c_2})^+$.*

4.3 Remarks

The discussion in Sect. 3.3 has indicated that the idea of packetizer has been adopted in [1,2,4] to account for the packetization effect. In particular, for the corresponding bounds as shown in Propositions 4 and 5, the suggested adjustments can be found in [1,2,4].

More specifically, for the constant bit case, the service curve is adjusted to be the same as shown in Proposition 4, and the service curve for the concatenation system, the adjustment is also the same. In addition, the output is upper-bounded by, $\forall s, t \geq 0, A^*(s, s+t) \leq \rho t + \sigma + l^M$ and the backlog is upper-bounded by $\forall t \geq 0, B(t) \leq \sigma + l^M$, while for virtual delay, it is upper-bounded by $\forall t \geq 0, D(t) \leq \frac{\sigma}{c}$. Comparing with the bounds shown in Corollary 1, our output and backlog bounds are tighter. However, for virtual delay, the bound derived from ignoring the packetizer effect is better. For the strict priority case, similar comparison can be conducted, and it is also observed that the packetizer approach gives the same service curves, looser output and backlog bounds, but tighter delay bound.

A final remark is that the approach of taking the packetization effect directly into account in service-modeling has been exploited in the network calculus literature, e.g. in [1,16,17]. Recent work [17] particularly indicates that the same delay bounds can also be derived for the two basic systems using this approach. For a more detailed discussion, which is beyond the scope of the present paper, interested readers are referred to [1,16,17].

5 Conclusion

Network calculus analysis has been applied to two basic systems that are fundamental or default settings in time-sensitive networks. The focus has been on analyzing their service curve characterizations and performance bounds. It was shown through counterexamples that the service curves, which have been widely adopted in some recent literature for the two fundamental settings, are actually faulty. Additionally, it was also shown that for the output bound, backlog bound and concatenation service curve results derived from the faulty service curves, counterexamples can also be constructed. This implies that both the service curve characterizations of the two fundamental settings and the correspondingly derived performance bounds need to be adjusted or re-investigated to account for the packetization effect. To this end, the service curves and performance bounds were corrected by exploring the idea of factoring packetization directly into service-modeling. The results exemplify not only that if the packetization effect is overlooked, network calculus analysis can produce faulty results, but also how the packetization effect can be factored in the analysis.

References

1. Chang, C.-S.: Performance Guarantees in Communication Networks. Springer-Verlag (2000)
2. Le Boudec, J.-Y., Thiran, P.: Network Calculus: A Theory of Deterministic Queueing Systems for the Internet. Springer-Verlag (2001). https://doi.org/10.1007/3-540-45318-0_1

3. Jiang, Y., Liu, Y.: Stochastic Network Calculus. Springer (2008). https://doi.org/10.1007/978-1-84800-127-5
4. Bouillard, A., Boyer, M., Le Corronc, E.: Deterministic network calculus: from theory to practical implementation. Wiley-ISTE, Deterministic network calculus (2018)
5. Cruz, R.L.: A calculus for network delay, part I: network elements in isolation. IEEE Trans. Inf. Theory **37**(1), 114–131 (1991)
6. Cruz, R.L.: A calculus for network delay, part II: network analysis. IEEE Trans. Inf. Theory **37**(1), 132–141 (1991)
7. IEEE standard for local and metropolitan area networks–bridges and bridged networks. IEEE Std 802.1Q-2022 (Revision of IEEE Std 802.1Q-2018), pp. 1–2163 (2022)
8. Finn, N., Thubert, P., Varga, B., Farkas, J.: Deterministic networking architecture. In: IETF RFC 8655 (2019)
9. De Azua, J.A.R., Boyer, M.: Complete modelling of AVB in network calculus framework. In: Proceedings of the 22nd International Conference on Real-Time Networks and Systems, RTNS 2014, pp. 55–64, New York, NY, USA, 2014. Association for Computing Machinery
10. Zhao, L., Pop, P., Zheng, Z., Li, Q.: Timing analysis of AVB traffic in TSN networks using network calculus. In: 2018 IEEE Real-Time and Embedded Technology and Applications Symposium (RTAS), pp. 25–36 (2018)
11. Mohammadpour, E., Stai, E., Mohiuddin, M., Le Boudec, J.Y.: Latency and backlog bounds in time-sensitive networking with credit based shapers and asynchronous traffic shaping. In: 2018 30th International Teletraffic Congress (ITC 30) (2018)
12. Zhao, L., Pop, P., Zheng, Z., Daigmorte, H., Boyer, M.: Latency analysis of multiple classes of AVB traffic in TSN with standard credit behavior using network calculus. IEEE Trans. Industr. Electron. **68**(10), 10291–10302 (2021)
13. Zhao, L., Pop, P., Steinhorst, S.: Quantitative performance comparison of various traffic shapers in time-sensitive networking. IEEE Trans. Netw. Serv. Manage. **19**(3), 2899–2928 (2022)
14. Zhao, L., Yan, Y., Zhou, X.: Minimum bandwidth reservation for CBS in TSN with real-time QoS guarantees. IEEE Trans. Industr. Inf. **20**(4), 6187–6198 (2024)
15. Miserez, J., Colle, D., Pickavet, M., Tavernier, W.: Exploiting queue information for scalable delay-constrained routing in deterministic networks. IEEE Trans. Netw. Serv. Manage. **21**(5), 5260–5272 (2024)
16. Goyal, P., Lam, S.S., Vin, H.M.: Determining end-to-end delay bounds in heterogeneous networks. Multimedia Syst. **5**, 157–163 (1997)
17. Jiang, Y.: Network calculus bounds for time-sensitive networks: a revisit. CoRR abs/2403.13656 (2024)

Demonstration of Effective UCB-Based Routing in Skill-Based Queues on Real-World Data

Sanne van Kempen[1(✉)], Jaron Sanders[1], Fiona Slothaak[1], and Maarten G. Wolf[2]

[1] Eindhoven University of Technology, Eindhoven, The Netherlands
s.f.m.v.kempen@tue.nl
[2] Koninklijke KPN N.V., Amsterdam, The Netherlands

Abstract. We consider the challenge of optimally controlling skill-based queueing systems such as data centers, cloud computing networks, and service systems. By means of a case study using a real-world data set, we investigate the practical implementation of a recently developed reinforcement learning algorithm for optimal customer routing. Our experiments show that the algorithm efficiently learns and adapts to changing environments and outperforms static benchmark policies, indicating its potential for live implementation. We also augment the real-world applicability of this algorithm by introducing a new heuristic routing rule to reduce delays. Moreover, we show that the algorithm can optimize for multiple objectives: next to payoff maximization, secondary objectives such as server load fairness and customer waiting time reduction can be incorporated. Tuning parameters are used for balancing inherent performance trade–offs. Lastly, we investigate the sensitivity to estimation errors and tuning parameters, providing valuable insights for implementing adaptive routing algorithms in complex real-world queueing systems.

Keywords: Skill-Based Queues · Machine Learning · Optimal Routing · Multi-Armed Bandits

1 Introduction

In skill-based queues, different customer types request service from heterogeneous servers, and compatibility relations determine which customer–server matches are allowed. Because such queueing systems are used in many places—for example, in data centers, healthcare applications, and service systems—efficient resource allocation in them is highly valuable [8]. A full theoretical understanding of such systems, however, is difficult to attain due to the challenging queueing dynamics resulting from the compatibility relations [1,2,27].

Canonical routing policies such as First–Come–First–Served (FCFS) Assign–the–Longest–Idle– Server (ALIS) and Serve–the–Longest–Queue policy are typically static by design [2]. Although such policies are easy to implement, they

A. Remke et al. (Eds.): Valuetools 2025, LNICST 691, pp. 255–274, 2027.
https://doi.org/10.1007/978-3-032-23901-3_16

do not account for long-term performance trade–offs or stability constraints. Moreover, they offer limited robustness and adaptability to optimize for various objectives such as maximizing the quality of customer–server matches, waiting times, and fairness. Other policies such as the $c\mu$ rule [24], MaxWeight scheduling [25], and Whittle index policies [18] rely on system parameters which might *a priori* be unknown in real-world applications. This limits their direct applicability in practice, especially in complex service systems with uncertainty.

To address these challenges, there has been a growing interest in data-driven control policies that can deal with unknown system parameters [17,23,29]. In particular, recent works underline the potential of machine learning algorithms. For example, [12] applies proximal policy optimization for routing in multiclass queueing networks, [26] optimizes congestion control in a data center using a reinforcement learning algorithm, [20] introduces an actor–critic method for multi-resource job scheduling, and [11] introduces new score-aware gradient estimators which are applied in policy-gradient methods for stochastic optimal control problems.

Optimization of skill-based queues is crucial in many practical settings. While minimizing customer waiting times is a commonly used performance objective, the quality of customer–server matches is also an important measure [8]. To capture such trade–offs, researchers have increasingly adopted multi-objective optimization approaches that balance efficiency, service quality, and resource utilization [4,9]. When working with real operational data, additional challenges arise due to time-varying arrival rates and dynamic server availability, which necessitate the use of accurate forecasting techniques to support effective decision making [15].

We focus on a recently developed utility-maximizing reinforcement learning algorithm called "UCB–Queue Routing (UCB–QR)", meant for routing in skill-based queueing systems [16]. This algorithm integrates multi-armed bandit techniques and Upper Confidence Bound (UCB estimators [5,19] to make routing decisions under uncertainty. It is shown in [16] that the algorithm is nearly optimal in the sense that its regret accumulation matches the asymptotic lower bound up to logarithmic terms. While [16] analyzes the theoretical performance of UCB–QR, its potential for real-world queueing systems was not demonstrated. For example, queue lengths, delays, and fairness aspects are not considered in [16]. To this end, we perform a numerical study of the potential applications and extensions for practical use of the algorithm in a realistic setting. We also prepare the algorithm for implementation in practice: this includes the incorporation of an action space reduction technique, and the ability to deal with temporary system instability and time-varying arrival rates and service capacities. While these phenomena are often neglected in synthetic experiments, they are critical for realistic applications.

To prepare for implementation of the algorithm in a real-life setting, we provide a simulation framework that supports arbitrary compatibility relations and general arrival and service processes. This makes it a valuable tool for testing performance and robustness of learning-based routing policies in complex environments. The simulation is publicly available[1] and relies on standard open-source Python libraries such as `NumPy` and `pandas`. To demonstrate the practical use of the UCB–QR routing algorithm, we use data from a large-scale U.S. bank call center, made publicly available by the Technion Laboratory for Service Enterprise Engineering (SEELAB)[2]. This extensive data set, also used in prior studies such as [3,6], serves as benchmark for call center operations research.

We demonstrate that the modified UCB–QR routing algorithm (Algorithm 1) is well-suited for implementation in a large, realistic queueing system, even when the environment is changing. The algorithm successfully accumulates high payoffs while learning the payoff parameters and estimating the (time-varying) arrival and service rates. We show that the algorithm consistently outperforms the benchmark policies in terms of payoff accumulation, including a "greedy" policy and a variant of the $c\mu$ rule that is modified for payoff maximization [24]. In one representative scenario, our algorithm closes the optimality gap by over 70% when compared to naive random routing (see Fig. 5). By also developing a new heuristic routing rule, which takes inspiration from [14], customer waiting times can be reduced significantly. Moreover, we show that multiple objectives can be optimized simultaneously, with tuning parameters balancing the trade–offs. Lastly, the algorithm is neither black-box nor computationally heavy: the algorithm's runtime is comparable with those of other routing policies like FCFS–ALIS or random routing.

2 Algorithm Description

We consider a skill-based queueing system with customer types $\mathcal{I} = \{1, \ldots, I\}$, servers $\mathcal{J} = \{1, \ldots, J\}$, and compatibility lines connecting customers to servers $\mathcal{L} = \{(ij) : i \in \mathcal{I}, j \in \mathcal{J}\}$. Type-$i$ customers arrive with rate $\lambda_i > 0$ and wait in the queue of their type until they start service at one of the compatible servers. The service rate of type-i customers at server j is $\mu_{ij} > 0$ and each service completion generates a random Bernoulli payoff with mean $\theta_{ij} \in [0, 1]$. Payoffs represent quality of service. In practice, this can be measured in terms of e.g. a customer satisfaction score. Other queueing related performance measures, such as e.g. delay minimization or server load balancing, can be integrated as well. We discuss this in Sect. 3.3.

We present a modified version of the routing algorithm developed by [16], called UCB–QR, in Algorithm 1. UCB–QR maximizes the total average payoff $\sum_{(ij)\in\mathcal{L}} \theta_{ij}\mathbb{E}(D_{ij}(t))$, where $D_{ij}(t)$ is the number of type-(ij) departures, while learning the payoff parameters θ_{ij} and maintaining queue stability. Algorithm 1 considers the following optimal transport Linear Program (LP) that maximizes the average payoff (1a) using routing rates x_{ij}. Constraints (1b) guarantee that all customers are routed to some server and that server loads are not exceeded. Here, $\mathcal{S}_i \subseteq \mathcal{J}$ are the compatible servers for customer type i and $\mathcal{C}_j \subseteq \mathcal{I}$ are the compatible customer types for server j.

---

[1] See https://github.com/SannevanKempen/UCBQR.

[2] See https://seelab.net.technion.ac.il/data/.

$$\text{LP}(\lambda, \mu, \theta, \varepsilon): \max_{x \geq 0} \sum_{(ij) \in \mathcal{L}} \theta_{ij} x_{ij}, \tag{1a}$$

$$\text{s.t.} \sum_{j \in \mathcal{S}_i} x_{ij} = \lambda_i, \quad \forall i \in \mathcal{I}, \qquad \sum_{i \in \mathcal{C}_j} \frac{x_{ij}}{\mu_{ij}} \leq 1 - \varepsilon, \quad \forall j \in \mathcal{J}. \tag{1b}$$

Algorithm 1 divides the time horizon into episodes. At the start of episode k, the estimators for (i) the average payoffs $\hat{\theta}_{ij}^k$, (ii) the arrival rates $\hat{\lambda}_i^k$, and (iii) the service rates $\hat{\mu}_{ij}^k$ are updated using collected samples. We use UCB estimators [5,19] for the payoff parameters in (7). Consequently, the set of routing rates $\hat{x}_{ij}$, $(ij) \in \mathcal{L}$ is chosen that maximize $\text{LP}(\hat{\lambda}^k, \hat{\mu}^k, \hat{\theta}^k, \varepsilon)$. During the episode, customers are routed to servers according to the rates $\hat{x}$ using virtual queues (Algorithm 2).

Practical Adaptations. Algorithm 1 is an adaptation of the algorithm by [16]. We briefly discuss the most significant changes to make the algorithm more suitable for practical implementation.

- **Action space reduction.** The algorithm in [16] considers the set of all Basic Feasible Solutions (BFSs) of the LP as its action space, i.e., the set of candidate solutions. Each episode, the algorithm chooses the solution (action) with the highest estimated payoff based on the UCB estimators $\hat{\theta}$. Since the number of BFSs scales exponentially with the number of customer types I, servers J, and lines $|\mathcal{L}|$, this approach can be computationally prohibitive for large queueing systems. To reduce the complexity of the algorithm, we instead solve (1) directly at the start of each episode using current payoff estimates, and use its maximizer as the desired routing rates (Line 5). This approach avoids the need to enumerate or store the full set of BFSs. For fixed values $\lambda, \mu, \theta, \varepsilon$, (1) can be solved efficiently by modern solvers that rely on, e.g., the simplex method or interior-point methods [7], making this a scalable alternative.
- **Arrival and service processes.** In [16], the analytical model assumes that arrivals are independent and stationary Poisson processes. The arrival process in the data, however, is time-varying; see Fig. 1. To capture both the level and trend, we use Holt's linear trend model to forecast the call volume of episode k using the realizations of previous episodes [15]:

$$\hat{\lambda}_i^k = \max\Big(\frac{\ell_i^{k-1} + b_i^{k-1}}{h}, 0\Big). \tag{2}$$

Here, h is the episode length and ℓ_i^k and b_i^k are the level and trend estimators, respectively, defined by $\ell_i^k = \alpha y_i^k + (1-\alpha)\hat{y}_i^{k-1}$, and $b_i^k = \beta(\ell_i^k - \ell_i^{k-1}) + (1-\beta)b_i^{k-1}$, with y_i^k the number of type-i arrivals in episode k. The smoothing parameters $\alpha, \beta \in [0,1]$ control the balance between reactivity to new data points and previous trends. By analyzing the forecast error for various values of α and β, we found that large values make the forecast overly reactive to noise, while small values miss trend changes, particularly for type-1 customers. By fitting the model and analyzing the mean squared error for the arrival pattern over one week, we found that there is not one set of parameter values with minimal error over all days. We therefore take $\alpha = 0.5$ and $\beta = 0.2$, which perform reasonably well over all days.

The theoretical model in [16] assumes independent and exponential service times for analytical tractability. The service times in the data are unlikely to be actually distributed as such (see Fig. 2). We therefore instead estimate the empirical service rate,

$$\hat{\mu}_{ij}^k := \frac{M_{ij}^k}{\sum_{\ell=1}^{M_{ij}^k} m_{ij}^\ell}, \tag{3}$$

where M_{ij}^k is the number of type-(ij) service completions up to episode k, and $(m_{ij}^\ell)_{\ell=1}^{M_{ij}^k}$ are the realized service times of those completions.

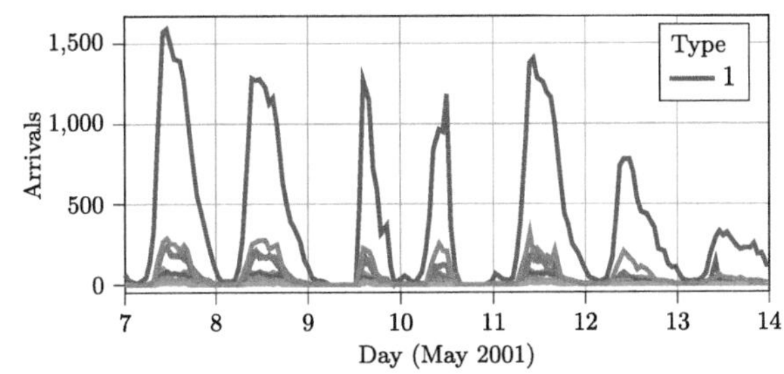

Fig. 1. Customer arrivals accumulated per 30-minute intervals. The call center is closed on the morning of May 9 and the afternoon of May 10.

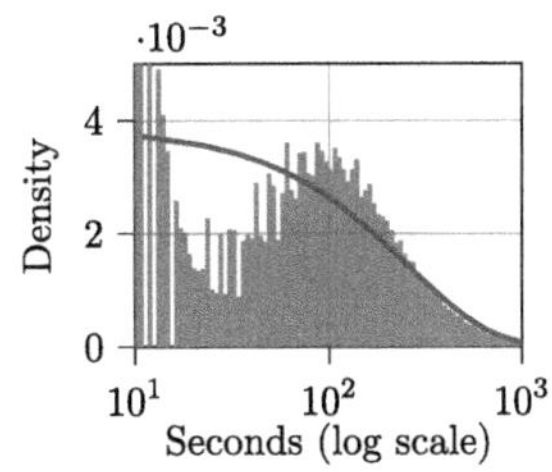

Fig. 2. Type-(11) service times in May 2001 (252,103 samples) with best-fitting exponential fit (Akaike Information Criterion (AIC)).

– **Stability.** In [16], a notion of stability is assumed. However, (1) can be infeasible if the arrival volume exceeds the service capacity. In practice, such situations are expected in real-life systems, since temporary overloads can and do occur. Additionally, estimation errors in $\hat{\lambda}$ and $\hat{\mu}$ can also lead to infeasibility of (1). If (1) is infeasible, we consider the following alternative LP:

$$\mathrm{LP^a}(\lambda, \mu, \theta, \varepsilon): \quad \max_{x \geq 0} \; \& \sum_{(ij)\in\mathcal{L}} \theta_{ij} x_{ij} - \sum_{i\in\mathcal{I}} p x_{iz}, \tag{4a}$$

$$\text{s.t.} \; \& \sum_{j\in\mathcal{S}_i} x_{ij} + x_{iz} = \lambda_i, \quad \forall i \in \mathcal{I}, \qquad \sum_{i\in\mathcal{C}_j} \frac{x_{ij}}{\mu_{ij}} \leq 1 - \varepsilon, \quad \forall j \in \mathcal{J}. \tag{4b}$$

$\mathrm{LP^a}$ introduces a fictitious "rejection" server z with infinite capacity. Type-i customers can be routed to server z, but this is penalized with a negative payoff p. If p is large, weight is given to x_{iz} only when no other feasible solution exists. (4) is always feasible and provides a robust alternative to (1). Server z is not actually used when making routing decisions: after obtaining the optimal solution x from (4), we normalize the rates according to Line 1 in Algorithm 2.

Algorithm 1. Modified UCB–Queue Routing (UCBQR).

Initialize $k = 1$. For all $(ij) \in \mathcal{L}$, initialize $T_{ij}(0) = \bar{\theta}_{ij}(0) = 0$ and $\hat{\theta}_{ij}(0) = \infty$.
for each episode $k = 1, 2, \ldots$ of length h **do**
  Set $\hat{\lambda}^k$ according to (2) and $\hat{\mu}^k$ according to (3).
  if LP$(\hat{\lambda}^k, \hat{\mu}^k, \hat{\theta}^k, \varepsilon)$ (1) is feasible **then** ▷ Determine routing rates.
    Solve LP$(\hat{\lambda}^k, \hat{\mu}^k, \hat{\theta}^k, \varepsilon)$ in (1); denote its maximizer by $\hat{x}^k$.
  else
    Solve LP$^{\mathrm{a}}(\hat{\lambda}^k, \hat{\mu}^k, \hat{\theta}^k, \varepsilon)$ in (4); denote its maximizer by $\hat{x}^k$.
  end if
  Serve customers according to $\hat{x}^k$ by applying Algorithm 2: FCFS–RR$(\hat{x}^k, h)$. ▷ Route customers.
  For each line $(ij) \in \mathcal{L}$, observe $N_{ij}^k \in \mathbb{N}_{\geq 0}$ payoff samples $(Y_{ij}^\ell)_{\ell=1,\ldots,N_{ij}^k}$.
  For each line $(ij) \in \mathcal{L}$, update ▷ Update estimators based on samples.

$$T_{ij}(k) = T_{ij}(k-1) + N_{ij}^k, \tag{5}$$

$$\bar{\theta}_{ij}(k) = \frac{\bar{\theta}_{ij}(k-1)T_{ij}(k-1) + \sum_{\ell=1}^{N_{ij}^k} Y_{ij}^\ell}{T_{ij}(k)}, \tag{6}$$

$$\hat{\theta}_{ij}^k = \begin{cases} \bar{\theta}_{ij}(k) + \sqrt{\frac{\ln(k)}{T_{ij}(k)}} & \text{if } T_{ij}(k) > 0, \\ \infty & \text{if } T_{ij}(k) = 0. \end{cases} \tag{7}$$

end for

Algorithm 2. FCFS–RR(x, h).

1: Set $p_{ij} = x_{ij} / \sum_{m \in \mathcal{J}} x_{im}$ for all $(ij) \in \mathcal{L}$. ▷ Compute routing probabilities.
2: Empty all virtual queues. ▷ Shuffle virtual queues.
3: Assign each waiting type-i customer to virtual queue j with probability p_{ij}.
4: Order customers in each virtual queue $j \in \mathcal{J}$ by arrival time.
5: **for** $t = 0, \ldots, h$ **do** ▷ Route customers.
6:   **for** each arrival of a type-i customer at time t **do**
7:     Assign customer to virtual queue j with probability p_{ij}.
8:     If the server is idle, start service.
9:   **end for**
10:   **for** each service completion of customer type i at server j at time t **do**
11:     Obtain a payoff $Y_{ij} \sim \mathrm{Bern}(\theta_{ij})$.
12:     If the virtual queue of server j is non-empty, start service of the head customer.
13:   **end for**
14: **end for**

2.1 Data Set and Implementation Challenges

Data Set. The data set (130 gigabytes) contains call logs and agent shifts from a U.S. bank call center between April 2001 and October 2003. On a typical weekday, approximately 1.200 agents handle around 50.000 calls. Customers are processed by a Voice Response Unit, which classifies their service request as a customer type. New services introduced in mid-2002 increase the total to 17 types. Service is skill-based and agents are partitioned into 47 groups based on their capabilities. The data also records their work hours, call handling, and idle times.

Since service categories and agent populations vary over time, we define customer type–agent group compatibility per month: we call a pair *compatible* if it appears in at least 100 calls. At most 1% of customers abandon before reaching an agent, and about 3% interact with multiple agents. We neglect both effects and treat each call as a unique customer.

Defining Payoff Parameters. To apply Algorithm 1, we need to define payoff parameters θ_{ij}, since no cost or satisfaction measures are available in the data. Call outcomes include *transfer* (customer redirected to another group) and *conference* (agent consults a colleague or supervisor). We let θ_{ij} be the ratio of successful type-(ij) calls not ending in transfer or conference. Concretely, $\theta^d_{ij} := s^d_{ij}/n^d_{ij}$ with s^d_{ij} the number of type-i calls routed to j without transfer or conference and n^d_{ij} the total number of type-(ij) calls on day d.

Time-varying agent populations Agent groups in the data set contain multiple agents, typically ranging from a few to nearly 500. For simplicity, we use one server for each agent group in the simulation, with service speed scaled proportionally to the number of working agents. This is similar to approximating an $M(\lambda)/M(\mu)/n$ system by an $M(\lambda)/M(n\mu)/1$ system, which has nearly identical stationary probabilities for states with n or more customers [10]. The number of available agents is updated hourly from the data.

3 Experiments

This section demonstrates UCB–QR (Algorithm 1) in practical situations. Section 3.1 compares against commonly used benchmark policies. The results show higher customer waiting times than the benchmarks. We therefore introduce a new heuristic routing rule in Sect. 3.2 to replace Sect. 2. Section 3.3 discusses extensions of UCB–QR to account for multiple objectives. Section 3.5 analyzes the sensitivity to estimation errors in arrival and service rates and Sect. 3.6 tests the sensitivity to the episode length.

To analyze the performance of UCB–QR, we consider the following benchmark policies:

- **Oracle:** Similar to UCB–QR, but with oracle knowledge of the payoff, arrival and service time parameters. In particular, this is Algorithm 1, but replacing $\hat{\theta}$, $\hat{\lambda}$, and $\hat{\mu}$ in Lines 5 and 7 by the actual θ, λ, and μ as obtained from the data.

- **FCFS–ALIS:** If a server is idle while compatible customers are waiting, assign the customer with the longest waiting time. If there are idle compatible servers upon a customer arrival, assign it to the server with maximal idle time. This policy is widely used in practice since it is easy to implement and both customers and servers experience fairness [2].
- **Greedy:** If server j is idle while compatible customers are waiting, assign the First–In–Line (FIL) customer with maximal expected payoff, i.e., a customer of type $\text{argmax}_{i\in\mathcal{I}}\,\theta_{ij}$. If there are idle compatible servers upon a customer arrival, assign it to server $\text{argmax}_{j\in\mathcal{J}}\,\theta_{ij}$. This policy maximizes the instantaneous payoff without considering long-term effects or stability.
- **Random:** If a server is idle while compatible customers are waiting, assign the FIL customer from a queue uniformly at random. If there are idle compatible servers upon a customer arrival, assign the customer to a server uniformly at random. This policy serves as a most naive benchmark since it makes uninformed decisions.
- $\theta\mu$ **rule:** If server j is idle while compatible customers are waiting, assign the FIL customer of type $\text{argmax}_{i\in\mathcal{I}}\,\theta_{ij}\mu_{ij}$. If there are idle compatible servers upon a customer arrival, assign it to server $\text{argmax}_{j\in\mathcal{J}}\,\theta_{ij}\mu_{ij}$. This policy is a variation of the $c\mu$ rule [24], which is known to minimize holding costs in a multi-customer single-server setting, and has been well-studied in multi-customer multi-server settings [21,28] and even in adaptive learning settings [17]. Instead of holding costs, we balance the average payoff θ_{ij} with service speed μ_{ij}.
- **Data:** We include the results from the data set which follow from the routing policy used by the call center. The policy that was applied is unknown to us.

3.1 Proof of Concept

We apply UCB–QR to the data of June 2001. The arrival pattern and agent schedules are shown in Figs. 3 and 4 and θ is given in Appendix A. We set the episode length to $h = 2$ minutes, and $\varepsilon = 10^{-6}$ and $p = 10^3$ in (1) and (4). Our results are based on 50 independent runs.

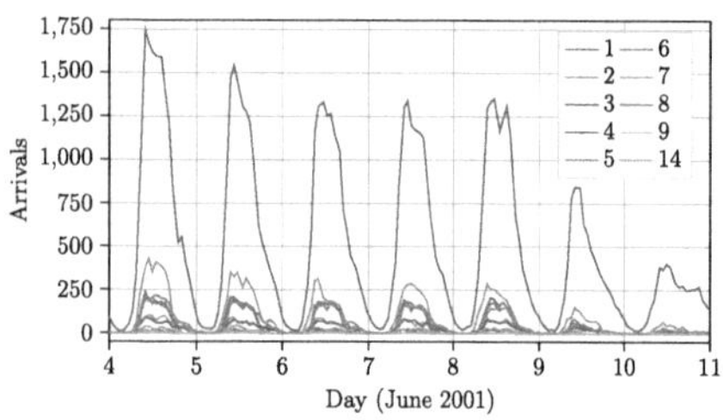

Fig. 3. Customer arrivals per type.

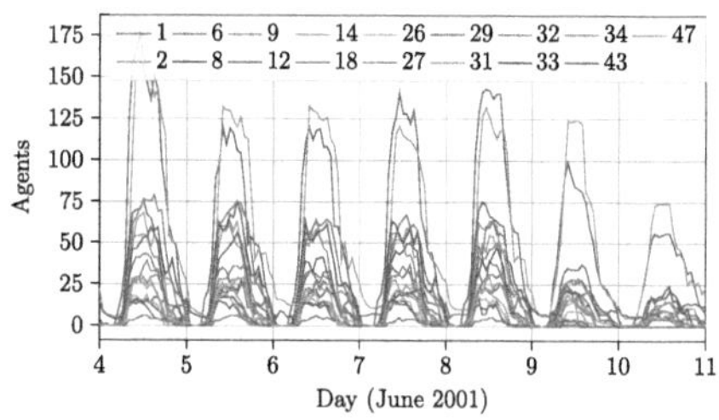

Fig. 4. Number of working agents per group.

UCB–QR Exhibits Little Day-to-Day Fluctuations. Figure 5 shows the average payoff per day. The values are scaled by those of the Oracle policy, i.e., the plot shows $r_{\pi,i}/r_{O,i}$ where $r_{\pi,i}$ is the average payoff for policy π on day i, and O indicates the Oracle policy. The call volume is different for each day, as shown in Fig. 3, with fewer calls on weekends. The payoffs reflect the quality of the customer–server matches; higher values indicate better performance. Observe that UCB–QR performs close to the Oracle across all days. The loss in payoff due to learning θ and estimating λ and μ is $0.7 - 1\%$ on weekdays and $1 - 2\%$ during weekends. The FCFS–ALIS, Random, $\theta\mu$ policies and the policy from the data set obtain lower payoffs and show strong fluctuations over the month in contrast to the stable performance of UCB–QR. Especially on June 25, most policies show a decrease in payoff except for UCB–QR. We inspected the routing rates of all policies and found that exploration of UCB–QR leads to different routing decisions when compared to the Oracle policy, although the overall payoff accumulation is competitive. This showcases the potential of the algorithm to learn and adapt under different load patterns.

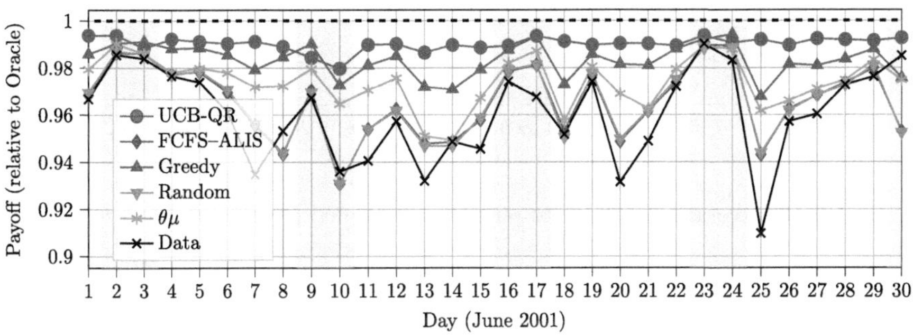

Fig. 5. Average payoff relative to the Oracle policy. The variance is negligible and therefore omitted. Days highlighted in yellow are weekends. (Color figure online)

UCB–QR Consistently Reduces the Optimality Gap. The Random policy performs quite well in terms of payoff and accumulates on average 96.5% of the Oracle payoff. The room for improvement is therefore small: the optimality gap between Random and Oracle is just 3.5%. However, observe that the UCB–QR policy obtains on average 99.0% of the Oracle payoff, closing the optimality gap of the Random policy by approximately 71.4%. The small optimality gap can be explained by the value of the payoff parameter θ (see e.g. Table 2 in Appendix A): the variance of θ is small, especially for type-1 customers while these dominate the call volume.

UCB–QR Outperforms Benchmarks Under High Variance Payoffs. To gain further insight in the payoff accumulation of UCB–QR, we conduct the same experiment using transformed payoffs θ'. We normalize the values to $[0, 1]$ and apply a power transformation to amplify the relative differences: let $\theta'_{ij} = \sqrt{(\theta_{ij} - m_i)/(M_i - m_i)}$, where $m_i := \min_k \theta_{ik}$ and $M_i := \max_k \theta_{ik}$. For example, θ' for June 4, 2001 is shown in Appendix A.

We run the same simulation but now using θ'. Figure 6 shows that UCB–QR outperforms the benchmark policies in terms of payoff: the UCB-QR policy achieves at least 98% of the Oracle payoff while other policies obtain as little as 60% on some days. The ordering of the policies is the same as in Fig. 5, i.e., the Greedy and $\theta\mu$ policies perform similarly and better than the FCFS–ALIS and Random policies. To conclude, UCB–QR achieves overall the best payoff accumulation, and the relative difference in payoff gain depends on θ.

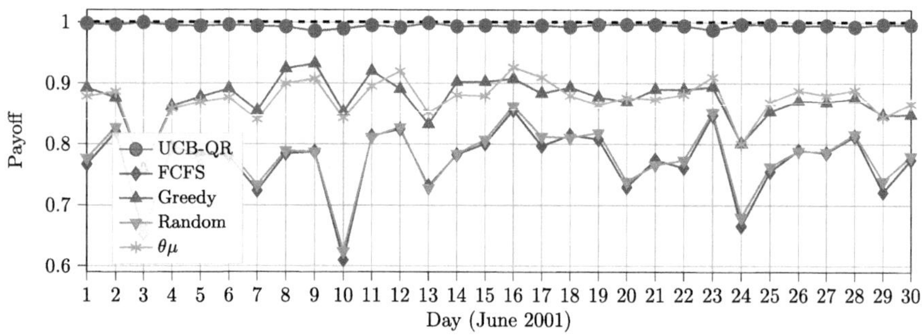

Fig. 6. Average payoff based on the transformed payoff parameter θ'.

UCB–QR Does not Minimize Waiting Times. Figure 7 shows customer waiting times and Fig. 8 shows the average waiting times during office hours (6am-9pm) when applied to the data of June 4, 2001. The policy of the data set shows a peak around midnight, while all other policies maintain more evenly distributed waiting times during the night. Around 6am, the offered load increases and many agents start working. Between 6pm and 9pm the policy from the data set shows another peak, which is handled more smoothly by the Oracle policy and UCB–QR, indicating a better way of adapting to a change in load. The benchmark policies FCFS–ALIS, Greedy, Random, and $\theta\mu$ consistently give low waiting times, which is why the plots are at some places indistinguishable. Overall, waiting times for UCB–QR and the Oracle policy are higher than those of other policies.

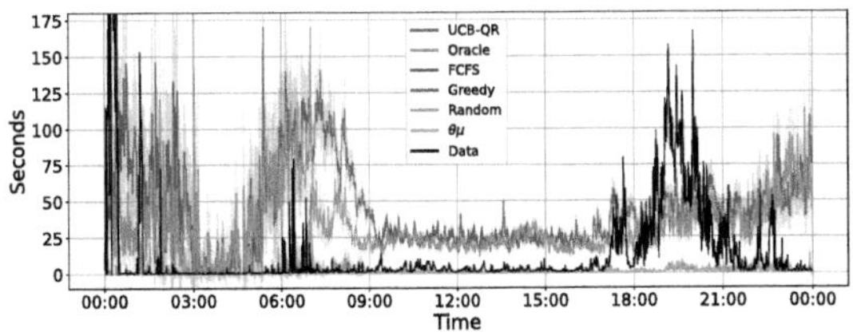

Fig. 7. Average customer waiting times over all types with 95% confidence intervals.

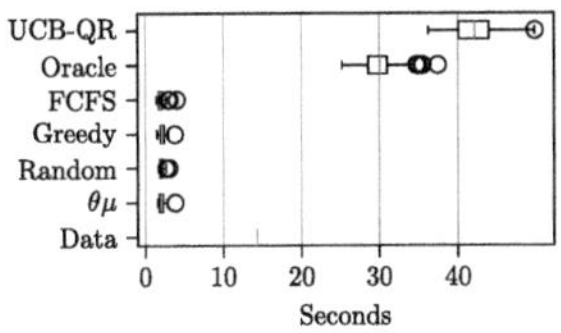

Fig. 8. Average waiting time during office hours.

Computational Complexity of UCB–QR Matches Benchmarks. All simulations were performed on separate threads using an Apple M1 Pro-chip with 8-core CPU. Running a full-day simulation with UCB–QR takes about 20 s. Although this is twice as long as the typical runtime of roughly 10 s for the benchmark policies, the difference is insignificant for a simulation covering 24 h.

3.2 Alternative Routing Rule to Decrease Waiting Times

Recall that we just observed that UCB–QR and the Oracle policy lead to long delays. Routing rule Algorithm 2 is not very adaptive, since customers are assigned to a server (via the server's virtual queue) upon arrival and cannot be routed to another idling server even when the assigned server has a long virtual queue. Moreover, the reshuffling of the virtual queues between episodes (Line 4) can be experienced as unfair by both customers and servers, since service is not FCFS (not even for customers of the same type) nor ALIS.

We may therefore try to construct an improved routing rule with fewer delays, while still routing according to the desired rates described by the LP. Concretely, the empirical routing rates $\mathbb{E}(D_{ij}(t))/t$, where $D_{ij}(t)$ is the number of type-(ij) departures up to time t, should converge to the desired rate x_{ij}. To the best of our knowledge, not many such rules exist in the literature, since routing rates and even stability conditions are generally difficult to determine for arbitrary routing rules for skill-based queues [1,27].

It is more feasible to heuristically justify a routing rule that approximates the desired routing rates. To this end, we propose and test Algorithm 3, inspired by the heuristic Join–the-Shortest–Queue–K (JSQ–K) policy used in [14] (not to be confused with the JSQ–K algorithm of [13]). Consider the bipartite graph $(\mathcal{I} \cup \mathcal{J}, \mathcal{L})$ of customer types $\mathcal{I}$, servers $\mathcal{J}$, and lines $\mathcal{L}$. Let x be a BFS of (1), then lines with $x_{ij} > 0$ induce a spanning forest on $(\mathcal{I} \cup \mathcal{J}, \mathcal{L})$ [14, Proposition 2]; see also [7]. In such a forest, parent and child nodes of servers are queues and *vice versa*. The root of the tree is a server with *slack*: $\sum_{i \in \mathcal{I}} x_{ij}/\mu_{ij} < 1 - \varepsilon$. This is possible because every tree in the spanning forest contains at least one slack server and exactly one slack server if x is non-degenerate [14, Proposition 2]. Algorithm 3 routes based on this spanning forest: upon service completion, a server serves its child queue(s) first, and only if those are empty, its parent queue (if any). Thus, non-slack servers are highly utilized, and the priority rule encourages routing toward the target rates x.

Algorithm 3. Tree-based routing(x, θ, h).

Consider the spanning forest of the bipartite graph $(\mathcal{I} \cup \mathcal{J}, \mathcal{L})$ induced by x.
for time $t = 0, \ldots, h$ **do** ▷ Route customers.
    for each service completion at server j at time t **do**
        if server j has non-empty children queues **then**
            Start service of the FIL customer of the non-empty child queue i that maximizes θ_{ij}.
        else if server j has a non-empty parent queue i **then**
            Start service of the FIL customer of the parent queue.
        else
            Server j remains idle.
        end if
    end for
    for each arrival of a type-i customer at time t **do**
        if queue i has idling children servers in the spanning forest **then**
            Start service at the idle child server j that maximizes θ_{ij}.
        else if the parent server of queue i is idle **then**
            Start service at the parent server.
        else
            Customer joins queue i.
        end if
    end for
end for

Minimal Payoff Loss from Heuristic Routing Rule. We compare UCB–QR with an adapted version, called UCB–QR–Tree, which uses Algorithm 3 instead of Algorithm 2. We found that the empirical routing volumes of customers to servers for UCB–QR–Tree are similar to those of UCB–QR, hence the payoff is minimally affected; see Fig. 9. By construction, we can intuitively argue that within each episode the empirical routing rates of Algorithm 3 should approximate their target x. Yet, as Remark 1 shows, the empirical rates $\mathbb{E}(D_{ij}(t))/t$ converge only approximately to x_{ij}. A theoretical analysis of the empirical routing rates remains open for future work. For a practical implementation, however, minor deviations have little impact on performance measures including payoff and waiting time, especially due to inherent noise in arrival and service rate estimators.

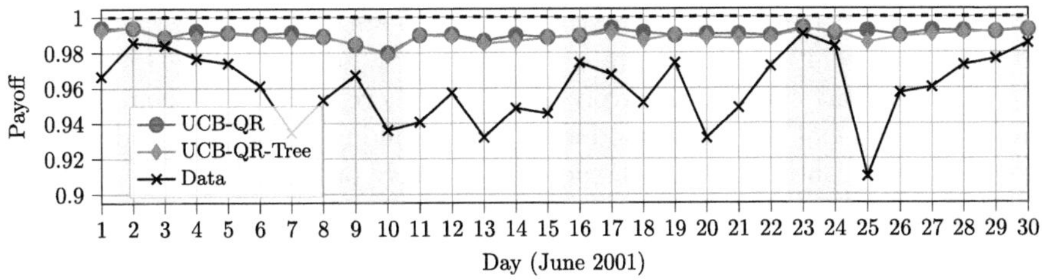

Fig. 9. Average payoff for the UCB–QR and UCB–QR–Tree policies.

Remark 1. We illustrate Algorithm 3 on the queueing system in Fig. 10 with the following non-degenerate BFS x^ε of (1): $x^\varepsilon_{11} = 1 - \varepsilon, x^\varepsilon_{12} = 2 + \varepsilon, x^\varepsilon_{22} = 3 - 6\varepsilon, x^\varepsilon_{23} = 4 + 6\varepsilon, x^\varepsilon_{33} = 5$.
We apply Algorithm 3 to route customers according to rates x^ε. Observe in Fig. 11 that the empirical routing rates have converged numerically to approximately $D_{11}(t)/t \approx 0.863, D_{12}(t)/t \approx 2.153, D_{22}(t)/t \approx 2.649, D_{23}(t)/t \approx 4.338, D_{33}(t)/t \approx 5$. There does not exist a value of $\varepsilon > 0$ such that the empirical routing rates agree with the analytical solution x^ε. Hence, the routing rates converge approximately to the target x^ε, but not exactly.

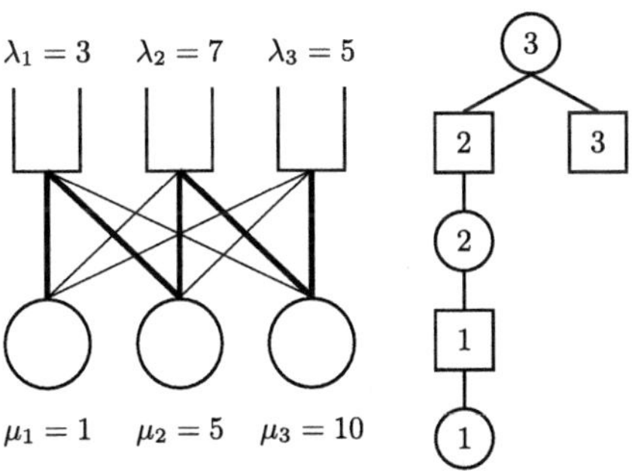

Fig. 10. Queueing system with Poisson arrivals and exponential service times (left), where the lines with non-zero mass in x^ε are shown in bold, and the spanning forest induced by x^ε (right), with customer types represented by squares and servers by circles.

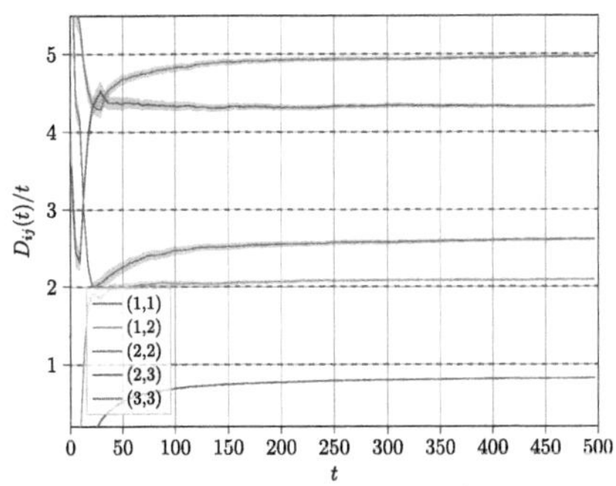

Fig. 11. Empirical routing rates $D_{ij}(t)/t$ over time t for the different lines (ij), based on 100 independent simulations with $h = 10$.

UCB–QR–Tree Significantly Reduces Waiting Times. In Fig. 12a, UCB–QR–Tree achieves waiting times almost as low as those of FCFS–ALIS. On the depicted day, the load is relatively low since there are many agents at work while the total call volume is moderate for a Monday (see Figs. 3 and 4). However, on days with a higher load, the average delay of UCB–QR–Tree is slightly worse than FCFS–ALIS. It still outperforms UCB–QR as shown in Fig. 12b.

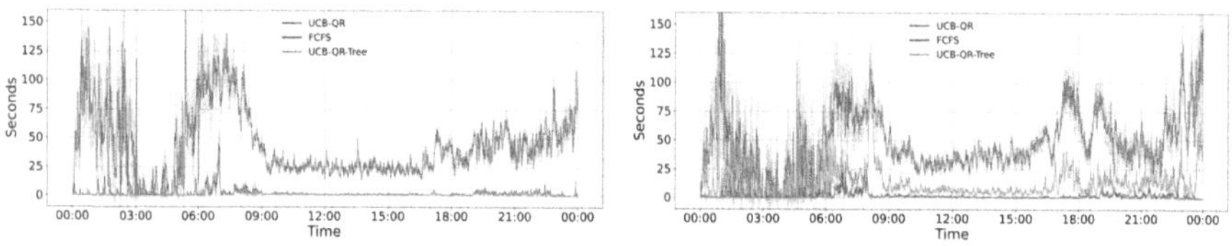

(a) June 4, 2001. (b) June 5, 2001.

Fig. 12. Average customer waiting time for the UCB–QR and UCB–QR–Tree policies.

Similar Runtimes for UCB–QR and UCB–QR–Tree. The computational complexity of UCB–QR–Tree is lower than UCB–QR, since virtual queues and reshuffling are omitted. However, at the start of each episode, the spanning forest must be determined based on the LP maximizer. The runtimes were consequently not substantially affected in our specific experiments.

In conclusion, Algorithm 3 is an alternative to Algorithm 2 for practical applications where exact convergence to target routing rates is not crucial while low waiting times are. The UCB–QR–Tree policy still accumulates high payoff similar to UCB–QR while waiting times are reduced significantly. It additionally promotes customer fairness in the sense of FCFS service for customers of the same type.

3.3 Combining Different Performance Objectives

UCB–QR is designed to maximize the total payoff, as reflected in objective (1a). In practice, however, service system management typically accounts for multiple performance criteria simultaneously. By expressing a performance measure in terms of x_{ij}, $(ij) \in \mathcal{L}$, and adding it to the objective function or constraint set of (1), our algorithm can be extended to integrate such objectives. Examples include waiting time, server load, penalty for deviation from a fixed set of routing rates, or encouraging dense or sparse routing. We illustrate this next using an example that balances payoff maximization and server fairness.

To balance payoff maximization and server fairness, we adapt the objective function of the LP (1); see optimization problem (8). Here, $\rho_j := \sum_{i \in \mathcal{I}} x_{ij}/\mu_{ij}$ represents the load of server j, and the penalty terms $\rho_j - \bar{\rho}$ penalize deviation from the mean $\bar{\rho} := \sum_{j \in \mathcal{J}} \rho_j / |\mathcal{J}|$. The parameter $\gamma \in \mathbb{R}$ controls the balance between server fairness and payoff maximization: larger γ gives more weight to server fairness at the cost of loss in payoff. Note that Algorithm 1 can simply be applied with this alternative optimization problem (8) replacing LP (1). For our simulation results next, we used the convex solver MOSEK [22].

$$\text{OPT}(\lambda, \mu, \theta, \varepsilon, \gamma): \quad \max_{x \geq 0} \sum_{(ij) \in \mathcal{L}} \theta_{ij} x_{ij} - \gamma \sum_{j \in \mathcal{J}} (\rho_j - \bar{\rho})^2, \quad \text{s.t. (1b).} \tag{8}$$

Load Balancing Decreases Waiting Times with Minimal Payoff Loss. Observe in Fig. 13 that the server loads become more concentrated as γ increases. As a result, the variance in load per server also decreases. Here, $\gamma = 0$ represents the original LP (1). This redistribution of work also affects customer waiting times: when more servers are actively involved in processing customers, the system is less likely to develop long queues at critically loaded servers. This in turn reduces the overall waiting time as γ increases. However, because customers are not always matched to their highest payoff server, the total accumulated payoff is slightly lower. This trade–off is illustrated in Fig. 14, which shows how increasing γ leads to shorter waiting times with only a modest decline in total payoff.

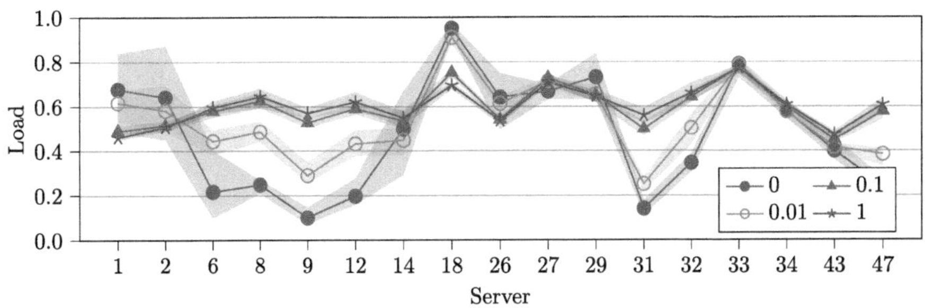

Fig. 13. Empirical server loads during office hours for UCB–QR with objective function (8) for different values of γ when applied to the data of June 4, 2001.

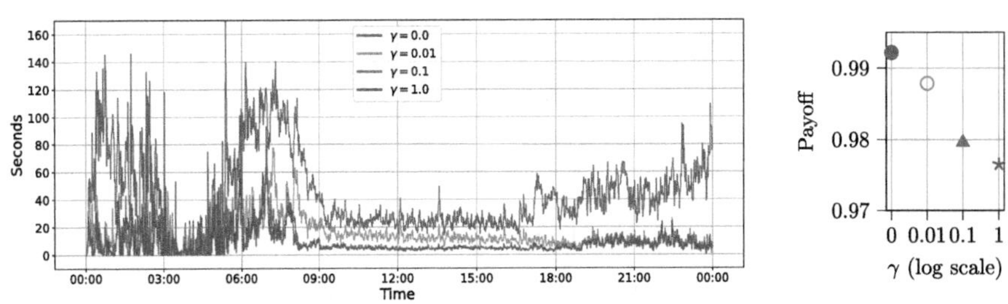

Fig. 14. Average customer waiting time and average payoff of UCB–QR with objective function (8) for different values of γ when applied to the data of June 4, 2001.

3.4 Resilience in Bursty Scenarios

We consider December 31, 2001, a day with many arrivals and few available agents. To mimic three customer surges during office hours, we add additional arrivals: 2,000 type-2 customers between 10:00–10:10am, 2,000 type-3 customers between 11:00–11:10am, and 2,000 type-5 customers between 12:00–12:10pm. The resulting bursty process is shown in Fig. 15. As UCB–QR can yield high waiting times, we only test UCB–QR–Tree in this experiment.

Delayed Recovery of UCB–QR–Tree After Customer Surges. All policies exhibit waiting times peaks after the surges; see Fig. 16. The benchmarks FCFS–ALIS, Greedy, Random, and $\theta\mu$ recover by about 12:30pm, while UCB–QR–Tree shows the highest peak and only returns to pre-surge levels around 3pm. This delay arises because decisions depend only on current episode estimators of arrival and service rates, ignoring customers already waiting. Since the surges occur in a small time interval, the arrival rate estimators recover quickly, and the routing rule is chosen that optimizes the future customer arrivals, not the backlog. Still, cumulative payoff of all policies is similar, UCB–QR–Tree attains the highest (99.1% of Oracle), slightly above the Greedy (98.8%) and $\theta\mu$ (98.1%) policies.

We conclude that UCB–QR–Tree (and similarly UCB–QR) is not yet well-suited to handle bursty customer arrival processes, and that further research is required. To address this, the episode length can be reduced or the values of α and β in the arrival rate estimators (2) can be adjusted to make the routing algorithm more responsive to such surges. Alternatively, the LP (1) can be adapted to account for the current queue lengths.

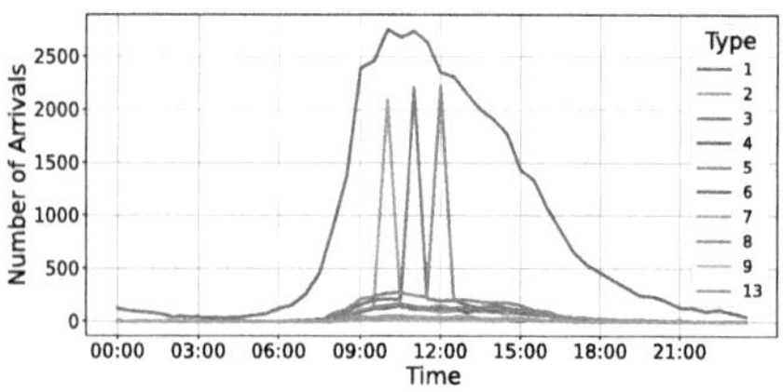

Fig. 15. Customer arrivals with artificial bursty arrivals for December 31, 2001.

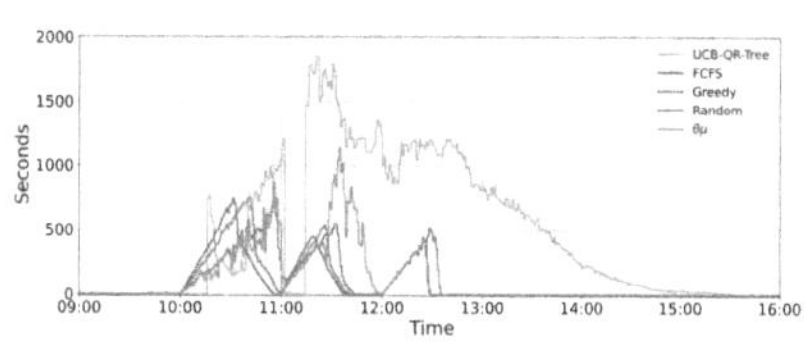

Fig. 16. Average customer waiting time when applied to the bursty arrival process on December 31, 2001.

3.5 Robustness Against Estimation Errors

We analyze the sensitivity of UCB–QR to errors in arrival and service rate estimation. To this end, we compare four variations of Algorithm 1. The algorithms follow the same steps as described in Algorithm 1, but differ in the knowledge of system parameters.

$(\hat{\theta}, \hat{\lambda}, \hat{\mu})$ UCB–QR, which uses UCB estimators $\hat{\theta}$, estimators $\hat{\lambda}$ in (2) for the arrival rates, and empirical estimators $\hat{\mu}$ in (3) for the service rates.
(θ, λ, μ) Oracle, which uses the true values θ, λ, μ.
$(\hat{\theta}, \hat{\lambda}, \mu)$ UCB–QR-μ, which uses estimators $\hat{\theta}$ and $\hat{\lambda}$, but the true service rates μ.
$(\hat{\theta}, \lambda, \hat{\mu})$ UCB–QR-λ, which uses estimators $\hat{\theta}$ and $\hat{\mu}$ but the true arrival rates λ.

Estimation Error in Arrival and Service Rates has Little Impact. We found that both UCB–QR-μ and UCB–QR-λ perform close to UCB–QR in terms of payoff accumulation. By granting access to the true arrival rate or service rate, the cumulative payoff is only increased in the order of 0.1%. Next to that, the average waiting times are comparable, as shown in Fig. 17. We conclude that the algorithm's performance can be improved only slightly by reducing the estimation errors in the arrival and service rates.

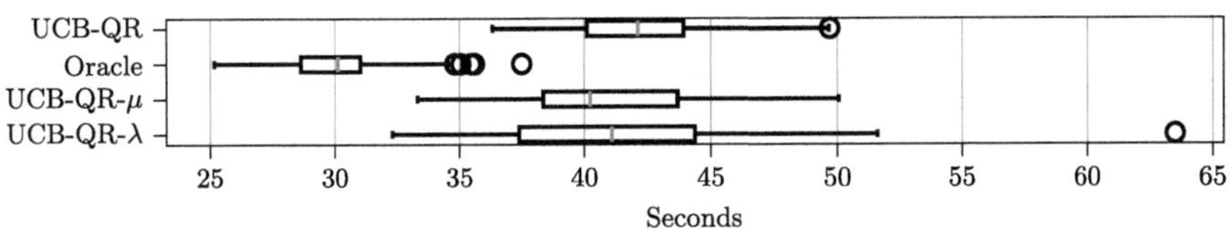

Fig. 17. Average waiting time during office hours for different variants of UCB–QR relying on different system information when applied to the data of June 4, 2001.

3.6 Balancing Reactivity and Complexity

We analyze the sensitivity of UCB–QR to the episode length h. Shorter episodes accelerate learning of payoff parameters θ and adaptation to arrival rate changes, but increase complexity since (1) is solved and queues are reshuffled each episode.

Large h Leads to Significant Delays. As seen in Table 1, simulation runtimes stabilize for $h > 10$ minutes. This shows that episode updates do not dominate computational complexity. Moreover, the cumulative payoff is insensitive to h. The average waiting time in Fig. 18 increases with the value of h. Especially the morning and evening hours are chaotic with large peaks in waiting times, since the algorithm is not able to pick up changes in traffic volume adequately fast.

A practical choice of h should reflect the timescale at which arrival rates vary. In our data, call volumes show fluctuations within 10–15 minutes on a typical day, while remaining approximately stationary over shorter intervals. In other operational settings, h could be tuned automatically. For example, by selecting the smallest h for which the error of Holt's model remains below a threshold.

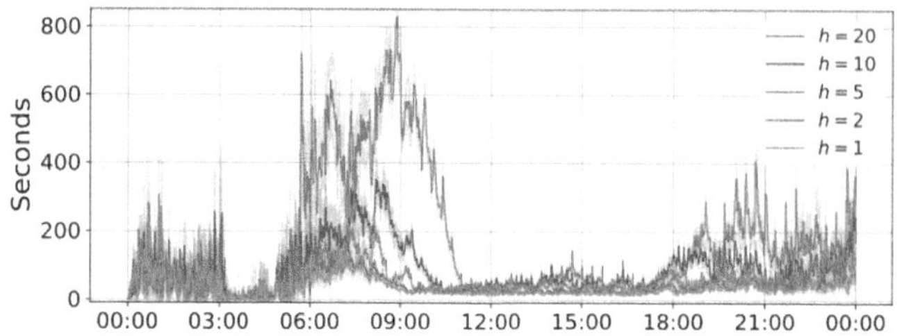

Fig. 18. Average customer waiting time of UCB–QR for different h (min).

Table 1. Average runtime (s) and payoff of UCB–QR for different h.

h	Time	Payoff
1	48	0.9914
2	30	0.9922
5	20	0.9931
10	17	0.9934
20	17	0.9922

Conclusion. We demonstrated that UCB–QR effectively achieves high payoff in realistic, time-varying environments while learning payoff parameters. We extended the algorithm to reduce customer delays and allow for multi-objective optimization. Future work includes improving robustness to customer surges, and extending the approach to settings like cloud networks.

Acknowledgments. This work is part of *Valuable AI*, a research collaboration between the Eindhoven University of Technology and the Koninklijke KPN N.V. Parts of this research have been funded by the EAISI's IMPULS program, and by Holland High Tech — TKI HTSM via the PPS allowance scheme for public-private partnerships.

A Payoff Parameters

Tables 2 and 3 show the true payoff parameter θ and the transformed value θ', respectively.

Table 2. Payoff parameter θ_{ij} for 4 June, 2001.

j	i									
	1	2	3	4	5	6	7	8	9	14
1	0.84									
2	0.84	0.82	0.93					0.67		
6	0.81		1.00							
8	0.84					0.71				
9	0.87		0.89				0.97			
12	0.85	0.89	0.84					0.61		
14	0.80								0.69	
18		0.86								
26			0.90							
27		1.00	0.90	1.00						
29			0.91	0.91						
31	0.88				0.84					
32					0.84	0.69			0.90	
33						0.86				
34								0.78		
43										0.95
47	0.92									0.96
Var	0.001	0.006	0.002	0.004	0	0.009	0	0.007	0.022	0

Table 3. Transformed payoff θ'_{ij} for 4 June, 2001.

j	i									
	1	2	3	4	5	6	7	8	9	14
1	0.60									
2	0.59	0.00	0.76					0.59		
6	0.37		1.00							
8	0.58					0.40				
9	0.76		0.54				0.98			
12	0.69	0.61	0.00					0.00		
14	0.00								0.00	
18		0.45								
26			0.61							
27		1.00	0.58	1.00						
29			0.65	0.00						
31	0.84				1.00					
32					0.00	0.00			1.00	
33						1.00				
34								1.00		
43										0.00
47	1.00									1.00
Var	0.08	0.17	0.09	0.25	0.25	0.25	0	0.25	0.25	0.25

References

1. Adan, I., Weiss, G.: Exact FCFS matching rates for two infinite multitype sequences. Oper. Res. **60**(2), 475–489 (2012). https://doi.org/10.1287/opre.1110.1027
2. Adan, I., Weiss, G.: A skill-based parallel service system under FCFS-ALIS – steady state, overloads, and abandonments. Stochastic Syst. **4**(1), 250–299 (2014). https://doi.org/10.1214/13-ssy117
3. Aktekin, T., Soyer, R.: Call center arrival modeling: a Bayesian state-space approach. Nav. Res. Logist. **58**(1), 28–42 (2011). https://doi.org/10.1002/nav.20436
4. Ali Rezaee, A., Akbari, M.: A multi-channel queue model to optimize service level and staff availability in bank industry. RAIRO - Oper. Res. **59**, 219–237 (2024)
5. Auer, P., Cesa-Bianchi, N., Fischer, P.: Finite-time analysis of the multiarmed bandit problem. Mach. Learn. **47**(2–3), 235–256 (2002). https://doi.org/10.1023/A:1013689704352
6. Bertsimas, D., Doan, X.V.: Robust and data-driven approaches to call centers. Eur. J. Oper. Res. **207**(2), 1072–1085 (2010). https://doi.org/10.1016/j.ejor.2010.05.040
7. Bertsimas, D., Tsitsiklis, J.N.: Introduction to Linear Optimization. Athena Scientific, Belmont, MA (1997)
8. Chen, J., Dong, J., Shi, P.: A survey on skill-based routing with applications to service operations management. Queueing Syst. **96**(1-2), 53–82 (2020). https://doi.org/10.1007/s11134-020-09669-5
9. Cildoz, M., Ibarra, A., Mallor, F.: Accumulating priority queues versus pure priority queues for managing patients in emergency departments. Oper. Res. Health Care **23**, 100224 (2019). https://doi.org/10.1016/j.orhc.2019.100224
10. Cohen, J.E., Kelly, F.P.: Reversibility and Stochastic Networks (1981). https://doi.org/10.2307/1268051
11. Comte, C., Jonckheere, M., Sanders, J., Senen–Cerda, A.: Score-aware policy-gradient methods and performance guarantees using local lyapunov conditions: applications to product-form stochastic networks and queueing systems. ArXiv: 2312.02804 (2023)
12. Dai, J.G., Gluzman, M.: Queueing network controls via deep reinforcement learning. Stochastic Syst. **12**(1), 30–67 (2022). https://doi.org/10.1287/stsy.2021.0081
13. Ephremides, A., Varaiya, P., Walrand, J.: A simple dynamic routing problem. IEEE Trans. Autom. Control **25**(4), 690–693 (1980). https://doi.org/10.1109/TAC.1980.1102445
14. Fu, X., Modiano, E.: Joint learning and control in stochastic queueing networks with unknown utilities. In: Proceedings of the ACM on Measurement and Analysis of Computing Systems **6**(3) (2022). https://doi.org/10.1145/3570619
15. Hyndman, R.J., Athanasopoulos, G.: Forecasting: Principles and Practice. OTexts, Melbourne (2021)
16. van Kempen, S., Sanders, J., Sloothaak, F., Wolf, M.G.: Learning payoffs while routing in skill-based queues (2024)
17. Krishnasamy, S., Arapostathis, A., Johari, R., Shakkottai, S.: On learning the $c\mu$ rule in single and parallel server networks. In: 2018 56th Annual Allerton Conference on Communication, Control, and Computing, Allerton 2018, pp. 153–154 (2018). https://doi.org/10.1109/ALLERTON.2018.8636001
18. Larrnaaga, M., Ayesta, U., Verloop, I.M.: Dynamic control of birth-and-death restless bandits: application to resource-allocation problems. IEEE/ACM Trans. Netw. **24**(6), 3812–3825 (2016). https://doi.org/10.1109/TNET.2016.2562564

19. Lattimore, T., Szepesvári, C.: Bandit Algorithms. Cambridge University Press, Cambridge (2020). https://doi.org/10.1017/9781108571401
20. Liang, S., Yang, Z., Jin, F., Chen, Y.: Data centers job scheduling with deep reinforcement learning. In: Lauw, H.W., Wong, R.C.-W., Ntoulas, A., Lim, E.-P., Ng, S.-K., Pan, S.J. (eds.) PAKDD 2020. LNCS (LNAI), vol. 12085, pp. 906–917. Springer, Cham (2020). https://doi.org/10.1007/978-3-030-47436-2_68
21. Long, Z., Zhang, H., Zhang, J., Zhang, Z.G.: The generalized c/μ rule for queues with heterogeneous server pools. Oper. Res. **72**(6) (2023). https://doi.org/10.1287/opre.2023.2472
22. MOSEK ApS: MOSEK optimizer API for Python (2023). https://www.mosek.com
23. Shah, V., Gulikers, L., Massoulié, L., Vojnović, M.: Adaptive matching for expert systems with uncertain task types. Oper. Res. **68**(5), 1403–1424 (2020). https://doi.org/10.1287/opre.2019.1954
24. Smith, W.E.: Various optimizers for single-stage production. Naval Res. Logist. Quart. **3**, 59–66 (1956)
25. Tassiulas, L., Ephremides, A.: Stability properties of constrained queueing systems and scheduling policies for maximum throughput in multihop radio networks. IEEE Trans. Autom. Control **37**(12), 1936–1948 (2002). https://doi.org/10.1109/9.182479
26. Tessler, C., et al.: Reinforcement learning for datacenter congestion control. SIGMETRICS Perform. Eval. Rev. **49**(2), 43–46 (2022)
27. Weiss, G.: Scheduling and Control of Queueing Networks. Cambridge University Press, Cambridge (2021)
28. Xia, L., Zhang, Z.G., Li, Q.L.: A c/μ-rule for job assignment in heterogeneous group-server queues. Prod. Oper. Manag. **31**(3), 1191–1215 (2022). https://doi.org/10.1111/poms.13605
29. Zhong, Y., Birge, J.R., Ward, A.: Learning the scheduling policy in time-varying multiclass many server queues with abandonment. SSRN Electron. J. (2022). https://doi.org/10.2139/ssrn.4090021

Rewriting for Efficient Multiformalism Performance Modeling of a Smart City Edge Server

Lorenzo Capra[1], Marco Gribaudo[3], Mauro Iacono[2], and Michele Mastroianni[4(✉)]

[1] Dip. di Informatica, Università degli Studi di Milano, via Celoria 18, 20133 Milano, Italy
capra@di.unimi.it

[2] Dip. di Matematica e Fisica, Università degli Studi della Campania"L. Vanvitelli", viale Lincoln 5, 81100 Caserta, Italy
mauro.iacono@unicampania.it

[3] Dip. di Elettronica, Informatica e Bioingegneria Politecnico di Milano, via Ponzio 51, 20133 Milano, Italy
marco.gribaudo@polimi.it

[4] Dip. di Scienze Agrarie, Alimenti, Risorse Naturali e Ingegneria, Via A. Gramsci 89/91, 71122 Foggia, Italy
michele.mastroianni@unifg.it

https://di.unimi.it, https://www.matfis.unicampania.it, https://www.deib.polimi.it/ita/home, https://www.agraria.unifg.it/

Abstract. Performance modeling of reconfigurable architectures may challenge well established methods, such as Petri nets and queuing networks: this may limit their applicability and the consequent advantages. These issues may be mitigated by adopting a rewriting approach, in which the model complexity is reduced by adapting the model whenever a reconfiguration occurs in the system. In this paper, we apply a multiformalism modeling approach based on rewriting to the performance evaluation of a reconfigurable and scalable edge server that monitors a portion of a smart city, a crucial subsystem from a national, EU funded research project (This research has been partially funded by MUR PRIN PNRR 2022 PaB-PIF research project, grant number P20227W8ZC, and by *Shift2SDV*, GA 101194245 - NextGenerationEU - ChipsJU 2024 1-IA-Topic 3 - MIMIT DM 16/12/2022 N. 186485 PNRR M4C2I2.2). The proposed case study shows the effectiveness of the approach.

Keywords: Edge computing · smart city · performance evaluation · Petri nets · model rewriting

1 Introduction

Smart cities pose interesting design challenges in terms of the complexity of both the information streams and the architecture of the system-of-systems needed

A. Remke et al. (Eds.): Valuetools 2025, LNICST 691, pp. 275–298, 2027.
https://doi.org/10.1007/978-3-032-23901-3_17

to implement and coordinate. Monitoring and information acquisition coverage must be continuous, complete, and inexpensive, both with reference to apparel and energy consumption: this is a requirement that requires a correct balance since the first phases of the design cycle. Component systems should be carefully designed to allow the overall system-of-system to be efficient under all profiles.

The design of complex systems relies on models to control the process and support decisions. Performance models are a well established tool, useful for both preliminary evaluation and successive verification of design assumptions and decisions. Among the most common techniques adopted in performance evaluation are the ones based on the use of Petri nets (in any of the many variants, according to specific needs) and queuing networks, typically suitable to evaluate the effects of design decisions about the consequences of functional specifications on some non-functional specifications. While the Petri net family allows modeling most of the behavioral aspects of a system, they suffer from the state-space explosion problem, which limits the possibility of applying those to complex or detailed designs without a very deep expertise on them. Several mitigation strategies exist in the literature for this problem, ranging from clever use of modularization of models with evaluation by parts [23], to folding by means of "colors" [14], to advanced multiformalism modeling [3], to resorting to simulation [6] instead of analytical model evaluation techniques. Non-trivial models may benefit of both the features and advantages of Petri nets and queuing networks combined, but, as for complex Petri nets models, also multiformalism models require a very deep expertise.

In this paper, we demonstrate the use of model rewriting, in combination with modularity, to allow an easier approach to complex models design of reconfigurable systems, to allow the use of adaptive multiformalism modeling solutions. Model rewriting is applied to performance evaluation of a reconfigurable edge computing node in charge of storing in a blockchain all information obtained by monitoring the traffic and the state of an area of a smart city, to support decisions in the architectural design of the node, which must operate adapting its configuration to the actual workload, generally depending on vehicular and pedestrian traffic in the monitored area, also in view of successive optimization of energy consumption. Making a step further with respect to our previous methodological proposals, the case study presented here is part of the preliminary results of a national, EU funded research project, included in the design of a system presented in [11], and allowed to explore performance and energy aspects of the main portion of the data acquisition interface of the system, which is meant to be spatially distributed over a whole city settlement.

This paper is organized as follows: Sect. 2 provides background and related work; Sect. 3 describes the application scenario; Sect. 4 presents the analysis of the proposed case study; Sect. 5 describes the use of rewriting in the context of multiformalism modeling for performance evaluation, with a hands-on approach based on the case study, and results; Sect. 6 presents the analysis of the evaluation of the case study to demonstrate the proposed approach; the conclusions close the article.

2 Background and Related Work

2.1 Smart Cities

The constant and continuous increase in population in cities led to the need to go further with respect to informed policy design, towards the definition of a paradigm that allows administrators and policy makers to close a feedback loop on policies through continuous observation of cities, defining the concept of smart city [30]. In smart cities, data are continuously collected to monitor the state of the affairs on a local and global scale, providing the means to observe the effect of decisions and define adaptive solutions and dynamic contexts to adapt to traffic, people behavior, events, transportation demand or to anticipate needs. ICT is one of the main resources that allow these possibilities [1], with a key role played by the Internet of Things (IoT) and edge computing [21,24].

The fact that monitoring data include explicit or implicit information about habits, movements, gatherings, and visits of people makes the problem subject to privacy issues [28]. However, this information is of paramount importance for improving safety, producing deterrence against law infringement, and protecting people, so it must be collected and kept immutable to turn it into means of proof, in addition to its importance for policy verification. Notwithstanding the known tension between privacy regulations (in UE, GDPR) and blockchain [7], blockchain features (persistence, tamper-resilience, dependability, trustability) may be a good solution to guaranty immutability of collected data [26,31] together with compliance with privacy regulations [10]. Of course, performance issues should be carefully considered [18].

2.2 Multiformalism Modeling

The multiformalism modeling approach [5,19,23,27,32,33] aims to dominate complexity by giving the possibility of using the most suitable modeling formalism for each component of a system while guaranteeing the overall coherence of the model of a system and exploiting modularity and formalism features to properly manage the evaluation process (for example, by adopting *multisolution*). The perspective on multiformalism in this work is based on OsMoSys [22] and SIMTHESys [3,25], which respectively use the orchestration of a workflow [29] (properly exploiting external independent tools to evaluate submodels using different formalisms), and allow the definition of custom formalisms through formalism elements specific behavior generating a specific tool for the evaluation. In [4] an overall view of the main issues of these tools is presented.

The potential of rewriting engines in multiformalism modeling has been preliminarily explored in [2] and [16]. In detail, the use of rewriting engines opens the possibility for the implementation of dynamic modification of submodels structure (OsMoSys *late binding* feature, enabled by workflow execution features) into SIMTHESys custom generated multiformalism solvers, by enabling *solution-time* rewriting of the actual model, to provide the basis for a more manageable and efficient solution process while keeping the complexity of the process limited and the extent of submodels lower, which result in an easier model design process, more accessible to a wider practitioners' audience. The contribution of rewriting engines is detailed in Sect. 5, which also contextualizes the adopted solution: to ease reading, a case study is introduced to use related submodels as examples to introduce the technique as well.

3 The Application Scenario

In a smart city, an edge server receives information from sensors of various nature (smart road side, cameras, vehicular black boxes, autonomous cars, etc.) which must be collected, processed, and stored in a blockchain [12]. Sources differ in nature (message, streams, burst) and the most of them generate data traffic with variable rates (smart road side sensors have a minimal data transmission rate which is increased according to vehicular traffic, cars join and depart the area controlled by the edge server and move at different speeds, there can be a raise of the rate of sensing frequency on demand of the authority because of specific events, etc.), and the vehicular traffic variates according to time of the day and traffic jams. The workload of the edge server is consequently variable.

The server has a data acquisition subsystem, a computing subsystem, a network interface to interact with the rest of the smart city information management system of which it is part, and a backup radio module, a temporary storage subsystem. The computing subsystem is equipped with a processor with multiple cores, which are activated or deactivated and modulated according to the workload, as it performs the data preprocessing and cleaning section and, periodically or when a given amount of data is ready to be stored, aggregates data into packets and interacts with the blockchain subsystem through the network interface to permanently store data. Blockchain operations may be suspended for a short time if network is not available or because of power outages, to maximize the duration of the backup power source, but, after a watchdog timer expires or data storage is full beyond a threshold, the backup radio module is activated, and blockchain operations are anyway performed, and if data storage triggered the operation, pending buffered data are processed and packed.

The edge server must operate in each instant with the minimum use of resources and energy, so that the backup radio module is generally off, data storage is not used, and the minimum required CPU are used at the lowest power level possible, that is, in a way that when 80% utilization of the CPU is reached, it increases the frequency to the maximum level or another CPU is activated, while when utilization falls down to 50% the immediately lower performance configuration is restored.

A performance model of the edge server is needed that allows one to monitor components utilization and overall energy consumption to understand the actual operating conditions, considering all adaptation mechanisms and scenario variability.

4 Case Study

The edge server is logically structured as in Fig. 1. The whole system behavior, technically equipped as described in Appendix A , is represented using a state diagram shown in Fig. 2. The states L_0,...,L_3 represent the behavior of the system at increasing load level. The transition rate from state L_i to L_j is denoted by q_{ij}. The states are detailed in the following:

- L0: in this state, the Buffer is active (it is the only state in which it is active), there is only 1 core active in the CPU, the CPU performs both computation and data encryption, and the only active network is the slow rate (A interface); The presence of the buffer is motivated by the blockchain, since this technique works best when a large amount has to be processed, rather than in small sets.
- L1: in this state there are 3 active CPU cores, the CPU performs both computation and data encryption, and the active network is the faster one (B);
- L2: in this state there are 6 active CPU cores and the network interfaces are all active (A+B), the CPU performs only computation, 1 of the GPU boards is active and performs data encryption;
- L3: in this state all the 8 CPU cores are active, both GPUs are active performing encryption, both network interfaces are active (A+B), and the Storage is active (this is the only state in which the Storage is active).

Figure 1 depicts the overall organization of the processing, in terms of functional blocks of the system, which are assigned to hardware components in a different way according to the operating conditions of the edge node. The transitions allowed between operating conditions are shown in Fig. 2, together with a summary of the active hardware components in each condition.

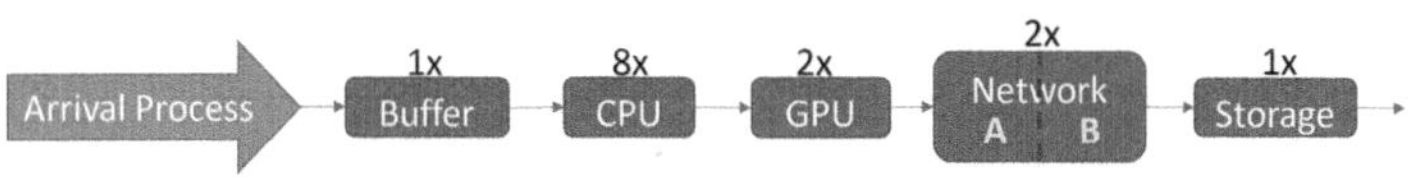

Fig. 1. The model of the considered scenario.

According to the chosen modeling approach, for each block, different submodels are actually used, depending on the operational condition. In the figures, dashed arcs are marking dependent arcs.

Figure 3a) presents the two related alternating submodels. When buffer is not included in the operational condition, this submodel is just absent (lower part of the figure); otherwise, the behavior of the buffer is modeled by means of the Petri net in the upper part of the figure. Incoming data packets are buffered in place with a n label, until the K packets needed to constitute a blockchain payload have been collected (enabling the transition $t_{collect}$) or until a timeout (represented by the timed transition $T_{timeout}$) is reached that allows tho keep the

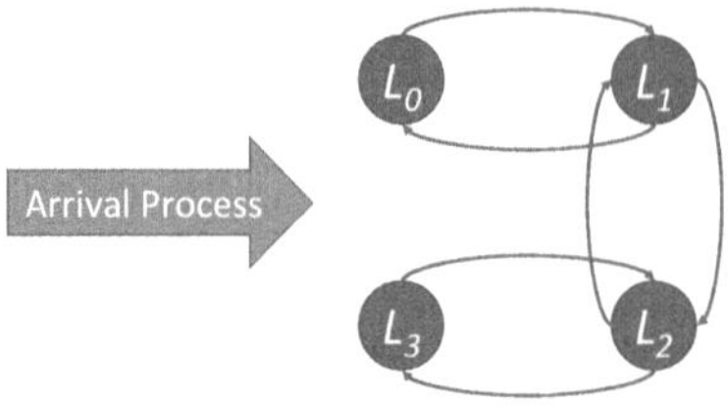

	Buf	CPU	GPU	Net	Stor
L_0	1	1	0	A	0
L_1	0	3	0	B	0
L_2	0	6	1	A+B	0
L_3	0	8	2	A+B	1

Fig. 2. The arrival process definition, and the corresponding configurations.

pace with the needs for blockchain synchronization. In both cases, the collected data packets are grouped (place with a label m) and ready to move to the CPU (as represented by the transition $t_{continue}$). Note the use of marking-dependent "flush" edges to simplify the description of the Net.

Figure 3b) presents two related alternative submodels, the second of which is actually a parametric representation, for the sake of space. In the upper part of the figure, the CPU is represented by a single queue CPU_1; in the lower part, the submodel, parametric with parameter N, represents all operating conditions in which N cores are active, with $N > 1$. In analogy to the previous case, each core is represented by a queue CPU_i $(1 \leq i \leq N)$, and incoming data packets are processed by the N cores, to which they are routed at arrival using a Join the Shortest Queue (element JSQ) allocation algorithm.

Figure 3c) presents two related alternating submodels to model GPU operations in the operational conditions in which the GPU is active, analogous to the submodels presented for the CPU component. Please note that, when the GPU is used, the demand of the CPU reduces accordingly.

Figure 3d) presents three related alternate submodels to model the operational conditions in which only the A module is used (upper part, queue Net_A), only the B module is used (middle part, queue Net_B) and both A and B modules are used (analogous to the 2 GPUs submodel).

Finally, Fig. 3e) presents two related alternate submodels to model operational conditions in which storage is not or is active: in the first case (upper part of the figure) the submodel is not present, while in the second it is represented by a queue $Storage_1$.

5 Using `Maude` as a framework for reconfigurable multi-formalism models

In this section, we discuss the use of `Maude` [20] (and its runtime support) as a rewriting engine for multi-formalism models. The advantages of this choice are multiple: flexibility and modularity of the modeling, efficiency, soundness, ease of integration with existing tools, and upgrade. We inherit the `Maude` facilities for formal verification; in addition, we can exploit a new quantitative analysis capability based on the association of a Markov process to `Maude` executable modules, introduced in [15,17] for rewritable SPN and fully developed in [13].

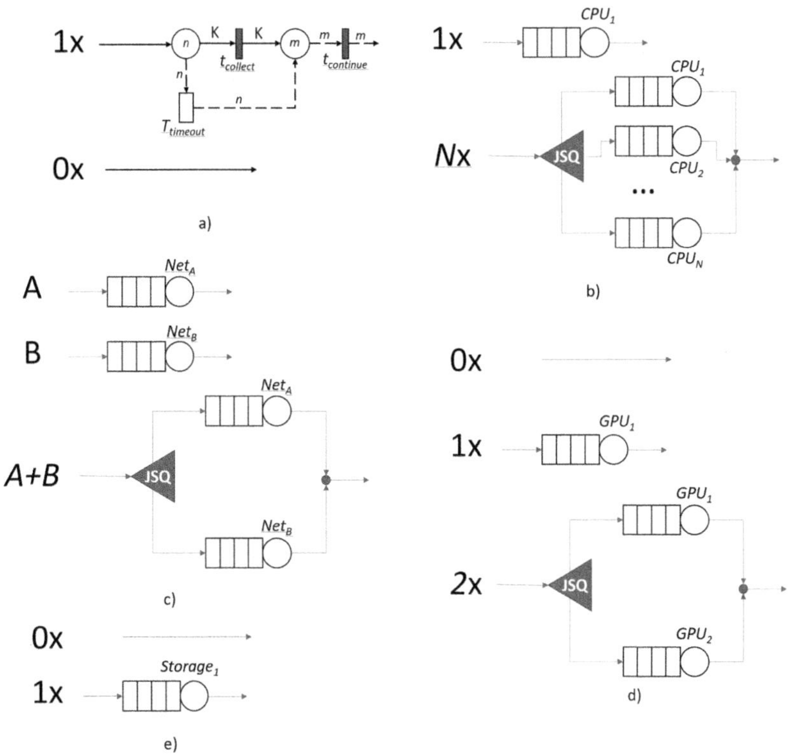

Fig. 3. The submodels for the subsystems: a) the *Buffer*; b) the *CPU*; c) the *GPU*; d) the *Network*; e) the *Storage*.

After intuitively describing the general approach to multiformalism modeling using Maude, we will instantiate it in the case study. We skip many technical details and refer to the online repository https://github.com/lgcapra/rewpt/tree/main/multiformalism for a complete description. However, we include code excerpts in the text and list a few modules in the appendix for the reader's convenience.

The Maude System. Maude [20] is a purely declarative language with high performance and rewriting logic semantics [9]. It achieves efficiency and expressiveness through pattern matching modulo axioms, subtyping, generic types, and reflection. A Maude system module is an executable specification for a distributed system. The Maude runtime engine provides various facilities for model-checking, LTL formula verification, and symbolic reachability. Maude has intuitive rewriting semantics. Statements are *equations* (utilized as simplifications) or *rewrite rules* (representing local concurrent transitions). A specification in Maude comprises *Functional* modules (which contain only equations) and *System* modules (which include rules and potentially equations). A functional module characterizes a *theory* $(\Sigma, E \cup A)$ within the framework of membership *equational* logic: Σ constitutes the signature (operators, sorts, subsorts), E comprises the set of axioms, and A encapsulates the operator equational attributes (such as AC). The model of an equational theory is the initial algebra, specifically, the ground terms' *quotient* algebra $T_{\Sigma/E \cup A}$, which, assuming that confluence and termination conditions are met, is isomorphic to the *canonical* term algebra made of simplified terms: thus, the mathematical and operational semantics align. A system module represents a *rewrite theory* $(\Sigma, E \cup A, R)$, R being a set of rewrite rules. The corresponding model is set forth as a *labeled transition system* (TS) associated with each term: therein, the distributed states are represented by *canonical* terms, whereas state transitions illustrate *classes* of equivalent rewrites.

5.1 Reconfigurable Multiformalism Models in `Maude`

The multiformalism encoding in `Maude` is based on a simple, compact, and extensible hierarchy of modules. We propose a simple, elegant, and concise solution, though based on a few advanced features of `Maude` module operations. Our aim is to reuse existing modules that encode particular formalisms as much as possible.

In the following, we focus on the generic part (the core) of the multiformalism framework and then explain how the single components used in the case-study (rather intuitively described and some of which are listed in the appendix for the reader's convenience) are linked to the framework in a standard way.

Parametrized modules have type parameters expressed by *theories*; these theories establish module interfaces by setting syntactic and semantic properties for parameter modules; a *view* links a source theory to a target module, detailing the mapping of sorts and operators of the theory. As usual, our formalization is based on multisets, or more generally, commutative monoids.

Multiformalism Framework. The framework we propose extends and refines that presented in [2]. The objective is to improve the characterization of the dynamics of nodes within a complex heterogeneous network, thus facilitating the modeler's endeavors, who can focus on the structural adaptation of the network.

We rely upon a fundamental concept: a multiformalism model is constructed by integrating multiple heterogeneous model components (e.g., Petri nets, queue networks, BPMN, activity diagrams, process algebra, etc.) that collectively maintain a notion of distributed state. This notion is formalized by the theory of commutative monoids (`C-MONOID`, see the excerpt below), which requires a sort `Elt` and an associative-commutative (AC) juxtaposition operation. This theory describes the parameter of the functional module `NETWORK{L :: C-MONOID}` , which provides the simple Abstract Data Type (ADT) of a multiformalism model.

The abstract syntax of the model is characterized by the sort `Network`, its subsort `Node`, and the AC juxtaposition (of SPSVERBc3s) `_,_`, which uses the ground term `emptyNetW` as its identity element. To put it another way, a multiformalism model functions as a multiset (or a commutative monoid) made up of potentially diverse `Network` components, referred to as nodes herein. The concept is simple: by appropriately "instantiating" the various node types through specific subsort relationships, we can construct a model composed of various concrete components that interact via shared state elements. A `NetSys` term consists of a `Network` and a term that pertains to the module's parameter sort (`S$Elt`), and it depicts a *network* of interconnected nodes with a distributed associated *state*.

In our example, the nodes in the network utilize a state concept similar to the *marking* of a Petri net, characterized by a multiset of places. This is efficiently represented using the `PBAG{PL ::TRIV}` module, where the trivial theory `TRIV` consists solely of the sort `Elt` declaration. The module's type parameter specifies the place label, and we use natural numbers to index places. This flexibility in place labeling is crucial, as we will detail later. The AC operator `_+_`, also designated as a constructor (which appears in canonical forms), describes multisets as weighted sums. For example, the term `3. p(1) + 1. p(2)` of type `Pbag`, derived from the instantiation of the module `PBAG{Nat}`, signifies a multiset with three instances of place p_1 and one of p_2.

The view `S-Pag{PL :: TRIV}` is used to instantiate the theory `C-MONOID` as a multiset of places through a suitable mapping. This view allows us to develop the ADT of heterogeneous networks that incorporate the distributed state notion of marking, as specified in `NETWORK{S :: C-MONOID}` .

A network of various nodes n_i with a shared distributed state B (made up of integer variables and formally expressed as a multiset of places) will intuitively be represented as a term `n1, n2,..., nk : B`.

```
fth C−MONOID is
   sort Elt .
   op 0 : −> Elt .
   op _+_ : Elt Elt −> Elt [assoc comm id: 0] .
endfth
```

```
fmod NETWORK{S :: C−MONOID} is
 protecting EXT−BOOL .
 sorts Node Network NetSys .
 subsort Node < Network .
 op emptyNetW : −> Network [ctor] .
 op _,_ : Network Network −> Network [ctor assoc comm prec 123 id: emptyNetW] .
 op _:_ : Network S$Elt −> NetSys [ctor prec 125] . *** heterogeneous network
 op netw : NetSys −> Network .
 op state : NetSys −> S$Elt .
 vars N N' : Network . var M : S$Elt .
 eq netw((N : M)) = N .
 eq state((N : M)) = M .
 op remove : Network Network −> Network .
 eq remove((N, N'), N) = N' .
 eq remove(N, N') = N [owise] .
 op in : Network Network −> Bool .
```

```
 eq in((N, N'), N) = true .
 eq in(N, N') = false [owise] .
endfm

view S-Pbag{PL :: TRIV} from C-MONOID to PBAG{PL} is
 sort Elt to Pbag .
 op 0 to nilP .
endv
```

Components used in the Case-Study. Three types of nodes are used: Stochastic Petri Nets (SPN) (extended with "flush" I/O edges), Queue Networks (MQN) (here simply used as pools of elementary queues), and JSQs. The Markov modulating MC is represented as a particular SPN (in which transitions' pre- and post-sets are singletons, except for a special place). We first briefly describe their signatures and then their link to the framework.

SPN We reuse and extend the signature of the (rewritable) SPN [15], which is based, in turn, on the (rewritable) Place-Transition (PT) nets provided in [17]. The SPN modules are available at https://github.com/lgcapra/rewpt.

SPN transitions (terms of sort `Tran`) are described through labels linked to adjacency lists, expressed as `Pbag` triples `[I, O, H]`. These labels include a descriptive tag (a `String` in our example), a `Float` (the rate parameter of a negative exponential firing delay), and a `Nat` (which specifies the firing policy). In addition, there can be flush arcs. For instance, the ground term,

```
t("a",1.5,0) |-> [2 . p(2), 1 . p(2), 2 . p(1)] f: p(3) >> p(4,7)
```

delineates a transition characterized by the label "a", an exponential firing rate $\mu = 1.5$, and an infinite-server type. This transition requires at least two tokens in place p_2, at least one token in p_3, and zero or one in p_1. Upon firing, it will remove one token from p_2, empty place p_3, and add to p_4 all the tokens previously in p_3, provided that the capacity of p_4 (7) is not exceeded. The net underlying an SPN, a term of kind `Net`, is defined in a modular way using the AC juxtaposition `_;_` and the relationship `Tran < Net` .

Using the operator `firingRate : Tran Pbag -> Float` , we can define marking dependent rates: The current definition is based on the enabling degree, which refers to the occurrences of a transition that are simultaneously enabled.

The Buffer (Fig. 3a) and the modulating Markov chain (Fig. 2) are SPNs, with the latter encoded as an SPN specialization in which the transitions' adjacency matrices have this layout: `[1 . P, 1 . P' + 1 . P'', 1 . P'']` , where `P''` is a "special" place shared by all transitions that is both output and inhibitor: This indicates that the transition from the MC place (state) `P` to `P'` , when `P''` is unmarked, halts the MC evolution until the triggered system quasi-instantaneous reconfiguration occurs.

Queue Networks. We reuse the multi-class queue networks (MQNs) signature. MQNs are built from single servers, or terms of sort `Server`, as defined in module

SERVER{PL :: TRIV} . Each term has a Place and a Float (exponential service rate), noted as P @ F. The MQN signature (QUEUE{PL :: TRIV }) is based on a predefined parametrized module LIST. A simple MQN, a term of sort SimpleQ, is a non-empty list of servers (terms of sort NeList{Server}) ending with a Place (MQN endpoint), noted as NeL > P. In our case-study, elementary queues (sort ElQueue) consist of one server. Generally, a MQN (sort Queue) is a SimpleQ with two Pbag terms (in []) for input and inhibitor enabling conditions (similar to PT nets). The relationship ElQueue < SimpleQ < Queue holds. The MQN time semantics is defined by firingRate, which calculates the service rate at each step based on the MQN population.

Queue networks can be composed in a flexible way using the Network juxtaposition (_,_) and shared places. We focus on creating pools of similar queues modeling the CPU (Fig. 3b)) and the GPU (Fig. 3d)) in various setups. The Network (Fig. 3c)) –distinct from Network– comprises two different queues, while the Storage (Fig. 3e)) consists of a single queue.

JSQ. This newly introduced component plays a pivotal role in the allocation of jobs to a set of queues according to the eponymous algorithm. The pertinent signature (module JSQ{PL :: TRIV}) is presented in Appendix B. A JSQ, which is a term of type Jsq, is characterized by an input place and an associated (potentially empty) set of output places, which serve as entry points for connected queues. We employ the intuitive notation P |> S, where S denotes a set of places. The JSQ is additionally equipped with a firingRate operator that facilitates a flexible state-dependent definition of the scheduling time.

Linking Nodes to the Network. A straightforward pattern allows us to interconnect any kind of node in a standardized way. We illustrate the method using SPN nodes. We need to define a functional module (SPN-NODE) that encapsulates both the node's signature (SPN-SIG) and the ADT of the network (NETWORK) appropriately instantiated, by establishing the proper subsort relationship between the specific node sort (Net) and Node. This newly defined functional module is then wrapped in a separated system module (SPN-NODE-SYS), for convenience, that defines the node dynamics (the SPN firing rule) in the network context.

With a sub-sort structure, the NODE mapping can vary. For the SPN nodes, the abstract sort Node can be bound to Net (our choice) or Tran. In the former case, both (t1 ; t2), t3 and t1, t2, t3 are different terms of type Network.

```
fmod SPN-NODE{PL :: TRIV} is
  extending NETWORK{S-Pbag{PL}} .
  protecting SPN-SIG{String, PL} .
  subsort Net < Node .
endfm

mod SPN-NODE-SYS{PL :: TRIV} is
  including SPN-NODE{PL} .
  var N : Network . vars PN PN' : Net . vars M M' : Pbag .
  var K : NzNat . var rate : Float . var T : Tran .
```

```
crl [firing−t] : (N , PN) : M => (N , PN) : M' if T ; PN' := PN /\ enabled(T, M) /\
  M' := firing(T, M) /\ overCap(M') = false /\ rate := firingRate(T, M) .
endm
```

We link JSQs and QUEUEs to the network via modules defined similarly (see the appendix).

Getting a Concrete Model: The Case Study. The formalization of the case study is divided into a few system modules for convenience. The core module (listed hereinafter) includes three modules `<NTYPE>-NODE-SYS` characterizing the dynamics of each node type present in the network, as explained. Through the view `Plab` we use place labels containing a descriptor (a `String`) with associated index (a `Nat`), and possibly a value (a `NzNat`) indicating the place capacity (unbounded, if omitted).

```
*** blockchain with separated modulating MC
mod MM−BLOCKCHAIN is
  including SPN−NODE−SYS{Plab} .
  including QUEUE−NODE−SYS{Plab} .
  including JSQ−NODE−SYS{Plab} .
  including SPN−EMU{String,Plab} . *** represents the MC

  sort MMnetwork . *** Markov modulated network
  op MM:_N:_ : System NetSys −> MMnetwork [ctor] .
  op mc : MMnetwork −> System .
  op sys : MMnetwork −> NetSys .
  var MC : System . var Sys : NetSys .
  eq mc (MM: MC N: Sys) = MC .
  eq sys(MM: MC N: Sys) = Sys .
endm
```

For example, the buffer timeout is described as (`K` is an alias for the place capacity):

```
t("timeout", 0.2, 1) |-> [nilP, nilP] f: ("in" 0, K) >> p("b" 0, K)
```

The core module `MM-BLOCKCHAIN` wraps a fourth system module (`SPN-EMU`) that represents the modulating MC encoded as a particular SPN. This components is not linked to the `Network` (even if it could have been) due to the particular role it plays. In fact, it should be considered a sort of meta-component that drives the evolution of the underlying network. `Maude` is a reflective language provided with meta-level modules; However, using these predefined modules is cumbersome and introduces significant overhead in terms of rewriting.

Through the constructor `MM:_N:_ : System NetSys -> MMnetwork`, we represent the MC and the network as two distinct components. This approach formulates a term `MMnetwork` as the amalgamation of these elements. Note that the `System` sub-term represents an SPN with an associated state (a multiset of places): The system module `SPN-EMU` includes the SPN firing rule, which activates the local rewrite that encodes a state transition of the MC. We aim to integrate Maude strategy language to control rewrite rule execution, facilitating a more elegant interaction between the MC and the network.

Two additional modules (based on MM-BLOCKCHAIN) complete the case-study formalization by defining compositional operators and rules for the network reconfiguration modulated by the Markov chain. In particular, the operators:

```
    op pool : ElQueue NzNat -> Network
op connect&link : Jsq Network -> Network
```

allow us to build a pool of similar elementary queues with a single exit point (helpful, in particular, in the CPU component) and to connect them to a JSQ.

Compositional operators are essential for facing scalability both in modeling and, above all, in analysis, as we shall briefly discuss.

We conclude this description with a small excerpt of the case-study's "final" module (BLOCKCHAIN-EXE, listed in the appendix) that illustrates the two rewrite rules that implement the system reconfiguration from state L_0 to L_1, and vice versa (Fig. 1).

```
var MC : System . var Q : Net . var S : Pbag . var Nw : Network . var B : Pbag .
crl [S0>S1] : MM: Q S N: (Nw : B) => MM: Q 1 . L(1) N: (netWork1 : B)
      if S == 1 . L(1) + 1 . s−tran /\ in(Nw, buffer) .

crl [S1>S0] : MM: Q S N: (Nw : B) => MM: Q 1 . L(0) N: (netWork0 : set(B,
   pin(cpu1), k)) if S == 1 . L(0) + 1 . s−tran /\ in(Nw, cpu3) /\
   k := allClients(cpu3, B) /\ k <= cap(cpu1) .
```

We massively use aliasing for clarity (e.g., A0 represents the component A of the submodel in Fig. 3, cpu3 indicates three CPUs in a pool, netWork0 the system configuration in state L_0, netWork1 that in state L_1, and so forth) and apply compositional operators. The rewrite is activated when the MC place s-tran holds one token (indicating a change in the MC state) and is deactivated immediately afterwards by removing this token from s-tran. Transitioning from L_1 to L_0, CPUs decrease from three to one, with a policy of potentially waiting to shift jobs based on the single CPU capacity, challenging the assumed immediate reconfiguration; alternatives exist, here not described.

This methodology offers a flexible means to build a multiformalism model with reconfigurable components. Allows for easy automation of some steps. Modularity enables isolated testing of the network for specific setups (MC states). In the example, MC modulation governs network reconfiguration, but in complex scenarios resembling a feedback-loop, the MC itself could change dynamically.

5.2 Results

The analytical resolution of the Maude model within the case study must address the inherent complexity of a highly dynamic setting along with the presence of extensive collections of analogous components. The approach detailed in [15,17] for rewritable SPNs utilizes algebraic operators, both compositional and modifying, to identify and preserve model symmetries, particularly automorphisms of Petri nets, through automatic structured node labeling. This procedure enables the development of modular and hierarchical model architectures, as well as the derivation of a quotient transition system by efficiently normalizing states in accordance with strong bisimulation criteria, thereby ensuring *exact lumpability* of the associated CTMC.

This approach has been extended to the multiformalism framework by modifying the automorphism concept for heterogeneous, hierarchical graph structures. Furthermore, efficient normalization has been integrated through automated node labeling, facilitated by symmetric algebraic operators such as the previously referenced `pool`, which constructs a collection of similar CPUs. The `Maude` modules used to produce a quotient transition system from multiformalism models—created and transformed with symmetric operators—can be accessed at https://github.com/lgcapra/rewpt/tree/main/multiformalism/MODmulti.

The results appear to be promising, as evidenced by the table below. The data pertain to the performance of the `Maude` run-time shell command, which identifies final states within the comprehensive multiformalism model of the reconfigurable edge-server (refer to Sect. 4). (`mmc` serves as an alias for the SPN encoding the modulating MC.) The command demonstrates that the system is devoid of deadlocks. For ease of analysis, a model with a single parameter (N) is employed, which denotes the capacity of the majority of places in the model.

```
Maude> search MM: mmc 1 . L(0) N: netWorkSys0  =>! M:MMnetwork .
```

Without the utilization of symmetries via modular operators, the analytical resolution of model configurations is feasible only for systems of medium to small scale. Consequently, in such cases, the application of simulation methods becomes imperative (Table 1). In contrast, the normalization procedure introduces an operational overhead, which is deemed acceptable given the scale of the problem. For example, the setup described in $N = 32$ pertains to a standard TS characterized by a magnitude on the order of hundreds of billion states.

6 Case Study Analysis

To show the effectiveness of the approach on the proposed case study, we consider the parameters shown in Table 2. The solution has been calculated with Discrete Event Simulation of the components considered in Sect. 5, using a custom solver based on the Java Modeling Tools (JMT) engine [8]. The simulator engine also computes confidence intervals, which have not been reported to simplify the presentation. With the parameters considered, each configuration can handle the maximum arrival rate shown in the first row of Table 3. We first consider a constant variable workload $\lambda = 0 \ldots 6$ requests per second, and we consider to switch the configuration to the next one, when utilization reaches around 80% , as shown in the second line of Table 3 . Figure 4a) shows the evolution of the response time for each configuration and for the actual case, when the best is considered. It is interesting to note the classical U-shaped behavior of the buffer: with low load, the response time is dominated by the timer. As the load increases, the required quantity of requests is accumulated faster and faster, making the response time initially decrease, until it reaches a point where queue starts to form, and it finally increases as in a normal server. It is also interesting to see that as soon as the configuration is upgraded, there is an immediate drop in response time.

Figure 4b) instead focuses on the cost of each configuration. Each resource is the sum of two factors, a constant required just for having the component running in the system, and another proportional to its utilization. The costs considered per month are shown in Table 4. As can be seen, each configuration follows an almost linear behavior and the switch causes a jump in the actual expense. If we consider instead the cost per request, as shown by the green line on the secondary axis, we see that it decreases as the volume increases. We also see that the cost of maintaining the blockchain is very high when the load is very small, and becomes justifiable only when the number of requests to handle is sufficiently high. We then take the modulation into account and we analyze the complete system. In particular, we consider a parameter $0 < \alpha < 1$, to control how much the modulating process stays in a given configuration. If we define a base switching time $T_{base} = 6$ [h], then we set:

$$q_{i\ i+1} = \frac{1}{\alpha T_{base}} \qquad q_{i\ i-1} = \frac{1}{(1-\alpha)T_{base}} \tag{1}$$

Table 1. ordinary vs normalized Transition System as the capacity varies (with a 11th Gen Intel Core i5 32 GB RAM)

N	TS		Quotient TS	
	states(final)	time (sec)	states(final)	time (sec)
2	789,456(0)	145	2,345(0)	10
4	10,092,458(0)	3689	5,534(0)	67
8	interrupted	–	20,842(0)	420
16	interrupted	–	189,496(0)	1070
32	interrupted	–	1,954,408(0)	7910

Table 2. Parameters used in the considered scenario

Description	Parameter	Value
Buffer size	K	10
Timeout	$T_{timeout}$	1 [min]
CPU Demand (no GPU)	CPU_i	2 [s]
CPU Demand (with GPU)	CPU_i	1.2 [s]

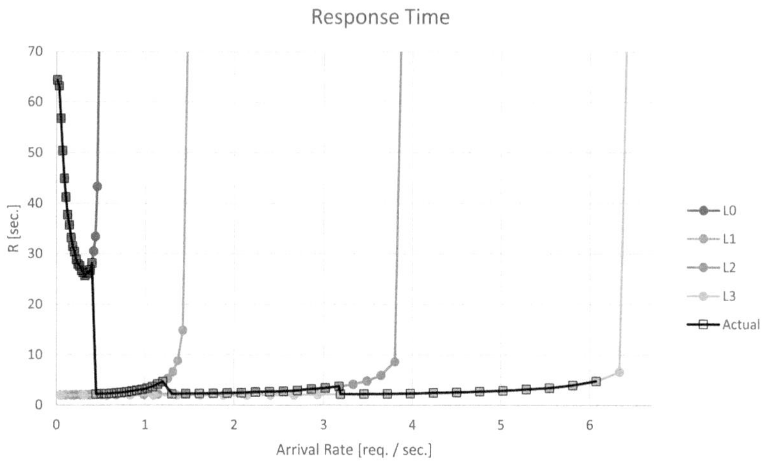

a)

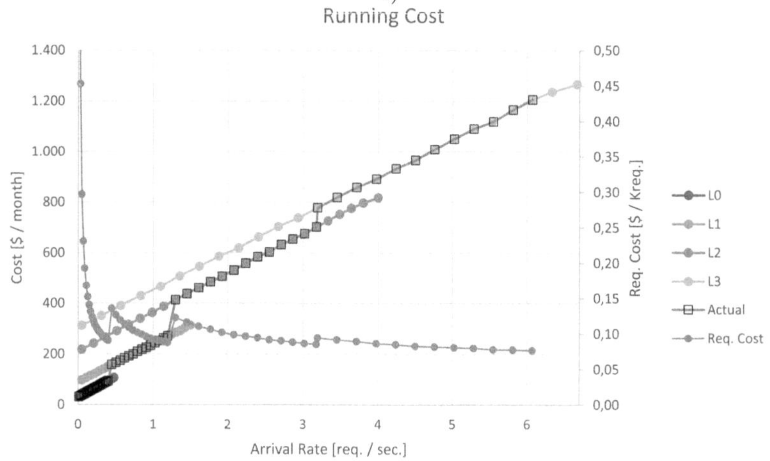

b)

Fig. 4. Simulation results: a) comparison of system response time with different arrival rates for configurations L0, L1, L2, L3 and the actual configuration; b) comparison of running cost with different arrival rates for configurations L0, L1, L2, L3 and the actual configuration, with the indication of the cost per request.

Figure 5a shows the probability of each configuration as a function of α: in particular, when $\alpha \rightarrow 0$ the system tends to be more crowded, leading to higher probability for configuration L_3. In contrast, as $\alpha \rightarrow 1$, the system becomes less and less crowded, increasing the probability of using the configuration L_0.

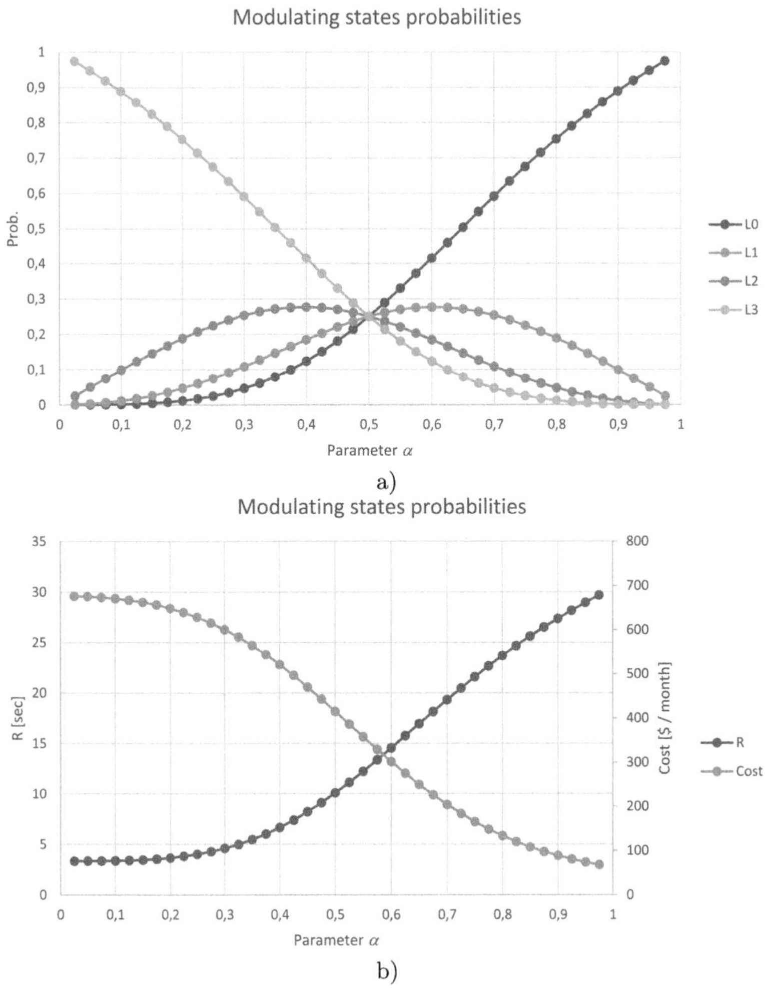

Fig. 5. Results for the considered parameter α a) Comparison of probabilities for different values of parameter α in configurations L0, L1, L2 and L3 ; b) Response time and costs for different values of parameter α.

Figure 5b shows the response time (primary axis) and the total cost per month (secondary axis), considering the arrival rate in each modulating state as reported in the third row of Table 3. The response time remains sufficiently controlled as long as the system is not too long in configuration L_0 where the buffer is used. In contrast, the cost increases by almost an order of magnitude when the system remains in configuration L_3 for longer periods.

Table 3. Arrival rate parameters per modulating state: maximum allowed arrival rate, switching rate, considered arrival rate in this study

	L0	*L1*	*L2*	*L3*
Maximum λ [req./sec.]	0.5	1.5	4	6.667
Switch point λ [req./sec.]	0.4	1.2	3.6	n.a.
Considered λ [req./sec.]	0.2	1	3	5

Table 4. Considered fixed and variable costs

	CPU	GPU	Net. Mod. A	Net. Mod. B	Storage
Fixed	20 $	50 $	10 $	30 $	5 $
Variable	60 $	200 $	50 $	100 $	30 $

7 Conclusion and Future Work

In this paper we presented, with the support of a real-world case study, the potential of model rewriting techniques to support more efficient performance evaluation besed on multiformalism modeling. In particular, we have shown how rewriting features can handle riconfiguration events in a clear and compact way. Future works include a further integration of `Maude` into the SIMTHESys Multi-solution Framework to extend the experimentation and make this feature available in its context, as well as an improved model-based description of the reconfiguration events.

Appendix A

The EDGE server is made up as follows:

- Buffer: a DRAM buffer;
- CPU: Intel XEON Gold 6250 8-core;
- GPU: 2x NVIDIA A2 Tensor Core;
- Network: two different network interfaces, a slow "backup" interface (A), which is a LoraWAN link with 50 Kbps of maximum speed, and a faster "default" interface (B), which is a WiMAX link with 10 Mbps of maximum speed;
- Storage: a generic storage unit.

As the main CPUs engine of the server, we select the XEON 6250, despite the fact that it is not the most recent CPU model, due to the very high clock speed (higher than newer CPUs from Intel) and to the availability of accurate benchmarks from which it is possible to estimate simulation parameters. The main characteristics of the XEON 6250 are listed in the following Table 5:[1]

[1] https://www.intel.com/content/www/us/en/products/sku/198652/intel-xeon-gold-6250-processor-35-75m-cache-3-90-ghz/specifications.html.

Table 5. Intel XEON Gold 6250 main characteristics

Cores	8 (16 Threads)
Base Clock freq.	3.6 GHz
Turbo boost freq.	4.4 GHz
Cache	35.75 MB
TDP	185 W

The choice of GPU is centered on NVIDIA A2 Tensor Core[2], due to its low cost and power consumption, which are ideal for equipping servers that need to be deployed in large quantities and in hostile environments where failures can be frequent.

Appendix B

Example of Model-Specific Component: JSQ

```
*** signature
fmod JSQ{PL :: TRIV} is
  protecting PSET{PL} .
  protecting FLOAT .
  vars P P' : Place . var S : Pset . var L : PL$Elt .
  sort Jsq .
  op _|>_ : Place Pset -> [Jsq] [ctor] .
 cmb P |> S : Jsq if cap(P) = 1 /\ P in S = false . *** a JSQ has capacity 1
  op In : Jsq -> Place .
  eq In(P |> S) = P .
  op Out : Jsq -> Pset .
  eq Out(P |> S) = S .
  op newJsq : Place -> [Jsq] . ***create an "empty" JSQ
  eq newJsq(P) = P |> emptyPset .
  op newJsq : PL$Elt -> Jsq .
  eq newJsq(L) = p(L, 1) |> emptyPset .
endfm

*** link to the network
fmod JSQ-NODE{PL :: TRIV} is
  extending NETWORK{S-Pbag{PL}} .
  protecting JSQ{PL} .
  subsort Jsq < Node .
endfm

mod JSQ-NODE-SYS{PL :: TRIV} is
   including JSQ-NODE{PL} .
```

[2] https://www.nvidia.com/content/dam/en-zz/solutions/data-center/a2/pdf/a2-datasheet.pdf.

```
  var N : Network . var B : Pbag . vars P P' : Place . var S : Pset . var NeS : NePset .
  op firingRate : Jsq Pbag -> Float .
  eq firingRate(P |> NeS, B) = 100.0 . *** dummy implementation
  crl (N , P |> NeS) : 1 . P + B => (N , P |> NeS) : B + 1 . P' if P' U S := emin(B,
      NeS) /\ rate:Float := firingRate(P |> NeS, B).
endm
```

Case Study's Final Module

```
mod BLOCKCHAIN-EXE is
 inc BLOCKCHAIN-OP .
 var i : Nat . var k : NzNat . var P : Place .
 op mmc : -> Net . *** the modulating MC
 op L : Nat -> Place . *** alias for the MC states
 op s-tran : -> Place .
 eq L(i) = p(< "mc" ; i >) . *** states of the MC
 eq s-tran = p(< "s-tran" ; 0 >) .
 *** the modulating MC
 eq mmc = t("",1.0,1) |-> [1 . L(0), 1 . L(1) + 1 . s-tran, 1 . s-tran] ;
    t("",2.0,1) |-> [1 . L(1), 1 . L(0) + 1 . s-tran, 1 . s-tran] ;
    t("",2.0,1) |-> [1 . L(2), 1 . L(1) + 1 . s-tran, 1 . s-tran] ; t("",1.0,1)
        |-> [1 . L(1), 1 . L(2) + 1 . s-tran, 1 . s-tran] ;
    t("",2.0,1) |-> [1 . L(2), 1 . L(3) + 1 . s-tran, 1 . s-tran] ; t("",1.0,1)
        |-> [1 . L(3), 1 . L(2) + 1 . s-tran, 1 . s-tran] .
  *** model's parameter(s)
 op N : -> NzNat [memo] . *** timeout parameter (place capacity)
 eq N = 2 .
  *** simulates new arrivals in the system
 op pin : NzNat -> Place [memo] .
 eq pin(k) = p(< "in" ; 0 >, k) .
 ops in out : -> Tran [memo] .
 eq in = newTin(pin(N), 2.0) .
  *** "in" is the input place of the system (and of the buffer)
 ops cpuI cpuO A B : -> Place .
 eq cpuI = p(< "cpu" ; 0 >, N) .
 eq cpuO = p(< "cpu-Out" ; 0 >, N) .
  *** the BUFFER component
 op buffer : -> Net [memo] .
 eq buffer = t("collect", 1.0, 1) |-> [N . pin(N), N . p(< "b" ; 0 >, N)] ;
    t("timeout", 0.2, 1) |-> [nilP, nilP] f: pin(N) >> p(< "b" ; 0 >, N) ;
    t("continue", 1.0, 1) |-> [nilP, nilP] f: p(< "b" ; 0 >, N) >> cpuI .
  ***CPU (pools)
 op cpu1 : -> ElQueue [memo] .
 eq cpu1 = newElQueue(cpuI, cpuO, 5.0) .
 ops cpu3 cpu6 cpu8 : -> Network [memo] .
```

```
eq cpu3 = pool(cpu1, 3) .
eq cpu6 = pool(cpu1, 6) .
eq cpu8 = pool(cpu1, 8) .
*** GPU
op gpu : -> ElQueue [memo] .
eq gpu = pool(newElQueue(p(< "GPU" ; 0 >, N), p(< "GPU-O" ; 1 >, N),
    20.0), 2) .
*** NETWORK
ops A0 B0 : -> ElQueue [memo] .
ops A B : Place -> ElQueue . *** parametric in the input place
eq A(P) = newElQueue(P, p(< "A" ; 0 >, N), 2.0) .
eq B(P) = newElQueue(P, p(< "B" ; 0 >, N), 4.0) .
eq A0 = A(out(cpu1)) .
eq B0 = B(out(cpu1)) .
*** JSQ
op jsq1 : -> Jsq [memo] .
eq jsq1 = p(< "cpu" ; 1 >, N) |> p(< "q" ; 1 >, N) U p(< "q" ; 2 >, N) .
*** Storage
op storage : -> ElQueue [memo] .
eq storage = newElQueue(p(< "St" ; 0 >, N), p(< "St-O" ; 0 >, N), 0.2) .

*** the network (blockchain) in the state L0
op netWorkSys0 : -> NetSys .
ops netWork0 netWork1 : -> Network [memo] .
eq out = newTout(out(A0), 1.0) .
eq netWork0 = in, buffer, cpu1, A0, out .
eq netWork1 = newTin(pin(1),2.0), connect&link(newJsq(pin(1)), cpu3),
    B0, newTout(out(B0), 1.0) .
eq netWorkSys0 = netWork0 : nilP .

*** rewrites governed by mmc -- istantaneous upon MC change state
var MC : System . var Q : Net . var S : Pbag . var Nw : Network . var B : Pbag .
crl [S0>S1] : MM: Q S N: (Nw : B) => MM: Q 1 . L(1) N: (netWork1 : B)
      if S == 1 . L(1) + 1 . s-tran /\ in(Nw, buffer) .
crl [S1>S0] : MM: Q S N: (Nw : B) => MM: Q 1 . L(0) N: (netWork0 : set(B,
   pin(cpu1), k)) if S == 1 . L(0) + 1 . s-tran /\ in(Nw, cpu3) /\
   k := allClients(cpu3, B) /\ k <= cap(cpu1) .

*** the other network rewrites driven by the MC
***
***
*** initial configuration (used in searches)
op MMsys0 : -> MMnetwork .
eq MMsys0 = MM: mmc 1 . L(0) N: netWorkSys0 .
endm
```

References

1. Alshekhly, I.: Smart cities: survey. J. Adv. Comput. Sci. Technol. Res **2**, 79–90 (2012)
2. Barbierato, E., Capra, L., Gribaudo, M., Iacono, M.: Enhancing multiformalism models with rewrite engines. In: Proceedings of EPEW 2025, Catania, Italy, 26–27 June 2025 (2025)
3. Barbierato, E., Gribaudo, M., Iacono, M.: Modeling hybrid systems in SIMTHESys. Electron. Notes Theor. Comput. Sci. **327**, 5–25 (2016). https://doi.org/10.1016/j.entcs.2016.09.021
4. Barbierato, E., Gribaudo, M., Iacono, M., Jakóbik, A.: Exploiting CloudSim in a multiformalism modeling approach for cloud based systems. Simul. Model. Pract. Theory **93**, 133–147 (2019)
5. Bause, F., Buchholz, P., Kemper, P.: A toolbox for functional and quantitative analysis of DEDS. In: Puigjaner, R., Savino, N.N., Serra, B. (eds.) TOOLS 1998. LNCS, vol. 1469, pp. 356–359. Springer, Heidelberg (1998). https://doi.org/10.1007/3-540-68061-6_32
6. Beccuti, M., Franceschinis, G.: Efficient simulation of stochastic well-formed nets through symmetry exploitation (2012). https://doi.org/10.1109/WSC.2012.6465256
7. Belen-Saglam, R., Altuncu, E., Lu, Y., Li, S.: A systematic literature review of the tension between the GDPR and public blockchain systems. Blockchain: Res. Appl. **4**(2) (2023). https://doi.org/10.1016/j.bcra.2023.100129
8. Bertoli, M., Casale, G., Serazzi, G.: JMT: performance engineering tools for system modeling. SIGMETRICS Perform. Eval. Rev. **36**(4), 10–15 (2009). https://doi.org/10.1145/1530873.1530877
9. Bruni, R., Meseguer, J.: Generalized rewrite theories. In: Baeten, J.C.M., Lenstra, J.K., Parrow, J., Woeginger, G.J. (eds.) ICALP 2003. LNCS, vol. 2719, pp. 252–266. Springer, Heidelberg (2003). https://doi.org/10.1007/3-540-45061-0_22
10. Campanile, L., Iacono, M., Marulli, F., Mastroianni, M.: Privacy regulations challenges on data-centric and IoT systems: a case study for smart vehicles, pp. 507–520 (2020)
11. Campanile, L., Iacono, M., Marulli, F., Mastroianni, M.: Designing a GDPR compliant blockchain-based IoV distributed information tracking system. Inf. Process. Manag., **58**(3) (2021). https://doi.org/10.1016/j.ipm.2021.102511
12. Campanile, L., Iacono, M., Mastroianni, M., Riccio, C.: Performance evaluation of an edge-blockchain architecture for smart city, vol. 2025-June, pp. 620–627 (2025). https://doi.org/10.7148/2025-0620
13. Capra, L.: Associating a Markov process with Maude executable modules. In: Proceedings of the 15th International Conference on Simulation and Modeling Methodologies, Technologies and Applications, pp. 106–116. SciTePress (2025)
14. Capra, L., Dutheillet, C., Franceschinis, G., Ilie, J.M.: Towards performance analysis with partially symmetrical SWN, pp. 148–155 (1999)
15. Capra, L., Gribaudo, M.: A lumped CTMC for modular rewritable PN. In: Doncel, J., Remke, A., Pompeo, D.D. (eds.) Computer Performance Engineering - 20th European Workshop, EPEW 2024, Venice, Italy, 14 June 2024. Lecture Notes in Computer Science, vol. 15454, pp. 106–120. Springer, Heidelberg (2024). DOI:
16. Capra, L., Gribaudo, M., Iacono, M., Köhler-Bußmeier, M.: Using rewriting systems for performance analysis. QualITA 2025: The Fourth Conference on System and Service Quality, Catania, Italy, 25–27 June 2025, Proceedings (2025)

17. Capra, L., Köhler-Bußmeier, M.: Modular rewritable petri nets: an efficient model for dynamic distributed systems. Theor. Comput. Sci. **990**, 114397 (2024). https://doi.org/10.1016/j.tcs.2024.114397
18. Chinnasamy, P., Vinothini, C., Arun Kumar, S., Allwyn Sundarraj, A., Annlin Jeba, S.V., Praveena, V.: Blockchain technology in smart-cities. In: Panda, S.K., Jena, A.K., Swain, S.K., Satapathy, S.C. (eds.) Blockchain Technology: Applications and Challenges. ISRL, vol. 203, pp. 179–200. Springer, Cham (2021). https://doi.org/10.1007/978-3-030-69395-4_11
19. Ciardo, G., Miner, A.S.: SMART: the stochastic model checking analyzer for reliability and timing. In: International Conference on Quantitative Evaluation of Systems, pp. 338–339. IEEE, Los Alamitos (2004)
20. Clavel, M., Durán, F., Eker, S., Lincoln, P., Martí-Oliet, N., Meseguer, J., Talcott, C.: All About Maude - A High-Performance Logical Framework. LNCS, vol. 4350. Springer, Heidelberg (2007). https://doi.org/10.1007/978-3-540-71999-1
21. Far, A.Z., Far, M.Z., Gharibzadeh, S., Zangeneh, S., Amini, L., Rahimi, M.: Artificial intelligence for secured information systems in smart cities: collaborative IoT computing with deep reinforcement learning and blockchain. arXiv preprint arXiv:2409.16444 (2024)
22. Franceschinis, G., Gribaudo, M., Iacono, M., Mazzocca, N., Vittorini, V.: DrawNET++: model objects to support performance analysis and simulation of systems. In: Field, T., Harrison, P.G., Bradley, J., Harder, U. (eds.) TOOLS 2002. LNCS, vol. 2324, pp. 233–238. Springer, Heidelberg (2002). https://doi.org/10.1007/3-540-46029-2_18
23. Gribaudo, M., Iacono, M.: An introduction to multiformalism modeling (2013). https://doi.org/10.4018/978-1-4666-4659-9.ch001
24. Guo, S., Qi, Y., Yu, P., Shao, S., Qiu, X.: Edge network resource synergy for mobile blockchain in smart city. In: 2020 International Wireless Communications and Mobile Computing (IWCMC), pp. 1272–1277. IEEE (2020)
25. Iacono, M., Gribaudo, M.: Element based semantics in multi formalism performance models, pp. 413–416 (2010). https://doi.org/10.1109/MASCOTS.2010.54
26. Khan, A.A., et al.: Secure remote sensing data with blockchain distributed ledger technology: a solution for smart cities. IEEE Access (2024)
27. Lara, J., Vangheluwe, H.: AToM^3: a tool for multi-formalism and meta-modelling. In: Kutsche, R.-D., Weber, H. (eds.) FASE 2002. LNCS, vol. 2306, pp. 174–188. Springer, Heidelberg (2002). https://doi.org/10.1007/3-540-45923-5_12
28. Mezquita, Y., González-Briones, A., Casado-Vara, R., Wolf, P., de la Prieta, F., Gil-González, A.-B.: Review of privacy preservation with blockchain technology in the context of smart cities. In: Corchado, J.M., Trabelsi, S. (eds.) SSCTIC 2021. LNNS, vol. 253, pp. 68–77. Springer, Cham (2022). https://doi.org/10.1007/978-3-030-78901-5_7
29. Moscato, F., Flammini, F., Di Lorenzo, G., Vittorini, V., Marrone, S., Iacono, M.: The software architecture of the OsMoSys Multisolution Framework (2007)
30. Okai, E., Feng, X., Sant, P.: Smart cities survey. In: 2018 IEEE 20th International Conference on High Performance Computing and Communications; IEEE 16th International Conference on Smart City; IEEE 4th International Conference on Data Science and Systems (HPCC/SmartCity/DSS), pp. 1726–1730. IEEE (2018)
31. Padma, A., Ramaiah, M.: Blockchain based an efficient and secure privacy preserved framework for smart cities. IEEE Access **12**, 21985–22002 (2024)

32. Sanders, W.: Integrated frameworks for multi-level and multi-formalism modeling. In: Proceedings of 8th International Workshop on Petri Nets and Performance Models, 1999, pp. 2–9 (1999)
33. Trivedi, K.S.: Sharpe 2002: Symbolic hierarchical automated reliability and performance evaluator. In: DSN '02: Proceedings of the 2002 International Conference on Dependable Systems and Networks, p. 544. IEEE, Washington, DC (2002)

Localized Statistical Learning of Cell Loads in Cellular Networks

Lucas Darlavoix[1,2,3](✉), Bartłomiej Błaszczyszyn[2,3], and Mohamed Kadhem Karray[1]

[1] Orange Research, 40-48 avenue de la République, 92320 Châtillon, France
{lucas.darlavoix,mohamed.karray}@orange.com
[2] INRIA Paris Centre, 48 rue Barrault, 75013 Paris, France
[3] ENS Paris, 45 rue d'Ulm, 75005 Paris, France
bartek.blaszczyszyn@ens.fr

Abstract. Accurate cell load prediction is crucial for efficient wireless networks. This paper investigates localized statistical learning, using a varying number of input neighboring cells k to optimize load estimation. Using real-world operational data, different prediction methods are benchmarked, such as neural networks (NNs), linear fitting and ridge regularization.

Experiments compellingly show that NNs incorporating activation functions achieve superior prediction performance. An optimal range for k is identified to be around 20-30 neighbors, demonstrating an essential balance between model complexity and generalization. Notably, the study affirms the robustness of this approach against stochastic training variations and highlights the benefits of sufficient training data. Thus, this work underscores the efficacy of localized, non-linear models, offering robust insights and paving the way for deep learning approaches to cell load prediction.

Keywords: QoS Prediction · Wireless Networks · Statistical Learning · Spatial Localization · Structural Regularization · Data-Efficient Learning

1 Introduction

In modern wireless cellular networks, the ability to predict, infer, and control the *load of base stations* is crucial for ensuring efficient resource allocation, quality of service (QoS), and energy-aware operation [1,7]. As user demand and network density increase, *cell load* becomes a complex, spatially distributed quantity that reflects the local user environment, interference and traffic dynamics.

Available physics-based mathematical models of network dynamics are inherently complex. They require an intricate engineering approach that integrates the performance of wireless links, the complexity of data connections, and the geographical deployment of base stations within dense network infrastructures. These models rely on deep theoretical foundations such as information theory,

A. Remke et al. (Eds.): Valuetools 2025, LNICST 691, pp. 299–317, 2027.
https://doi.org/10.1007/978-3-032-23901-3_18

queuing theory, and stochastic geometry, offering insights into different layers of the system [4].

While such models can deliver accurate global performance predictions, they often lack precision at the cell level, unless detailed location-specific propagation data is available. This limitation motivates the exploration of alternative, data-driven methods to achieve accurate, localized predictions of cell load.

Recent advances in *statistical learning* [2] offer promising avenues for estimating cell loads based on observed data. An initial effort in this direction was presented in [6], where a method was proposed to learn individual, cell-specific loads in operational wireless networks as a function of cellwise traffic demand, using real-world measurements.

However, applying statistical learning in this context poses several challenges. In particular, the *spatial localization* of the learned function emerges as a critical principle, closely tied to the limited scalability of training data in large networks comprising thousands of cells. Both aspects are essential to achieve robust *generalization* across diverse and dynamic network conditions. Without careful localization, there is a significant risk of *overfitting*: the learned function memorizes patterns specific to the training data rather than capturing the true underlying physical relationships.

In this work, the localization approach is investigated and formalized in the context of cell load learning. This article proposes a family of localized estimators, whose spatial range can be tuned to match the amount of available training data. Analyses of how localization influences prediction error are also carried out. This is done in several frameworks, including ridge regularization, thereby complementing the previous work presented in [6]. Theoretical insights are supported by numerical experiments using real-world datasets from operational cellular networks, highlighting trade-offs between *locality*, *model capacity*, and *prediction accuracy*.

From a learning-theoretic perspective, localization acts as a form of *structural regularization*, serving as an alternative rather than a complement to traditional techniques such as ridge regularization. In the present study, it not only significantly reduces the true prediction error but also enables the discovery of an effective spatial influence range of traffic demand on cell load. This insight represents a crucial first step toward uncovering the underlying geometry of the learning problem and opens the door to unifying physics-based and statistical modeling approaches.

2 Related Works

This section surveys prior research foundational to the present work, addressing various topics such as cell load prediction in cellular networks, localization principles within stochastic geometry and the application of localization as a regularization technique.

2.1 Cell Loads in Cellular Networks

The accurate prediction of cell loads is fundamental for efficient network operation, as it empowers various activities, such as dynamic resource allocation, energy saving and interference management [3,8]. Predictions have been achieved using physics-based models, often leveraging information theory, stochastic geometry and queueing theory to capture complex interactions between user distribution, channel conditions, and scheduling policies [4]. Several *machine learning* (ML) techniques have also been explored, ranging from classical time-series forecasting models to more advanced deep learning architectures. For example, Long Short-Term Memory (LSTM) networks were employed to capture temporal dependencies in traffic patterns for load prediction [17]. Graph Neural Networks (GNNs) have also been investigated to model network topology and inter-cell dependencies, in order to improve traffic prediction accuracy [10]. Surveys such as [13] provide overviews of ML applications in network traffic analysis in optical networks, which may also prove useful for load prediction. Despite the promise of these methods, challenges related to model complexity and generalization remain, thus motivating research into techniques like localization, as explored in this article.

2.2 Localization and Regularization in Stochastic Geometry

In stochastic geometry, the principle of *localization* plays a key role in establishing theoretical guarantees for statistics of spatial point processes. A central concept is that of *stabilizing functionals*, whose value at a point depends only on the configuration within a finite, typically exponentially decaying neighborhood [5,14,15]. These ideas are pivotal in proving laws of large numbers, central limit theorems, and concentration inequalities for geometric quantities such as coverage, connectivity, or load. Recent developments have also connected stabilization to *regularization*, particularly in spatial statistical inference. For instance, spatial score functions and localized estimators have been used to construct asymptotically optimal estimators and to control variance in the estimation of intensity or interaction potentials [11]. These methods naturally complement physics-based models by enabling scalable, data-driven inference under geometric constraints. The present work builds on these ideas by viewing spatial localization as a structural regularizer for learning spatially distributed functions, such as cell load in wireless networks.

2.3 Localization as Regularization

The idea of using spatial localization as a form of regularization has appeared in various areas of geometric statistics, including the analysis of stabilizing functionals in stochastic geometry and spatial inference. In particular, localization has been shown to control the variance and complexity of estimators in models based on point processes, such as in the estimation of intensity functions or interaction potentials [11,15]. In the context of learning theory, localization can be interpreted as a structural prior that limits the effective capacity of the hypothesis space by enforcing spatial constraints on the support of the function being learned. This reduces the risk of overfitting when data is scarce or unevenly distributed, especially in high-dimensional or networked settings. Despite these connections, explicitly learning spatially distributed functions in networks under localization constraints does not appear to have been addressed in previous works and, to the best of the authors' knowledge, this has not been explored in the context of wireless networks.

3 Localization of Cell Load Functions: Spatial Influence Range and Data Tradeoffs

In wireless cellular networks, a core performance indicator is the cell load θ_i, defined as the fraction of time/frequency resources used by the base station of some cell C_i to serve its users. Similarly, traffic demand ρ_i for cell C_i represents the volume of data its users are requesting from the network. This quantity depends on the spatial distribution of *traffic demand* $\{\rho_j\}_{j\in\mathcal{N}}$ across the network (with $\mathcal{N}$ the set of indices of all cells), inter-cell interferences [4] and user association mechanisms.

The load at cell C_i is modeled as a function $f_i\colon \mathbb{R}^{|\mathcal{N}|} \to \mathbb{R}$, mapping the network-wide traffic demand to the local load:

$$\theta_i = f_i(\{\rho_j\}_{j\in\mathcal{N}}).$$

However, for both computational and statistical reasons, it is often advantageous to approximate this global function with a localized version $\tilde{f}_i$, depending on traffic demand of cell C_i and its local neighborhood $\mathcal{N}_i^k \subset \mathcal{N}$ containing k other cells:

$$\theta_i \approx \tilde{f}_i(\{\rho_j\}_{j\in\{i\}\cup\mathcal{N}_i^k}).$$

In practice, these k closest neighbors are identified by measuring the Euclidean distance between the base station of cell C_i and those of other cells.

3.1 Spatial Influence Range and Function Complexity

The size of the *spatial influence range* k controls the input dimension of the localized function $\tilde{f}_i$, which is $k+1$ (cell C_i and its k closest neighbors). Let $\mathcal{F}_k$ be the class of functions, with $k+1$ inputs, defined over spatial influence range k (also sometimes called *receptive field* of radius k in the literature).

As k increases, so does the number of traffic demand variables it depends on, and correspondingly, the *complexity* of the hypothesis class $\mathcal{F}_k$.[1] This complexity can be quantified by the *Vapnik–Chervonenkis dimension* $\mathrm{VC}(\mathcal{F}_k)$.[2]

[1] Throughout the paper, emphasis is placed on linear functions, possibly followed by a non-linear activation. This choice is motivated by the physics-based model, cf. [4].
[2] In the class of affine functions, $\mathrm{VC}(\mathcal{F}_k) = (k+1)+1 = k+2$.

Moreover, this problem being grounded in statistical learning theory, which provides the following generalization bound for a class of predictors with finite VC dimension. With probability at least $1-\delta$, for any function $f \in \mathcal{F}_k$, the true (expected) prediction error $R(f)$ satisfies:

$$R(f) \leq \hat{R}(f) + \sqrt{\frac{1}{M} \max\left(\mathrm{VC}(\mathcal{F}_k) \log\left(\mathrm{VC}(\mathcal{F}_k)/2\right), \log\left(\gamma/\delta\right)\right)}. \tag{1}$$

Here:

- $\mathcal{F}_k$ is the hypothesis class,
- $\hat{R}(f)$ is the empirical prediction error on the training set of size M,
- δ is the confidence level and γ is a constant, that depends only on $\mathrm{VC}(\mathcal{F}_k)$.

This inequality stems from [16] and [9, Section 7.1.2 p. 112]. It shows that for a fixed training size M, a smaller VC dimension yields a tighter generalization bound and thus, a model less prone to overfitting [12]. Here, this observation translates to learning *localized functions* with limited spatial input dependencies, especially when historical training data is limited in volume or diversity.

Finally, as discussed earlier, the complexity of the hypothesis class varies as follows:

$$\mathrm{VC}(\mathcal{F}_k) \uparrow \quad \text{as} \quad k \uparrow .$$

Consequently, the number of training samples M required to learn $\tilde{f}_i \in \mathcal{F}_k$ with generalization guarantees also increases.

3.2 Structural Regularization via Localization

Restricting the spatial influence range acts as a form of *structural regularization*: it limits the function's input domain, thereby constraining its complexity and reducing the amount of training data required to learn it reliably. This property is particularly beneficial in real-world deployments, where data can be scarce or noisy.

However, this gives rise to a fundamental tradeoff. A small spatial influence range k, and consequently a low capacity of the function class $\mathcal{F}_k$, may result in a large true error, primarily because the model is too simple to capture the underlying patterns, leading to a large empirical prediction error $\hat{R}(f)$. This situation is commonly referred to as *underfitting*. On the other hand, a large radius k, and thus, a high capacity of $\mathcal{F}_k$, may also lead to large true error, this time due to the complexity penalty in (1), corresponding to the *overfitting* regime.[3]

In the numerical study based on real network data, including traffic demand and measured cell loads, this tradeoff is empirically investigated. For instance, Fig. 6 clearly exhibits the regime switch between underfitting and overfitting, while also displaying the influence of the number of training samples M. Using

[3] Rigorously speaking, the impact of the capacity of $\mathcal{F}_k$ on the penalty term in (1) can be ensured provided that $\mathrm{VC}(\mathcal{F}_k)\log(\mathrm{VC}(\mathcal{F}_k)/2) \geq \log(\gamma/\delta)$.

simple function models within $\mathcal{F}$, motivated by physical insights into interference and resource usage, this work aims at quantifying the interplay between model complexity, influence range size, and generalization performance.

4 Statistical Load Prediction with Varying Number of Neighbors

The following section briefly recalls the context of this study and presents the two statistical frameworks used, linear fitting and ridge regularization, before focusing on the results obtained and comparing the performance of these two methods.

4.1 Context and Prior Work

Physical studies of networks demonstrate that while neighboring base stations (BS) influence metrics like load, this influence attenuates with distance. In practice, assuming a network model where BS are arranged in a hexagonal grid (as depicted in [7, Fig 5(a) p. 11]), a widely accepted and practically applied guideline in cellular network engineering when accounting for interference is to consider one or two *layers* around every BS. Each layer here refers to a successive ring of neighboring hexagonal BS. In this study, the BS are tri-sectorial, meaning that each of them contains three cells.

Due to overfitting issues mentioned in [6] when accounting for the whole network (the *multidimensional* case), one may wonder if there exists an optimal number of neighboring cells that improves the prediction performance, compared to a framework with no neighbors considered (the *unidimensional* case), without exhibiting the effects of overfitting previously observed. Using the same statistical methods as in [6] but now leveraging geographical positions of BS to *localize* the data, the number of neighbors is incrementally increased, from $k = 2$ cells (only one BS) to $k = 100$ cells (≈ 34 BS). Thus, the frameworks are multidimensional, but this dimension is now varying and different for each value of k.

4.2 Multidimensional Linear Fitting

Let N be the number of cells in a cellular network. For each cell C_i, with $i \in \{1, \ldots, N\}$, the multidimensional linear fitting framework uses a traffic matrix[4] $\rho \in \mathbb{R}^{(k+2)\times M}$, with k the number of neighboring cells considered and M the number of training samples (here, one sample is a single average value over one hour), and a load vector $\theta \in \mathbb{R}^{1\times M}$, containing load values of cell C_i only. Least-squares fitting parameters $\hat{\beta}$ are obtained by:

$$\hat{\beta} = (\rho\rho^T)^{-1}\rho\theta^T. \tag{2}$$

[4] An additional input equal to 1 is introduced to incorporate the intercept. The weight learned for this extra input becomes the intercept $\hat{\beta}_0$.

Load prediction $\hat{\theta}_i$ for cell C_i is then computed using some testing data. Thus, for a given testing hour h with a traffic vector $\rho'_h = (1, \rho_1, \ldots, \rho_{k+1})$, the load prediction is:

$$\hat{\theta}_i(\rho'_h) = \hat{\beta}_0 + \hat{\beta}_1 \rho_1 + \cdots + \hat{\beta}_{k+1} \rho_{k+1} \tag{3}$$

This process is then repeated for all cells on the network (i.e., in (3), $\hat{\beta}_j = \hat{\beta}_{ij}$, $i \in \{1, \ldots, N\}$, $j \in \{0, \ldots, k+1\}$).

4.3 Ridge Regularization

Ridge regularization adds a penalty term when computing the loss between predicted and measured load. Using the same notations as in Sect. 4.2, parameters $\hat{\beta}$ are the solution to a minimization process defined by:

$$\min_{\beta} \|\theta - \beta^T \rho\|_2^2 + \alpha \|\beta\|_2^2 \tag{4}$$

where α is a scalar value called *regularization parameter* and the norm of choice is the *Euclidean norm.* The coefficients can be expressed as:

$$\hat{\beta} = (\rho\rho^\top + \alpha \mathrm{I})^{-1} \rho \theta^\top. \tag{5}$$

Finally, load predictions are computed using the same formula as (3).

4.4 Performance Evaluation

In order to assess the performance of these methods, the median over all cells of the relative prediction error was chosen as the key indicator. This error, computed between prediction values and testing data, gives an insight into the true prediction error, defined in (1). While this choice remains arbitrary, the median is a reliable indicator as it is not easily skewed by outliers, in contrast to the average which can be heavily influenced by extreme values. Moreover, the relative error is preferred since it offers a more practical interpretation than the absolute error. Indeed, the relative error scales against the empirical mean of the true value, yielding a percentage-like figure that is easier to understand and compare.

For each cell C_i, load predictions are calculated using testing data. The prediction vector $\hat{\theta}_i(\rho')$ is computed as in (3), using a traffic matrix $\rho' \in \mathbb{R}^{(k+2)\times Q}$, with Q the number of testing hours. These predictions are then compared to field measurements of loads $\theta'_i \in \mathbb{R}^{1\times Q}$.

The relative error is computed as:

$$\frac{\sqrt{\mathbf{m}[(\hat{\theta}_i(\rho') - \theta'_i)^2]}}{\sqrt{\mathbf{m}[\theta'^2_i]}} \tag{6}$$

where the numerator is the absolute error[5] (computed as RMSE) and $\mathbf{m}$ is the empirical mean over all testing hours. The median of this metric over all cells is then used to gauge performance.

The dataset, confidential due to company restrictions, is made of 4G 2600 MHz downlink traffic and load values for $N = 7979$ cells, stemming from a large area representative of some European country and comprising a mix of urban, suburban and rural zones. Experiments were conducted using a setup mindful of data representativeness and respecting the machine learning heuristic of the 80-20 train-test split. Consequently, the dataset was split between 23 days of training and 7 days of testing, focusing on daytime hours only, that is between 8 AM and 8 PM included. Thus, the size of the training dataset is $M = 23 \times 13 = 299$ hours per cell (versus $Q = 7 \times 13 = 91$ hours per cell for testing).

Note that choosing a setup that trains exclusively on daytime hours is still sufficient to obtain an estimation of the network behavior, via the acquisition of functions linking traffic to load, each corresponding to a single cell. It is crucial to understand that these functions describe the behavior of each cell and by extension, of the entire network, when faced with a traffic input. This means that further investigating temporal variability, namely looking at various hours or various days independently, would only have a marginal impact on these functions, as they fundamentally depend on the network itself. For instance, a cell might experience less traffic at certain hours of the day or on certain days of the week, but the relationship between traffic and load remains essentially unchanged across these temporal variations.

Multidimensional Linear Fitting. The performance of multidimensional linear fitting can be observed in the blue curve on Fig. 1, giving a first insight into network geometry and its impact. Indeed, the nature of this curve is very informative as it validates two main hypotheses: first, the initial decrease in prediction error demonstrates that considering nearby cells does improve the estimation, and second, the curve reaching a minimum confirms that there exists an optimal number of neighbors yielding the lowest error.

This behavior can be partly explained by the intuitive idea that neighboring cells have a non-negligible impact on the load computation process. Thus, adding their traffic information as an input to the model should improve performance, as shown here. However, the reason why the error starts rising after $k = 10$ neighbors is a consequence of overfitting, as mentioned in [6] and explained in Sect. 3. Indeed, passed a certain input dimension $k + 1$, the model's learning capabilities are hindered, as the negligibility condition $k \ll M$ is not strictly met. Instead of learning, the model *memorizes* the training data and its quality of prediction decreases.

[5] This absolute error is an estimation of the true prediction error $R(f)$ (cf. Equation 1).

Ridge Regularization. Applying the same training and testing conditions as the multidimensional linear fitting framework, ridge regularization however requires an appropriate choice for the regularization parameter α. After experimenting with various values, its value was heuristically set to $\alpha = 10^9$.

The results displayed in Fig. 1 are particularly interesting, as both frameworks exhibit the same curve shape. For ridge regularization, a minimum is reached for $k = 30$ neighbors, further than the linear fitting case. After this value of k, increasing the number of neighbors considered leads to poorer prediction performance.

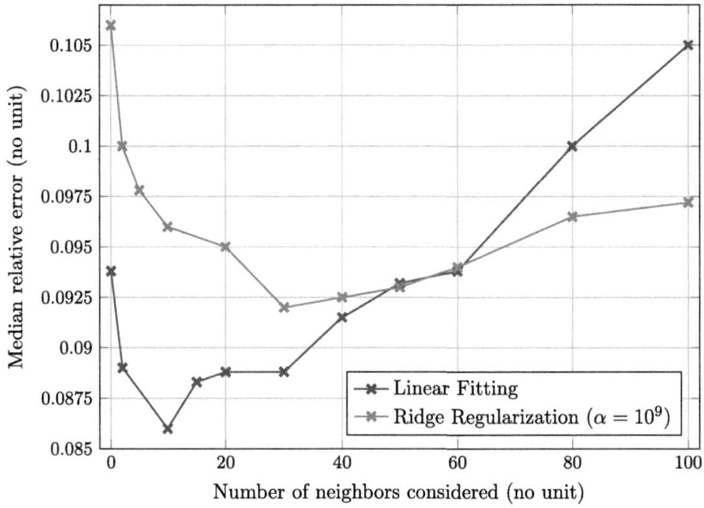

Fig. 1. Median relative error using linear fitting (in blue) and ridge regularization (in orange) for load prediction versus number of neighbors considered. Learning on 23 days (daytime) – Testing on 7 days (daytime). (Color figure online)

A second observation can be made regarding the improvements offered by ridge regularization. Indeed, this method was used in hopes to mitigate any overfitting effect that may result from using large coefficients to weigh the influence of faraway cells. For low values of k, this effect is less potent, as the condition $k \ll M$ still holds. For numbers of neighbors higher than $k = 30$, where it would seem that overfitting effects start to appear, ridge regularization manages to limit degradation and maintain the error at a lower level than linear fitting. Notably, this $k = 30$ threshold also coincides with the orange curve increasing, giving even more credit to the hypothesis that this upturn is due to overfitting. After a transition phase between $k = 40$ and $k = 60$, ridge regularization clearly outperforms linear fitting for later values of k and proves its superiority when considering larger number of neighbors.

5 Load Prediction Using Neural Networks with Varying Number of Neighbors

Prediction methods such as linear fitting and ridge regularization revolve around the idea of computing the load of a given cell by attributing weights to its own traffic and to that of its neighboring cells; an intercept value is also added to the computation. In practice, these approaches require training a model for every individual cell on the network, thus becoming more and more costly as network size increases. Moreover, when searching for a relation between load and traffic, these methods restrict their exploration to the class of linear functions, which may be a limitation when trying to find the optimal function to achieve best performance.

Thus, exploring neural networks may be a useful approach. Firstly, they offer a more efficient computation of the weights for each cell by design, as the whole network is slowly refined towards an optimal solution. They also allow function searches within broader classes than linear methods, which may be achieved by the addition of activation functions, thereby providing non-linear outputs. Finally, the possibility of adding intermediate layers within the network itself increases the complexity of the relationships between neurons. This *deep learning* approach is another crucial advantage of neural networks and may lead to even more precise function evaluation.

5.1 Structure of the Neural Network

The bare structure of the neural network can be viewed as a complete graph containing all the cells as an input and all the cells as an output. Each cell C_i is represented by a neuron and is linked to every cell C_j on the network with a weight w_{ij}.[6] This structure is displayed in Fig. 2, albeit slightly simplified, as all the edges are not represented for readability. Here, in order to account for cell neighborhoods, these weights have been set to zero for cells further than a certain distance from cell C_i. Namely, once the desired number of neighbors k in the neighborhood has been fixed, any cell C_j with a larger distance to C_i than its k-th neighbor harbors a weight $w_{ij} = 0$, represented here grayed out with a dotted line. This choice was made to observe the impact of specific cells within a restricted neighborhood, using a masking effect.[7]

Therefore, load predictions for any cell C_i are computed using the following equation:

[6] Interestingly, a network containing this simple structure could be used to confirm the results obtained in the previous sections. Indeed, by using a neural network with no intermediate layer and no activation function, the approach is essentially equivalent to a linear fitting framework: the coefficients are the weights of neurons, while intercept values can be equated to the bias.

[7] Nonetheless, an argument could be made that this mask may also have been more progressive than zeroing the weight: for example, a fading coefficient could have been applied to these distant cells, whose attenuation increases with distance and effectively rendering the influence of faraway cells residual.

$$\hat{\theta}_i(\rho'_h) = \sum_{j \in \mathcal{I}_i} \hat{w}_{ij}\rho_j + \hat{w}_{i0} \tag{7}$$

where notations are defined as such:

- $\hat{\theta}_i$ is the estimated load for cell C_i,
- $\rho'_h = \left(1, (\rho_j)_{j \in \mathcal{I}_i}\right)$ is the traffic vector for testing hour h,
- $\hat{w}_{ij}$ is the weight connecting the traffic from cell C_j (with $j \in \mathcal{I}_i$) to the load of cell C_i, while $\hat{w}_{i0}$ is the bias term. These coefficient values are converged upon using gradient descent (cf. Section 5.3).
- $\mathcal{I}_i = \{i\} \cup \mathcal{N}_i^k$ is the set of indices including cell C_i itself and $\mathcal{N}_i^k$, which denotes the set of indices of the k nearest distinct neighboring cells to C_i.

5.2 Generation of Non-Linear Outputs

In order to enable the network to learn complex patterns and non-linear relationships, the previous output must be transformed by a non-linear activation function. For this purpose, the hyperbolic tangent function (tanh) is introduced, defined by:

$$\tanh(x) = \frac{e^x - e^{-x}}{e^x + e^{-x}}.$$

The tanh function is a common choice for activation due to its sigmoidal nature, which normalizes values within the range of $(-1, 1)$. This can prove beneficial for the performance of the network, especially in order to clip load predictions that may be above 1.

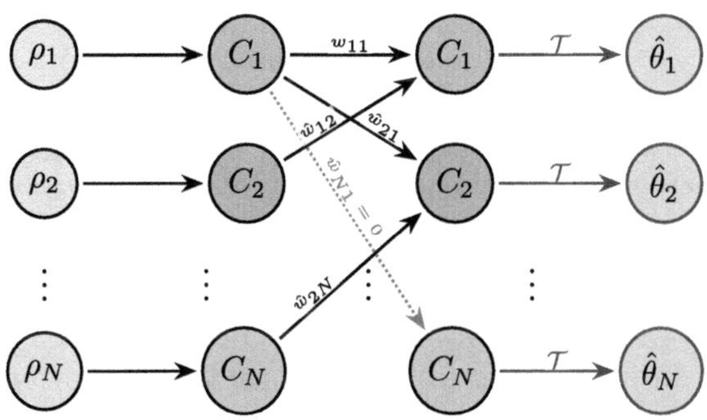

Fig. 2. Simplified structure of the neural network computing load estimations $\hat{\theta}$ based on testing traffic values. For example here, C_1 is linked to itself by $\hat{w}_{11}$, $\hat{w}_{12}$ is active (because C_2 is in C_1's neighborhood) and $\hat{w}_{N1} = 0$, as C_1 is outside of C_N's neighborhood. The function $\mathcal{T}$, which can be an identity map or an activation function like tanh, is applied to the output of the network before obtaining load predictions $\hat{\theta}$.

Using the same notations as (7), for any cell C_i, load prediction $\hat{\theta}_i$ is now computed using this formula:

$$\hat{\theta}_i(\rho'_h) = \tanh\left(\sum_{j \in \mathcal{I}_i} \hat{w}_{ij}\rho_j + \hat{w}_{i0}\right). \tag{8}$$

5.3 Performance Evaluation

Using the same training and testing conditions as previously, Fig. 3 superimposes the results obtained using a neural network, with and without activation, to the results observed previously with linear fitting and ridge regularization.

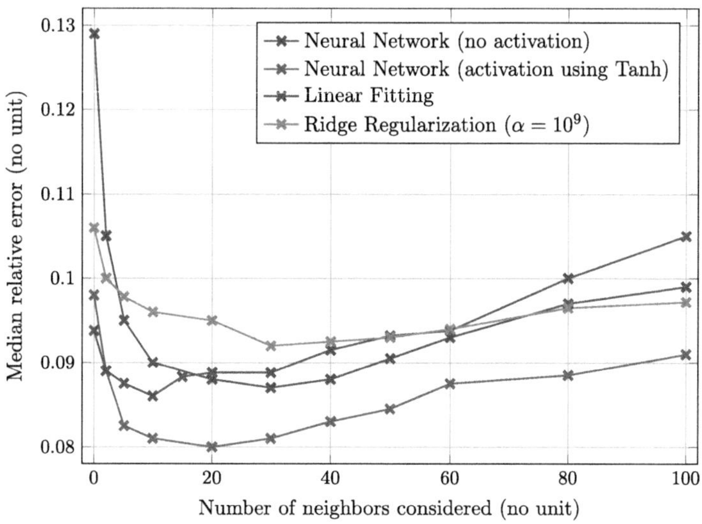

Fig. 3. Median relative error using linear fitting (in blue), ridge regularization (in orange), neural network (in green) and neural network with activation (in red) for load prediction versus number of neighbors considered. Learning on 23 days (daytime) – Testing on 7 days (daytime). (Color figure online)

Two primary insights emerge from the comparative results presented in Fig. 3. Firstly, the neural network incorporating the hyperbolic tangent activation function (shown in red) demonstrates a notably superior performance. Indeed, it achieves the lowest median relative error across almost the entire range of neighbors considered, significantly outperforming all other methods. This substantial improvement over the non-activated neural network (in green), as well as the linear fitting and ridge regularization techniques, validates the introduction of non-linearity. Such a result suggests that the underlying relationship between cellular load and traffic patterns possesses complex, non-linear characteristics.

This further highlights limitations of linear approximations in this context, particularly when knowing the real nature of the cell-load equations linking traffic and load and described in [4, Equation (15)].

Secondly, the performance curve of the neural network without activation exhibits a similar overall shape to that of the standard linear fitting method. This expected result provides a degree of confidence in the basic structural implementation of the neural network and serves as a valid baseline of comparison with other methods, even without the introduction of the non-linear activation layer.

However, it is worth noticing that the performance of the neural network is highly degraded when considering no neighbors. In fact, it is also the only case for which the neural network with activation is outperformed. This may be explained by the fact that this configuration is ill-suited for a neural network, as it is essentially forced to operate in a *unidimensional* setup and unable to capture complex relationships. Moreover, the suboptimal nature of the neural network's training process, reliant on stochastic gradient descent, may be more apparent in this scenario.

Impact of Stochastic Gradient Descent (SGD). Regular *gradient descent* iteratively refines each weight w_{ij} to minimize a loss function L defined as

$$L = \sum_{i \in \mathcal{N}} \sum_{m \in \mathcal{M}} (\hat{\theta}_{i,m} - \theta_{i,m})^2 \tag{9}$$

with $\mathcal{N}$ the set of all cells on the network and $\mathcal{M}$ the set of all M training instants. The loss function measures the error between the predicted load $\hat{\theta}_i$ and the measured load θ_i for any cell C_i at training instant m. The update uses the gradient, computed according to the following formula:

$$(w_{ij})_{t+1} = (w_{ij})_t - \eta \frac{\partial L}{\partial w_{ij}}\bigg|_t$$

where:

- At iteration t, the weight $(w_{ij})_t$ links the traffic of cell C_j (with $j \in \mathcal{I}_i$) to the load of C_i and $(w_{i0})_t$ is the bias term,
- η is the learning rate,
- $\frac{\partial L}{\partial w_{ij}}$ is the partial derivative of the loss function L with respect to w_{ij} evaluated at t.

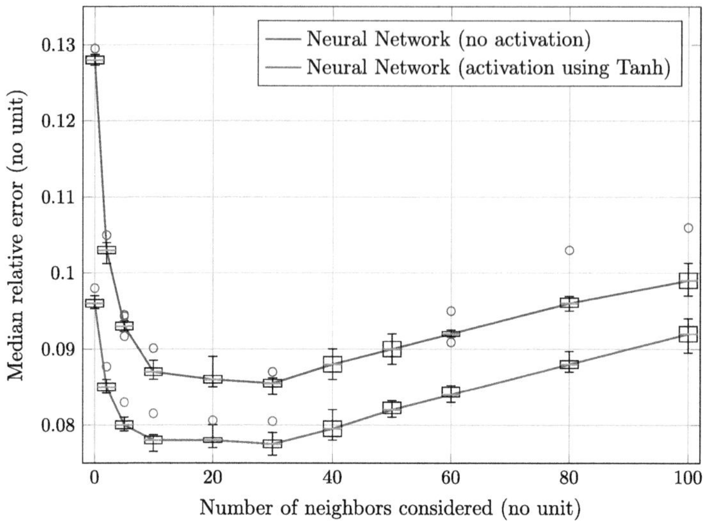

Fig. 4. Median relative error versus number of neighbors for neural network (in blue) and neural network with activation (in red). The box and whisker plot gives results for 10 different realizations of the SGD procedure. (Color figure online)

In Stochastic Gradient Descent (SGD), stochasticity arises because the gradient is computed using only some terms of the total loss function L defined in (9), chosen at random. In order to investigate the variations due to this randomness, the model is trained 10 times for each value of k. Results can be observed on Fig. 4.

This box-and-whisker plot demonstrates that the variance introduced by the stochastic nature of SGD is not substantial enough to significantly alter the trends previously observed in Fig. 3. Indeed, the curves preserve their general shape and the systematic improvement offered by activation remains noticeable throughout the process. The optimal number of neighbors seems to revolve around $k = 30$, although one may more cautiously refer to an optimum *plateau* around $k = 20$ and $k = 30$.

Impact of the Testing Dataset. Following the investigation of variability attributable to SGD, these results were also found to be highly dependent on the testing dataset. Indeed, as mentioned prior, testing is conducted over a dataset containing a full week of data in daytime hours. In order to have a smaller, more digestible number of points, a random selection of points from this dataset was used. This randomness is however "fixed", as the same reduced dataset has been used to test all the methods so far[8].

[8] This exact reduced dataset has also been used to conduct all the performance comparison tests that were discussed in [6].

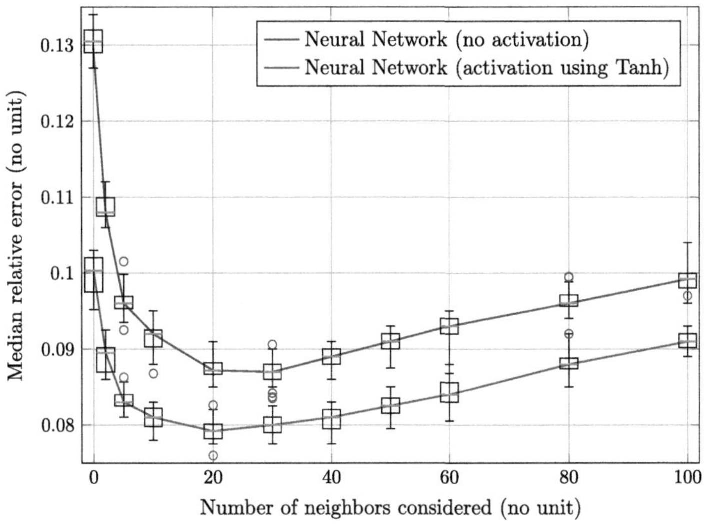

Fig. 5. Median relative error versus number of neighbors for neural network (in blue) and neural network with activation (in red). The box and whisker plot gives results for 30 different testing subsets, picked randomly within the testing week. (Color figure online)

Results in Fig. 5 examine any variability that may arise from variations in the testing conditions. Once again, the global trend of the curves is preserved and the systematic gap is clearly observed. Since there are now 30 repetitions, the curves appear smoother and exhibit once again an optimum plateau around $k = 20$ and $k = 30$. The main takeaway is that these methods are robust and despite some stochasticity in the gradient descent process and some randomness in the choice of the testing sample, the curves remain rather similar, at least in their shapes and their relative gap to each other.

Impact of Training Dataset Size. One may also be interested in investigating training datasets, or more particularly, how does the training period affect performance in these scenarios. Using the regular neural network (without activation), experiments were conducted to slowly increase the training period from 6 to 23 days. The shortest training period (6 days) is comparable to the testing period (7 days), while the longest (23 days) is approximately three times longer.

The results in Fig. 6 confirm the intuition that increasing the training period offers better results, as adding more learning days keeps improving performance.

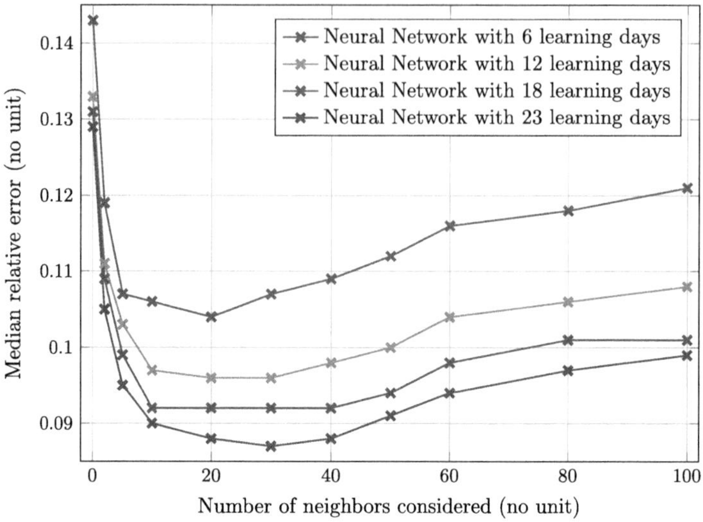

Fig. 6. Median relative error versus number of neighbors for neural network. The training period grows incrementally by approximately 6 days. It features durations of 6 days (in blue), 12 days (in orange), 18 days (in green) and 23 days (in purple). (Color figure online)

Moreover, despite increases in the number of learning examples M, the optimal number of neighbors remains around $k = 20$ and $k = 30$. This leads to the conjecture that considering further than $k = 30$ neighboring cells ($\approx$ 10 base stations) seems to be of marginal utility to achieve accurate load predictions, which makes physical sense when accounting for attenuation in cellular networks.

6 Algorithmic Implementation

All algorithms were coded in Python 3.11.12 and employed various *machine learning* libraries that support the implementation of the techniques presented in the article.

6.1 Linear Fitting and Ridge Regularization

Both the multidimensional linear fitting and the ridge regularization frameworks were developed via the *scikit-learn* library, which provides tools for several ML applications.

The first one was implemented using the *LinearRegression* function, training one model per cell and relying on a dataset (described in Sect. 4.4) offering cellwise traffic and load values at each of the M training instants.

The second one was coded using the *Ridge* function, which natively lets the user choose the regularization parameter α that suits the problem best. After examining various values of α and observing a performance curve similar to [2, Fig 3.3, p. 58], the value was set at $\alpha = 10^9$.

Finally, the various cell neighborhoods could be computed thanks to an $N \times N$ matrix of inter-cell distances, allowing the algorithm to define, for each cell, the k closest cells to consider.

6.2 Neural Network

Neural networks were developed using the *PyTorch* library. As described in Fig. 2, they consist of a single layer and have N neurons as inputs and N neurons as outputs, with N the number of cells on the network. For any cell C_i, the $N - k - 1$ cells that are not within its neighborhood are identified, through the matrix of inter-cell distances. The weights linking them to cell C_i are then set to zero.

The training process consisted of 100 epochs, which proved sufficient for the total loss L, defined in (9), to reach a stable level. The learning rate was set to $\eta = 10^{-11}$ through trial and error and the network was optimized via SGD. As detailed in Sect. 5.3, SGD gradient updates are computed by using only some terms of L. In practice here, the updates were computed by randomly choosing a single term of L, which is considered to be the true SGD approach, also called *online learning*. This process is repeated 64 times for each epoch, on different terms of L picked at random.

Several activation functions have been explored (ReLU, Sigmoid, Softmax...) and tanh proved to be the most fit for the problem, achieving the lowest total loss L over all epochs.

6.3 Execution Time Comparison

In addition to offering a better prediction performance, the neural network approach is also considerably faster than the other methods studied here. Using a system containing four NVIDIA Tesla T4 GPUs, the running time of an epoch is of approximately 5 seconds, which gives a total running time of 8 minutes 15 seconds, versus 38 minutes 8 seconds for the scikit-learn based methods (approximately 4.6 times slower).

7 Conclusion

Investigating network geometry using localized functions has been useful to thoroughly improve load prediction capabilities. Moreover, the use of neural networks has proven instrumental in achieving higher prediction performance, particularly by leveraging network activation to search for non-linear functions linking load and traffic.

The natural next step of this work is to further investigate neural networks, by using intermediate layers. This *deep learning* approach may allow an even finer evaluation of traffic-load functions and consequently, more accurate load predictions on future networks.

Acknowledgments. The authors extend their sincere thanks to Zeinab Nehme. Her efforts in developing some elements of the codebase were instrumental to the progress of this project.

References

1. Andrews, J.G., et al.: What will 5G be? IEEE J. Sel. Areas Commun. **32**(6), 1065–1082 (2014)
2. Bach, F.: Learning Theory from First Principles. MIT press (2024)
3. Bega, D., Gramaglia, M., Banchs, A., Sciancalepore, V., Costa-Perez, X.: DeepCOG: cognitive network management in sliced 5G networks with deep learning. IEEE J. Sel. Areas Commun. **37**(10), 2260–2272 (2019). https://doi.org/10.1109/JSAC.2019.2933074
4. Blaszczyszyn, B., Karray, M.K.: Performance analysis of cellular networks with opportunistic scheduling using queueing theory and stochastic geometry. IEEE Trans. Wirel. Commun. **18**(12), 5952–5966 (2019). https://doi.org/10.1109/TWC.2019.2940938
5. Błaszczyszyn, B., Yogeshwaran, D., Yukich, J.E.: Limit theory for geometric statistics of point processes having fast decay of correlations. Ann. Probab. **47**(2), 835–895 (2019)
6. Darlavoix, L., Blaszczyszyn, B., Karray, M.K., Nehme, Z.: Apprentissage Statistique Cellule par Cellule de la Charge à Partir de la Demande de Trafic dans les Réseaux Cellulaires Sans Fil. In: CORES 2025 - 10èmes Rencontres Francophones sur la Conception de Protocoles, l'Evaluation de Performances et l'Expérimentation des Réseaux de Communication. Saint Valery-sur-Somme, France (2025). hal-05030767
7. ElSawy, H., Hossain, E., Haenggi, M.: Stochastic geometry for modeling, analysis, and design of multi-tier and cognitive cellular wireless networks: a survey. IEEE Commun. Surv. Tutorials **15**(3), 996–1019 (2013)
8. Imran, A., Zoha, A., Abu-Dayya, A.: Challenges in 5G: how to empower son with big data for enabling 5G. IEEE Netw. **28**(6), 27–33 (2014). https://doi.org/10.1109/MNET.2014.6963801
9. Karray, M.K., Blaszczyszyn, B., Darlavoix, L.: Data science: from statistics to machine learning and deep learning, with applications to wireless networks. Working paper or preprint (2025). hal-05294023
10. Khalid, M.: Traffic prediction in cellular networks using graph neural networks (2023). https://doi.org/10.48550/arXiv.2301.12605
11. Lavancier, F., Møller, J., Rubak, E.: Determinantal point process models and statistical inference. J. Royal Stat. Soc. Ser. B (Stat. Methodol.) **77**(4), 853–877 (2015)
12. Mohri, M., Rostamizadeh, A., Talwalkar, A.: Foundations of Machine Learning. MIT Press, 2nd edn. (2018)
13. Macaluso, I., et al.: An overview on application of machine learning techniques in optical networks. IEEE Commun. Surv. Tutorials **21**(2), 1383–1408 (2019). https://doi.org/10.1109/COMST.2018.2880039
14. Penrose, M.D.: Random Geometric Graphs. Oxford University Press (2003)
15. Penrose, M.D., Yukich, J.E.: Central limit theorems for some graphs in computational geometry. Ann. Appl. Probabil. **11**(4), 1005–1041 (2001)

16. Shalev-Shwartz, S., Ben-David, S.: Understanding Machine Learning: From Theory to Algorithms. Cambridge University Press (2014)
17. Zhang, C., Zhang, H., Qiao, J., Yuan, D., Zhang, M.: Deep transfer learning for intelligent cellular traffic prediction based on cross-domain big data. IEEE J. Sel. Areas Commun. **37**(6), 1389–1401 (2019). https://doi.org/10.1109/JSAC.2019.2904363

Author Index

A. Remke et al. (Eds.): Valuetools 2025, LNICST 691, pp. 319–320, 2027.
https://doi.org/10.1007/978-3-032-23901-3

GPSR Compliance

The European Union's (EU) General Product Safety Regulation (GPSR) is a set of rules that requires consumer products to be safe and our obligations to ensure this.

If you have any concerns about our products, you can contact us on ProductSafety@springernature.com

In case Publisher is established outside the EU, the EU authorized representative is:

Springer Nature Customer Service Center GmbH
Europaplatz 3
69115 Heidelberg, Germany

Batch number: 10634094

Printed by Printforce, the Netherlands